21/11/2017

To Ala
with bbe. ...

UPROOTED

Uprooted

How 3,000 Years of Jewish Civilisation in the Arab World Vanished Overnight

Lyn Julius

VALLENTINE MITCHELL

LONDON • PORTLAND, OR

First published in 2018 by Vallentine Mitchell

Catalyst House,
720 Centennial Court,
Centennial Park, Elstree WD6 3SY, UK

920 NE 58th Avenue, Suite 300
Portland, Oregon
97213-3786 USA

www.vmbooks.com

Copyright © 2018 Lyn Julius
Foreword © 2018 Tom Gross

British Library Cataloguing in Publication Data:
An entry can be found on request

ISBN 978 1 910383 64 3 (Cloth)
ISBN 978 1 910383 66 7 (Paper)
ISBN 978 1 910383 65 0 (Ebook)

Library of Congress Cataloging in Publication Data:
An entry can be found on request

Printed by Clays Ltd, Bungay, Suffolk

Toleration is not the opposite of Intoleration,
but is the counterfeit of it. Both are despotisms.

Thomas Paine, *The Rights of Man*

Dedicated to my parents,

Bertha Bekhor and the late Maurice Bekhor, Jewish refugees from
Iraq, and to the memory of my friend Névine Rose (née Savdié),
a Jewish refugee from Egypt.

Contents

A Note on Terminology		viii
Foreword: A People Ignored		ix
Introduction		xiii
Preface: First the Saturday People		xvii
1	Over a Millennium before Islam	1
2	The Myth of Peaceful Coexistence	24
3	The European Colonial Revolution	48
4	The Legacy of the Nazi Era	79
5	A Virulent Nationalism	100
6	What Came First: Anti-Semitism or Anti-Zionism?	119
7	Jewish Refugees: Forgotten No More?	148
8	'My House is your House'	169
9	Mizrahi Wars of Politics and Culture	196
10	Myths, Lies and Omissions	223
11	The Quest for Justice for Indigenous Peoples	242
Appendices		263
Bibliography		323
Index		327

A Note on Terminology

Ashkenazi: Jews from medieval Germany and northern France. The term has now come to refer to Jews of central and eastern European descent.

Mizrahi: modern Hebrew term deriving from *Edot Ha'Mizrah*, Jews from the East. It denotes 'eastern' or 'oriental' Jews who have been settled in the Middle East and North Africa since Biblical times. It also refers to the Jews of the greater Babylonian diaspora (present-day Iraq, Afghanistan, Iran and the southern ex-Soviet republics). Nowadays it also encompasses Jews from Yemen, the Indian subcontinent and Ethiopia – any Jew who is not Ashkenazi. This book uses 'Mizrahi' as a catch-all, although the term is technically inaccurate when describing North African (Maghrebi) communities since these are geographically westerly (Morocco is to the west of much of western Europe).

Sephardi: literally, Spanish. Jews expelled from Spain (Sefarad) and Portugal after 1492. Most Middle Eastern and North African communities are now mixed Sephardi and Mizrahi.

The term is often used to describe any community that is not Ashkenazi. 'Sephardi' also means following the broad traditions of Sephardi Judaism.

Foreword

A People Ignored

It is not surprising, given the sheer scale of the Holocaust and its sadism, that it has dominated contemporary discourse among Jews and others.

But while the extermination of European Jews has rightfully (though belatedly) generated a great deal of study and research, the ethnic cleansing of the Jews of the Arab world has been all but ignored.

This ignorance extends to policymakers at the highest level. Some journalists at leading news outlets, as well as politicians I have spoken to, have expressed surprise when I have even mentioned that Jews lived in sizeable numbers in the Middle East before Israel's independence.

In fact Jews have lived in what is now the Arab world for over 2,600 years, a millennium before Islam was founded, and centuries before the Arab conquest of many of those territories. In pre-Islamic times, whole Jewish kingdoms existed, for example Himyar in Yemen.

Up until the seventeenth century, there were more Jews in the Arab and wider Muslim world than in Europe. In Baghdad, in 1939, 33 per cent of the population were Jews making it at the time, proportionately more Jewish than Warsaw (29 per cent) and New York (27 per cent). Jews had lived in Baghdad since the destruction of the first temple in Jerusalem in 586 BCE. Today only five Jews reportedly remain there.

Before they were driven out en masse, the Jews of the Arab world, like Jews in Europe, were often important figures in their societies.

The first novel to be published in Iraq was written by a Jew. Iraq's first finance minister was a Jew, Sir Sasson Heskel. The founder of Egypt's first national theatre in Cairo, in 1870, was a Jew, Jacob Sanua. Egypt's first opera was written in 1919 by a Jew. Many of the classics of Egyptian cinema were directed by Jews and featured Jewish actors. The pioneer of Tunisian cinema was also Jewish (he was one of the first in the world to film underwater sequences), as was Tunisia's leading female singer.

The world bantamweight boxing champion was also a Tunisian Jew and so were many other leading boxers and swimmers – including Alfred Nakache, the Algerian swimming champion who later survived Auschwitz. (Hundreds of Jews died in Nazi camps set up in Libya and some other Libyan Jews were deported to Bergen-Belsen.)

Even the less prominent Jews were often interwoven into the wider societies. As a Moroccan proverb put it, 'A market without Jews is like bread without salt.' (In the West, there are many prominent Jews with roots in the Arab world. The American comedian Jerry Seinfeld has a Syrian Jewish mother; Bernard-Henri Levy's parents were Algerian Jews, and so on.)

In Israel, 160,000 Arabs stayed after the country's rebirth in 1948 and took Israeli citizenship. (That number is now 1.7 million, representing over 20 per cent of Israel's population, and Israeli Arabs serve in posts ranging from Supreme Court justices to Israeli diplomats). And when Israel declared independence following the UN partition plan, many of the Palestinian Arabs who departed were not pushed out, but left on the orders of their own leadership so as to stay out of the way when several Arab armies marched in with the aim of wiping out the Jews.

In sharp contrast, the ethnic cleansing of hundreds of thousands of Jews from the Arab world in the mid-twentieth century was systematic, absolute and unprovoked.

There were 38,000 Jews in western Libya before 1945. Now there are none, forty-seven synagogues are gone and a highway runs through Libya's main Jewish cemetery. In Algeria there were 140,000 Jews. Now there are none. In Iraq, there were about 150,000 Jews. Five remain. There were 80,000 Jews in Egypt. Almost all are gone.

Many Jewish refugees still suffer the trauma of armed men arriving at their door, and being marched away without explanation and without being able to take their possessions.

Unlike Palestinian refugees who left in smaller numbers (between 1948 and 1951, according to UN statistics, 711,000 Palestinian Arabs left what became Israel although many historians put the numbers at fewer than this) the 856,000 Jews who were made refugees from Arab countries have never received any proper recognition or international financial help. Instead, there is wilful ignorance. So for example, in Cairo today, the Swiss, German, Canadian, Dutch, South Korean and Pakistani embassies all occupy the stolen homes of wealthy expelled Jews. Similar situations exist in some other Arab capitals.

Adding to the injustice, some Middle East commentators like to propagate the myth that the Jews of the Arab world were never discriminated against or persecuted or attacked.

Not only were Jews often treated as second-class citizens with discriminatory laws and additional taxes imposed on them, but many were killed or injured in pogroms: for example, in Fez in Morocco, 45 Jews were killed in 1912; in Constantine in Algeria in 1934; in Rabat in Morocco in 1934; in Gabès in Tunisia in 1941; in Aden in 1947, when 87 Jews were killed and hundreds of shops destroyed; in Iraq in 1941, when at least 180 Jews were murdered and many others raped and injured and thousands of homes looted;

in Libya in 1945, when 130 Jews were killed; in Aleppo in 1947, when as many as 75 Jews were said to have lost their lives. In 1939, bombs were planted at a Cairo synagogue.

Nor can such attacks be excused as somehow being merely in reaction to Zionism. There were many attacks before this period. In 1807, in Casablanca, there was a massacre of Jews. In 1840, the infamous Damascus blood libel led to the kidnapping and torture of dozens of Jewish children. (As late as 1986, the Syrian Defence Minister, Mustafa Talas, published a book, *The Matzah of Zion*, in which he claimed that the Jews did indeed use the blood of a Christian monk to bake matzah, and therefore he said the 1840 pogrom was justified.) In 1857, an innocent Tunisian Jew, Batto Sfez, was beheaded and his head was tossed around like a football by a mob, leading the French authorities to intervene.

Other pogroms occurred in Aleppo in 1850 and 1875, in Damascus in 1848 and 1890, in Beirut in 1862 and 1874. In Cairo, Jews were set upon by mobs in 1844, 1890, and 1901–2, and in Alexandria in 1870, 1882 and 1901–7.

In Morocco, as far back as the eighth century, whole communities were wiped out by Idris the First. In 1033, about 6,000 Jews were murdered in Fez by a Muslim mob. In 1465, another massacre took place in Fez, which spread to other cities in Morocco. There were pogroms in Tetuan in 1790 and 1792, in which many children were murdered. Between 1864 and 1880, there was a series of attacks on the Jews of Marrakesh, and hundreds died. In 1903, there were pogroms in Taza and Settat, in which over forty Jews were killed.

In 1907, in Casablanca thirty Jews were killed and many women raped. There was also a series of massacres in Algeria in 1805, 1815 and 1830, and in Libya in 1785. And so on.

By the 1880s the situation for Yemeni Jews was so bad, that many started to walk to Palestine to join European Jews there and 15,000 Yemeni Jews had arrived by the late 1930s.

Today the only Middle Eastern state where Jews and Arabs cohabit in any numbers is Israel. (Indeed the Arab population in Israel is now much larger than it was during the British mandate period.)

Some Arab reformers have lamented the loss of Jews, giving it as key a reason why the Arab world is now in such disarray. The Egyptian-born journalist Magdi Allam says that 'by losing their Jews the Arabs have lost their roots and have ended up losing themselves.'

All this and more is explored by Lyn Julius in this significant new book.

A deeper understanding about the fate of the Jews of the Arab world is not just important because a great injustice has been done to them, but because by ignoring their plight, and history, and concentrating only on the Palestinian Arabs who in 1947–8 were made refugees from Israel, policy makers from US Secretary of States downwards have formed a lopsided view of the conflict.

If it were better understood that there were two sets of suffering here – Jewish and Arab – then grievances surrounding the Palestinian question could be more easily reconciled and a resolution to the Arab-Israeli conflict made less hard to achieve.

Tom Gross
Former Middle East correspondent, *Sunday Telegraph*;
contributor to *The Guardian* and *Wall Street Journal*

Introduction

The issue of Jewish refugees from Arab countries pursued me, the daughter of Jewish refugees from Iraq, throughout my childhood. In adulthood, 9/11 jolted me back to the observation of just how dysfunctional certain parts of the Arab and Muslim world could be. Now, though, the threat which had begun with the destruction of Middle Eastern minorities has gone global. It could target Madrid commuters, passengers on a London bus, revellers in a Bali disco or rock fans in a French music hall.

Back in 1969, as a schoolgirl, I remember attending a very emotional vigil outside the Iraqi embassy in London just after nine Jews had been executed in Liberation Square in Baghdad. It was addressed by Percy Gourgey MBE, who fought like a lion all his life to raise awareness of the plight of Jews from Arab countries. The fate of Iraq's remaining 3,000 Jews was a source of great personal anxiety to my family: my four grandparents and several cousins and aunts were trapped in Baghdad under Saddam Hussein's reign of terror.

In England, my father, who had fled Iraq in 1950 as a refugee with his new wife, my mother, acted as guardian to the three children of his absent sister. Widowed at thirty-five, my aunt had returned to Iraq in 1964 to sell some property, but had ended up unable to leave the country, a helpless hostage of the Ba'ath regime. In those dark days after the Baghdad hangings, my father devoted much energy to trying to secure the release of Aunt Marcelle, my grandparents Baba and Nana and great-uncle Amou Sasson. He went to see MPs – or anyone he thought might listen – and wrote frantic letters to the French senator Alain Poher, who headed a human rights committee. Eventually my Aunt Marcelle was smuggled by Kurds out of northern Iraq into then-friendly Iran; she was disguised in an *abaya* as a Muslim called Khadija. After six long years, she was reunited with her family in London. She had missed the wedding of her eldest son by four months. Baba, Nana and Amou managed to secure passports, hitherto rarely granted to Jews. They gained admission to England helped by Joan Stiebel, a non-Jewish heroine of the Central British Fund, now known as World Jewish Relief. At about the same time, cousins on my mother's side of the family also escaped Baghdad for Canada, and my parents acted as surrogates until my cousins were reunited with their parents twenty years later.

In typical oriental style, the whole *hamula* was resettled with us – my grandparents and great-uncle on the ground floor of our London home, and my aunt and her children next door.

Reams have been written about the Arab-Israeli conflict, but the story of the Jews from Arab and Muslim countries remains shockingly neglected. Yet there have been more Jewish refugees from Arab countries than Arab refugees from Palestine. Most of these Jews resettled in Israel. Although they comprised only 10 per cent of the worldwide Jewish population before the Holocaust, Jews from Arab and Muslim countries and their descendants comprise just over half of Israel's six million-strong Jewish population today.[1]

The reasons for such neglect are complex. Few Jewish refugees have wanted to talk about their past experiences, being too busy adapting to their new lands. Israel has failed to mention their plight. Arab historians have avoided mentioning their flight. Eurocentric Jews have rarely discussed Jewish refugees from Arab lands too, their story being crushed under the weight of the Holocaust. Finally, the problem appeared to have been solved: whereas Palestinian refugees still languish in camps, not a single Jew still claims to be a refugee. Moreover, too many interests are vested in denial. Myths abound: no Jews ever lived in the Muslim world; the 'ethnic cleansing' didn't happen; if it did happen, outside factors – the Zionists, the colonial powers, even the Jews themselves – are to blame.

The story of the displacement of Jews from the Middle East drew renewed attention with the flight of Christians from the Middle East in the wake of the 2011 Arab Spring. The mass departure of almost a million Jews – also known as the Jewish *Nakba* (catastrophe) – preceded the Christian exodus. As the Islamist saying goes, 'First the Saturday people, then the Sunday people.'[2] In other words, first rid these countries of Jews and next, drive out the Christians.

The public debate about Israel never seems to pan outwards from a narrow focus on the ongoing dispute with the Palestinians. Yet the plight of Jewish refugees from Arab lands is an unresolved injustice. It is also central to an understanding of the Arab and Islamist struggle against Israel and Jews, and minorities in general. It constitutes a vital context capable of transforming opinion.

The issue of the Jewish refugees has been gathering momentum in recent years and came blinking out of the darkness of oblivion on 30 November 2014. This was the date designated by the Israeli Knesset as the Day of Remembrance for Jewish refugees from Arab Countries and Iran.[3] Henceforth, this date, which coincides with the anniversary of the outbreak of vicious riots in Arab countries against Jewish communities following the approval of the 1947 UN Partition Plan for Palestine, will memorialise the near-total extinction of an ancient civilisation. It will provide a focus in Israel and across the world for telling a hitherto untold story.

It has long been necessary to put Jewish refugees on the map. And this book is the result of that need. The importance of exploding certain myths has crystallised out of material I have collected for my blog, *Point of No Return*,[4] which, in 2015, marked its tenth birthday. Who are the Jews from Arab countries? What were relations with the Muslims like? What made the Jews leave countries where they had been settled for thousands of years? What became of the majority who settled in Israel, and how can their cause contribute to peace and reconciliation? What lessons can we learn from the mass exodus of minorities from the Middle East?

Although Jews have been displaced as a result of anti-Semitism in Afghanistan, Iran, Pakistan and even Turkey (countries where religious diversity is much diminished), I have chosen mainly to focus on Arab countries.[5] This is because the bulk of displaced Jews from Muslim countries came from the Arab world. In 1948, Iran was still an ally of Israel: it was not until 1979 that the Islamic revolution precipitated the exodus of four-fifths of Iran's Jews.

There have, of course, been several academic histories of Jews in Arab lands, and I do not intend to compete with them. I make no secret of the fact that I have been advocating for the rights of Jews from Arab lands through Harif, the UK Association of Jews from the Middle East and North Africa. Readers will, I hope, find useful a reference section of maps, tables, testimonies and timelines. My main motivation is to tell the truth, and to equip others with the knowledge to tell the truth, in the hope that truth will lead to greater understanding, even reconciliation.

I would like to acknowledge those who have read all or parts of the manuscript: Dr Edy Cohen, Dr Henry Green, Dr Stan Urman, and Nathan Weinstock (any errors are all my own). Special thanks go to Tom Gross for writing the Foreword and for his advice and encouragement, and to Levana Zamir for her wisdom and patient assistance. Thanks too go to Michelle Huberman for her inspiration, Lisette Shashoua Ades, Niran Bassoon-Timan, Lily Amior and Ralph Assor for their help, and the staff at Vallentine Mitchell. Finally, I would like to express my appreciation to those friends of the Jewish people who are striving to preserve its memory in the Middle East, often at personal risk.

I am indebted to Joseph Alexander Norland for starting me off on this eventful journey by setting up my blog *Point of No Return*. I have learned much along the way, not least from my regular commenters.

I should like to thank my family and especially my son Gideon for his help with footnotes and sources. Last but not least, this book would not have seen the light of day without the steadfast and dedicated support of my husband Laurence.

Notes

1. 50.2 per cent according to the Statistical Abstract of Israel, 2009, Central Bureau of Statistics. 'Table 2.24 – Jews, by country of origin and age' (PDF).
2. 'After Saturday comes Sunday' is an expression commonly heard in the Arab world or scrawled as graffiti. It is referenced in Bernard Lewis's prescient essay, 'The Return of Islam', *Commentary*, 1 January 1976.
3. 'For the first time, Israel marks day for Jewish refugees from Arab lands'. *i24 news*, 30 November 2014 at http://www.i24news.tv/en/news/international/middle-east/52889-141130-israel-marks-day-for-jewish-refugees-from-arab-lands. (Last accessed 26 April 2017).
4. *Point of No Return: Jewish Refugees from Arab countries* at http://jewishrefugees. blogspot.co.uk/. (Last accessed 26 April 2017).
5. I have not treated Sudan separately as it was effectively administered by Egypt with British approval. I have not mentioned the communities in Bahrain, Asmara or other Red Sea or Gulf ports. This book does not cover the Jewish communities of India, Pakistan, Singapore, Burma, Hong Kong and Shanghai founded by Baghdadi and Aleppan Jews.

Preface

First the Saturday People

Suppose a man leaps out of a burning building ... and lands on a bystander in the street below. The burning building is supposed to be Europe, the jumper is the Jew, and the unfortunate bystander the Palestinian Arab. This metaphor for the Arab-Israeli conflict was apparently coined by writer Jeffrey Goldberg and has been approvingly cited by the late polemicist and author Christopher Hitchens.[1]

Whilst it is a striking image, this analogy is, of course, inherently problematic. It propagates the assumption that Jews came from Europe to displace innocent natives. Now try a different analogy. Imagine that the building is actually situated in the Middle East, a short distance from a homestead by the sea originally settled by the Jew. Some 3,000 years ago and until recent times, the Jew inhabited the main house alongside other indigenous residents of the Middle East. The homestead was seized by the Romans in 70 CE and most of its residents dispersed. An occupier arrived in the seventh century, and took over the whole region. In the twentieth century, arsonists set fire to the main building, forcing the Jew to jump out of the window. *'First the Saturday people, then the Sunday people'*: Armenians, Assyrians, Chaldean Christians, Maronites, Copts also jumped for their lives. And not just the Sunday people: Mandaeans, Yazidis and 'heretical' and sectarian Muslims have been jumping out of the windows too. The difference is that the Jew found refuge in the embattled homestead, his original abode. Populating it continuously through 2,000 years, Jews had never surrendered its title.

More than 99 per cent of Jewish residents have fled from the Arab world in the last sixty years. Some 650,000 went to Israel and 200,000 to the West.[2] Their exodus took two forms: those better equipped with foreign passports and connections generally engineered their private exits, mainly to Europe, Australia or the Americas. Together with a minority of ideological Zionists, the rest went to Israel. Although the diaspora remains overwhelmingly Ashkenazi, over 50 per cent of Israel's Jews today are Mizrahi or Sephardi refugees from Arab and Muslim countries or their descendants.[3]

Mass refugee movements have been a feature of conflicts in the first half of the twentieth century: upwards of fifty-two million people have been displaced.[4] The Arab-Israeli conflict is no exception. However, the root causes of the mass displacement of the Jews predate the Arab-Israeli conflict, and it may be argued that the inability of Arabs and Muslims to accept Israel belongs in deep-seated cultural, religious and ideological prejudice.

The twentieth century produced 135 million refugees[5] as a consequence of the self-determination of peoples through violence. Population exchanges were common in the twentieth century – roughly equal numbers of Jews from the Middle East and North Africa, and Palestinian Arabs swapped places. There were also exchanges of refugees between Greece and Turkey, India and Pakistan, and Greek and Turkish Cyprus, not forgetting the mass migration of ethnic Germans and others in the wake of the Second World War.

However, while all these refugee populations have been absorbed in their new countries, only the Palestinian Arabs are still, according to the UN, considered refugees and allowed to pass on their refugee status to succeeding generations *ad infinitum*.[6] Their leaders have constantly kindled the vain hope of a 'Right of Return' to Palestine in their hearts, even though most were not born there and some had been resident for no more than two years. Arguably, these refugees have been deliberately deprived of civil rights in their adopted countries in order to remain a standing reproach to Israel and a weapon in the decades-long Arab and Muslim struggle against the Jewish state.

Although two refugee populations exchanged places, the circumstances of their displacement were very different. Palestinian Arab refugees were caught up in a war zone in 1948. Many chose to flee but expulsions did take place, for instance at Ramle and Lydda,[7] but the fact that 160, 000 Arabs out of about 870,000 in western Palestine[8] chose to stay indicates that the newly-proclaimed Israeli state had no systematic policy of 'ethnic cleansing'.[9] By contrast, Jordan, which took over territory after the 1948 war, 'ethnically cleansed' the West Bank of Jordan (Judea and Samaria) and the Old City of Jerusalem, where the Jews had been the largest constituent group; every last Jewish inhabitant was displaced.[10] Almost a million Middle Eastern and North African Jews, hundreds or thousands of miles from the theatre of battle, on the other hand, were singled out for persecution and dispossession because they were Jews. While Palestinian refugees were internally displaced a few miles or relocated to countries which, like the great majority of them, were Sunni Muslim and Arabic-speaking, Jews were forced to abandon their age-old heritage, languages and culture, and start afresh.

On 29 November 1947, the United Nations passed UNGA resolution 181, approving the Partition of Palestine into

Jews pour out of the Old City of Jerusalem in 1948. Every last Jew was expelled following the Arab conquest.

Four generations of the Jewish Habbani tribe from the Arabian peninsula, Ein Shemer camp, Israel, 1950 (Fritz Cohen/Israel Government Press Office)

a Jewish and an Arab state. The Arabs fiercely rejected the plan; anti-Jewish riots broke out in Syria, Bahrain and Aden. The five Arab League countries – Syria, Lebanon, Egypt, Iraq and Jordan – which had launched the 1948 war against Israel (Yemen and Saudi Arabia sent expeditionary forces) waged a second war against their own non-combatant Jewish citizens, whom they referred to as the Jewish 'minority of Palestine'.[11] They lost the war against Israel, but won the war decisively against their own Jews. Except when they were treated as hostages and forbidden to leave the country, these Jews had no alternative but to move away.

In 1948, the countries of the Maghreb, including Morocco, home to the largest population of Jews in the Arab world, were not yet members of the Arab League and were still under the colonial yoke, having not yet achieved independence. These countries were not contiguous with Palestine and their governments not at war with Israel, but their populations were, nevertheless, swept up in a powerful wave of anti-Jewish hostility. Most of Libya was under British control but the 1945 Tripoli riots had displaced thousands of Jews, already traumatised, exhausted and decimated by the Second World War. Angered by a wave of Moroccan Jews streaming into Algeria on their way to Palestine, professional agitators instigated rioting against the border Jewish communities of Oujda and Jerrada (and forty-four Jews were killed).[12] These pogroms, the worst since the *Fez Tritl* of 1912, had a grave psychological effect: Jews questioned if they had a future in Morocco now that they had an alternative in Israel.

Whilst Jews fleeing Nazi Germany found the gates to most countries shut in their faces, the establishment of Israel gave Jews fleeing the Arab and Muslim world – usually the poorest, sickest and most vulnerable – somewhere secure to go.

As soon as Israel was born, the Zionist underground and the American Joint Distribution Committee, determined after the Holocaust never again to leave Jews in the diaspora to their fate, rescued great numbers of refugees

Yemenite Jews arriving in Israel (Fritz Cohen/ Israel Government Press Office)

Child at the Caesarea *Ma'abara*, 1954 (Fritz Cohen/Israel Government Press Office)

in some of the largest airlifts in history. Operation Magic Carpet (Wings of Eagles) in Yemen, Operation Ezra and Nehemiah in Iraq, and Operations Mural and Yakhin in Morocco, shifted tens of thousands of Jews to Israel.[13]

The Jews of Arab lands faced two sorts of 'ethnic cleansing'. Yemen, Syria, Libya, Iraq, post-Suez Egypt and Algeria disgorged the majority of their Jews in one precipitous go. In Lebanon, Morocco and Tunisia, Jews were ushered over a longer period towards the exit, their flight peaking at periods of heightened tension in the Israeli-Arab conflict. All these countries criminalised Zionism, exposing their Jewish minorities to accusations of being a fifth column.

Jews who stayed on frequently became prisoners in their countries of birth, where discriminatory travel bans operated. When the pressure for emigration became unbearable, Yemen and Iraq made a deal with the Israeli Mossad to allow their Jews to leave. Their liberation by airlift was achieved with hard cash. In effect, Israel paid a ransom for each Jew, paying to transport them out of the country. Iraqi officials had to be bribed to the tune of several times their monthly salaries.[14] It cost £12 a head (equivalent to £400 today) to fly each and every passenger to safety. When a five-year Moroccan emigration ban on Jewish families was lifted, an agreement was reached in 1961 whereby the World Jewish Congress paid a ransom of up to $250 a head secretly to transport Jews out of the country in the early sixties, equivalent to $1,600 today. The total cost of the indemnities paid to the Moroccan authorities was somewhere between $5 million and $20 million.[15]

'Those Zionists were delegated by the Messiah. They saved thousands of lives', said Penina Elbaz, who witnessed how Zionist operatives came to collect poor Jews from the southern town of Safi in Morocco.[16]

The Iraqi government agreed to release its Jews because it thought that thousands of destitute Jews arriving on Israel's doorstep with little more than the shirts on their backs would lead to economic collapse.[17] The airlifts were lucrative for the governments and civil servants of these countries who received generous bribes. Arabs were sometimes major shareholders in the transport companies. At the end of the day, Arab states and individuals reaped a short-term bonanza in Jewish assets seized and property deemed to have been abandoned or sold for peanuts. The long-term costs to the economy and culture of Arab states are unquantifiable.

The mass airlifts to Israel were unprecedented. The nightmare journey in a ramshackle cargo plane huddled with other air-sick passengers began for these Jews well before they stepped on board. Jews in Yemen made a long and risky trek on foot down to the British crown colony of Aden: emissaries paid various Yemeni tribal chiefs a head tax to permit Jewish refugees to pass through the country.[18] They arrived half-starved and destitute and spent weeks in makeshift camps in the heat and dust. Some 150 died on the way and 700 perished in the camps.[19]

Egyptian Jews arriving by ship in Greece on their way to Israel.

In total, 4,000 of the 38,000 Jews in Libya had been made homeless by lethal riots in 1945 and had been sleeping in the synagogues.[20] Some 120,000 Jews leaving Iraq were stripped by decree of their citizenship in 1950, and later of their property by a parliamentary law passed in secret session.[21] Jews in Egypt – the community numbered 80,000 – left in two main waves: 20,000, including communists and Zionists, in 1948; 25,000, comprising the middle classes, summarily expelled in 1956 and given just hours to leave with only 50 dinars in their pockets.[22] All but 5,000 of the 30,000 Jews of Syria fled violent riots in 1947.[23]

Many were marked for life by the trauma of their uprooting. Heads of families had had their work permits rescinded. Egyptian Jews remained haunted by the abusive or obscene phone calls they had received or calls with no-one at the other end of the line, the threatening letters received, the bribes demanded, the ominous knock at three in the morning, the shock of armed men at the front door, male relatives taken away without explanation. Plans for leaving had to be made in secret, without the usual goodbyes, especially if the final destination was Israel – which some Egyptian Jews called '*chez nous*'. When the time came for their hurried departure, Egyptian Jews would have their passports confiscated and replaced with a *laissez-passer* marked with the words: 'one way – no return'.

Jews were stripped of their citizenship in Iraq and permitted to leave with 50 dinars ($80 today), one suit, a wedding ring, a cherished bracelet, a watch and one suitcase. There was no guarantee that those suitcases would arrive at their destination. The Mossad emissary Mordechai Ben-Porat discovered a porters' racket at Baghdad airport to spirit the suitcases off the passenger buses.[24] Departing Jews complained that malicious customs men would confiscate a last piece of jewellery, ransack their bags or ruin the contents.

Having reached safety, the refugees faced the challenge of building their lives all over again. The mental and physical cost was considerable. 'Exile broke him', writes Raphael Luzon of his father in his autobiography *Libyan Twilight*.[25] 'The mourning for a lost life never left him, so he remained what he had always been – a Libyan Jew.'

There is anecdotal evidence that a shocking number died soon after displacement, unable to cope with the trauma of uprooting and stress of providing for their families. City dwellers had to rebuild their lives in the country. Camille Fox, from a wealthy Egyptian family, describes how she exchanged the fragrance of Chanel for the stench of the cowshed on a *moshav* (cooperative farm) in the south of Israel.

The refugee generation was known as the 'desert generation' – it did not possess the language or professional skills to prosper in its adopted country. Fathers especially found their authority suddenly eroded in a society less patriarchal than the one they had come from. The Iraq-born author Eli Amir describes the dashed expectations of his father, who had a dream to plant rice-fields in Israel's Hula Valley. Men who were merchants or administrators in their country of birth took off their suits and joined construction gangs. Women went out to work for the first time and were often more resilient to change.

Relationships were turned upside down, with children taking responsibility for their disorientated parents. Israel paid special attention to the children, sending them to youth villages and kibbutzim in order to prepare them for life in the Jewish state. Refugee families were atomised and siblings dispersed across the globe. At one stage, my mother in England had a sister in Iraq (until 1991), a brother in Iran,[26] a sister in France, a sister in the US and a brother in Canada.

Naturally, the harsh conditions awaiting the 650,000 Jews who went to Israel –the stinking *ma'abarot* (transit camps), the shortage of food and jobs, and the alien language and culture – were hardly encouraging. Israel was struggling to cope with an influx of refugees and Holocaust survivors which doubled its 600,000-strong population overnight.[27]

In the chaos of the camps there were stories of babies and children stolen and never seen again.[28] Some refugees remained in the tin shacks and wooden huts of the *ma'abarot* for up to thirteen years. These were often on the country's northern and southern borders. The camps slowly turned into permanent towns and cities. The border town of Sderot, a notorious target for Hamas short-range missiles, began life as the *ma'abara* of Gevim-Dorot. It housed Kurdish, Iranian and North African Jews.

The new state did not always show sensitivity to the needs of these immigrants. Yiddish was a prerequisite for some jobs. New accommodation in Israel was not designed for large families. The state had little use for dozens of shoemakers and shopkeepers. Jobs had to be invented for Moroccan immigrants with little education and no transferable skills: for instance, carting grass from a neighbouring kibbutz to Ashdod beach.[29]

In spite of the hardships and suffering of the early years, these Jews had escaped anti-Jewish riots, synagogue burnings, kidnappings, internment and executions. But conditions in Israel for the new arrivals were dire. The few thousand Jews, usually the wealthier ones, who stayed behind in Arab countries, congratulated themselves at the time that they had not joined the mass exodus. For a short time they continued to live calm and comfortable lives. But even worse torment and terror lay in store for them: Jews in Egypt were brutally expelled after 1956, the few thousand Jews remaining in Iraq and Syria, who had to carry special identity cards, were stripped of their rights and livelihoods in the 1950s and 1960s. Until 1961, Jews were banned from leaving Morocco. All that Jews who chose to stay behind in Arab countries were doing was postponing their inevitable departure.

In Iraq, desperate conditions demanded desperate measures, and after 1970, following the horrific hangings of nine Jews in Baghdad's main square and the disappearance of scores more, 1,900 Jews were smuggled *Kachagh* (illegally) through Kurdistan with the complicity of the Israeli authorities. Syrian Jews were virtual prisoners, restricted in their movements with their every move watched by the secret police. Those who could, risked the treacherous smugglers' route to Israel – some of them on foot – until 2,000 were liberated as a result of international pressure in the 1990s.

In Morocco, poverty could also trap those Jews who did not join the mass emigrations. The last Jews of Meknes were compelled to pay $125 for a passport: many could not afford both a passport and an airplane ticket.[30] A common government ruse in other countries was to allow foreign travel for one member of a family, with the others being forced to remain behind as hostages.

If hundreds of thousands of Jews had not been transported to Israel, what would have happened to them? It is highly likely they would have remained at the mercy of their host countries, vulnerable to episodes of mob violence, arbitrary arrests and rampant injustice. If Jews had remained in the areas of Syria and Iraq occupied by Da'esh (Islamic State) they would have met a similar fate to Yazidis and Assyrian Christians: executed, with their women and children raped and sold as slaves. At the very least, many would have languished, vulnerable to pogroms, struggling to feed their children, deprived of jobs and livelihoods by state-sanctioned and more subtle discrimination.

It is undeniable that some of these Jews encountered prejudice on arrival in Israel and were isolated in remote development towns; however, Israel accepted these dispossessed and huddled masses unconditionally – on the basis that they were Jews. It gave them citizenship. It gave them freedom. It cured them of tuberculosis and trachoma. Above all, it gave them the safe haven and political ability to defend themselves, which minorities in Arab countries sorely lack.

Until the mass flight of Middle Eastern Christians after the 2003 invasion of Iraq, the largest number of non-Muslim refugees in the Middle East and North Africa was Jewish.[31] They outnumbered Palestinian Arab refugees from what is now Israel.[32] The vast majority are unequivocally thankful that they got out and rebuilt their lives in the free world: 'They took everything, but the one thing they could not take was inside our heads', Maurice Mizrahi, an Egyptian Jew who became a Pentagon engineer, said of the Egyptian authorities.[33] Many are, however, increasingly frustrated that their story has been neglected or forgotten.

In the twentieth century, the Jewish refugees in Arab lands were among the first victims of totalitarianism, its seeds planted in the 1930s, its tendrils still wrapping themselves around the Arab and Muslim world today. The world has ignored the Jewish refugee story and the Jewish quest for justice. But the scope of this book extends far into the past, contextualising the Jewish story of minority submission.

If we are ever to reach a point of understanding and even reconciliation, it is essential to look more closely at the plight of the Jews from Arab countries and bust the myths that have been allowed to take root during decades of silence. The existence of pre-Islamic Jewish communities has been erased, or their history rewritten and distorted to fit post-modern agendas. Too many people are in denial about Arab and Muslim anti-Semitism and bigotry, the engine of 'ethnic cleansing' within the region. The story is not just a niche Sephardi or Mizrahi one – it is more relevant than ever to an understanding of the Arab/Islamist struggle against Israel and the non-Muslim Other.

This book takes a closer look at Mizrahi integration into Israel and at the politicisation of their struggle. It charts the growing clamour for recognition, redress and memorialisation for Jewish refugees.

Notes

1. Benny Morris, 'No love for Muslims, unless they are Palestinians', *Haaretz*, 29 September 2010 at http://www.haaretz.com/no-love-for-muslims-unless-they-re-palestinian-1.316295. (Last accessed 26 April 2017).

2. Maurice Roumani, *The Jews from Arab Countries: A Neglected Issue* (Tel Aviv: World Organization of Jews from Arab Countries (WOJAC), 1983), p.2.

3. Statistical Abstract of Israel, 2009, CBS. 'Table 2.24 – Jews, by country of origin and age' (PDF).

4. Ben-Dror Yemini, 'Why do Palestinian refugees get so much more attention than others?' *Ynet News*, 4 December 2015, http://www.ynetnews.com/articles/0,7340,L-4734742,00.html. (Last accessed 26 April 2017).

5. Eli Hertz, *Arab and Jewish Refugees – the Contrast, Myths and Facts,* 2007, p.37.

6. Daniel Pipes, 'Eventually, all Humans will be Palestinian Refugees', *Washington Times*, 21 February 2012, http://www.danielpipes.org/10695/unwra-palestine-refugees. (Last accessed 26 April 2017).

7. Benny Morris, 'Israel conducted no ethnic cleansing in 1948', *Haaretz*, 10 October 2016, http://www.haaretz.com/opinion/.premium-1.746676. (Last accessed 26 April 2017).

8. UNWRA was responding to the needs of about 750,000 refugees in 1950. (www.unwra.org).

9. Ibid.

10. See Michael J. Totten, 'Between the Green line and the Blue line', *City Journal*, summer 2011, http://www.city-journal.org/html/between-green-line-and-blue-line-13397.html. (Last accessed 26 April 2017).

11. Political committee of the Arab League, Draft Law regarding Jewish Residents, 1947, http://zionism-israel.com/hdoc/Arab_League_Law_Jews.htm. (Last accessed 26 April 2017).

12. David B. Green, 'This Day in Jewish History: Anti Jewish Rioting in Morocco Leaves 44 Dead', *Haaretz*, 8 June 2014, http://www.haaretz.com/jewish/features/.premium-1.597458. (Last accessed 26 April 2017).

13. Israeli Ministry of Aliyah and Immigrant Absorption, http://www.moia.gov.il. In the 1990s, the Israeli government continued to pursue its policy of rescuing Jews in distress by airlifting thousands of Ethiopian Jews in Operations Moses and Solomon.

14. Mordechai Ben-Porat, *To Baghdad and Back* (Gefen, 1998), p.122.

15. Xavier Cornut, 'The Moroccan Connection', *Jerusalem Post*, 22 June 2009, http://www.jpost.com/Features/The-Moroccan-connection. (Last accessed 26 April 2017).

16. 'The truth about Morocco: fear made Jews leave', *Point of No Return*, 11 September 2016, http://jewishrefugees.blogspot.co.uk/2016/09/the-truth-about-morocco-fear-made-jews.html. (Last accessed 26 April 2017).

17. See Elie Kedourie's essay, 'The Break between Arabs and Jews', in Mark R. Cohen and Abraham L. Udovitch (eds), *Jews Among Arabs* (Darwin, 1989).

18. Joe Spier, 'Alaska Airlines and the Jews of Yemen', *San Diego Jewish World*, 1 May 2015.

19. Vered Lee, 'The Frayed Truth of Operation Magic Carpet', *Haaretz*, 28 May 2012, http://www.haaretz.com/jewish/books/the-frayed-truth-of-operation-magic-carpet-1.432991. (Last accessed 26 April 2017).

20. Shmuel Trigano, '1920–1970: A History of Ongoing Cruelty and Discrimination', *Jerusalem Center for Public Affairs* (JCPA), 4 November 2010, http://jcpa.org/article/the-expulsion-of-the-jews-from-muslim-countries-1920-1970-a-history-of-ongoing-cruelty-and-discrimination/.(Last accessed 26 April 2017).

21. Itamar Levin, *Confiscated wealth: the fate of Jewish property in Arab lands*, Policy Forum 22, Institute of the World Jewish Congress, 2000, p.11.
22. Michael Laskier, *Jews of Egypt* (New York: NY University Press, 1992), p.144.
23. Itamar Levin, *Locked Doors* (Westport, CT: Praeger, 2001), p.173.
24. See Ben-Porat, *To Baghdad and Back,* (Jerusalem: Gefen, 1998), p.122.
25. Raphael Luzon, *Libyan Twilight* (London: Darf, 2016), p.26.
26. He had to flee a second time from the Islamic revolution in 1979.
27. Jonathan Kaplan, 'The Mass Migration of the 1950s', *Jewish Agency for Israel*, 27 April 2015, http://www.jewishagency.org/society-and-politics/content/36566. (Last accessed 26 April 2017).
28. The Yemenite Children Affair (not all were Yemenite, some were Iraqi and some even Ashkenazi) concerns children who were taken away alive from their parents. Parents were told they had died, but this was not always the case. The Affair has been the subject of three Israeli official inquiries. A 2001 probe examined more than 1,000 cases and concluded that most of the children in question had died natural deaths. While it stated that some of the remaining ones were probably adopted — and did not reach conclusions in a number of cases — it found no evidence of kidnapping or an organised conspiracy. In 2016, the government ordered files which had been sealed until 2071 to be declassified. In 2017, revelations that unauthorised tests had been carried out on Yemenite children caused an outcry.
29. Simon Skira interviewed in the film: *Les destins contrariés* by Younes Laghrari (2015).
30. D. Sitton, *Sephardi Communities Today,* (Jerusalem: Council of Sephardi and Oriental Communities, 1985), p.166.
31. Eliza Griswold, 'Is this the end of Christianity in the Middle East?', *New York Times*, 22 July 2015, http://www.nytimes.com/2015/07/26/magazine/is-this-the-end-of-christianity-in-the-middle-east.html. (Last accessed 26 April 2017).
     Griswold notes that over a million Christians have left the Arab world since 2003 – slightly more than the Jewish exodus of 850,000.
32. Bernard Lewis quotes the 30 September 1949 UN Economic Survey for the Middle East figure of 726,000 Palestinian refugees in *Semites and Anti-Semites* (Norton, 1999), p.184.
33. Elliot Malki (producer) & Ruggero Gabbai (director), *Starting Over Again*, 2015.

1

Over a Millennium before Islam

Each year for the Feast of the Sacrifice (Eid al-Adha), Umm Mariam visits the Mashhad al-Shams shrine at Kifl near the town of Hillah in southern Iraq to decorate its walls with henna. She is one of dozens of pilgrims packing the grassy, palm-fringed courtyard in the shadow of a ziggurat and newly-restored, ornate minaret. She tells the Arabic electronic medium *Al-Monitor* that the shrine cured her daughter of a chronic illness after she slept there for one night. Some believe the shrine also has the power to make infertile women bear children.[1] The site is resplendent with carved colonnades and opulent marble, reminiscent of many Shi'a mosques in the region. There are mosaic domes with Qur'anic inscriptions. Nothing would suggest that this place has ever been other than a Muslim place of pilgrimage.

Yet the pan-Arab publication *Al-Monitor* admits that Kifl has not always been Islamic. Before Islam, we are told, it was associated with the Babylonian sun god Shams. The newly-renovated shrine, under the control of the Shi'a *Wakf* (Endowment) is lined with photos of Shi'ite Imams and inscriptions indicating that the Fourth Imam Ali ibn Abi Talib had prayed and stayed there in the seventh century: 'The space's sacredness derives from this Islamic event and has superseded its importance as a historic Babylonian monument.'[2]

Courtyard of the refurbished shrine of Ezekiel.

Unbeknown to Umm Mariam, her fellow pilgrims and most readers of
Al-Monitor, before it was re-invented as Mashhad al Shams, Kifl was the
shrine of Ezekiel, one of six Jewish prophets' shrines in Iraq. By one stroke
of his pen, the *Al-Monitor* reporter had elided 2,700 years of Jewish history.

Holy shrine of Prophet Ezekiel Kifil

אדוניגו הנביא יחזאל זייעא

J.S. Hoary, Baghdad

View of Ezekiel's shrine before Islamisation.

Aerial view of Ezekiel's shrine at Kifl today.

The renovated shrine of Ezekiel has been transformed into a classic Shi'a holy site.

Benjamin of Tudela visited the site in 1170, and described seeing a synagogue, a *tebah* (reading platform) and a room filled with books dating back to the First and Second Temples. Until their mass flight in 1951, the local Jews, and some from as far afield as Persia and India, converged on the tomb – especially between New Year and the Day of Atonement when the book of Ezekiel was read.[3]

Ezekiel, whose name, Yehézq'el, signifies 'strong as God' or 'whom God makes strong', was the son of Buzi. He was one of the priests who, in the year 598 BCE, was deported, together with King Jehoiachin, as a prisoner from Jerusalem. He seems to have spent the rest of his life in Babylon. Ezekiel foretold the complete destruction of the Kingdom of Judah. After his prophecies were fulfilled, he was commanded to announce that the people would return from exile to their ancestral land, and the coming of the Messiah.

So important was Ezekiel the prophet to the Jews of Iraq that Yehézq'el was traditionally the most popular name for Jewish boys. For Muslims in Iraq, Heskel became a generic name for 'Jew'.

Ezekiel's tomb became a favourite place of pilgrimage with Muslims, being on the route of the *Hajj* to Mecca. It is thought to have become a Jewish centre after the Muslim conquest and the cult of the Shi'ite saints in Islam took hold. Before the latest renovation by the Shi'a *Wakf*, Muslims referred to Ezekiel's shrine as the tomb of Dhu al-Kifl, a minor character in the Qur'an. He has now been demoted in importance as the *Wakf* inflates the connection of the site with Imam Ali, to reinforce the legitimacy of Shi'a Islam.

Some 5,000 Jewish pilgrims used to visit the prophet's tomb at Shavu'oth (Pentecost). They would stay in accommodation adjoining the shrine. Thousands of Jews lived and owned land in the town of Hillah. On a visit to the tomb in 1910,[4] David Solomon Sassoon, grandson of the great entrepreneur and philanthropist David Sassoon, kept a diary in Hebrew. 'Hillah is a very small town surrounded by a wall built not in very good fashion from bricks taken from the ruins of ancient Babylon', he wrote. 'The colour of the water is so bad that one is frightened to drink. To the north and south, the city is surrounded by date palms.'[5]

David Sassoon Junior found the Jews of Hillah oppressed by the local sheikhs. They had rigorously applied the strictures of *dhimmitude* (including the Shi'a idea that a Jew was 'unclean' or *najas)* until a few years before. He wrote in his diary:

> The lovely building over the grave is extremely old, built from very big stones said to be the work of King Jehoiachin. Above the doorway was a plaque dated 1809/10, which has inscribed on it – '*this is the tomb of our master Yehezkel the prophet, the son of Buzi the Kohen, may his merit shield us and all Israel. Amen.*'[6]
>
> The room with the grave is very high and has flowers painted on the walls and the names of important visitors to the grave. It is mentioned that my grandfather David Sassoon repaired the building in 1859. The grave is very large: 12 feet 9 inches long, 5 feet 3 inches wide and 5 feet 1 inch high. It is covered with a decorated *parochet* (curtain) which was sent by David Sassoon from Bombay. It is also written on the walls of the visit of Menahem Saleh Daniel to the grave in 1897/8; and his donation to redecorate the grave. Nearby, another room has five tombs of *Geonim* (Sages).[7]

The tomb of Ezekiel, with its Hebrew inscriptions still visible on the walls, is draped in green to signify its importance to Muslims.

We do not know the post-makeover fate of the tombs of the *Geonim*, nor do we know if the floral decoration and Hebrew inscriptions will survive. A green covering embroidered with Arabic script, denoting the tomb of Dhu al-Kifl, has replaced the *parochet*. In any event, David Sassoon would hardly recognise the shrine today.

Today, no Jews remain in Kifl, and only five reside in the whole of Iraq[8]. In the space of one generation, the Jewish community has become extinct. History has been rewritten to wipe out the Jewish presence from Iraq's past altogether.

An Uprooting without Precedent

In 1945, 856,000 Jews lived in the Middle East and North Africa.[9] Only about 4,500 remain – almost all of them in Morocco and Tunisia. The numbers of Jews in Egypt, Syria, Lebanon, Yemen, Bahrain and Iraq may be counted on the fingers of one or two hands. In Libya and Algeria there are none at all.[10]

More than 99 per cent of Jews who once lived in the Arab countries have left them.[11] According to the historian Nathan Weinstock: 'there is no precedent for so dramatic an elimination of Jewish communities around the world, even when compared with the flight of the Jews from Tsarist Russia, Germany in the Thirties or massive immigration from Eastern Europe after World War II.'[12]

People in the West tend to apply a common misconception to all Jews, borrowing the European Christian notion that Jews have been guests, wandering from land to land throughout history, with no country to call their own. It is a misunderstanding: not only have Jews always lived in the patch of land in the Mediterranean which the Romans named Palestine, they have had an unbroken presence in the Middle East and North Africa for over 2,000 years, predating Islam and the Arab conquest by at least a millennium.[13]

Until their expulsion fifty years ago, Jews had been settled in Iraq since the Babylonians had exiled Jews from Jerusalem and Judea to the land of the two rivers in 586 BCE. In the early twentieth century, Baghdad was amongst the most Jewish cities in the world. Comprising up to 40 per cent of the city's population, Jews constituted the largest single ethnic group: even the market shut down on the Sabbath.[14]

There were five exiles from the land of Israel to Mesopotamia, and the Babylonian exile led to the foundation of the world's oldest diaspora. Jews were taken from Jerusalem to captivity in Babylon in 586 BCE. They wept on the banks of the Tigris 'when they remembered Zion'.[15] A sizeable minority chose to remain there after the Persian King Cyrus defeated the Babylonians and declared that the Jews were free to return to Jerusalem to rebuild their Temple.

The Jews of the Middle East and North Africa belonged to an indigenous patchwork of ethnicities, languages and communities. In pre-Islamic times, the Jewish kingdom of Himyar existed in Yemen, where Christians and Jews were powerful and influential. In Egypt, at the time of the Pharaohs, there was a wealthy and well-established Jewish garrison on the island of Elephantine. History recounts that the High Priest Omnias fled to Egypt and constructed a Temple identical in every way to the one in Jerusalem. The Jewish historian Flavius Josephus records that a million Jews lived in Egypt 2,000 years ago, before they were decimated by the Romans.

Over the centuries, large numbers of non-Muslims adopted Islam: Berbers in North Africa, Copts in Egypt, Byzantine Orthodox in Syria, Zoroastrians in Persia and Hindus in India. It is said that, until the fifteenth century Spanish Inquisition, 90 per cent of Jewry lived under Muslim rule.[16] Following the expulsion of Jews and Muslims from Spain, large numbers of Sephardi Jews went east and south as well as west and north, and reinforced the existing Jewish communities around the Mediterranean basin, bringing with them their own distinctive traditions, intellectual vitality and medieval Spanish dialects.

Islam married religious universalism with political imperialism. From the seventh century, Muslim conquerors burst forth from the Arabian Peninsula and set about imposing a new order on the Christians, Jews and pagans of the Middle East and North Africa.

The Arab conquest subjugated indigenous peoples, colonised their lands and expropriated their wealth. Under the Pact of Omar, modelled on Byzantine Christian rules, Jews, Christians and Mandaeans became *dhimmis*.[17] This term, meaning 'protected ones', originates from the Qur'an, but was later refined and developed to have a precise meaning in Islamic jurisprudence. To be a *dhimmi* was not a privilege; in effect, non-Muslim monotheists subcontracted their right to self-defence to the Muslim authorities by paying a 'protection' tax. It begs the question: protection from whom?

The *dhimma* system, the historian Darío Fernández-Morera asserts, was a gangster-like protection racket profitable to the Muslim rulers.[18] The non-Muslim had to be continuously reminded that he was the defeated party in *jihad* – to give just a few examples, he had to wear special clothing and badges (the yellow patch, later to be obligatory in the sixteenth century Venice ghetto and the ancestor of the Nazi yellow star, was mandated by the Caliph al-Mutawakkil),[19] and step aside for Muslims on the street. In addition, he could not build synagogues or homes higher than the Muslim, nor testify against him in court, nor marry a Muslim woman, nor ride a horse, nor make a show of himself.

Conditions for Jews under Byzantine and Visigoth rule, however, were often worse, and Jews sided with their Muslim conquerors. Arabs were also pragmatists, and especially in the early centuries of the Arab conquest, were outnumbered by the peoples they had conquered. They were far less interested in the mass conversion of vanquished peoples than securing their tribute.[20] The ninth century was a time of tolerance because the Arab rulers represented a minority. In the Middle Ages, Barbarians and non-Arabs took military control of Muslim lands, spreading mayhem; but non-Muslims remained legal and social inferiors.

Abbasid Baghdad became a centre of science, philosophy and culture. It ushered in a dazzling period of Muslim-Jewish cross-fertilisation and fruition. The Arabs revived the position of Exilarch, the honorific title given to the leader of the Babylonian-Jewish community. Exilarchs continued to be appointed until the eleventh century and were treated with great pomp and circumstance.

The Arab conquerors allowed their subjugated peoples freedom to practise their skills and talents under their rule. They exploited their skills and labour. Muslim rulers welcomed Jews into their domains, not because they loved them, but because they needed them to do the jobs they would not, or could not, do.

Very soon Jews and other minorities left agriculture to escape poll and land taxes. They became the economic backbone of society: craftsmen, artisans, traders and middlemen. (The great international trade represented by polyglot Jewish merchants such as the Radhanites, predates Islam and even the Babylonian exile, going back to the silk trade at the time of King Solomon.)[21] Jews were 'despised but indispensable'.[22] As the Moroccan proverb states: 'A market without Jews is like bread without salt.'[23]

Institutionalised inequality put non-Muslims at an economic disadvantage and placed them under pressure to convert in order to avoid paying the dreaded *Jizya* and other taxes. Only through conversion could they become fully socially accepted. It was always a one-way street: apostasy from Islam was punishable by death. Muslim men could take non-Muslim wives and convert them to Islam. The reverse did not apply. On this uneven playing field, pagan, Christian and Jewish majorities became minorities. In North Africa, Christianity was wiped out altogether.

It could be argued that it is a tribute to Muslim 'tolerance' in the Middle East that a kaleidoscope of ancient religions and non-Muslim communities survived for so long. On the other hand, they survived in much reduced numbers.

There were times when Jews flourished: the rules of *dhimmitude* were more honoured in the breach than the observance. Jews and Christians became physicians in violation of a Muslim prohibition.[24] Although the Jews were allowed no political power, they were appointed to government posts because there were no suitable Muslim candidates.[25] Jews were employed because of their extreme vulnerability and dependability for the same reason that Muslim rulers depended on Turkish guards, black slaves and eunuchs.[26] Jews were prohibited from carrying arms, putting their safety entirely in the hands of the dominant Muslims. There were, however, exceptions: Jews in Muslim Spain were often armed. Jews in the (Berber) Rif and Atlas mountains (Morocco) could be armed, ride horses and be exempt from *jizya*, alongside other Jews who were serfs of their Muslim masters.[27] The Jews of Daghestan were respected by their Muslim neighbours as fierce warriors. They even carried weapons when sleeping.[28] In the twentieth century, the Hashemite King Abdullah of Jordan trusted only Circassian bodyguards or guards from the Jewish Habbani warrior tribe of southern Yemen.[29]

An enlightened ruler who treated his Jewish subjects well could be out of step with his deeply religious Muslim population. It was for the Jews' own protection that the Jews of Fez were locked up in their own ghetto in 1438.[30] (Naturally, their concentrated numbers also made them especially vulnerable to mob violence.) Nevertheless, Jews had few rights and occupied a place near the bottom of the social ladder.

The Pentagon adviser and Islamic specialist Harold Rhode has an arresting metaphor to describe the treatment of Jewish *dhimmis* by Islam by reference to the manure market in Isfahan in central Iran:

> There are different types of manure available for sale – actually different qualities – each used for different purposes. There are

different grades/levels, but no matter how one defines it, it is manure. Which roughly corresponds to the way non-Muslims were treated in the Muslim world – a higher level than in the Christian world, but in the end, they were treated as inferiors or worse.[31]

On top of the usual *dhimmi* disabilities, Shi'a Islam added an obsession with ritual purity. Jews were *najas* or impure.

When conditions were good, both rulers and ruled benefited. The regime's legitimacy was bolstered by its commitment to protecting its minorities. When things were bad, they could be terrible. Life for vulnerable minorities was always precarious if not dangerous, especially in times of trouble or turmoil. Although expulsions were rare, pogroms erupted when an interregnum power vacuum arose, at times of drought or starvation, or when the regime was weak, insecure, economically shaky or driven to impose heavy taxes to pay for its wars.

In Yemen, Kurdistan and the Berber lands, Jews were considered 'tribal protégés': the system imposed on tribesmen, as a matter of honour, the protection of the 'weak'. A feudal relationship governed nineteenth century relations between Jewish serfs and Muslim lords in the lawless *bilad al-siba* of Berber Morocco.[32] Often Jews were little more than unpaid labourers or slaves to the tribal chieftains;[33] in Tripolitania they were serfs, passed on to a master's heirs following his death.[34] Some chiefs sold Jews or gave them away as gifts. The existence of Kurds with Jewish grandmothers seems to testify to great numbers of Jewish girls sold or abducted.[35]

Shapers of Judaism

The Jews are a unique people, one of the few to have preserved their identity and language since ancient times. Although there have always been Jews in Jerusalem, Hebron, Safed and Tiberias in Palestine, their mass return in the twentieth century from 120 countries to their ancestral homeland has no precedent. In spite of being scattered to the four corners of the globe, diaspora Jewish communities maintained continuity and links with each other and with the small numbers in *Eretz Yisrael*. History shows that when Jews in one corner of the world are oppressed, Jews in the opposite corner hasten to show solidarity.

Jews living under Muslim rule shaped Judaism as we know it. With few exceptions, Jewish communities both East and West formally accepted the Babylonian Talmud as binding, written in the pre-Islamic academies of present-day Iraq; indeed, modern Jewish practice follows the Babylonian Talmud. For centuries, Babylon was the spiritual and religious hub of Judaism.

When the tenth century ended, other centres sprang up: Jerusalem, Fostat, Córdoba. In North Africa, the city of Kairouan was an important centre for medieval Talmudic scholarship until fundamentalists turned it into a Holy City of Islam, from which Jews were banned. Except when 300 Ashkenazi rabbis arrived in 1210 –11 from France and England – to settle the city of Acre in order to help reconstruct Jewish life after the ravages caused by the Crusaders, oriental and Sephardi Jews were the mainstay of the Jewish community in *Eretz Yisrael*. The communities of Tiberias and Safed, which experienced a sixteenth century revival under the Ottomans, remained under the Sephardi rabbinical authorities and followed Sephardi *halacha* (Jewish practice).[36]

Sephardi thinkers pioneered 'Zionist' thought even before this movement appeared in eastern and western Europe, namely, Joseph Levy of Adrianople, Turkey; Rabbi Yehuda Bibas of Gibraltar; Marko Baruch of Sofia and Rabbi Yehuda Alcalay of Sarajevo.[37]

Eastern Jews belong to ancient communities predating the Arab conquest by a millennium or more. Nevertheless, Israel's opponents, often abetted by the Western media, are wont to deny the 'rootedness' that Jews feel after at least 2,000 years in the Middle East and North Africa. These Jews were Middle Eastern and North African long before they, along with other indigenous peoples, were 'arabised' in terms of language and culture. Yet it is the Arabs who claim to be indigenous – in Palestine 'since time immemorial'. So widespread is this misconception that, when reporting the terrorist attack on the ancient synagogue in Djerba, Tunisia, in 2002, the French media spoke of the Jewish 'settlement' of Djerba, although the Jews preceded the Arabs on the island by 1,000 years.[38]

Jews underwent a gradual process of linguistic assimilation and cultural synthesis representing what the great historian Bernard Lewis has termed the Judeo-Islamic tradition. The much-vaunted Golden Age of cultural flowering in Jewish philosophy and poetry in medieval Spain was a succession of mini-Golden Ages. Hasdai ibn Shaprut, Solomon Ibn Gabirol, Judah Halevi, Samuel Hanagid, as well as the great Maimonides, contributed to a period of intellectual interplay and spiritual collaboration. From such fertile soil sprang Jewish geographers, cartographers and mathematicians.[39]

The medieval philosopher and rabbi Moses Maimonides became private physician to the Viceroy of Ayyubid Egypt. His prominence was less a sign that Jews could attain the very highest office under Muslim rule – it demonstrated that the community as a whole was hostage to the good behaviour of these individual Jews: Jews could be trusted not to poison or betray their masters, otherwise they risked unleashing a massacre of their co-religionists.

During the centuries when both Muslim and Christian states existed in the Iberian peninsula, there were times and places, as in Maimonides' own birthplace, when it was the Muslims who persecuted the Jews and the Christians who offered refuge.[40] The thirteenth century Mongols waived the *dhimmi* rules, but proceeded to massacre tens of thousands, if not millions. It is not clear how Jews survived these dark times.

Arabic replaced local languages and place names. It became the *lingua franca*. However, 30 million non-Arab Kurds have clung on to their language, culture and identity. Amazighen (Berbers) seek to revive their tongue and identity in Algeria and Morocco. Arabic never replaced Farsi and Turkish in the mountainous regions of Persia and Turkey. Until recently, Jews from the relatively isolated Kurdish mountains might have spoken Aramaic.[41] The rugged Berber hinterland helped preserve the Tamazight language. Even where Arabic was their native tongue, it was not the only language Jews knew. Hebrew was the language of prayer. Until the end of Ottoman rule, the Alliance Israëlite Universelle school system taught Turkish as well as European languages and Arabic. Even before Arabic became dominant, Jews in Arab countries spoke *Qiltu*, an Arabic predating the Mongol invasion and unadulterated by the *Gilit* dialect spoken by the waves of Bedouin immigrants who poured into the cities from the desert. So autonomous were the communities that each developed a distinct dialect and accent. The Judeo-Arabic dialect became replete with Hebrew, Persian and Turkish words (and in modern times, even French, English and other European languages) and was written in Hebrew characters.

A small number of Jews could rise to become advisers to the ruling sultans and, in turn, enjoyed their protection. In later centuries, thanks to their trading contacts and mastery of foreign languages, Jews of Sephardi origin became ideal intermediaries with the European powers.

The collapse of the Ottoman Empire pitted the tyranny of the Muslim majority against minorities, who hitherto had gained a degree of protection from the self-contained Ottoman *millet* system. Anti-Zionists reproach Zionism for creating a dichotomy between 'Jews' and 'Arabs': in the Ottoman Empire, people defined themselves as Ottoman subjects belonging to a faith community – as Jews, Muslims and Christians. Until the rise of nationalism, however, each community governed itself. The Jewish community had its own *Haham Bashi* (chief rabbi) and *Beth Din* courts. Jews married among themselves and voluntary conversions to Islam were rare. Communities were segregated but Jews and Muslims mixed in the world of work. In North Africa and Persia, Jews lived in their own ghettoes. Nonetheless, the Jews had a sense of belonging to a distinct tribal-ethnic group (often politely known as 'Israelite' in the colonial era) with its own values, culture, dialect, accent, customs and festivals.

A Plurality without Pluralism

The twentieth century Syrian ultra-nationalist Sati al-Husri once said, 'Every person who speaks Arabic is an Arab!' His dictum became an article of faith for Arab nationalists.[42] His disciple Michel Aflaq (1910–89), founder of the Ba'ath Party, advocated violence and cruelty against those Arabic speakers who refused to conform to his prescribed, all-encompassing, Arab identity.

The twentieth century experiment by pan-Arabists to forge a single nation, based on a common language, from a delicate ecosystem of different ethnic groups and religions, coexisting in multi-ethnic empires, has been a catastrophe. The Middle East and North Africa are a plurality without pluralism. Although non-Muslims were in the forefront of its construction, a further factor caused non-Muslims to be excluded from the Arab national project. Islam is inextricable from Arab nationalism. It is the bedrock of Arab identity. Islam is a source of Arab constitutional law in all modern Arab states today, hence the difficulty that Christians, and even Jews who declared themselves patriots, have had in being accepted. Leading Christian Arab nationalists, like Michel Aflaq, have ended up converting to Islam.

Pan-Arabism died out with the failure of Egyptian President Gamal Abdel Nasser to forge a United Arab Republic and the Arab defeat by Israel in 1967. The Western-educated 'secular' elite, with its colonial connections, had already been driven from power. The rise of political Islam has supplanted nationalism with a purely religious identity, propagating the idea that borders will collapse as the Islamist utopia takes shape according to the slogan: 'One God, One Caliph, One *Umma* (nation). [43]

However, even at its most tolerant, Islam believes it is the ultimate revealed religion: non-Muslims suffer a constant reminder that humiliation is the price they must pay for not following the true path. On the other hand, Islam is Judaism's younger brother and the two faiths share a kindred approach to prayer, charity, permitted foods, ritual slaughter, burial (with none of Christianity's theological hostility to Jews as Christ killers). Judaism and Islam have many affinities, and overlap linguistically and culturally. The Geniza store of ancient documents found in a Cairo synagogue attic testifies to the vast amount of fruitful interaction between Jews and Muslims in medieval times.[44] One scholar writes: 'Jews and Muslims had lived in proximity for so long that they shared a religious ambience even when members of one group knew relatively little about the precise behaviour and beliefs of the other'.[45]

As a mark of respect for Judaism, Muslim notables in Tunisia and Algeria would attend the synagogue service on the Jewish festival of Shavu'oth in order to hear Sa'adia Gaon's commentary on the Ten Commandments in Arabic.[46] And, as examples of cultural symbiosis, hardly a Jewish shrine or holy place exists that is not also considered sacred to Muslims. Thirty-one saints' tombs in North Africa are revered by both Jews and Muslims.

However, the conviction that Islam is the ultimate revelation impels it to become supercessionist and thereby 'colonise' Jewish religious sites, appropriate them as Muslim sites, and even deny, at times in collusion with bodies such as UNESCO,[47] that the Jews have ever had any connection with them. The Tomb of the Patriarchs in Hebron (now the Ibrahimi mosque), the Tomb of Rachel (renamed Bilal ibn-Rabah) and Temple Mount (known to Muslims as the Haram al-Sharif) in Jerusalem are the obvious examples. This same appropriation applies to Christian, Zoroastrian and Hindu sites.

The Jewish History of Iraq

Iraq – the Biblical Mesopotamia – is almost as rich in Jewish history and landmarks as the Land of Israel. Here Abraham first discovered the one God, and the Biblical prophets Ezra, Nehemiah, Nahum, Jonah and Ezekiel walked the dusty land of the two rivers. In neighbouring Iran, Jewish shrines include the tombs of Habakkuk, Daniel, Esther and Mordechai.

The shrine most closely associated with the Jews of Iraq was the tomb of Ezekiel at Kifl, some two hours' drive south of Baghdad. I have described it earlier in this chapter but let us return, for a moment, to its story. On the face of it, Ezekiel's shrine constitutes a 'shared Jewish-Muslim heritage'.[48] Throughout its history, however, the shrine conceals a bitter struggle for control.

The synagogue at Ezekiel's tomb became significant as a symbol of national identification under the Abbasids, when the Jews of the lands of Islam united under the leadership of the Jews of Babylonia. The growing importance of the site aroused Muslim envy. Some Muslim writers attributed the burial place of the prophet Ezekiel to their 'mysterious and controversial' Qur'anic prophet Dhu-al-Kifl. Under the fourteenth century Mongol sultan Oljeitu the Muslims took over the synagogue of the prophet Ezekiel and turned it into a Muslim prayer house. Oljeitu also began to build a mosque, later ruined by flooding, but its minaret exists to this day.[49]

For five centuries, not much was heard about the synagogue at Ezekiel's tomb, but it is assumed that control of it and the access yards to the tomb itself were in Muslim hands.

Around 1778, when the mosque was destroyed by floodwater, the local Muslims tried to turn the outer yard into a mosque. Until the 1820s the Jews were banned from passing through the yard – now converted into a mosque – to the tomb.

In the 1840s, the Jews managed to regain control of the synagogue next to Ezekiel's tomb.[50] At the time, the Turkish authorities needed the Jews to pay for repairs to the outer yard. In spite of protests by the Shi'ite Muslims who controlled the tomb precincts, the Jews seized the opportunity to remove the Muslim symbols and ritual items from the outer yard and turn it into a synagogue again. The Turks (allegedly plied with generous Jewish bribes) expelled the Shi'ite caretakers and allowed the Jews to erect new buildings. To reinforce their hold on the site, the Jews set up a *yeshiva* staffed by scholars from Baghdad and their families. Jewish traders and craftsmen from Hillah, Baghdad and elsewhere went to settle in Kifl.

In the 1850s, the Turks expelled the last of the Shi'ite caretakers. The Jewish official now in charge was elevated to the same status as the keepers of the Shi'ite shrines. Jewish control was complete. The Muslims made two more attempts to wrest control of Ezekiel's yards – in 1860 and in the 1930s when they took over the synagogue for prayers. After a few months, the occupation of the synagogue ended. Until their mass departure for Israel in 1951, the Jews of Kifl continued to maintain the yards of the prophet Ezekiel's tomb.

With no Jews left in the area to preserve the shrine, the site has been converted into a mosque on the orders of the Shi'a *Wakf*. Qur'anic inscriptions now adorn it. The unique Hebrew inscriptions are in jeopardy. After 2010 the Iraqi ministry of Heritage and Tourism lost its battle with the Shi'a *Wakf* to restore the original character of the shrine and its adjoining town of Kifl as a Jewish tourist destination.[51]

However, the emergence in Iraq and Syria of the jihadists of Islamic State (Da'esh) presented a still greater threat: this group would destroy all religious heritage – including Shi'a Muslim shrines and mosques – as symbols of idol worship. Their aim was to wipe out the cultural identity of all those who did not accept the new caliphate which they intended to establish on the ruins of nation states. Da'esh blew up parts of the ancient Assyrian site of Nimrud, the Roman heritage site at Palmyra and the shrines of Jonah and Seth.

The Erasure of Jewish Heritage

History suggests that 'ethnic cleansers' never stop at eradicating the physical presence of a group: they are not satisfied until every last vestige of that group's religious heritage is wiped out – so much so that people will say that Jews never lived in, much less made their mark, on the Arab Middle East and North Africa.

In Tunisia there are six synagogues worth preserving, three rabbis' mausoleums, three cemeteries, and of course, the fifth century mosaic floor at Kelibia, attesting to the 2,000-year-old Jewish presence.

In Syria, the fate of the twenty-four Damascus synagogues recorded as standing in 1990 is unknown, although the spectacular murals of the ancient synagogue of Dura-Europos are preserved in the national museum.[52] The Jobar synagogue, the site of the shrine of the Prophet Elijah, was largely

Mural of Samuel crowning David at Dura Europos, one of Syria's earliest synagogues. (Lucien Gubbay)

destroyed by bombing during the civil war. The Franji synagogue is the only one still in use. The Aleppo Great synagogue was looted and burnt in the 1947 riots, and it is not known if the building survives in 2016. The Ezra synagogue at Tadef, once a place of pilgrimage, is in ruins.[53]

The Franji Synagogue, Damascus (Lucien Gubbay)

Of sixty synagogues in Egypt, sixteen are still standing (the Rambam synagogue has been renovated), four of which are in good order – the rest are crumbling to dust or have been converted to other uses. Sewage flows through the Bassatine cemetery in Cairo (whose marble headstones have been pillaged); three cemeteries in Alexandria also suffer from neglect.

Of fifty synagogues in Baghdad only one working synagogue, Meir Tweg, remains. It is almost permanently shut.

In Libya, very few of the seventy-four synagogues are still recognisable, while a highway runs through the main Tripoli cemetery.[54]

Service at the Eliyahu Hanavi (Nebi Daniel) Synagogue, in the heyday of the Alexandria community (Nebi Daniel Association)

The only bright spot in this bleak picture has been in Morocco, where the government has invested heavily in restoring Jewish quarters, synagogues and 167 cemeteries. Cynics would say that memorialising the Jews is in Morocco's own interest, since these sites attract tourism. Unfortunately, the

Morocco has restored 167 Jewish cemeteries. Tomb of Rabbi Moshe Meir Hai Eliyakim, Bab Marrakesh, Casablanca.

synagogues will not be more than empty buildings as barely 1 per cent of Morocco's post-War Jewish population remains.

The expulsion of the Jews proved to be a portent of other calamities to come: more than half of the Christians of the Middle East have been forced to flee.[55] The Muslim world has unravelled into its tribal components. Islam, in turn, is riven with sectarian conflicts. The Kurds have turned their back on Iraq in an attempt to assert their independence by setting up their own state.

A Mutilated Identity

The Arab world losing its Jewish and other minorities is like a person with an amputated limb who still feels its ghostly presence. Soon after seeing the film *Silent Exodus*, the Egyptian-born Italian journalist and Euro-MP Magdi Cristiano Allam reflected on the Arab world's truncated identity:

> In a flash of insight I could see that the tragedy of the Jews and the catastrophe of the Arabs are two facets of the same coin. By expelling the Jews who were settled on the southern and eastern shores of the Mediterranean centuries before they were arabised and Islamised, the Arabs have in fact begun the lethal process of mutilating their own identity and despoiling their own history. By losing their Jews the Arabs have lost their roots and have ended up by losing themselves. As has often happened in history, the Jews were the first victims of hatred and intolerance. All the 'others' had their turn soon enough, specifically the Christians and those who do not fit exactly into the ideological framework of the extreme nationalists and Islamists. There has not been a single instance in this murky period of our history when the Arab states have been ready to condemn the steady exodus of Christians, ethnic-religious minorities, enlightened and ordinary Muslims, while Muslims plain and simple have become the primary victims of Islamic terror.[56]

Since the 2011 Arab Spring, Arabs have been lamenting their loss of the Jews and the enormous cost to their countries. More than twenty novels have been published which feature Jewish characters.[57] Arab intellectuals, especially in Iraq and Egypt, are beginning to recognise the wrongs done to their Jewish minorities. Film directors are making nostalgic forays into the pluralistic past. In 2015, protesters in Baghdad held placards commending Iraq's first finance minister, the Jew Sir Sasson Heskel, for his loyalty and accomplishments in the 1920s: he conceived of tying Iraq's oil revenues to the Gold Standard.[58] The finance ministers since 2003, on the other hand, have been rated 'zero' for achievement.

In 2015 Baghdad demonstrators held placards giving full marks to Sir Sasson Heskel, Iraq's 1920s Jewish finance minister, while those since 2003 rated zero for achievement.

Sir Sasson Heskel, Iraq's Jewish finance minister, in state uniform.

With its Jews driven to extinction, Islam's colonisation of the Middle East and North Africa, beginning with Muhammad's conquest, is almost complete – but it has been achieved at the cost of cultural richness and diversity. Something miraculous has come out of this tragedy: the Jews have flourished in the tiny corner of the region on the Mediterranean coast to

Hebrew inscription at the crumbling tomb of the Prophet Nahum, Al-Kosh, northern Iraq (Edwin Shuker)

Scribes at the shrine of Ezekiel, 1930s.

The Hebrew inscriptions of the shrine of Joshua the High Priest in Baghdad have now been painted over (*Scribe* Journal)

which they have been driven, where they have proclaimed their sovereignty. But that sovereignty has been continuously challenged and is dangerously fragile.

Twenty years after he published the first novel of his *Alexandria Quartet* in 1957, Lawrence Durrell returned to find Alexandria 'listless', and 'depressing beyond endurance'.[59] Had he returned in the early twenty-first century, Durrell would have found Alexandria even more dull and monochromatic. He would no longer recognise the city, devoid of its Greeks, Armenians and assorted Europeans, and with its five Jews, where once religions and cultures flourished to create a rich and lively mix. As the columnist Mark Steyn once put it, 'Islam is king on a field of corpses'.[60]

Notes

1. Adnan Abu Zeed, 'Babylonian temple now Islamic healing shrine', *Al-Monitor*, 18 January 2016, http://www.al-monitor.com/pulse/originals/2016/01/iraq-babylonian-shrine-turned-islamic.html#ixzz40FoDZoDs. (Last accessed 26 April 2017).
2. Ibid.
3. See Zvi Yehuda, 'The synagogue at the Tomb of the Prophet Ezekiel' in Zvi Yehuda (ed.) *Tombs of Saints and Synagogues in Babylonia* (Or Yehuda: The Babylonian Jewry Heritage Center, 2006), pp. 33–46.
4. *The Scribe*, Issue 75, Autumn 2002.
5. Ibid.
6. Ibid.
7. Ibid.
8. James Glanz and Irit Pazner Garshowitz, 'In Israel, Iraqi Jews reflect on Baghdad Heritage', *New York Times*, 27 April 2015.
9. Maurice Roumani, *The Jews from Arab Countries: A Neglected Issue* (Tel Aviv: World Organisation of Jews from Arab Countries (WOJAC), 1983) and *WOJAC'S Voice*, Vol. 1, No. 1, January 1978.
10. Ibid.
11. Ibid.
12. Nathan Weinstock, *Une si Longue Présence: Comment le Monde arabe a perdu ses juifs 1947–1967* (Paris: Plon, 2008), p.10.
13. Legend has it that Jews arrived in Yemen at the time of King Solomon in 900 BCE. Biblical-era Israelites travelling with Phoenician traders established Jewish communities in the Maghreb. The Jews of modern-day Iraq and Iran trace their ancestry back to the destruction of the first Biblical Temple. In 2014, researchers found inscriptions in Saudi Arabia testifiying to the region's pre-Islamic Jewish and Christian roots in 470 CE. See Ariel David, 'Before Islam: When Saudi Arabia was a Jewish kingdom', *Haaretz*, 15 March 2016.
14. Daniel Khazzoom, *The Journey of a Jew from Baghdad*, Part One (2010).
15. Book of Psalms, 137:1.
16. Sarina Roffé, 'A History of Italian Jewry', JewishGen Sephardic Genealogy Website, http://www.jewishgen.org/sephardic/coliseum.htm. (Last accessed 26 April 2017).
17. 'Pact of Umar', available on Fordham University website, http://sourcebooks.fordham.edu/halsall/source/pact-umar.asp. (Last accessed 26 April 2017).
18. Darío Fernández-Morera, *The Myth of the Andalusian Paradise* (Wilmington, DE: ISI, 2016), p. 21.

19. Georges Bensoussan, *Juifs en pays arabes: le grand déracinement 1850–1975* (Paris: Tallandier, 2012), p. 236.
20. Efraim Karsh, *Islamic Imperialism* (New Haven, CT: Yale University Press, 2006), p. 21.
21. S.D. Goiten, *Jews and Arabs: Their Contacts Through the Ages* (New York: Schocken, 1974), p.107.
22. Paul Fenton lecture at The Jews of Morocco conference, UCL, 20–22 June 2011, reported in *Point of No Return*, http://jewishrefugees.blogspot.co.uk/2011/06/18th-c-jews-tried-and-failed-to.html. (Last accessed 26 April 2017).
23. Aomar Boum quoted in 'Remembrance of things past: Moroccans talk about the Jews who once lived among them', *Vox Tablet*, 16 March 2013.
24. See Goiten, *Jews and Arabs*, p. 70.
25. Ibid., p.69.
26. Norman A. Stillman, *The Jews of Arab Lands: A History and Source Book*, Vol.1 (Philadelphia, PA: Jewish Publication Society of America, 1979), p.179.
27. See Weinstock, *Une si longue présence*, p. 125.
28. Martin Gilbert, *In Ishmael's House* (New Haven, CT: Yale University Press, 2010), p.124.
29. 'Habbani Jews', *Wikipedia*, https://en.wikipedia.org/wiki/Habbani_Jews#cite_note-24. (Last accessed 26 April 2017).
30. See Stillman, *The Jews of Arab Lands*, Vol.1, p. 79.
31. Harold Rhode, 'Minorities in the Muslim World', Fall 2015, http://www.jewishpolicycenter.org/5678/minorities-muslim-world. (Last accessed 26 April 2017).
32. Michel Abitbol, *Le passé d'une discorde: Juifs et Arabes depuis le VIIe siècle* (Paris: Perrin, 2003), p. 206.
33. See Gilbert, *In Ishmael's House*, p.119.
34. Bat Ye'or, 'The *Dhimmi* factor in the Exodus of Jews from Arab Countries' in Malka Hillel Shulewitz (ed.), *The Forgotten Millions* (London: Continuum, 2000), p. 41.
35. Judit Neurink, 'Iraq under my skin', blog, 29 October 2015, http://www.iraqundermyskin.com/2015/10/making-space-for-jews-again-in-kurdistan.html. (Last accessed 26 April 2017).
36. 'De-legitimizing Israel: an outsider perspective', *Fernando* blog, 1 January 2011, http://topicperspectiva.blogspot.co.uk/2011/01/de-legitimizing-israel-outsider.html. (Last accessed 26 April 2017).
37. Ibid.
38. Alexandre del Valle, 'Preface' in Moïse Rahmani, *L' exode oublié: Juifs des pays arabes* (Paris: Raphaël, 2003), p. 17.
39. David de Sola Pool, *Old Faith in the New World: Portrait of Shearith Israel 1654–1954* (New York: Columbia University Press, 1955), pp.487–8.
40. Bernard Lewis, *The Jews of Islam* (Princeton, NJ: Princeton University Press, 2014), p.106.
41. See Ariel Sabar, *My Father's Paradise* (Algonquin, 2009) for an account of the life of his father, one of the last Aramaic-speaking Kurdish Jews.
42. Franck Salameh, 'Does anyone speak Arabic?' *Middle East Quarterly*, Fall 2011, http://www.meforum.org/3066/does-anyone-speak-arabic. (Last accessed 26 April 2017).
43. A slogan quoted by Islamic fundamentalists. See for example Hizb ut Tahrir video, http://www.hizb-ut-tahrir.info/en/index.php/multimedia/video/1864.html (Last accessed 26 April 2017).
44. Malka Hillel Shulewitz, 'Introduction' in *The Forgotten Millions*.
45. Harvey E. Goldberg, *Sephardi and Middle Eastern Jewries: History and Culture in the Modern Era* (Bloomington, Ind: Indiana University Press, 1996), p. 20.
46. Harvey E. Goldberg, 'Ritual Mutuality in North Africa: Jews and Muslims listen to the Ten Commandments in Synagogue', lecture, 15 September 2014, http://judaicstudies.uconn.edu/2014/09/05/ritual-mutuality-in-north-africa/. (Last accessed 26 April 2017).

47. Samuel Osborne, 'Temple Mount: Jerusalem's most holy site has nothing to do with Judaism, UNESCO rules', *The Independent*, 14 October 2016, http://www.independent. co.uk/news/world/middle-east/israel-jerusalem-unesco-motion-jewish-ties-temple- mount-noble-sanctuary-el-harem-al-sharif-a7360776.html. (Last accessed 26 April 2017).
48. Peter Ford, 'In Iraq, Reverence for Ancient Tomb of a Jewish Prophet', *Christian Science Monitor*, 2 June 2003, http://www.csmonitor.com/2003/0602/p08s01-woiq.html. (Last accessed 26 April 2017).
49. See Yehuda, *Tombs of Saints and Synagogues in Babylonia*, p. 34.
50. Ibid., p.36.
51. Steven Lee Myers, 'Crossroads of antiquity can't decide on a new path', *New York Times*, 19 October 2010, http://www.nytimes.com/2010/10/20/world/middleeast/20ezekiel. html?pagewanted=1&_r=1. (Last accessed 26 April 2017).
52. 'National Museum, Damascus', *Wikipedia*, https://en.wikipedia.org/wiki/Dura- Europos_synagogue. (Last accessed 26 April 2017).
53. Robert Lyons, 'Silent Sacred Spaces: selected photographs of Syrian Synagogues' (pdf), http://www.isjm.org/country/syria/Silenced%20Sacred%20Spaces.pdf. (Last accessed 26 April 2017).
54. Justice for Jews from Arab Countries (JJAC), Document presented to UNESCO, June 2014.
55. Eliza Griswold, 'Is This the End of Christianity in the Middle East?', *New York Times*, 22 July 2015, http://www.nytimes.com/2015/07/26/magazine/is-this-the-end- of-christianity-in-the-middle-east.html. (Last accessed 26 April 2017).
56. 'Arabs without Jews: Roots of a Tragedy', *Point of No Return*, 24 July 2013, http://jewishrefugees.blogspot.co.uk/2013/07/arabs-without-jews-roots-of-as- tragedy.html. (Last accessed 26 April 2017).
57. Marcia Lynx Qualey, 'True Histories: The Renaissance of Arab Jews in Arabic Novels', *The Guardian*, 29 October 2014, http://www.theguardian.com/books/booksblog/ 2014/oct/29/renaissance-arab-jews-arabic-novels-ali-bader-mohammad-al-ahmed. (Last accessed 26 April 2017).
58. 'Sir Sasson Heskel tops loyalty list', *Point of No Return*, 17 August 2015, http://jewishrefugees.blogspot.co.uk/2015/08/sir-sasson-heskell-tops-loyalty-list- in.html. (Last accessed 26 April 2017).
59. Mark Steyn, *National Review*, 25 February 2013, https://www.nationalreview. com/nrd/articles/340075/ghost-cities. (Last accessed 26 April 2017).
60. Ibid.

2

The Myth of Peaceful Coexistence

J'ai quitté mon pays, j'ai quitté ma maison
Ma vie, ma triste vie se traîne sans raison
J'ai quitté mon soleil, j'ai quitté ma mer bleue
Leurs souvenirs se réveillent, bien après mon adieu
Soleil, soleil de mon pays perdu

****

I left my country, I left my home
My life drags on sadly as I am left to roam
I left my sun, I left blue sea and sky
Their memory awakens long after I said goodbye
Sun, sun of my lost country

Enrico Macias[1]

On 13 February 2015, the city of Algiers witnessed a strange spectacle: the burial in the Jewish cemetery of St Eugene (Bologhine) of the famous French actor Roger Hanin, star of TV, film and stage.[2] Hanin, who died at the age of eighty-nine, was laid in the ground not far from his father. He was the first Jew to be buried in the cemetery since the funeral of Freha Touboul in 2001. Unlike Freha Touboul's, Roger Hanin's funeral was a celebrity affair, with a guard of honour from the Algerian state, the French ambassador and the Algerian president and minister of culture attending his funeral.

What makes a Jew want to be buried in a country he hasn't lived in for forty years? In a country where there are officially no Jews left of the original community of 130,000? In a cemetery whose tombstones have been vandalised and spray-painted with graffiti? Where his French-based family will not easily be able to visit? Hanin's decision to choose Algiers as his last resting place is the 'expression of his attachment to his native land; many Jews feel a similar attachment to Algeria and a deep sense of familial belonging', the president of CRIF (the representative body of French Jewry) Joel Mergui proclaimed at Hanin's funeral.[3] The Algerian President Abdelaziz Bouteflika paid homage to the actor, 'a symbol of the friendship between the Algerian and French peoples'.[4]

Hanin was not the only one to want his last resting place to be in the country of his birth. The singer Georges Moustaki also entertained a last wish to be buried in his native Alexandria,[5] where five Jews remain, but the idea was abandoned.

Hanin embodies the answer to the question 'Why?' in his very name: Hanin means 'nostalgia' in Arabic. Nostalgia is a recurrent theme amongst Jews born in Arab countries. How often have you heard Jews lament, with tears in their eyes, the gardens filled with orange blossom, the *samak masgouf* carp, charcoal-grilled on the banks of the river Tigris, the softly flowing waters of the Nile...?

A group of Iraqi Jews, some ex-communists, think of themselves as exiles in Israel and have dedicated their life's work to writing about their country of birth. Authors Sami Michael and Sasson Somekh define themselves as 'Arab Jews'. One, the late Samir Naqquash, continued to write in Arabic. The younger generation, born in Israel, is also rediscovering its roots: over 40,000 have joined the Facebook page entitled: *Preserving the Iraqi-Jewish Language.*

So powerful a sentiment is nostalgia that Jews who were not even born in Arab countries experience it. Author of *How to be a Heroine* Samantha Ellis, for example:

> For as long as I remember I've been homesick for a place I've never seen. My parents are Iraqi Jews. I was born in London, but my past was quite literally another country. At four, my party trick was to say, in imperfect Judeo-Arabic, 'You can put the curly tail of the dog inside a sugar cane tube for forty days and forty nights and when you take it out, it will still be curly'.[6]

Memory: A Mechanism for Forgetting

It's a well-worn paradox: one day, a Jew from an Arab country swears that he lived happily alongside Arabs. He paints a picture of harmony and coexistence. Another day, he might say life was awful. So which is the truth?

Eli Mayo remembers his Egyptian childhood in Port Said as 'wonderful', at least until 1948:

> My father owned a large shop and was one of the most respected men in the city.
>
> He was sometimes invited to events at the home of the governor of Egypt. My best friend was a Muslim named Jamal. Our families got along well. But when the War of Independence broke out, Jamal was the first to throw rocks at my house and shout, 'Death to the Jews'.[7]

These experiences, opposing as they are, are not, however, contradictory, they are complementary. When Egyptian Jews met the Egyptian ambassador in Brussels in the 1990s, what was expected to be 'a hail of reproach and recrimination in a climate of lynching, dissolved into a wave of irrepressible nostalgia among deracinated and inconsolable Egyptian-Jewish patriots'.[8] And this response is consistent with what anthropologists have identified as a tendency to suppress memories of fear and escape. 'Memory is a mechanism for forgetting', says the historian Georges Bensoussan.[9] It filters out what one does not wish to remember. In any event, it makes for unreliable history.

Robert Satloff wrote *Among the Righteous* in order to open a crack in the wall of Holocaust denial rampant in the Arab world. Satloff's book began as a simple effort to find a righteous Arab who saved a Jew. What he didn't expect, though, in the course of his research, was *Jewish denial* – a tendency to deny or gloss over Jewish suffering. Satloff even met a Jew who claimed to have 'nice memories' of the Nazis. He comes up with an interesting explanation for this strange phenomenon. He concludes that denial was a mechanism which allowed generation after generation of Jews to survive as *dhimmis*.[10] Unswerving loyalty to the ruler provided the only safety shield against the capriciousness of the Muslim masses. Satloff's theory not only explains why some Jews were anxious to put a positive spin on the way they were treated by the Nazis, but by Arab society generally: 'Generally, when I asked Jews in Morocco and Tunisia about their own and their families' experiences during the war, the usual refrain was: "It wasn't so bad." Only

The Cairo family of Lucette Lagnado, author of T*he Man in the White Sharkskin Suit*. The man in question is her father, standing tall on the left (Courtesy L. Lagnado).

after several of these conversations did it occur to me that this sort of denial among Jews from Arab lands is part of their overall strategy for survival.'[11]

The researcher Bat Ye'or identifies a type of *dhimmi* syndrome in which unpleasant memories are erased: 'Reduced to an inferior existence in circumstances that engender physical and moral degradation, the *dhimmi* perceives and accepts himself as a devalued human being.'[12] This syndrome of alienation and fourteen centuries of humiliation is not easily overcome after living for two generations in the free world.

Yet Samantha Ellis acknowledges the profound impact that persecution had on her family in Baghdad: her mother was arrested as she tried to escape the country illegally through Kurdistan. She has transmitted her fear of having her hair touched to her daughter who writes: 'I hated having my hair touched by strangers. Recently I worked out why; my mother had said that when interrogated in prison, they pulled her hair. No wonder I flinched.'[13] Hebrew University Emeritus Professor Shmuel Moreh, born Sami Muallem in Baghdad, is determined to put the past behind him: 'For me, Iraq is like an ex-spouse. Who would want to keep in touch with one's former spouse? You just want to forget and move on.'[14]

Many of those who lived through the terror of Saddam's executions in Iraq are unequivocally *not* nostalgic. Some still quake at the memory. Giving her testimony forty years later, one woman wanted it to be anonymous, so entrenched is the fear that the Iraqi secret police might be out to get her. For others the process of remembering is too painful. The trauma experienced by Egyptian Jews, for example – imprisonment, accusations of Zionism, sequestration, street assaults, rights violations and mass expulsion – is not reflected in the memoirs of Egyptian Jews, argues Dr Daphne Tsimhoni.[15]

The Alexandria-born author of the memoir *Out of Egypt* André Aciman, whose sufferings were relatively mild, writes:

> Egypt is not my home. It hasn't been my home in decades. In fact, Egypt was never my home. I didn't belong in Egypt. Most of my childhood and adolescence in Egypt consisted of finding ways to pretend I was already out of Egypt. New York is my home now – or almost my home. Maybe 'home' is a foreign concept for exiles – was already a foreign concept as I was growing up in Egypt.[16]

The need to talk about negative memories publically has only come about after decades of silence. Published and self-published memoirs by Jews driven from Arab lands began pouring out in the twenty-first century, perhaps because to flaunt one's ethnic roots is fashionable, perhaps because people felt they were ready to revisit their past, perhaps because they wanted their grandchildren to be aware of their origins.

The Happy Memories of Childhood

Those Jews who are nostalgic for life in Arab lands know deep down that they are visiting a country of the mind. They know that their uprooting was final, even if, like the Tunis-born writer Colette Fellous, they are still able to visit their place of birth in order to make the disconnect easier to bear.[17] Yet, in spite of all of this evidence, the myth of the enchanted history of the Jews refuses to die. Since their mass exodus in the second half of the twentieth century, the exiled Jews themselves have spread the perception of the Jewish idyll in Arab countries because they were children at the time, and childhood is associated with happy memories. And the further you went up the social scale, the happier the memories. These Jews were growing up in the colonial era in the Middle East and North Africa, an age of comfort and upward Jewish mobility. Jews dominated literature, culture and sport, excelled in finance and commerce. The wealthy families were shielded from the outside world. They had servants and belonged to exclusive clubs. They threw lavish parties, made shopping trips to Paris, and the women especially enjoyed a life of coffee-sipping and bridge-playing leisure.

Jews and Muslims mixed in the business world. The well-to-do elite – Jewish, Muslim and Christian – socialised (Muslim men came to play bridge with Iraqi Jews, but never brought their wives).[18] There were occasional cases of intermarriage with Christians and Muslims among the haute bourgeoisie in Egypt. The Jewish aristocracy in Egypt and Morocco even mixed with the royal family. Their servants were often loyal and devoted. Jewish children

Jewish boys visiting the Pyramids, 1940s.

had Muslim and Christian school friends and often acquired a detailed knowledge of each other's' religions.[19] Jews and Muslims invited each other to their important family occasions – circumcisions, barmitzvahs, weddings. They visited each other on religious festivals. Muslim neighbours were honoured to be asked to share *tbeet*, the classic Sabbath dish, with their Iraqi-Jewish neighbours. (Muslim neighbours did not reciprocate, because of the strict Jewish dietary laws.) It was not unusual for Jewish babies in poorer families to have Muslim wet-nurses. Moroccan Jews invited their Muslim neighbours into their homes for the *Mimouna*, the feast that concludes the Jewish Passover.

However, invisible social and religious boundaries remained firmly in place. The writer Naim Kattan, a Jewish boy growing up in the Baghdad of the thirties, would, for

Khatoun Meir, the author's grandmother, after a shopping trip to Paris, 1920s.

Groppi Café, a favourite haunt for Cairene Jews.

A Syrian-Jewish wedding.

The Piazza Municipio quarter of Benghazi, Libya, was home to many Jews in the 1920s.

Marriage of Gloria and Abe Sofaer in Baghdad (Eli Saleh collection)

example, never dare to venture alone into a cinema.[20] The Jewish author and academic Benjamin Stora describes the situation in his native Constantine, Algeria: 'Segregation between communities prevailed and, as is well known, later caused problems in that country. The Jews lived among themselves, with their own customs and beliefs; the Muslims and Europeans did the same. There was not really any exchange in the private sphere.'[21]

Memories were far from rosy, however, if you were born, as was the Tunisian writer and philosopher Albert Memmi, *without* a silver spoon in your mouth: 'The much vaunted idyllic life of the Jews in Arab lands is a myth! The truth, since I am obliged to return to it, is that from the outset we were a minority in a hostile environment; as such, we

Menu at the Groppi Café, Cairo (Laurence Julius collection)

Succoth lunch in the Jewish Recreation Club, Khartoum, Sudan, c.1948 (Courtesy Daisy Abboudi)

underwent all the fears, the agonies, and the constant sense of frailty of the underdog.'[22] The vast majority of Jews were poor and vulnerable. Memmi lost his friend Bissor in a pogrom in Tunis:

> For us poor Jews, enjoying the demise of arbitrary feudalism, cinemas, cars and doctors, we still had to put up with policemen hunting down petty traders and the humiliation of the slightest contact with

Postcard showing Jewish women at Tin-mel in the Atlas mountains, Morocco (Laurence Julius Collection)

bureaucracy. If the pogrom never reached the plush neighbourhoods with their mixed Jewish, Muslim and Christian homes, the huge ghetto, forgotten in its sordid misery by the anti-Semites, was under permanent threat of death. Breaking down any door would reveal Jews behind it. Having never left this side of the Mediterranean, we felt cut off, exposed to all sorts of local disasters. [23]

Memmi recalls one such particular disaster: 'Playing together boisterously in the rue Tarfoune, a young Jewish boy caught the earring of a young Muslim girl. The blow caused the jewel to sever her earlobe. For three days, the whole street besieged the Jewish boy's home, refusing all monetary compensation. They wanted to get their hands on the boy so they could tear off his ear.'[24]

Victor Hayoun, a young survivor of the Gabès pogrom in 1941, learned early on that his own father could not protect him against the wrath of his Arab neighbours:

Our Arab neighbours, whose conduct toward us ranged from sincere fraternity to humiliation and even pogroms (The Gabès 1941 pogrom was still fresh in my young memory), had sharpened my childish feeling that we were tolerated by the 'masters of the place' and they could get so angry as to make my status precarious. My destiny was not in the hands of my father.[25]

Penina Elbaz accuses rich Moroccan Jews of downplaying the anti-Semitism which poor Jews, particularly those who lived cheek-by-jowl with Muslims, suffered during her childhood:

Because some rich people wanted to play at being ambassadors for Morocco and talk about their good life, they failed to report, or denied, the persecutions endured by the majority, especially those who had to live in Muslim areas. Our lives were put at risk every day. I have so many examples: My elderly aunt was pushed against the wall by Muslims and they broke her shoulder. My 14-year-old cousin was pushed against the wall with a knife to her throat.[26]

Whereas some upper middle-class Iraqi Jews remember a comfortable, even idyllic life with servants, Salim Fattal's childhood was marked by grinding poverty. The boy was forced to earn a living from an early age, while attending night school. His widowed mother cherished the dream that her five sons would someday be doctors, lawyers, engineers, poets and scientists. The dream would come to pass – but not in Iraq. Salim became the poet and later made a successful career as a journalist, filmmaker and one of the

Jewish mothers and children who stayed behind in Baghdad, 1950s.

founders of Israel TV's Arabic service. His childhood memoir is entitled *In the Alleys of Baghdad.*[27]

In his book, Salim describes episodes of brutality and hardship. More affluent Jews were more likely to escape the First World War Ottoman draft, but Salim's Tatran neighbourhood is caught up in a dragnet: despite Salim grandfather's best efforts to hide young Jewish men, his brother Menashe is taken into the Turkish army, freezing to death on the front.

Tragedy strikes the family again when Salim's uncle Meir is kidnapped and murdered during the 1941 *Farhud* pogrom. Meir's body was never found. The family survives a night of murder and rape by bribing a policeman with a shotgun into protecting them, paying him half a dinar per shot. Another uncle drinks and smokes himself to an early death and a third is lured into the desert and murdered by two Bedouin associates.

The Tunisian writer Albert Memmi, who also grew up in a family of straitened means, recalls: 'As far back as my childhood memories go – in the tales of my father, my grandparents, my aunts and uncles – coexistence with the Arabs was not just uncomfortable, it was marked by threats periodically carried out.'[28]

Rich or poor, happy or unhappy, the result was the same. All Jews ended up leaving Arab countries. In the words of Robert Satloff, 'nostalgia can only smooth over the hard edges of memory. These Jews left for a reason.'[29]

Competing Historical Narratives

Jews and Muslims lived side-by-side for fourteen centuries, but two competing narratives jostle for attention: on the one hand, the 'neo-lachrymose conception of Jewish-Arab history' interprets the exodus as a response to a long history of Arab persecution, culminating in the ethnic cleansing of Jewish communities after Israel's establishment.[30] The neo-lachrymose version takes at its watchword Maimonides' twelfth century epistle to the persecuted Jews of Yemen:

Little girl, Baghdad, 1950s.

> You know, my brethren that on account of our sins our God has cast us in the midst of these people, the nation of Islam who persecute us severely and who devise ways to harm us and to debase us. Never did a nation molest, degrade, debase, and hate us as much as they [...] No nation has done more to harm to Israel.[31]

Maimonides had himself fled persecution from the fanatical Berber Almohads, and is even thought to have temporarily converted to Islam in Morocco, before fleeing to Egypt. Less than a hundred years after the Ottoman Sultan invited Jews fleeing the Spanish Inquisition to settle in his empire, Murat III ordered 'the liquidation of the Jews'.[32]

The converse narrative is *convivencia* – faiths lived side by side during the 'Golden Age', with its apogee in medieval Muslim Spain. Al-Andalus was the centre of Jewish life during the early Middle Ages. It produced a renaissance of Arabic and Hebrew literature and learning, leading to a flowering of Spanish culture. María Rosa Menocal, a specialist in Iberian literature, claims that 'tolerance was an inherent aspect of Andalusian society'. Menocal's book, *The Ornament of the World*,[33] argues that the Jewish *dhimmis* living under the caliphate, while allowed fewer rights than Muslims, were still better off than those Jews living in the Christian parts of Europe. The Jewish communities of Al-Andalus had so intimate a grasp

El Tránsito Synagogue, Toledo.

of Arabic culture and language that it fundamentally redefined their own relationship to Hebrew. Hebrew developed its grammar and vocabulary on the Arabic model. The Qur'anic inscriptions on the walls of the el Tránsito synagogue in Toledo, built by Samuel Halevi Abulafia, are remarkable because they were added about 300 years after the city was no longer ruled by Muslims.[34]

It was through translators in Muslim-ruled medieval Spain that the learned men of France, Italy and England discovered the treasures of Greek heritage. It was thanks to Jewish translators that works by Averroes and Al Farrabi were translated first into Hebrew then Latin. Between the eleventh and fifteenth centuries, Arabic texts were translated from the original, from Syriac or from Greek. In spite of this, Peter Cole, an expert on the poetry of the Golden Age of Al-Andalus, takes a sanguine view: 'At its best, the culture gave Jews greater religious, social, economic, and intellectual freedom than they knew in any other medieval (non-Muslim) society; at its worst, it led to heavy taxation and serious oppression. When the bottom fell out of it, forced conversion, emigration, and slaughter weren't long in coming.'[35]

According to the historian Bernard Lewis, the myth of Muslim tolerance is one of the great myths of history propagated by nineteenth century intellectuals. Jewish historians wanted to embarrass the West into giving European Jews greater civil rights. Belief in the myth of Muslim tolerance was a result, more than a cause, of Jewish sympathy for Islam. According to Lewis, the myth was invented by Jews in nineteenth-century Europe as a reproach to Christians – and taken up by Muslims in our own time as a reproach to Jews:

> If tolerance means the absence of persecution, then classic Islamic society was indeed tolerant to both its Jewish and Christian subjects – more tolerant perhaps in Spain than in the East, and in either incomparably more tolerant than was medieval Christendom. But if tolerance means the absence of discrimination, then Islam never was or claimed to be tolerant, but on the contrary insisted on the privileged superiority of the true believer in this world as well as the next.[36]

To say the Muslim world was more tolerant is to set the bar pretty low. Yet the myth of greater Muslim tolerance stubbornly persists among Jews. The writer Paul Berman recalls that every Jewish home had the classic work by Heinrich Graetz, *The History of the Jews,* on its bookshelf.[37] Graetz wrote: 'This religion [Islam]… has exercised a wonderful influence on the course of Jewish history and on the evolution of Judaism.'[38] The Golden Age of Jewish–Muslim coexistence in Spain has become the Muslim 'calling card'.[39] Its proponents contend that Jews and Muslims lived happily side by side until their brotherly ties were torn asunder by foreign influences – colonialism, tribal nationalism and Zionism – rendering them 'intimate strangers'.[40]

Dissenting voices argue that the paradise of al-Andalus was a myth, that the much-praised Umayyad period in medieval Spain was, in fact, an age of persecution, beheadings and crucifixions.[41] Proponents of the Golden Age gloss over the era when fundamentalist Berber Muslims, the Almoravids and Almohads, ruled Spain for over one hundred years, causing a mass flight of Jews, including the great rabbi Maimonides. For the full seven centuries that Muslims ruled Spain, until the fall of Granada in 1492, the regime was under continuous pressure from the Christian *Reconquista*, causing it to behave, at times, in cruel and unpredictable ways.

The Golden Ageists claim that Jews did not complain as much about persecution by Muslims as they did when Christians were responsible – so it could not have been so dire. According to the scholar Mark Cohen, where Jews did chronicle their suffering the material is 'lean': the main episodes were the Granada pogrom in 1066, the Almohad persecution and the persecution of the Jews of Yemen: 'The dearth of literary sources devoted to persecution of Jews of the Islamic world during the classical centuries reflects a milieu in which there was much less of the kind of violent persecution of Jews as Jews than that which kindled the doleful literature and other memorialising traditions of Christian lands.'[42]

Cohen argues that non-Muslims were granted 'an aura of embeddedness' in society and 'enjoyed substantial security during the formative and classical periods of Islam'. He cites the incident when, under the 'mad' caliph Al-Hakim in eleventh century Egypt, a Muslim mob attacked a Jewish funeral procession – a not uncommon event because it violated the anti-*dhimmi* public display of religious ceremonies. When the Jews protested, Al-Hakim found the Muslims at fault for giving false testimony. The Jews proclaimed an annual fast: the only Jewish writings that survive about this episode are the celebratory *piyyutim* and *selihot* to be recited during the fast.[43]

Cohen appears to downplay the mass apostasy of Jews to Islam by the fundamentalist Almohads: it was not *that* bad. He quotes Maimonides, who tells the Jewish converts not to be plagued by guilt. Unlike Christianity, Islam is not idolatrous and does not demand that Jews martyr themselves rather than convert. They may still retain their links to Judaism and even revert to their ancestral religion, as Maimonides himself was thought to have done in more tolerant climes.

Cohen's thesis has already resulted in an intellectual stand-off with Bat Ye'or, the pioneering author of *The Dhimmi*. She claims that Cohen cannot even bring himself to use the word *dhimmi*.[44] The relative protection granted to the non-Muslim who submits to the *dhimma* can only ever be a temporary suspension of the ideological *jihad* against the infidel, Bat Ye'or argues. Indeed, the absence of theological anti-Semitism in Islam – there were no burnings of the Talmud in the Muslim world[45] – does not absolve Islam from anti-Semitism *per se*.

One explanation for the lack of 'memorialisation' in Jewish sources of the darker persecutions in their history is this: the essence of being a *dhimmi* is to 'diminish' oneself. Why would the Jews have rubbed their rulers up the wrong way with lachrymose accounts of how they had been treated? Non-Muslims chose to downplay their persecution and extol their Muslim saviours for reasons of survival – because it was politically expedient to do so. Even when they are not living under Muslim rule today, Jews have been known to display this *dhimmi* syndrome.[46]

As for the myth that Islam was more tolerant of Jews than Christendom, the scholar Paul Fenton claims that more Jews (3,000) were massacred in Granada, Spain, in 1066 – in a Muslim backlash against the Jewish vizir Joseph ibn Naghrela – than lived in the Rhineland towns of Speyer, Worms and Mainz at the time of the Crusades.[47] Where Jews were the most conspicuous minority – in Yemen and Iran for instance – they suffered massacre, degradation and conversion under Shi'ism. In the Maghreb, Malikite Sunnism treated Jews particularly harshly, after wiping out the Christian presence in North Africa.[48]

A comparison between pogroms in the Christian and the Muslim worlds is not easy to make, but Albert Memmi claims that, if you put all the pogroms end to end, you finish up with a picture of violence little different to that perpetrated under Christendom:

 If we except the massacres of the twentieth century (the pogroms in Russia after Kishinev and later by Stalin, as well as the Nazi crematoria), the total number of Jewish victims from Christian pogroms over the centuries probably does not exceed the total of the victims of the smaller and larger periodic pogroms perpetrated in Arab lands under Islam over the past millennium.[49]

Others claim that pogroms did not break out as often in the Muslim world as they did under Christendom. Expulsions were rare.[50] Throughout fourteen centuries of Jewish-Muslim interaction, there were periods of history when Muslim rulers welcomed Jews with open arms: Sultan Saladin called on Jews to return to settle in Jerusalem in 1190 after they were banned by the Crusaders. The Christians, who had expected to be massacred, were permitted to ransom their lives and the penniless to go free. Maimonides,

Statue of Maimonides in his birthplace, Córdoba.

one of Judaism's greatest thinkers, became court physician to Saladin. The Ottomans welcomed Jews (and other minorities) fleeing the Spanish inquisition into Constantinople. The sixteenth century ushered in an era of relative religious freedom when the Sultan's aristocratic Sephardi allies, Doña Gracia and her nephew Joseph Nasí, encouraged Jews from Spain to settle in Tiberias and Safed.

Much is made of the fact that Jews fled the Spanish Inquisition for the Maghreb, Turkey and *Eretz Yisrael*, all under Muslim rule, but Sephardim also went to Christian Holland and northern Europe, and re-established the British-Jewish community in the seventeenth century.

Supernatural Attributes

The Ottoman motive for welcoming the fugitives from the Spanish Inquisition was not altruistic, it was pragmatic. The Jews had trade links and skills of value to the new rulers. Jews had business acumen, worth as middlemen, contacts with other Jews in other lands. The Jews had a reputation for honesty. *Haqq-al-Yahud* on the Tunisian island of Djerba was the equivalent of giving an oath following a discussion on the price or quality of an object – a kind of Jewish version of 'scout's honour', implying honesty and reliability.[51] Muslim society had a sense that the Jews had a special relationship to God. When the first autumn downpours came to Baghdad following fervent praying for rain during the Jewish festival of Succoth, Iraqi Muslims could be overheard telling each other: 'the feast of the Jews must be over.'[52]

Ordinary folk, particularly in the Maghreb, viewed Jews as possessing certain supernatural attributes. In Morocco, curing sickness was, in many cases, the exclusive province of Jewish rabbis and saints. Barren Muslim women turned to local Jewish 'saints' in the hope of becoming pregnant; families sometimes sought rabbis' blessings to cure infertility, mental illness, paralysis, and epilepsy.[53] These traditions persist to this day: rabbis are still summoned to pray at the bedside of ailing Moroccan kings.

Yet for all the Jews' talents and skills, the abiding image of the Jew, prior to the establishment of Israel, was not as an object of hatred, but as weak and worthy of contempt. Barriers between the faith communities, and a certain amount of mutual suspicion, existed. Jews were at once natives and strangers. Take the Jews of Fez in Morocco, for example: 'They were Moroccans, just like us', was a sentiment researcher Oren Kosansky heard repeatedly. Yet, at the same time that Jews are remembered as native, they are also remembered as distinct: 'they were engaged in typically Jewish trades, they lived in a segregated quarter and they spoke a peculiar dialect.'[54] The Jewish settlement of Akka in the Sahara predates Islam: nevertheless, the Muslims viewed the Jews of the town as 'outside the Arab Islamic national narrative of Morocco.'[55]

For all their usefulness, Jews and sometimes Christians – their fellow outsiders in the Muslim world – could also, at times, be associated with evil:

> The curse of a Jew was believed to be more fearsome than those from fellow Muslims; religious pilgrims went to great lengths to avoid seeing Jews before traveling to Mecca. Jews were asked to provide preventive charms for protection against evil eye and bad spirits, but it was also believed that when a Jew entered a Muslim's house, the angels deserted it.[56]

While Muslim attitudes were those of 'tolerance', 'trouble arose when Jews or Christians were seen to be getting too much wealth or too much power' and more particularly when they were enjoying them too visibly. Any troublesome courtier to whom this applied was usually executed, and if this did not quell popular resentment, pogroms could break out.[57] The best known example of this is the massacre of Jews in Granada in 1066, usually ascribed to a reaction among the Muslim population against a powerful and ostentatious Jewish vizier.[58]

The Friendly Neighbour: Last Line of Defence

The periodic violence that erupted in the Middle East and North Africa tested interpersonal relations to the hilt. In modern times, Jewish-Arab coexistence broke down completely with the outbreak of murderous riots and state-sanctioned persecution. While the authorities failed to intervene to protect Jews – or even incited the rioting (see Chapter Three) – the friendly neighbour stood as the last line of defence. Just as Righteous Gentiles saved Jews from the Nazis, Arabs saved Jews: 300 Jews sheltered in twenty-eight Arab homes during the Hebron massacre of 1929. There are similar reports from the 1941 *Farhud* (Arabic for 'violent dispossession') in Iraq and in the 1945 Libyan pogrom. Had Muslims not rescued Jews from rioting mobs in Arab countries, the death toll would have been far higher. Honourable Muslims who performed these acts of rescue in the twentieth century often belonged to an old-school elite which has since been destroyed or banished into exile.[59]

This kind of hopeful story is countered more often than not, however, by horrifying tales of treachery and violence; the neighbour could just as easily betray the Jew: familiarity can breed contempt, resentment and greed. Among such stories in Hebron in 1929 was that of the Jewish doctor murdered by his own patients. The Makleff family near Jerusalem was slaughtered by the Arabs they worked with.[60] Jews terrorised by the 1941 *Farhud* in Iraq and the Libyan pogrom in 1945 recognised, among their assailants, the local policeman, butcher and milkman.

A reliance on benevolent neighbours was not good enough for the Zionist movement. The underground in Iraq and in North Africa began stockpiling weapons precisely to put an end to the Jewish community's traditional vulnerability and, in several instances, it did manage to contain the violence.[61]

Modern Coexistence Projects

Against this backdrop, it is surprising that coexistence projects between Arab and Jews are touted as the solution to the Arab-Israeli conflict in microcosm. If Jews and Arabs talk to each other, live together, play music together – so the thinking goes –peace will break out. The idea that familiarity leads to mutual respect underpins the work of some thirty Arab-Jewish coexistence projects in Israel alone.

There is a place for coexistence initiatives, especially when a Muslim stands scant chance of ever meeting a Jew. Projects such as Daniel Barenboim's East-West Divan Orchestra play a role in humanising Arabs to Israelis, and Israelis to Arabs. The cooperative village of Neve Shalom/Wahat al-Salam in Israel introduces Arabs and Jews to each other's cultures. There is a place for Mizrahim in coexistence projects: people familiar with Arab culture and mentality who can serve, at best, as bridge-builders, at worst, as interpreters of Arab mentality and cultural norms.

Some frustrated Arabic-speaking Jews believed that conflict in the 1920s and 1930s might have been mitigated in Palestine, had they been granted a greater role to play. Such individuals complained that the Ashkenazi-dominated Zionist movement would not listen to them.[62] Yet Mizrahim *have* been involved in diplomatic peace initiatives since before Israel's independence. Consider Ezra Danin, Eliyahu Sassoon – a Syrian nationalist-turned-Israeli diplomat – Moshe Sassoon, and others. In the 1920s, Yosef Eliyahu Chelouche, along with other Arabic-speaking Tel Avivians, founded Hamagen ('The Shield'), an organisation dedicated to persuading Arabs that they and Jews share economic and cultural interests and can only improve each other's lot.[63] But the efforts of Arabic-speaking 'bridge-builders' have all run aground on the fundamental unwillingness of the Arab leadership to make peace.

The myth of peaceful coexistence trumpets Arab/Muslim 'tolerance', but history tells us that it is a conditional tolerance where Jews exist under sufferance. 'Tolerance is a form of discrimination', as the writer Eli Amir puts it.[64] It is not the same as respect. For fourteen centuries, life for a defenceless minority was precarious and insecure. Under *sharia* law it is intrinsically discriminatory.

Almost all coexistence projects in the Middle East originate as Israeli initiatives because Arabs fear intimidation from their peers or being labelled as traitors if they advocate 'normalisation' with Israel. These initiatives can become an exercise in Jewish *dhimmi* self-abasement.[65] They can lead to Jews suppressing their rights, identity and suffering while empowering Arab grievances. Jews may feel the pain of a Palestinian refugee and even 'understand' terrorism, while there is no corresponding shift on the Arab side. In practice, coexistence initiatives rarely take into account the bitter experiences of Mizrahi Jews and perpetuate the myth that Jews and Arabs lived together in harmony before the rise of Zionism.

There are other cultural differences: Jews are famously argumentative: Jewish views span an entire spectrum, as per the dictum 'two Jews, three opinions'. Arab opinion, on the other hand, tends to be monolithic.[66] Whereas Jews are often ready to feel guilt or take blame, the Arab shame/honour code would consider an admission of fault to be a 'humiliation'. Moreover, any dissenting voice from the prevailing view is open to charges of treason.

As Professor Richard Landes describes it, when discussing dominant negative Arab attitudes to Israel: 'this kind of testosterone-fuelled, authoritarian discourse imposes its interpretation of honour on the entire community, often violently.'[67]

The historian Mark Cohen questions whether the Jews' bitter experiences are rooted in historical memory. He ventures to suggest that animosity towards Arabs reflects the desire of Oriental Jews to differentiate themselves from Arabs, 'the object of deep prejudice among the Israeli public':[68] 'Oriental Jews perceive correctly that the Ashkenazim stake their claim to the fruits of Jewish independence in the Jewish state as compensation for the persecution they suffered in Christian lands ... Consciously or unconsciously, Oriental Jews have taken to accentuating their historic persecution ... in an attempt to justify their claim to an equal share of the Zionist dream.'[69]

The Nazi genocide of the Jews in Europe plumbed the depths of such persecution. One Egyptian-Jewish leader in Israel, Shlomo Kohen Tsidon, 'exploited vocabulary linking the Egyptian government to the Nazis to validate the history of his community and to make it understandable in Ashkenazi terms.'[70]

The view that Mizrahim distort their historical experiences in order to ingratiate themselves with the Ashkenazi-dominated Israeli establishment is not, however, borne out by fact: if it were true, Mizrahim would be aligning their (generally hawkish) political views with those of Israel's political doves, most of whom are 'dreamy-eyed' Ashkenazim. In an essay for *Commentary* on the fiftieth anniversary of the state of Israel, the historian Paul Johnson wrote: 'An irony here is that there were indeed plenty of Jewish Middle Easterners in Israel: the [misnamed] Sephardim who flocked there in fear and poverty after being driven out of the Arab world. But these arrivals, far from leavening the Western-formed majority with a local yeast, pushed in the opposite direction.'[71]

It is easy to confuse cultural symbiosis with coexistence. The lesson learnt from over fourteen centuries of 'coexistence' is that it is not enough for Jews and Arabs to live together – they must do so in mutual trust and security and as *political equals*. As evidence in this chapter has demonstrated, Islam is accustomed to dominating non-Muslims. But the age-old dynamic has been reversed in relatively recent history: Jews no longer exist as fearful and vulnerable minorities in Muslim-majority states. The Jew, in official Israel Defense Forces (IDF) uniform, has turned out, contrary to all expectations, to be a courageous warrior. Israel has inflicted the ultimate 'humiliation' on Arabs in successive wars.

Paradoxically, as Jewish communities in Arab states approach extinction, the only state where Jews and Arabs now live together is in Israel. Jews are the masters in their own sovereign state. Israel is a lively (albeit flawed) parliamentary democracy with a vigorous, independent judiciary: Israel's Declaration of Independence demands that non-Jewish rights should be fully respected.[72] A number of Arabs are yet to internalise that they belong to a minority in a Jewish state. A number of Jews are yet to discard the psychological baggage of being *dhimmi*.

So far, peace initiatives have failed to address these issues.

Notes

1. Enrico Macias, 'Adieu Mon Pays'(song), *La Fête à l'Olympia* (Album), 1996, lyrics at http://musique.ados.fr/Enrico-Macias/Adieu-Mon-Pays-t83431.html. (Last accessed 26 April 2017).
2. Le Dernier Hommage à Roger Hanin à Alger, *Le Parisien*, 5 February 2015, http://www.leparisien.fr/actualite-people-medias/en-images-alger-le-dernier-hommage-a-roger-hanin-13-02-2015-4530979.php?pic=2#contTitre. (Last accessed 26 April 2017).
3. Ibid.
4. Ibid.
5. Georges Moustaki Obituary, *The Guardian*, 24 May 2013, https://www.theguardian.com/music/2013/may/24/georges-moustaki-obituary. (Last accessed 26 April 2017).
6. 'You can take Baghdad out of the girl ...', *Point of No Return*, 16 April 2012, http://jewishrefugees.blogspot.co.il/2012/04/you-can-take-baghdad-out-of-girl.html. (Last accessed 26 April 2017).
7. Yariv Peleg and Lior Yaakobi, 'Escape from Port Said', *Israel Hayom*, 28 October 2016, http://www.israelhayom.com/site/newsletter_article.php?id=37459. (Last accessed 26 April 2017).
8. Nathan Weinstock, 'Ambiguïtés et ambivalences du statut de *dhimmi*', unpublished lecture notes, p. 5.
9. *Akadem* lecture, June 2012, http://www.akadem.org/sommaire/themes/histoire/diasporas/les-juifs-sefarades/juifs-en-pays-arabe-le-grand-deracinement-1850-1975-05-07-2012-45763_77.php. (Last accessed 26 April 2017).

10. Robert Satloff, *Among the Righteous* (New York: Public Affairs, 2006), p.178.
11. Ibid.
12. Bat Ye'or, *The Dhimmi: Jews and Christians under Islam* (London: Associated University Press, 1985), p.143.
13. Samantha Ellis, 'You can't take Baghdad out of the girl', *Night and Day: the Middle East*, Issue VI, p.4.
14. Ksenia Svetlova, 'Baghdad revisited', *Jerusalem Post*, 6 June 2010, http://www.jpost.com/Features/In-Thespotlight/Baghdad-revisited. (Last accessed 26 April 2017).
15. Dr Tsimhoni's work, 'Jewish-Muslim relations as reflected in Memoirs of Jews of Egypt' is quoted by Levana Zamir in A. Aharoni, A. Israel-Pelletier & L. Zamir (eds) *History and Culture of Jews of Egypt in Modern Times* (Tel Aviv: Keness Hafakot, 2008), p.32.
16. André Aciman, 'An Alexandrian in search of lost time', *Newsweek*, 2 June 2011, http://europe.newsweek.com/alexandrian-search-lost-time-68691?rm=eu. (Last accessed 26 April 2017).
17. Colette Fellous, *Pièces Détachées* (Gallimard: Paris, 2017), p.77.
18. Abdullah Dangoor, interviewed by Bea Lewkowicz, Sephardi Voices UK, 2015.
19. Ellis Douek, interviewed by Bea Lewkowicz, Sephardi Voices UK, 2016.
20. Naim Kattan, *Adieu Babylone* (Paris: Albin Michel, 2003), p.154; but for Naim Kattan, the greatest hostility came from Armenians and Assyrian Christians, themselves 'victims of the Muslims'.
21. A. Meddeb and B. Stora, *Encyclopaedia of Jewish-Muslim Relations from their Origins to the Present Day* (Princeton, NJ: Princeton University Press, 2013), p.15.
22. Albert Memmi, 'Who is an Arab Jew?', Sullivan County.com, February 1975, http://www.sullivan-county.com/x/aj1.htm. (Last accessed 26 April 2017).
23. Albert Memmi, *La Statue de Sel* (Paris: Gallimard,1966), p.276.
24. Ibid., p.287.
25. Victor Hayoun, 'Tisha (9ème jour) Be Av, jour de deuil', *Harissa* blog, 8 August 2016,t http://harissa.com/news/article/tisha%E2%80%99-9e-jour-be-av-jour-de-deuil. (Last accessed 26 April 2017).
26. Penina Elbaz, 'The Truth about Morocco: Fear made Jews leave', *Point of No Return* blog, 11 September 2016, http://jewishrefugees.blogspot.co.uk/2016/09/the-truth-about-morocco-fear-made-jews.html. (Last accessed 26 April 2017).
27. Salim Fattal, *In the Alleys of Baghdad* (Tel Aviv: Shlomo Levy, 2012).
28. See Memmi, 'Who is an Arab Jew?'
29. See Satloff, *Among the Righteous*, p. 179.
30. Mark R. Cohen, *Under Crescent and Cross* (Princeton, NJ: Princeton University Press, 1994), p.55.
31. Daniel H. Frank (ed.) *Jews of Medieval Islam* (E.J. Brill, 1995), p. 147.
32. Nathan Weinstock, *Une si longue présence: Comment le Monde Arabe a perdu ses Juifs 1947–1967* (Paris: Plon, 2008), p.24.
33. María Rosa Menocal, *The Ornament of the World: How Muslims, Jews and Christians Created a Culture of Tolerance in Medieval Spain* (New York: Little Brown, 2002).
34. Ibid.
35. Cited in Harold Bloom, 'The Lost Jewish Culture', *New York Review of Books*, 28 June 2007, http://www.nybooks.com/articles/2007/06/28/the-lost-jewish-culture/. (Last accessed 26 April 2017).
36. Bernard Lewis, *Islam in History: Ideas, Men and Events in the Middle East* (London: Alcove Press, 1973), p.137.

37. Paul Berman, *The Flight of the Intellectuals* (Melville House, 2011), p.81.
38. Henrich Graetz, *A History of the Jews* (Philadelphia, PA: Jewish Publication Society, 1891–8) cited in Paul Berman, *The Flight of the Intellectuals*, p.81.
39. Shmuel Trigano, 'Archéologie du "Miracle Andalou"', *Pardès* no. 55, p.251.
40. Karim Miske, 'Jews and Muslims: intimate Strangers', *Woolf Institute* blog, 2 June 2015, https://woolfinstitute.blog/2015/06/02/jews-and-muslims-intimate-strangers/. (Last accessed 26 April 2017).
41. Darío Fernández-Morera, 'The Myth of Ummayad Tolerance' in *Myth of the Andalusian Paradise* (Wilmington, DE: ISI, 2016), pp. 119–38.
42. See Cohen, *Under Crescent and Cross*, p.187.
43. Ibid., p.185.
44. Bat Ye'or, 'De la Dhimmitude à Eurabia. Le déni de Mark Cohen' in Shmuel Trigano (ed.) 'Qu'est-ce qu' un acte antisemite?', *Pardès* no.55, p. 256.
45. Georges Bensoussan, interviewed by Alain Finkielfraut in 'Répliques' (*France Culture Radio*) 13 April 2013, http://www.franceculture.fr/emissions/repliques/les-juifs-dans-le-monde-arabe. (Last accessed 26 April 2017).
46. See the work of Bat Ye'or, author of *The Dhimmi*.
47. Paul Fenton, 'Exile in the Maghreb', London lecture, 13 December 2015.
48. See Bernard Lewis, *The Jews of Islam* (Princeton, 1987) pp. 150–1.
49. See Memmi, 'Who is an Arab Jew?'.
50. Bensoussan, 'Répliques', *France Culture Radio*, 13 April 2013.
51. Abraham Ludovitch and Lucette Valensi, *The last Arab Jews: The Communities of Jerba, Tunisia* (London: Harwood 1984), p.118.
52. 'Succot in Baghdad, now and then', *Point of No Return* blog, 21 October 2008, http://jewishrefugees.blogspot.co.uk/2008/10/succot-in-baghdad-now-and-then.html. (Last accessed 26 April 2017).
53. A. Boum, 'Arab Demonization of Jews Is a Historical Anomaly – and Shows the Limits of Today's Leaders', *Tablet Magazine*, 21 February 2014, http://www.tabletmag.com/jewish-news-and-politics/163536/jews-post-arab-spring?recipient_id=14mcWCVNaKzrl0Wfp6DH7pP6ykcHtpQ76r; (Last accessed 26 April 2017).
    Boum adds that 'Visitors to the region around Errachidia in southern Morocco, also known as Ksar Souk, will notice piles of clothes, body hair, chains, and sometimes women's bras and underwear on a shrub around the tombs of three rabbis locally known as Yihia Lahlou, Moul Tria, and Moul Sedra'.
54. Oren Kosansky, 'Reading Jewish Fez: On the Cultural Identity of a Moroccan City', *Journal of the International Institute*, Volume 8, Issue 3, Spring/Summer 2001, http://quod.lib.umich.edu/j/jii/4750978. 0008.305/—reading-jewish-fez-on-the-cultural-identity-of-a-moroccan?rgn=main;view=fulltexthttp://quod.lib.umich.edu/j/jii/4750978.0008.305/—reading-jewish-fez-on-the-cultural-identity-of-a-moroccan?rgn=main;view=fulltext. (Last accessed 26 April 2017).
55. Aomar Boum, *Memories of Absence* (Stanford, CA: Stanford University Press, 2013), p.110.
56. See Boum, 'Arab Demonization of Jews Is a Historical Anomaly' *The Tablet*, 21 February 2014 http://www.tabletmag.com/jewish-news-and-politics/163536/jews-post-arab-spring. (Last accessed 26 April 2017).
57. Norman A. Stillman, *The Jews of Arab Lands: A History and Source Book*, Vol.1 (Philadelphia, PA: Jewish Publication Society of America, 1979), p.62.
58. Bernard Lewis, *The Jews of Islam* (Princeton, NJ: Princeton University Press, 2014), p.54.
59. Conversation with Moshe Kahtan, May 2016.

60. Suzy Eban, *A Sense of Purpose* (London: Halban, 2008), p.44.
61. See M. Roumani, *The Jews of Libya: Coexistence, Persecution, Resettlement* (Sussex Academic Press, 2008), p.58. Trained members of the Jewish defence movement resisted rioters in Tripoli, Libya in 1948 and contained the violence. They also thwarted a pogrom in the Tunis *Hara* in 1952. See Jacques Taieb in S. Trigano (ed.) *La fin du Judaisme en terres d'Islam* (Denoël, 2009) p.365.
62. See Aharoni, Pelletier-Israel, Zamir (eds) *History and culture of Jews of Egypt in Modern Times*, p.41.
63. 'Joseph-Eliyahu Chelouche: coexistence campaigner', *Point of No Return* blog, 12 April 2009, http://jewishrefugees.blogspot.co.uk/2009/04/yosef-eliahu-chelouche-coexistence.html. (Last accessed 26 April 2017).
64. Eli Amir, *The Dove Flyer* (London: Halban, 2010), p.67.
65. See Edward Alexander's assessment of the Jewish-Arab village of Neve Shalom, 'No, an exercise in Jewish Self-Abasement', *Middle East Quarterly*, December 1998, http://www.meforum.org/134/no-an-exercise-in-jewish-self-debasement. (Last accessed 26 April 2017).
66. Hunter Stuart, 'How a pro-Palestinian American reporter changed his views on Israel and the conflict', *Jerusalem Post*, 15 February 2017.
67. Richard Landes, 'Why the Arab world is lost in an emotional *nakba* and why we keep it There', *The Tablet*, 24 June 2014.
68. See Cohen, *Under Crescent and Cross*, p.13.
69. Ibid.
70. Joel Beinin, *The Dispersion of Egyptian Jewry: Culture, Politics, and the Formation of a Modern Diaspora* (Berkeley, CA: University of California Press, 1998), p.209.
71. Paul Johnson, 'The Miracle', *Commentary* 105, no.5 (May 1998).
72. Jonathan Adelman writing in 'The Israeli Arabs: Trailblazers of a better Middle East', *Huffington Post*, 19 August 2015, quotes a poll indicating that 77 per cent of Israeli Arabs prefer to live in Israel than a Palestinian state. http://www.huffingtonpost.com/jonathan-adelman/the-israeli-arabs-trailbl_b_8010020.html. (Last accessed 26 April 2017).

3

The European Colonial Revolution

In 1857, a Tunisian Jew named Batto Sfez was accused of being drunk, insulting a Muslim and cursing the Islamic religion. He was brought to justice under *sharia* law and sentenced to death. A few days before the arrest of Batto Sfez, Mohammed, Bey of Tunis, had executed a Muslim soldier who had murdered a Jew. To create an equivalence, the Bey ordered the same sentence on Batto Sfez, though his alleged crime was not murder. Western Jews and Christians were outraged by the cruelty of this sentence. They appealed to the European consular authorities to stop the execution and implored Mohammed Bey to show mercy. Sfez was beheaded on 24 June 1857 and his head was tossed around by an unscrupulous Arab gang as a football. Local Jews dug deep into their pockets to pay to retrieve Batto Sfez's decapitated head.[1]

The tragedy of Batto Sfez is just one of many instances of abuse, illustrating the helpless vulnerablility of the great mass of Jews living as a minority in the Muslim world before the colonial era. One nineteenth century traveller in Algeria, Signor Pananti, wrote: 'There is no species of outrage or vexation to which they are not exposed … the indolent Moor, with a pipe in his mouth and his legs crossed, calls any Jew who is passing, and makes him perform the offices of a servant … Even fountains were happier, at least they were allowed to murmur.'[2]

According to the eighth-century Pact of Omar, indigenous Jews and Christians were permitted to practise their faith as long as they acquiesced to the *dhimmi* condition of inferiority and institutionalised humiliation. Central to the concept of *dhimmi* is that the Jews owe their lives to Muslims. It is only under Muslim rule that Jews can fulfil their identity as Jews. By extension, Jews are a helpless and non-threatening minority. The traveller Joseph Halevy visited the *mellah* of Marrakesh in 1876 and confirms this assertion: 'All subjects, Jews and Muslims, are subjected to beatings … but an Israelite does not need to commit crimes in order to be outside the law – he is a criminal by birth, by his religious opinions, and it is already a great act of generosity to allow him to live and move among the true believers.'[3]

Jews surrendered their right to bear arms and defend themselves by paying 'protection money' – a poll tax called the *jizya*. The eleventh century Cairo Geniza records that the *jizya* was an exceedingly burdensome tax, and the source of terrible hardship.[4] In addition, the *dhimmi* rules underlined the absolute dependence and subservience of the 'protected one': 'The image of the Jew, slapped or beaten as he delivered the community's yearly tribute to the sultan's representative in nineteenth century Morocco, mirrors that of the tribute-bearing Jew upon whose neck the keeper of Rome, on orders of the Pope, placed his foot, before dealing him a sharp blow.'[5]

Dhimmi status was most strictly applied in the Maghreb, Yemen and Persia – parts of the Muslim world barely touched by European colonisation. Jews were regularly mobbed, robbed, beaten up on the slightest pretext, subject to a false charge brought by a jealous neighbour or having their possessions looted. Generally-speaking, Jews were better treated in the Levant, being one of several non-Muslim minorities, and treated more poorly where the Christian minority had died out.

Shi'a Persia was perhaps the most egregious in terms of its treatment of Jewish residents. Shi'ite law viewed religious minorities as *najas* (impure infidels), leading to the growing isolation and vulnerablility of Christians, Jews and Zoroastrians who lived there.[6] In the mid-nineteenth century, J.J. Benjamin wrote about the dwindling and poverty-stricken community of Persian Jews, describing conditions and beliefs that went back to the sixteenth century.[7]

> They are obliged to live in a separate part of town …; for they are considered as unclean creatures … Under the pretext of their being unclean, they are treated with the greatest severity and should they enter a street, inhabited by Mussulmans, they are pelted by the boys and mobs with stones and dirt … For the same reason, they are prohibited to go out when it rains; for it is said the rain would wash dirt off them, which would sully the feet of the Mussulmans … Sometimes the Persians intrude into the dwellings of the Jews and take possession of whatever please them. Should the owner make the least opposition in defense of his property, he incurs the danger of atoning for it with his life … If … a Jew shows himself in the street during the three days of the Katel (Muharram) …, he is sure to be murdered.

In Iraq, Jews avoided going out during Ashura – a ferocious Shi'a rite involving flagellation, commemorating the martyrdom of Muhammad's grandson Hussein. If a Shi'a came across a Jew during the procession, he would baptise himself in the river forty times, crying, 'I touched a Jew!'[8]

By their distinctive clothing, grovelling demeanour and modest housing Jews were targeted for humiliation under *sharia* law. Their testimony would be worth half that of a Muslim in a court of law.[9]

In Morocco 'the twilight of the Middle Ages was to continue well into the nineteenth century and for some into the second decade of the twentieth.'[10] Jews had to walk barefoot when passing a mosque. They were confined to ghettoes for their own safety – to protect them from popular violence. There are instances of Jewish women and children sold into slavery. The lucky ones were ransomed from their Arab or Berber captors.

In a similar way to their Ashkenazi counterparts in medieval Europe, Jews in Morocco were debarred from certain occupations by the Islamic guilds. As in Europe, they performed certain necessary economic functions like moneylending and associated tasks like metal-working, which were deemed reprehensible or unlucky by the non-Jewish majority.[11] The Jews were given the most menial of tasks: one such job assigned to them was the salting of the decapitated heads of executed captives.[12] In Yemen the job of cleaning the sewers was done by a sub-caste of Jews. (In Egypt today the Christian Copts are the rubbish collectors; in twentieth century Iraq, Christians also did menial jobs in conformity with their lowly status, like cleaning septic tanks.)

The small Sephardi community of Palestine was so abased under Muslim rule that a contingent of Ashkenazi followers of the 'false Messiah' Shabbetai Zvi, seeking refuge in Jerusalem in 1700, refused to put up with the humiliations suffered by the Sephardim. 'The Arabs behave as proper thugs towards the Jews ...' one wrote.[13]

In Palestine, Jews were not allowed to worship freely at their holy places. The Mamluk rulers forbade them from treading beyond the seventh step on the staircase to the burial place of the Patriarchs in Hebron. 'Nothing equals the misery and suffering of the Jews of Jerusalem', wrote Karl Marx. 'Turks, Arabs and Moors are the masters in every respect.' To be *a dhimmi* was to be continually reminded of Islam's supremacy over Judaism and Christianity.

Of course Jews performed an essential function as commercial go-betweens and could and did rise to lofty positions as courtiers, *sarrafs* (treasurers) and merchants. Some became fabulously rich, like Hayim Farhi, but like him, these Jews could just as quickly fall into disfavour – Farhi had his nose cut off and his eye gouged out by a treacherous Ottoman governor and was subsequently assassinated.[14]

J.L. Burkhardt, the Swiss traveller, noted in 1811: 'there is scarcely an instance in the modern history of Syria of a Christian or Jew having long enjoyed the power or riches he may have acquired. These persons are always taken off in the last moment of their apparent glory.'[15]

In his book, *Juifs en pays arabes: le grand déracinement 1850–1975*,[16] French historian Georges Bensoussan stands the modern trope of 'Jewish colonialism' on its head: it is the Jews who lived under Muslim rule who were the true victims of colonialism – of the Muslim variety. Significantly, he notes that women, minorities and slaves are curiously absent from Edward Said's postcolonial 'bible', *Orientalism*. Bensoussan observes that the Islamic order was built on a 'colonial' notion – submission. The Muslim submits to Allah, the Muslim woman submits to her husband, the non-Muslim *dhimmi* submits to the Muslim. At the very bottom of the pile is the slave. The slave trade was a huge Arab-run empire and the abduction of Jews so egregious that 'a whole corpus of Jewish law was devoted to the means of responding to these extortionist demands.'[17] Jews were still being sold as slaves in Morocco in 1890. In 1896, in the Saharan town of Ghardaïa, Jewish women and girls were sold in the public square.[18] The capture of Jews, among others, into slavery, was so serious a problem that the Spanish and Portuguese Jews' Congregation in London had a *Cautivos* fund for ransoming them.

In 1913, in the Atlas mountains in Morocco, families 'lived like slaves' and some even sold themselves to kinder Berber masters.[19] As late as 1934, Kurdish Jews were working for the local *agha* for no wage but a hunk of bread.[20]

Jews were feminised in the Muslim imagination as being cowardly, submissive and unable to stand up for themselves. They were animalised as *Yahudna Kalabna* – the dogs of the Arabs.[21] The modern rhyme became: *Filistin Baladna, Yahudna kalabna* (Palestine is our country, the Jews are our dogs!). In nineteenth century Palestine, it was customary to chide recalcitrant donkeys with *Emchi ya-ibn–el–Yahudi* ('come on, you son of a Jew!').[22] The theoretician of the colonial revolution Frantz Fanon coined a term for this – '*animalisation* of the internally colonised'.[23] It was pathetically appropriate that Jewish survivors of the 1912 pogrom in Fez, whose unenviable task it was to feed the royal beasts, should have taken refuge in the sultan's menagerie with the royal lions and tigers.[24]

These prejudices persisted well into the 1940s, when Shmuel Moreh was a schoolboy in Baghdad. Moreh confounded his schoolmates by winning wrestling matches with the schoolyard bullies: 'The students' attitude towards me showed me how much the Muslims and the Christians despised the Jews and mocked their notorious cowardice in a community which considers brutality as bravery', he wrote.[25] Similarly, 'Everyone knows you Jews are *masblool* (frozen by cowardice)', a Muslim tells Heskel Haddad, a Jewish medical student in Baghdad in the 1940s.[26] 'It was simply an accepted fact that Jews were frozen in the face of danger and couldn't raise a finger in their own defence.' Haddad challenges him and throws him to the ground.

Like women, Jews were considered to be 'dangerous' but controllable: indeed, while Jews could embody threatening forces in many traditional Middle Eastern world-views, their cultural identity in Arab societies tended to be associated with the same kind of danger presented by women – which meant that as long as Jews could be controlled, like women, then their Muslim patrons had nothing to fear. Jews and women alike were, for example, forbidden from entering granaries or gardens and barred from getting close to beehives, because their presence was thought to threaten the annual yield.[27] This explains why it was widely considered acceptable throughout many parts of the Arab world to leave a Jewish man in the presence of Muslim women without a male chaperone: the male was assumed to be weak and controlled and therefore safe. Jewish pedlars had access to Muslim households, while Muslim traders were denied it.[28]

Whilst Muslim women were considered to be safe in the presence of Jewish men, the same cannot always be said for Jewish women in the presence of Muslim men. Since Jewish women were not required to cover their faces, this was often considered to signal their availability to any Muslim who took a fancy to them. Instances abound throughout history of Jewish women kidnapped and forcibly converted to Islam: 'In Persia the condition of the Jews is worse even than in Syria ... and their women are unceremoniously taken from them, without their daring to murmur', writes a nineteenth-century European vicar.[29]

On the other hand, insolent *dhimmi* Jews had a reputation for being cunning and deceitful. Jews accused of having sexual designs on Muslim women were brutally made examples of: Victor Darmon, Moroccan-Jewish consul to Spain, was executed in 1845 for his adventures with Muslim women – a *casus belli* for war in 1860 with Spain.[30]

The Muslim image of the Jew was contradictory in other ways: Jews were thought of as rainmakers[31] who could bring a good harvest by guaranteeing the fertility of the soil. Arabs and Berbers alike attributed this power to the fact that Jews smelled bad, and so, therefore, God granted their wish for rain showers – but nevertheless, in times of drought, Jews were called upon to pray for rain, even though they were typically not allowed to get close to the village spring, out of fear that they might desecrate it.[32]

Jewess dressed for marriage in Algiers, painted by the French nineteenth-century artist Delacroix.

Jewish girl, Tunisia (Laurence Julius Collection)

According to the ethnographer Aomar Boum:

> Yet Jews and sometimes Christians – their fellow outsiders in the Muslim world –could also be associated with evil. The curse of a Jew was believed to be more fearsome than those from fellow Muslims; religious pilgrims went to great lengths to avoid seeing Jews before traveling to Mecca. Jews were asked to provide preventive charms for protection against evil eye and bad spirits, but it was also believed that when a Jew entered a Muslim's house, the angels deserted it.[33]

Today, as a result of saturation-levels of media and mosque anti-Semitic brainwashing, these stereotypes have been corrupted and replaced by European concepts of the demonic, manipulative and all-powerful Jew. Hitler's *Mein Kampf* and the *Protocols of the Elders of Zion* are best-sellers in Arab bookshops. As the historian Bernard Lewis observes, 'the empires and superpowers themselves are often depicted as helpless puppets manipulated by hidden Jewish hands, in pursuit of their plan to rule the world.'[34] Since Lewis wrote these words in the 1980s, levels of anti-Semitism have not diminished, and Jews have been blamed for all sorts of calamities, from 9/11 to shark attacks,[35] Even Da'esh leader Abu Bakr al-Baghdadi was claimed to be the Jew Simon Elliot.[36] Lewis adds:

> These attitudes color not only political discussion, but also literature and the arts, religion and scholarship. They are no longer confined to fringe and polemical publications, but appear in major newspapers, government television and radio programs, and in school and university textbooks. The level of hostility, and the ubiquity of its expression, are rarely equalled even in the European literature of anti-Semitism.[37]

Liberated from Dhimmitude

If the first wave of colonisation subjugated the non-Muslim to the Muslim in the eighth century, the second wave of colonisation – by the European powers – 'liberated' the Jews from the strictures of *dhimmitude.*

Nineteenth-century Jews, like Sir Moses Montefiore, who had benefited from the age of Enlightenment and the new era of religious emancipation in Europe, did their best to improve the lot of oppressed Jewish communities of the Middle East and North Africa. In 1864, Sir Moses undertook the first of his journeys to North Africa: he then tried (unsuccessfully) to intercede with the Ottoman Sultan.[38] The Anglo-Jewish Association and the Alliance Israëlite Universelle took a patronisingly 'colonial', but sincerely altruistic, interest in their less fortunate brethren in Muslim countries, as they tried to propagate European norms of emancipation and equality.

The case of Batto Sfez gave the French government a pretext to intervene in Tunisian affairs. There were others: the British government used 'gunboat diplomacy' to intervene in Greece on behalf of Don Pacifico, the victim of an anti-Semitic riot; and the Busnach affair (also known as the Fly-swatter Incident), an attempt by the Ottoman governor of Algiers to make France repay its debts to Jewish grain merchants,[39] backfired on him and resulted in the French invading Algeria in 1830. Generally speaking, ill-treatment and cruelty towards Jews in the Ottoman Empire and Maghreb became a catalyst for the Western powers to insist that reforms be introduced based on justice, security and freedom for all subjects.

The 1827 Fly-swatter Incident: the Dey of Algiers struck the French Consul in a row over debts owed by two Jewish grain merchants. The row precipitated the French invasion of Algeria.

By the late nineteenth century, the colonial powers had made inroads into the declining Ottoman Empire, extending protection primarily to the Christian minorities. Under Western pressure the *jizya* was abolished. It was small wonder that, in 1830, the Jews greeted the French in Algeria as saviours.

As the Ottoman Empire passed the Tanzimat reforms, heralding the emancipation of non-Muslims into society, life became incomparably better than before for the Jews of Iraq, Syria and Egypt. Jews sat in the Istanbul parliament after 1908. They served in the Turkish army. Like the Muslim majority, Jewish communities were swept up in broad social trends that saw an influx from smaller rural communities into the cities, migration across the Ottoman Empire and greater freedoms for women. Although Jews made up 3 per cent of the total population, the big cities of the Middle East and North Africa were heavily Jewish; along with other minorities, the Jews controlled trade and, in the British sphere of influence, established a business network linking Manchester, India and the Far East, as well as Latin America. As the European colonial powers gained footholds in the declining Ottoman Empire, Jews sought Western consular protection: the Turkish Capitulations conferred rights and privileges on subjects of European states resident or trading in the Ottoman Empire. Those traders lucky enough to become foreign nationals were exempt from local prosecution, taxation, conscription, and searches of their homes.

It cannot be emphasised enough that nineteenth century life was nasty and brutish for all, not just the Jews, but upward Jewish social mobility in the twentieth century inverted the traditional pecking order. Jews began dressing in European clothes, giving their children European first names and moving out of the Jewish ghettoes into the 'European quarters' of North African cities. Muslims saw Jews not just as collaborators with European colonialism, but there is a recurring theme of the time that Jews had become 'arrogant and reckless'.[40] The Muslim Arabs lagged behind in literacy by at least a generation.[41] Jews had the skills and education to take the best jobs, adding to Arab resentment. The final straw for some was when Jews began employing Muslim maids.

Unlike the German Jews, many of whom who aspired to assimilate into society at large, the Jews of the Middle East had no desire to be like the Muslim majority. Although they lacked political power, they felt drawn towards colonial society.[42] As the historian Michel Abitbol remarks:'Its values were open-minded and universal, but in effect it was rigid and racist'.[43] For example, Jews who were British colonial subjects could never be British enough to be admitted to imperial clubs. The *pieds noirs* settlers in Algeria, represented by such politicians as the deputy Edouard Drumont, author of the anti-Semitic tract *La France Juive*, were notoriously susceptible to anti-Jewish rhetoric.

The anti-Semitic tract *La France Juive* by Edouard Drumont, member of the French parliament representing Algiers.

For the historian Georges Bensoussan, the post-1948 exodus of almost a million Jews in one generation was not a break with the Muslim world, it was an 'aggravated divorce'. The process began a century earlier when Jews had started to educate their children in the Western-oriented Alliance Israëlite Universelle (AIU) schools. A sectarian crack became a gap, then a chasm. Jews provided the spine of the colonial regime – as civil servants, administrators and translators. During the twenties and thirties in Iraq,

Sir Elly Kadoorie opens the Alliance girls' school in Baghdad named after his wife Laura (Alliance Israëlite Universelle Photolibrary, Paris)

Muslim graduates of school and university could not find work. Yet the numbers of Jewish clerks continued to rise. Iraq's government inflated the civil service workforce, employing hundreds of unnecessary clerks.[44] This only served to fuel envy and a rising tide of anti-Jewish feeling.

The 210 Alliance Israëlite Universelle schools established after 1860 in 16 countries educated some 40,000 Jewish children.[45] The AIU hauled the Jews out of poverty and ignorance and turned them into an educated elite familiar with the works of Lamartine and Voltaire, and speaking English, French, Turkish, Arabic and Hebrew. For the first time, Jewish girls received an education. The AIU attempted to reach the most remote and disadvantaged of communities.

Although a minority of Jews were involved in Arab political life in Syria, Iraq and Egypt, it was but a short step for the Muslim majority to identify all Jews as proxies for the West and agents of the imperial powers. In the eyes of nationalists fighting for independence, Jews were indistinguishable from colonialists. They were considered neither to deserve to be integrated into the new Arab nations, nor to merit state protection. Paradoxically, the Jews were both rejected as collaborators with colonialism and spurned as rebellious *dhimmis*.

The golden age of the Jews under the colonial era was short-lived. Decolonisation heralded a process of 'ushering the Jews towards the exit'.[46] Marginalisation took place gradually and by stealth.[47] When Tunisia became independent there were few trained Muslim civil servants and technicians. The French went home to France and President Bourguiba bought time, appointing Jews, until the Muslims were ready to take over.

Jewish civil servants soon found obstacles strewn in their career paths. One Jewish lawyer was not allowed to sign off his work. Air-conditioning units were installed in all offices except his.[48] Muslims received promotion over Jews, and Jewish doctors were passed over in favour of their Muslim students.[49] Egyptian-born Ellis Douek, an ear-nose-and-throat surgeon who became head of department in both Guy's and St Thomas's hospitals in London, said Jews like him could never have risen to the rank of Professor at the Kasr-El Ayni hospital in the University of Cairo.[50]

Sheikh Roubine of Gabès (Tunisia) wearing traditional dress (A. Benattia/Harissa)

The Search for an Escape Route

It is a myth to assume that Jews did not begin leaving the Muslim world until the creation of the state of Israel. In the mid-nineteenth century, Jews were departing from Iraq for India and the Far East, or to seek their fortunes in the Americas. Moroccan Jews comprised a third of the Sephardi population of nineteenth century Jerusalem[51] (and 20 per cent of the British colony of Gibraltar).[52] The great Baghdadi entrepreneur and philanthropist David Sassoon did not leave just to seek economic opportunities in India and along the trade routes of the British Empire, but to escape religious persecution by Daoud Pasha in Iraq. In the late nineteenth century, Syrian and Turkish Jews fled blood libels, civil strife, economic depression and the Ottoman draft for the UK, the US and Latin America.

Until the Turks declared all the Sultan's subjects equal under the law in 1856, the best guarantee of one's inalienable rights and security was a Western passport. The Livornese Jews (Grana) of Tunisia were Italian since 1846.[53] However, the great mass of Jews in Arab and Muslim lands did not have any kind of passport, let alone the wherewithal to leave their countries of birth.

Algeria, part of metropolitan France since 1830, was an exception. Here most Jews even attained the Holy Grail – French citizenship. Accepting French citizenship was not a decision to be taken lightly, and the Jewish religious establishment resisted the idea for forty years, fearing it would lead to secularisation and assimilation. In the end, the *Décret Crémieux*, named after a famous French-Jewish politician and philanthropist, was imposed on the entire Jewish community in 1870.

The myth has since developed that only the Jews in Algeria were offered the privilege of French citizenship. The Muslims were offered it too, but overwhelmingly rejected it, as it would have meant compromising their personal status, which was governed by Muslim law.[54]

Not all Algerian Jews were naturalised French. In the south, the Jews of Ghardaïa in the M'zab remained in a state of fossilised *dhimmitude*. The culture of the M'zab, although Muslim, was a stronghold of Berber fundamentalism. Even in the 1950s, non-M'zabi Muslims were banned from spending the night in the city. With Algerian independence imminent, the Jews of Ghardaïa scrambled to get French citizenship.

In order not to fuel further Muslim envy and white colonial resentment, all-pervasive in Algeria in the 1890s at the time of the Dreyfus Affair, the French protectorates in Morocco and Tunisia refused to extend the Crémieux Decree to Moroccan and Tunisian Jews.[55] Jewish women tried to give birth on Algerian soil in the hopes of getting French citizenship for their babies. It was a bitter irony that the same French government which granted Algerian Jews citizenship put them through the trauma of being stripped of it during the Second World War. It was restored to them only a full year after the Allies re-occupied the Maghreb.[56]

In Libya, too, the interests of the colonial power and the local Jews diverged. The Italian colonials were suspicious of the Jewish community, some of whom supported the Arab rebellion against the Fascists.[57] Throughout the 1920s, an upsurge of anti-Jewish incidents in Italian-controlled Libya culminated in the so-called Sabbath crisis: the regime dictated that Jews were no longer exempt from attending school on the Sabbath. 'Jews', the *Israel* newspaper alleged, 'were being forced to assimilate while Arabs were allowed to preserve their religion unhindered.' The crisis deepened when Italo Balbo was appointed governor in 1934 and a decree was promulgated forcing Jewish shopkeepers to open on Saturdays. As punishment, twelve trade licenses were rescinded and two Jews were flogged in public.[58]

When the Second World War was over, North African Jewry felt that they had survived death and potential extermination by the skin of their teeth. Their colonial liberators had revealed themselves to be their greatest betrayers. The Jews who flocked to Israel in its early years had understood that they could not depend on colonial governments to ensure their security. Neither could Jews depend on the Muslim majority to safeguard their rights once the colonial era had ended. Far off in another part of the Arab world, the Babylonian Jews, the most ancient and most arabised of all Jewish communities, were anxious in case Arab independence brought disaster.

After the establishment of the British administration in Iraq in 1918, the Jews of Iraq pleaded with Sir Percy Cox, the British High Commissioner, to be granted British nationality on three occasions. The Arabs lacked administrative experience, they were fanatical and intolerant, the Jews claimed.[59] The British refused their request.

In Egypt, after 1860, Jews, along with Armenians, were denied Egyptian citizenship. The majority were left stateless, but a privileged 25 per cent of the Jews held foreign passports – although most had never visited, much less spoken the language of, the country in question. Until 1949, foreign subjects alone had the right to have their affairs adjudicated in mixed courts.[60]

The Colonial Blind Eye

Overall, Jews did have a measure of greater personal security under colonial rule, but there were limits to how far European colonialism was prepared to go to protect the Jew.

A typical response in times of trouble was for the colonial power not to be seen to apportion blame: in 1898 in Tunisia, Jewish homes were looted and shops wrecked, but the authorities pointedly arrested twenty Jews as well as sixty-two Muslims.[61]

In order not to antagonise the Muslim population, examples abound of anti-Jewish pogroms which the colonial forces of law and order were in no hurry to quell. It is helpful here to take a look at some specific incidents in order to assess the extent of the colonial blind eye.

There is evidence[62] that the British whipped up the 1920 anti-Jewish riots in Palestine – the mob is said to have chanted 'The government is with us.' In 1929, one lone British policeman defended the hapless Jews of Hebron during the massacre. The International League against Racism and Antisemitism (LICA) announced that 'Jews had died by the fault of the authorities' in the Constantine, Algeria pogrom of 1934: armed soldiers failed to intervene.[63] French forces of law and order were dilatory in quashing the Gabès, Tunisia riot of May 1941 in which seven Jews were killed, and later the Oujda and Jerrada pogroms in Morocco in 1948.[64] During the Iraqi *Farhud* of June 1941, British forces stood on the outskirts of Baghdad, under orders not to intervene until the rioting had spread to Muslim quarters.[65] During the Libyan pogrom of 1945, which claimed 130 Jewish lives, British soldiers were ordered to barracks.[66] Of the 550 Arab rioters arrested only 289 were actually tried in court: the majority were set free months later. To maintain a semblance of even-handedness the British also arrested ten Jews for daring to defend themselves.[67] Instead of protecting the Jews of Aden in the 1947 riots, the British-armed, Arab-staffed Aden Protectorate Levies turned their guns against them.[68] The French authorities took three hours to intervene in the anti-Jewish Oujda and Jerrada riots of 1948 in Morocco.[69]

With their policy of 'divide and rule', the colonial powers helped sow the seeds of conflict between Jews and Arabs in Palestine. There the British authorities embarked on a policy of Arab appeasement. As well as failing to quell violence for fear of upsetting the mob, they can also be accused of having incited it. In 1928, during a visit to Baghdad by Sir Alfred Mond, a mob was instructed to shout 'Down with Zionism' (*Zioniyya*). Instead, however, not knowing what Zionism was, they shouted 'Down with the security tax' (*Paswaniyya*)![70]

The Perennial Dhimmi

For the great mass of Jews, anti-*dhimmi* prejudice persisted. Indeed, the breakdown of the traditional *dhimmi* relationship seemed to aggravate the Israel-Palestine conflict. A notable incident took place in 1908, when the Hashomer Hatza'ir pioneers of Sejera replaced their Muslim Circassian guards – who protected their settlement against Bedouin raids – with Jewish guards. For the Jews, this was an ideological statement of self-sufficiency. But for the neighbouring Arab *fellaheen*, they had crossed a red line. They had reneged on their part of the bargain: the *dhimmi*, who was not allowed to bear arms, was always expected to look to the Muslim for protection.[71] For a Jewish officer to command Muslim troops was inconceivable. For this reason, in 1942, the French found it impossible to form mixed Jewish-Muslim battalions in Morocco.[72]

Whilst the Ottoman Turks had introduced the fez in Iraq in 1808, so that religious groups should not be immediately recognisable by their headdresses, in Tunisia, over a century later, the social rules of *dhimmitude* were still in force, even under French colonial rule, and Albert Memmi's grandfather was still expected to wear the obligatory and discriminatory Jewish garb. Persian Jews had to pay the *jizya* tax until the advent of the Pahlavi dynasty in 1925.[73] During the Second World War, the Turkish government passed a special Capital Tax Law that taxed Jewish professionals and merchants at a rate four times that of Muslims.[74] The effect was catastrophic: an estimated 30,000 Jews, unable to pay their debts, fled the country.[75]

Even under the French protectorate in Tunisia, every Jew could expect to be hit on the head by any passing Muslim, a ritual which even had a name: the *chtaka*.[76] Stone-throwing at Jews, usually by children, is a time-honoured ritual to this day.[77] *Dhimmi* modes of dress were re-introduced in Morocco's tribal regions at the behest of the Allies after the Second World War so as not to alienate the Muslim majority. For example, Jews were required to dress in black in the Warzazat region of the High Atlas. These and other forms of stigmatisation continued even after the Vichy anti-Jewish laws were abolished in March 1943.[78]

Shi'ites subscribed to ritual purity prejudices even in recent times. A Jewish friend who lived in Shi'a Bahrain tells how her grandmother once picked up some fruit to see if it was ripe. The fruit seller tipped his basket to the ground, crying out 'You have defiled it!'[79]

The Golden Age

In the main, however, coexistence and pluralism flourished in the 1920s and 1930s under colonial rule. It was a golden age. Middle Eastern and North

African Jews had been an organic part of the region's culture for thousands of years. But it was as modernisers that Jewish musicians and singers, actors and authors, lawyers and civil servants, entrepreneurs and bankers, made an immeasurable contribution to culture, society, industry, commerce, land and urban development, in the twentieth century.

Joseph Aslan Cattaoui was the only Jew to have achieved cabinet rank in Egypt in the 1920s as Minister of Finance to King Fuad, while others achieved high positions in various ministries.[80] The first bank established in Egypt was the Mosseri Bank. Jews were pioneers in cotton-spinning (a member of the Cattaoui family created the longest cotton thread in the world), founded the Salt and Soda Company, the Egyptian Petrol Company, the National Bank of Egypt, the Egyptian Real Estate Bank and the sugar refining industry.

The entrepreneurial Suarès, Cattaouis and Mosseris played a prominent part in land and urban development in Egypt, in competition with the Belgian Baron d'Empain. The Suarès family built the first public transport system in Cairo and the first national rail network. The Mosseris administered the new Cairo-Helwan railway, moving fifty Jewish families to Helwan: the trains did not run on the Sabbath. [81]

Emir Faisal, who was named king of Iraq by the British, appointed as his first finance minister Sir Sasson Heskel. Jews soon became the backbone of the civil service, transport, postal service, finance and trade in Iraq.

While the lives of remote and rural communities were relatively untouched by modernity, the urban Jewish middle class dominated culture and sport. The founder of Egypt's first national theatre in Cairo, in 1870, was the Jew Yacoub Sanua, dubbed the country's Molière; the first Egyptian opera was written in 1919 by a Jew, Daoud Hosni. Togo Mizrahi produced dozens of films that are considered classics of Egyptian cinema. Jewish performers such as Rakia Ibrahim (Rachel Levy), Naghra Salem (Ninette Shalom) and Camelia (Liliane Levy Cohen) were stars of the silver screen. Crowds flocked to see the Egyptian-Jewish singer and actress Leila Mourad.

In the field of music, the Jews of Iraq played a disproportionate role. When a puritanical nineteenth century Ottoman *wali* prohibited Muslims from playing music, the Jews stepped willingly into the breach. Although there were Muslim and Christian practitioners of music and singers of all faiths, the Jewish community ensured high standards of musical instruction. It set up a special school for the blind with the objective of teaching them an instrument rather than seeing them beg on the streets.[82] The Baghdadi Jewish performer Salima Murad bewitched both Jews and Muslims with her voice. Of all the instrumentalists in 1930s Iraq, 250 were Jews and only 3 were Muslims. In 1932, all the Iraqi instrumentalists who attended the first Arabic music congress in Cairo were Jews. In 1936, the Jewish al-Kuwaity brothers

Yacoub Sanua, Egyptian nationalist, journalist and playwright.

Egyptian screen star 'Camelia' (Liliane Levy Cohen) was rumoured to have been King Farouk's mistress. She died in a plane crash in 1950.

The Jewish film actress Leila Mourad starred in 'L'Amour Eternel' in 1952 with leading man Anwar Wagdi. (Poster designed by Hassan Mazhar Gasour and Ahmed Fouad). Mourad converted to Islam but ended her career amid accusations of disloyalty.

Girls from the Laura Kadoorie Alliance school in Baghdad dressed as Dakaka'at, female musicians, 1931 (Alliance Israëlite Universelle Photolibrary, Paris).

The band of Baghdad Broadcasting House (one Muslim and five Jews in addition to the singer), 1938.

were asked to found a band for the new Iraqi Radio Broadcasting Service: the entire ensemble, apart from the percussion player, was Jewish. On Yom Kippur in 1945, the Iraqi Prime Minister Nuri al-Said, himself a keen amateur musician, was furious when he switched on the radio and heard silence. When he was told that the Jews did not work on that day, he resolved to found a non-Jewish orchestra.[83]

North African Jewish artistes and musicians such as Reinette l'Oranaise, Blond Blond, Zohra el-Fassia, Salim Halali, Cheikh Raymond and Raymonde El-Bidouia, were pioneers of popular culture. Jews and Muslims developed Chaabi (popular) Andalusian music in Algeria. In Tunisia, the actress and singer Habiba Messika became a national heroine. The Jewish pioneer of Tunisian cinema was Albert Samama, nicknamed 'Chikly' after a small island on the lake of Tunis where he used to hold parties. Chikly became the first Tunisian film-maker, with eleven films to his name.

It was not uncommon for Jewish families, who had a virtual monopoly of trade in North Africa and the Middle East, to be the first to be exposed to new-fangled novelties and technological inventions from Europe. Thus, before he pioneered the Tunisian film industry, Chikly – a man of insatiable curiosity – introduced the bicycle, the wireless telegraph and the first X-ray machine to be installed in a Tunisian hospital. A keen photographer, he was instantly attracted to moving pictures, which the Lumière brothers had invented in 1895. Two years later, Chikly was running film shows in a Tunis shop with a photographer named Soler, and soon after he was making films himself.[84]

The Algerian albino singer Blond Blond (real name Albert Rouimi) was a popular exponent of 'Chaabi' music, influenced by tango and flamenco.

Albert Samama ('Chikly'), pioneer of Tunisian cinema.

Not content to film at ground level, Chikly filmed the region between Hammam-If and Grombalia from a hot-air balloon in 1908. He was among the first to film underwater sequences. He captured on film the Messina earthquake, a tuna-fishing expedition for the Prince of Monaco and the trenches at Verdun during the First World War.

Boxing was a sport Jews excelled at out of necessity – in case of they were picked on and beaten up at school or in the street. Alphonse Halimi became the world bantam weight boxing champion. Victor 'Young' Perez was Tunisian fly weight boxing champion in the 1930s; Jacques Chiche and Felix Brami were Tunisian-born boxing champions of France, together with Bob David, Kid Albert and Young Roger; Algerian-born Robert Cohen was the European bantam weight boxing champion; Zizi Taieb was a swimming and water polo champion. Other Tunisian-born champion swimmers were Gilbert Naim and Alain Hagege. Alfred Nakache was a world-class, Algerian-born swimming champion who later survived Auschwitz. Guido Asher was

Tunis-born boxer Victor 'Young' Perez died on the 1945 death march from Auschwitz.

Algerian-born swimming champion Alfred Nakache survived Auschwitz.

a star of the Egyptian national basketball team; a Miss Mashiah was Egyptian table tennis champion; Isaac Amiel was an Egyptian boxing champion. Tunis-born Pierre Darmon went on to become the eighth seed in the international tennis rankings.

European Colonial Anti-Semitism

The colonial era, in which Jewish culture blossomed, proved all too brief. Jews were at least one generation ahead of their Muslim counterparts in terms of education and social mobility[85], but Jews and Muslims competed for jobs. The window the Jews opened onto the West as modernisers was a boon – but also threatened traditional norms and old certainties. Arab resentment grew. The

Enjoying Stanley Beach, Alexandria, in the 1930s.

Girls of the Jacques Bigard school, Marrakesh, 1950 (Alliance Israëlite Universelle Photolibrary, Paris)

vast majority of Algerian Jews, nominally French, found themselves stranded between the rock of Arab hostility and the hard place of colonial anti-Jewish hatred. One 1883 anti-Semitic pamphlet declared: 'Turning a Jew into a Frenchman is like trying to change a sack of coal into flour.'[86]

French colonial anti-Semitism reached its zenith with the wartime abrogation of the *Décret Crémieux*. Under Vichy rule, Jews were not only stripped of their French nationality but were sacked from public service jobs and subject to quotas and restrictions.

A society wedding scene at the Nebi Daniel Synagogue in Alexandria, painted by Camille Fox.

The *Décret Crémieux* was reinstated in 1943. In some Jews, the trauma of having their French citizens' rights taken away created an absolute dread of being identified with Arabs: they were Frenchmen of the Jewish faith – *français israélites*. However, as the Algerian Arab nationalists embarked on an ever more brutal campaign of decolonisation in the 1950s, while the *pieds noirs* engaged in equally brutal counter-terror, the Jewish community was careful to maintain an official position of neutrality – although in retrospect, the killing of rabbis and bombings of synagogues suggests that the bombers made no distinction between *pieds noirs* and Jews. Some Jews supported the Front de Libération Nationale (FLN) independence fighters. A minority of anti-French Jewish communists earned the title *pieds rouges*.[87]

The Jews could sit on the fence no longer when two events forced them decisively into the French camp: the first was the burning of the Great Synagogue in Algiers in December 1960. Arabs went on the rampage ripping memorial plaques from the walls, and torching books and Torah scrolls. The second was the murder, in June 1961, while he was out shopping in the market, of the famous Jewish musician, Sheikh Raymond Leyris, a symbol of a shared Arab-Jewish culture and father-in-law of the singer Enrico Macias. Like the *pieds noirs*, the Jews were faced with a stark choice: suitcase or coffin. They scrambled to reach seaports and airports. Within three months of Algeria declaring its independence on 3 July 1962, all but 4,000 Jews had left for France.

Some see Jews and Muslims as helpless victims of forces beyond their control, tossed apart by the waves of history.[88] The flight of Jews from Arab countries can be ascribed to the *bêtes noires* of decolonisation and Zionism, both originating in nineteenth century Europe. The contemporary Western liberal view is that Jews are honorary 'whites' and collaborators with Western imperialists and colonialists and therefore 'deserve' to have been expelled. Although Jews were indigenous, their flight is, therefore, to be compared to the eviction of other 'foreign elements', and not to be pitied: *pieds noirs*, Italians, Greeks and Maltese, who were pressured to leave Arab countries when they became independent.

But to punish a constitutionally-protected minority for the actions of a foreign government was another matter entirely and this is exactly what happened in the aftermath of the 1956 Suez crisis when Israel, Britain and France colluded in the invasion of Sinai. The Egyptian regime took out its revenge on all Jews, not just British and French subjects, in spite of the fact that the Jews in Egypt were not Israeli citizens. George Naldrett-Jays, a senior police commander in Alexandria, fulminated: 'The motives of revenge and retaliation meted out to the British and French aggressors were all too apparent in the heartless harassing of those of Jewish faith – whatever the official spokesman may say to the contrary – to Jews of all nationalities, including Egyptian nationals and Jews residing in Egypt with no known national status.'[89]

Whilst the evidence points to the fact that Jews fared immeasurably better under European colonialism than they had under Muslim rule, the colonial powers were not above betraying Jewish interests out of anti-Semitic prejudice or in order to curry favour with the Muslim majority. In the eyes of the European colonists, Jews were useful but dispensable.

Post-modernists turn a blind eye to such inconsistencies. They treat the Palestinian struggle as typically anti-colonial. Israel is the last of the 'white' colonial powers. Zionism is viewed as a manifestation of European colonialism, foisted on the Jews of the Middle East and North Africa – yet the Zionists showed little interest in attracting Jewish immigration from Arab lands, a population which made up just 10 per cent of the global Jewish population, before the 1940s. Their main focus was on Europe, specifically on rescuing German Jewry from the Nazis. It was only after Israel's establishment, as conditions deteriorated for Jews in Arab lands, that the new state undertook the urgent rescue of Middle Eastern and North African Jews – the so-called '*Aliyot* of distress'.

The Jewish Natives Betrayed

The trend in academia and the media is to identify the Jews with colonialists – and nowhere more so than in relation to Algeria. The local Jews, who had

French citizenship, have been accused of casting in their lot with France in a supposed betrayal of Algeria's Arabs during the bloody war of independence. They 'got their comeuppance' with the expulsion of the *pieds noirs* in 1962. The Algerian war of independence is often held up as template for the Palestinian war of liberation, which will end with the expulsion of the 'colonialist' Israelis.

That these Jews predated the Arab conquest is conveniently ignored. As one Algerian-Jewish academic put it: 'If precedence gives one a prior claim in that land they call Algeria (this was not its original name), the Jews were there before any other monotheistic people – by this criterion alone.'[90]

Far from being colonial, Jewish roots in the Maghreb go back 2,000 years. Jewish traders arrived in North Africa with the Phoenicians, 1,000 years before Islam; and the first Jewish slaves and expellees from Judea settled among the Berbers soon after the destruction of the Second Temple. Some Berber tribes were said to have converted to Judaism. The most famous Jewish Berber of all, the warrior Queen Kahina, unsuccessfully fought off the Arab Muslim invaders in the seventh century. The *toshavim*, the settled indigenous Jews who managed to survive Islamisation, were joined in the fifteenth century by the *megorashim*, Jews escaping the Spanish Inquisition who settled mainly in coastal towns.

The historian Benjamin Stora, in his book *Les trois exils: juifs d'Algérie*, leads a contrarian school of thought: Jews were indeed natives, but they became traitors as their cordial ties with fellow native Muslims were torn asunder by French colonialism.[91] Jews in Algeria suffered a triple exile, Stora claims: the first was a moral exile, alienating them from their Arab Muslim brothers. The *Décret Crémieux*, in giving French citizenship to Jews in 1870, drove a wedge between Jews and Muslims. The Jews were thrust into a kind of limbo of identity and culture, denatured from their true Arabic roots. The second exile began the moment the Second World War Vichy government stripped Jews of their French nationality. The third exile was the physical exile from Algeria in 1962. At the end of this process, Jews were 'repatriated' to their 'motherland', France.

The French-Mauritanian film director Karim Miske[92] takes a similar view: invoking Hannah Arendt's expression 'tribal nationalism', he argues that two outside forces, Zionism and Arab nationalism, came to break the 'brotherly' bond between Jews and Arabs, turning them into *Intimate Strangers*, the title of a documentary film series he made. How then to explain anti-Semitism? According to Miske, anti-Semitism was imported into North Africa by European colonists.

It is indisputable that the French *petits-blancs*, many of them petty anti-Semites, stoked Arab violence against the Jews.[93] Algeria was a stronghold of the anti-Dreyfusards. Some of the worst riots were indeed caused by Europeans.[94] Stora and others eager to accuse Jews of betraying their Arab brethren do not appear, however, to hold the latter to account for treating Jews in pre-colonial North Africa as inferior *dhimmi* subjects living under Islam in abject misery, worsening poverty and as a minority vulnerable to outbreaks of mob violence. The one recurring sentiment amongst Jews from the nineteenth century onwards is 'fear'.[95] Jews lived with a permanent sense of insecurity and mistrust.

Independent Algeria was later to institutionalise discrimination in its constitution, excluding all but those with a Muslim father and grandfather from Algerian nationality. Yet, in spite of this, not all Jews left in 1962. A reader calling himself Benaya contacted *Point of No Return*:[96]

> My family sided with the Algerians in the late 1950s, when the FLN asked all Jews to choose [between the Algerians and the French]. There were only about 1,000 Jews in Oran. My father was well-loved in the city. We thought that nothing would happen to us. But in 1965 Islamists spread rumours about Jewish spies working for the Mossad. At that time we realised that we had better leave the country. But it all happened so fast. I was 15, and all I wanted to do was see my other cousins and friends in France.
>
> At school I used to be bullied because of my Jewish origins. People would ask me explanations for the suffering of the Palestinians. Everybody in the neighbourhood knew we were Jewish. The synagogues and graveyards had been vandalised. In 1967, when war broke out in Israel, my father's Algerian friends advised him to leave the country before it was too late. That is how, in a rush, I left my beloved city of Oran. I never saw it again.

Benaya's family threw in their lot with independent, post-colonial Algeria, but their reward was to be thrown out.

Historians like Gilbert Achcar are at pains to show that many Arabs make the distinction between anti-Zionism (good) and anti-Semitism (bad). The former is considered to be justified on the grounds that the Arabs should be morally entitled to protest Zionism's 'usurpation of their land'. However, in practice, the distinction is impossible to make, and Jews are punishable for being Jews.

Take, as a further example, the treatment of the passionately patriotic father of the last leader of the tiny Jewish community in Cairo, Magda Haroun. Maître Shehata Haroun (1920–2001) was an active anti-Zionist who was opposed to the partition of Palestine. He was the founding member of the Tagamu Party along with other leading Egyptian politicians. Yet it was for being a Jew that Haroun was arrested together with 400 Egyptian Jews as 'Israeli PoWs' in June 1967, following the Six-Day War, and sentenced to serve a long term in prison. When the time came for him to be released – on condition he left Egypt and boarded a ship directly out of the country – he refused to leave. He said: 'I am Egyptian, and I want to stay on in Egypt until my dying day.'[97]

In an interview on Egyptian TV at the time of her election, Magda recalled that when one of her sisters, then six-years-old, was very ill in the early 1960s, doctors said that she could be cured only in Europe. In order to be able to take her out of Egypt, her father was asked to give up his Egyptian identity – as all Jews were then asked to do. His Egyptian passport would be stamped with the notorious *Aller Sans Retour*: he would not be allowed to return to Egypt after his daughter was cured. So Maître Haroun decided not to leave Egypt and not to give up his Egyptian identity. He stayed with his daughter in Cairo where she died from her illness some months later.

In case you think Shehata Haroun suffered for his politics, not for his ethnicity – here's a further example: the tragic plight of Yemen's last Jews at the hands of the Houthi jihadists. These wretched people, whose antecedents have been in Yemen since the time of King Solomon, could not be accused of being communists or Zionists: they were simply Jews. Yet 'Convert or die!' was the stark choice facing the last 200 Jews in 2015.[98] In 2017, the ruling Houthis in the Yemen capital Sana'a were said to view the Jewish population of forty as an enemy and admitted to being 'engaged in a campaign of ethnic cleansing that includes ridding Yemen of its Jewish community'.[99]

Jew from Yemen, 1901 (Hermann Burchardt)

Yemenite children, 1901. The community is nearing extinction after 3,000 years (Hermann Burchardt)

With the possible exceptions of Tunisia and Morocco, matters have deteriorated so badly for the pitiful few Jews left in Arab countries that it is positively dangerous for them to self-identify. The Jews David Gerbi[100]and Raphael Luzon,[101] who have tried to return to Libya since the Arab Spring, were unceremoniously forced out of the country, the former to escape a lynching, the latter imprisonment.

Example after example abounds of how Jews have been singled out, not for what they believe, but what they were. Can this be construed as anything other than anti-Semitism?

Notes

1. Viviane Lesselbaum-Scemama, 'Les relations judéo-arabes en Tunisie de 1857 à nos jours: Le Pacte Fondamentale', *Harissa* blog, 3 June 2016, http://www.harissa.com/news/article/les-relations-jud%C3%A9o-arabes-en-tunisie-de-1857-%C3%A0-nos-jours-le-pacte-fondamental-par-viviane-l (http://jewishrefugees.blogspot.co.uk/2015/02/how-jews-beheading-led-to-equal-rights.html). (Last accessed 26 April 2017).
2. Signor Pananti, '*Narrative of a residence in Algiers*' (London: Edward Colburn, 1818) quoted in *Elder of Ziyon*, http://elderofziyon.blogspot.co.uk/2012/09/how-muslims-treated-jews-in-algiers-1818.html#.VqTLm_GU1JM. (Last accessed 26 April 2017).
3. Georges Bensoussan, *Juifs en pays arabes: le grand déracinement 1850–1975* (Paris: Tallandier, 2012), p.35.
4. S.D. Goiten, *A Mediterranean Society, An Abridgement in One Volume*, Revised and Edited by Jacob Lassner (University of California Press, 1999), pp. 182, 187–8 and 231.

5. Nathan Weinstock, *Une si longue présence: Comment le monde arabe a perdu ses juifs 1947–1967* (Paris: Plon, 2008), p.15.
6. David Yeroushalmi, *Light and Shadows, the story of Iranian Jews* (Tel Aviv: University of California and Beit Hatefutsot, 2012), p.24.
7. 'Persian Jews', *Wikipedia, https://en.wikipedia.org/wiki/Persian_Jews#cite_note-32*. (Last accessed 26 April 2017).
8. Ed Davies, quoted in W. Ellias, *Jewish Arabic of Baghdad* (JAB), Excerpts, p.8.
9. In the Islamic Republic of Iran today, *sharia* law dictates that the value of the life of a Muslim male, also called 'blood value', is much higher than that of a Jew. This is the compensation due to the victim or his relatives in case of loss of life and limb. The penalty for murdering non-Muslims by Muslims is much less, and can simply be bought by financial compensation, whereas the other way around carries a possible death penalty. The inheritance laws are skewed in favour of converts to Islam in a Jewish family. [Karmel Melamed interview with Frank Nikbakht, 'Q&A, Nikbakht on Iran's regime war on Christmas and Christians', *Jewish Journal of Los Angeles*, 17 January 2016, http://www.jewishjournal.com/iranianamericanjews/item/qa_nikbakht_on_iranian_reg imes_war_on_christmas_christians. (Last accessed 26 April 2017)].
10. N.A. Stillman, *The Jews of Arab Lands: A History and Source Book*, Vol.1 (Jewish Publication Society of America 1979) p.87.
11. Ibid.
12. Andrew G. Bostom, *The Legacy of Islamic Antisemitism* (Prometheus Books, 2008), p.46.
13. Alfred Morabia, 'Le Gihâd dans l'Islam médiéval', in *Le 'combat sacré' des origines au XIIe siècle* (Paris: Albin Michel, 1993), pp.267–8.
14. Elie Levi Abou Asal, *The Awakening of the Jewish World* (Cairo: 1934), http://www.farhi.org/Documents/HaimFarhi_1.htm. (Last accessed 26 April 2017).
15. See Bostom, *The Legacy of Islamic Antisemitism*, p.87.
16. See Bensoussan, *Juifs en pays arabes*, p.262
17. Edward Rothstein, 'Jerusalem Syndrome at the Met' *Mosaic* magazine, 6 February 2017, https://mosaicmagazine.com/essay/2017/02/jerusalem-syndrome-at-the-met/. (Last accessed 26 April 2017).
18. Fenton and Littman, *L'Exil au Maghreb* (Paris: PUPS, 2010), p.577.
19. See Bensoussan, *Juifs en pays arabes*, p.142.
20. Ibid.
21. Violette Shamash, *Memories of Eden* (London: Forum, 2008), p.166.
22. Weinstock, lecture notes: *Ambiguïtés et ambivalences du statut de dhimmi*.
23. Ibid.
24. See Weinstock, *Une si longue présence*, cover photo.
25. 'Baghdad Sami, champion of the world', *Point of No Return*, 15 June 2015, http://jewishrefugees.blogspot.co.uk/2015/06/baghdad-sami-champion-of-world.html. (Last accessed 26 April 2017).
26. Heskel M. Haddad, *Flight from Babylon* (McGraw-Hill, 1986), p.151.
27. Aomar Boum, 'Arab demonization of Jews is a historical anomaly – and shows the limits of today's leaders', *Tablet*, 21 February 2014, http://www.tabletmag.com/jewish-news-and-politics/163536/jews-post-arab-spring). (Last accessed 26 April 2017).
28. Ibid.
29. Revd J.W. Brooks, *History of the Hebrew Nation* (1841).
30. See Weinstock, *Une si longue présence*, p.132. The Jew Abraham Alalouf was burnt alive in Fez in 1880 because a Jewish anisette seller named Abecassis had pursued a Muslim woman.
31. The belief that Jews can bring rain has persisted up to the present day. See JTA and Gabriel Fiske, 'Moroccan king asks Jews to pray for rain', *Times of Israel*, 14 January 2014,

http://www.timesofisrael.com/morocco-king-asks-jews-to-pray-for-rain/.(Last accessed 26 April 2017).

32. See Boum, 'Arab demonization of Jews is a historical anomaly – and shows the limits of today's leaders'. *The Tablet*, 21 February 2014 http://www.tabletmag.com/jewish-news-and-politics/163536/jews-post-arab-spring (Last accessed 26 April 2017).

33. Ibid.

34. Bernard Lewis, *Semites and anti-Semites (Princeton*: 1999) p.195.

35. Nick Collins, 'Shark Sent to Egypt by Mossad', *The Telegraph*, 7 December 2010.

36. Mehdi Hasan, 'Why is the Muslim world in thrall to conspiracy theories?' *New Statesman*, 5 September 2014.

37. Bernard Lewis, *Semites and Anti-Semites* (Princeton: 1999) p.195.

38. See Bensoussan, *Juifs en pays arabes*, p.34.

39. In 1827, Hussein Dey, the Ottoman governor of Algiers, called in the loans of two Jewish merchants, Busnach and Bacri, but they claimed that they could not repay the Dey until they themselves were re-imbursed by the French. At a meeting between the Dey and the French consul Pierre Deval, Deval refused to discuss the matter, saying that His Most Christian Majesty could not deign to correspond with the Dey. Losing his temper, the Dey struck Deval with his fly swatter.

40. See Stillman, *Jews of Arab Lands*, Vol. I, p.100.

41. David Bensoussan, 'L' exode oublié des juifs des pays arabo-musulmans', *Harissa*, 16 June 2015, http://www.harissa.com/news/article/l%E2%80%99exode-oubli%C3%A9-des-juifs-des-pays-arabo-musulmans-par-dr-david-bensoussan. (Last accessed 26 April 2017).

42. Robert Assaraf, *Une certaine histoire des juifs du Maroc* (Jean-Claude Gawsewitch Editeur, 2005) p.354.

43. Michel Abitbol, *Le passé d'une discorde* (Paris: Perrin, 2003), p.268.

44. I. Levin, *Locked Doors* (Praeger, 2001), p.5.

45. Lucien Gubbay, 'How the Alliance remade the Jews of the East', lecture notes for *Point of No Return*, 9 June 2010, http://jewishrefugees.blogspot.co.uk/2010/06/how-alliance-re-made-jews-of-east.html. (Last accessed 26 April 2017).

46. See Weinstock, *Une si Longue Présence*, p. 96, quoting André Nahum, *L'exil des Juifs de Tunisie*, pp.244–5.

47. *Les réfugiés échangés* by Jean-Pierre Allali reviewed in *Point of No Return*, 15 October 2008, http://jewishrefugees.blogspot.co.uk/2008/10/how-bourguibas-tunisia-pushed-out-its.html. (Last accessed 26 April 2017).

48. Jean-Pierre Allali, *Les refugiés échangés* (JIPEA, 2007), p.107.

49. 'How Bourguiba's Tunisia pushed out its Jews', *Point of No Return*, 15 October 2008, http://jewishrefugees.blogspot.co.uk/2008/10/how-bourguibas-tunisia-pushed-out-its.html. (Last accessed 26 April 2017).

50. Interview by Bea Lewkowicz, *Sephardi Voices UK*, 2015.

51. See Weinstock, *Une si longue présence*, p.180.

52. See Assaraf, *Une certaine histoire*, p.28.

53. See Abitbol, *Le passé d'une discorde*, p.206.

54. The *senatus-consulte* of 1865 offered all natives (Muslims and Jews) the opportunity to acquire French citizenship, provided they gave up their 'personal status' (*Juifs d'Algérie*, Musée d'Art et d'Histoire du Judaïsme, 2012, p.93). See also 'Confusion over Algerian Jews' French nationality', *Point of No Return*, 7 March 2007, http://jewishrefugees.blogspot.co.uk/2007/03/confusion-over-algerian-jews-french.html. (Last accessed 26 April 2017).

55. See Bensoussan, *Juifs en pays arabes*, p.312.

56. The Jews who spearheaded the Algerian resistance and paved the way for a bloodless Allied landing in November 1942 were 'rewarded' with two months in a labour camp until finally released.

57. Maurice M. Roumani, *The Jews of Libya* (Sussex Academic Press, 2008), p.16.

58. See Roumani, *The Jews of Libya*, p.22.

59. See Bensoussan, *Juifs en pays arabes* p.519.

60. Beinin, *The Dispersion of Egyptian Jewry* (University of California Press, 1998), p.36.

61. Paul Sebag, *Histoire des juifs de Tunisie* (Harmattan, 1991), p.150.

62. Roberto Mazza, *Jerusalem: From the Ottomans to the British* (London: IB Tauris, 2012) quoting Colonel Meinertzhagen, p.176.

63. Ethan B. Katz, *Burdens of Brotherhood* (Harvard University Press, 2015), p.92.

64. Lyn Julius, 'Sixty-five years ago, panic swept Morocco's Jews', *Clash of Cultures* blog, *Jerusalem Post*, 7 December 2013, http://www.jpost.com/Blogs/Clash-of-Cultures/65-years-ago-panic-sweeps-Moroccos-Jews-364515. (Last accessed 26 April 2017).

65. Although the Jews were identified with the hated British colonial power, the theory has been advanced by the prominent Jewish civil servant Meir Basri that the British were no longer interested in protecting Jews as they had begun to trade with India and China and not Britain.

66. See Roumani, *Jews of Libya*, p.52.

67. Ibid.

68. M. Gilbert, *In Ishmael's House*, p.210.

69. André Chouraqui, *Between East and West: A History of the Jews of North Africa* (Varda Books, 2002).

70. Conversation with Maurice Bekhor, 2008.

71. Nathan Weinstock, *Histoires de Chiens* (Paris: Mille et Une Nuits, 2004), p.77.

72. G Bensoussan, *Le Nettoyage anti-Juif des pays arabes*, video uploaded 5 March 2013.

73. See Bensoussan, *Juifs en pays arabes*, p.271.

74. Rifat Bali, 'The slow disappearance of Turkey's Jewish Community, *Jerusalem Center for Public Affairs*, 6 January 2013, http://jcpa.org/article/the-slow-disappearance-of-turkeys-jewish-community/.(Last accessed 26 April 2017).

75. Erlend Geerts, 'The Jewish Community and Synagogues in Istanbul', *Istanbul Insider*, 15 March 2010, https://www.theistanbulinsider.com/the-jewish-community-and-notable-synagogues-in-istanbul/.(Last accessed 26 April 2017).

76. Memmi essay, *Who is an Arab Jew?* February 1975, http://www.sullivan-county.com/x/aj1.htm . (Last accessed 26 April 2017).

77. According to historian Benny Morris the practice of throwing stones at Jews is a venerable one in the Middle East, symbolic of Jewish degradation under Muslim rule. Morris quotes a nineteenth-century traveller: 'I have seen a little fellow of six years old, with a troop of fat toddlers of only three and four, teaching [them] to throw stones at a Jew." William Shaler, American Consul to Arab Algiers from 1815 to 1828, reported that the practice of Muslims throwing rocks at Jews was commonly seen. The practice of Arab rioters throwing stones at Jews was seen in the 1948 anti-Jewish riots in Tripolitania, Libya. It has been used as a weapon against colonialism in other Arab countries. https://en.wikipedia.org/wiki/Palestinian_stone-throwing#cite_note-Morris-37.(Last accessed 26 April 2017).

78. See Stillman, *The Jews of Arab Lands in Modern Times*,Vol. II., p.134.

79. Lyn Julius, 'Dilemmas of dhimmitude', *Jewish Quarterly*, autumn 2004.

80. See Stillman, *The Jews in Arab Lands in Modern Times*, Vol. II, p.54.

81. Levana Zamir, 'The Golden Era of the Jews of Egypt' in *History and Culture of the Jews of Egypt in Modern Times* (Keness Hakafot, 2008), p. 130.

82. The al-Kuwaity brothers are back!' *Point of No Return*, 1 September 2009.
83. Shlomo el-Kevity in Tamar Morad, Dennis Shasha and Robert Shasha (eds), *Iraq's last Jews* (US: Palgrave MacMillan, 2008), p.20.
84. Lyn Julius: 'Pining for La Goulette', *Jewish Quarterly*, Autumn 2005, http://jewishquarterly.org/issuearchive/article8110.html?articleid=159. (Last accessed 26 April 20017).
85. See Bensoussan, *Juifs en pays arabes*, p.393.
86. See Abitbol, *Le passé d'une discorde*, p.287.
87. Bensamy, 'Liste de juifs qui ont combattu pour le FLN', *Zlabia* blog, 5 March 2013, http://zlabia.com/forum/read.php?34,18173,18173#msg-18173. (Last accessed 26 April 2017).
88. This is the theme developed by Ethan B. Katz in *Burdens of Brotherhood* (Harvard, 2015).
89. FO 371/125602. UK National archives, Kew.
90. Raphael Draï, 'Racines', *Pardès*, https://raphaeldrai.wordpress.com/racines/Drai. (Last accessed 26 April 2017).
91. D. Sibony, 'La difficulté de voir la réalité' in S. Trigano (ed.), *Qu'est-ce qu'un acte antisemite? Pardès* 55.
92. 'Jews and Muslims: intimate strangers', *Woolf Institute* blog, 2 February 2015, https://woolfinstitute.wordpress.com/2015/06/02/jews-and-muslims-intimate-strangers/.(Last accessed 26 April 2017).
93. See Bensoussan, *Juifs en pays arabes*, p.482.
94. Miske blames the French for provoking the Constantine massacre of 1934 which claimed the lives of twenty-five Jews, implying that Arabs could never be responsible for these outbreaks of anti-Semitism – they were manipulated by European settlers. While there is some truth in this, the massacre, the culmination of a chain of violent incidents, started with an altercation between Muslims and a Jew by a mosque. The riot was premeditated – Arab tobacconists had cleared out their stock before the riot broke out [Richard Ayoun, 'De l'émancipation à l'exode brutale des juifs d' Algerie', in *La Fin du judaisme en terres d'Islam*, S. Trigano (ed.) (Denoël, 2012), p.212] – and trouble started simultaneously in several towns in the province. The rioters and looters were all Arab Muslims.
95. See Bensoussan, *Juifs en pays arabes*, p.212.
96. 'Last Algerian left as late as 1967', *Point of No Return*, 24 February 2008, http://jewishrefugees.blogspot.co.uk/2008/02/last-algerian-jews-left-five-years.html. (Last accessed 26 April 2017).
97. 'Goodbye Carmen, hello Magda', *Point of No Return*, 19 April 2013, http://jewishrefugees.blogspot.ie/2013/04/magda-haroun-is-next-cairo-jewish-leader.html. (Last accessed 26 April 2017).
98. Lyn Julius, 'The tragedy of the Yemeni Jews' *The Guardian*, 7 June 2009, https://www.theguardian.com/commentisfree/2009/jun/07/yemen-jews-exodus-arab-countries. (Last accessed 26 April 2017).
99. 'Yemen Minister says fate of country's last Jews unknown', *Times of Israel*, 16 April 2017.
100. Lisa Palmieri-Billig, 'Following calls for deportation, David Gerbi to return to Rome', *Jerusalem Post*, 10 October 2011, http://www.jpost.com/Middle-East/Following-calls-for-deportation-Gerbi-to-return-to-Rome. (Last accessed 26 April 2017).
101. Gil Stern Shefler, 'Libya Jew returns to UK Post-Benghazi jailing', *Jerusalem Post*, 31 July 2012, http://www.jpost.com/Jewish-World/Jewish-Features/Libya-Jew-returns-to-UK-post-Benghazi-jailing. (Last accessed 26 April 2017).

4

The Legacy of the Nazi Era

It is surely no coincidence that one of the most popular rallying calls at anti-Israel demonstrations around the world is *'khaybar khaybar ya yahud, jaysh Muhammad saya'ūd!'* ('remember the Khaybar, oh Jews, the army of Muhammad is coming now'). This genocidal chant recalls the first massacre of Jews under Islam: the ancient Jewish community of Khaybar (in present day Saudi Arabia) was almost wiped out by Muhammad and his first followers. Those that did survive had their land confiscated, their women sold into slavery, were humiliated with oppressive laws and forced to pay the *jizya* tribute tax.

Jews established themselves on the Arabian peninsula in Biblical times. Medina, Islam's second-holiest city, was originally named Yathrib. It was largely populated by Jewish tribes that had fled Judea after the Roman conquest. They rejected Islam, despite the fact that the Prophet Muhammad based the new religion heavily on Judaism and Christianity. He had hoped that the Jews he had cultivated would see the light and espouse his new religion – hence the verses favourable to the Jews in the first half of the Qur'an. But the Jews stubbornly resisted and were declared Muhammad's enemies.

The battle of Khaybar marked the ultimate defeat of the Jewish tribe of the Banu Qurayza. Jews were enslaved and murdered and, with the exception of a small group who continued to live at the southern tip, Jews were banished from Arabia.

Thereafter, the Jews, having been decisively defeated, posed little threat. They deserved only contempt for their failure to embrace the one true religion, Islam.

Bernard Lewis, an authority on the history of Islam, has written: 'On the whole, in contrast to Christian anti-Semitism, the Moslem attitude toward non Moslems [including Jews] is not one of hate or fear or envy but simply contempt.'[1]

Andrew Bostom in his *The Legacy of antisemitism in Islam*, together with Bat Yeʾor, pioneer historian of *dhimmitude*, firmly disputes this view. Bostom's book is part of an ongoing debate about the comparative situation of Jews under the Crescent and the Cross. The exodus of Jews from the Muslim world, both writers claim, can be explained by a litany through the centuries of mistreatment and massacre, fuelled by anti-Jewish verses in the Qur'an.

The battle of Khaybar has a resonance today with the Islamist *jihad* against the infidel.

Unlike Christianity, Islam has never had theological issues with Judaism, Bernard Lewis maintains. Islam, unlike Christianity, has not ever viewed Jews as Christ-killers: they were simply benighted unbelievers. Whatever the relative attitudes to Jews, it is illuminating to consider the question of whether they were better treated under Islam than Christendom. Bernard Lewis ponders this issue in *Semites and Anti-Semites*:[2] 'The situation of non-Muslim minorities in classical Islam falls a long way short of the standard set and usually observed in the present-day democracies. It compares, however, favourably with conditions prevailing in western Europe in the Middle Ages, and in eastern Europe for very much longer.'

The fortunes of Jews waxed and waned, depending on the place, time and ruler. It can be argued, however, that the utter degradation that, at times, came with extreme forms of the *dhimmi* condition of chattel slavery was far worse than anything that Jews in feudal Europe had experienced. For instance, the small Sephardi community of Palestine was so debased under a particular Muslim *qadi* that a contingent of Ashkenazi followers of the 'false Messiah' Shabbetai Zvi, seeking refuge in Jerusalem in 1700, refused to put up with the humiliations suffered by the Sephardim. 'The Arabs behave as proper thugs towards the Jews ...' Guedaliah de Siemiatycze of the *Hevrah Kadochah* wrote. 'Unlike the Sephardi Jews who are used to such treatment, Ashkenazim would never stand for such humiliation.'[3]

Lewis traces the infiltration of specifically Christian hostility towards Jews – with its blood libels, fears of conspiracy and domination, images of Jews poisoning wells and spreading the plague – to the high Middle Ages, when many Christians converted to Islam, and to the particular influence of Greek Orthodox Christians. It was not uncommon for one *dhimmi* community, especially where they were economic rivals, to try and turn their Muslim masters against another.[4] However, Jews were still viewed as powerless and insignificant. Unlike Christians and with few exceptions, they did not have the Western powers to protect them.

Dr Bostom and Bat Ye'or have also crossed swords with the German academic researcher Dr Matthias Küntzel, whom they accuse of turning Arab Muslims into 'passive victims of neo-colonialism'. Dr Küntzel argues that contemporary Muslim anti-Semitism is not all derived from the Qur'an. He remarks[5] that some hate-filled texts, such as al-Bukhari's so-called 'Doomsday Hadith', had been forgotten until comparatively recently:

> The Day of Judgement will not come about until Muslims fight the Jews, when the Jew will hide behind stones and trees. The stones and trees will say O Muslims, O Abdullah, there is a Jew behind me, come

and kill him. Only the Gharkad tree [the Boxthorn tree], would not do that because it is one of the trees of the Jews.[6]

According to one of Israel's leading Arabists, Yehoshua Porath, no mention of this *hadith* can be found anywhere in Arabic literature until after at least 1870. The *hadith* has been quoted countless times since. According to Küntzel, 'al-Bukhari's hate-filled *hadith* anticipates the rhetoric of modern anti- Semitism and for this very reason appears in the 1988 Hamas Charter'.[7] Küntzel and others insist that contemporary Muslim anti-Semitism owes a great deal to modern European purveyors of hate. Without doubt, Christian missionaries, traders, and officials in the nineteenth and early twentieth century saturated the region with their religious-ideological wares. The fraudulent *Protocols of the Elders of Zion* was translated by a Maronite Christian into Arabic and published in Cairo in 1925.

Historically, nonetheless, Jews have suffered during Islam's periods of intolerant fundamentalism. The Maliki and Hanbali schools of jurisprudence were very conservative applications of Islam. Salafism seeks to recreate the authentic atmosphere of piety around Muhammad and his early followers. The fourteenth century literalist scholar Ibn Taymiyyah sought to return Sunni Islam to what he viewed as earlier interpretations of the Qur'an, and is considered be the father of a narrow and puritanical strain of Islam.

In the twentieth century, however, Nazism exported a new element into the Muslim world: the idea of Jewish power, a hitherto alien concept.

The Eclipse of Muslim Moderation

Yet the rise of radical political Islam was not inevitable. Along with a current of secularism, it is easily forgotten that there was a strong and vibrant movement of modernist Muslim reformers in the nineteenth century. The European Enlightenment influenced Egyptian reformist Rifa'ah Rafi al Tahtawi (1801–73)[8] and Jamal Al-Afghani (1838–98). Afghani and his disciples sought to reconcile Islam with science and rationalist philosophy, much as Thomas Aquinas had done with Aristotle and Christianity. The nineteenth century Anglo-Indian Sayyid Ahmad Khan, the Indian Cheragh Ali and the Egyptian Muhammad Abduh, all thought Islam needed to be reformed. Sadly, after the break-up of the Ottoman Empire, their ideas were denounced as 'un-Islamic' and too Western-oriented. The *Umma* was reeling from the collapse of the Ottoman Empire and *Jihad* against Western colonialism was required to re-instate it.

Reactionary strains of Islam seeking to return to the purity of the religion's beginnings were embodied in the philosophy of an austere, narrow and intolerant Salafism in the Arabian peninsula, revived in the eighteenth century as Wahabism. Saudi Arabia was to use its fabulous oil wealth to finance the spread of this doctrine far and wide. The most important spiritual mentor of the Islamist movement was a pro-Nazi Egyptian religious scholar, Rashid Rida. Rida began his career as a philo-Semite, but performed an about-turn in the late 1920s. He 'legitimized his sympathy for Nazism by treating it as the instrument of God's will.'[9]

While Salafism was essentially quietist, the Islamism of the Muslim Brotherhood was revolutionary. The former tends to be a personal credo, the latter a political ideology.[10] Rather like Nazism, itself a response to unemployment and economic disaster, the Muslim Brotherhood was founded in Egypt in 1928 by Hassan al-Banna as a defensive reaction to modernity, the emancipation of women, the Great Depression and to re-instate the caliphate, which Turkey had abolished four years earlier. The fact that it was an anti-Western, mass movement did not make the Muslim Brotherhood's millennarian fundamentalism progressive. In fact, it showed that mass support could be mobilised for a thoroughly anti-modern and reactionary cause. Already in the 1930s it engaged in what the German scholar Matthias Küntzel called 'pogromist anti-Semitism'.[11]

The Muslim Brotherhood injected what the scholar Jeffrey Herf describes as 'a supposed, but actually false Jewish antagonism to Islam as a

Hassan al-Banna, founder of the Muslim Brotherhood.

religion.'[12] 'Otherisation' kicked in and lead to a loss of empathy to the point at which the 'Other' was no longer perceived as human. A narrative of oppression took over: the Jews were thought to want to take over the world, making it necessary to fight them at all costs.

The 1936 Arab Revolt in Palestine set off the Muslim Brotherhood campaign of violence. Between 1936 and 1938 the Brotherhood organised mass demonstrations in Egyptian cities under the slogans 'Down With the Jews!' and 'Jews Get Out of Egypt and Palestine!' Leaflets called for a boycott of Jewish goods and shops.[13] The Brotherhood's newspaper, *al-Nadhir*, carried a regular column on 'The Danger of the Jews of Egypt', which published the names and addresses of Jewish businessmen and (allegedly) Jewish newspaper publishers all over the world – attributing every evil, from communism to brothels, to the 'Jewish danger'. The Jews of Egypt were repeatedly called on to publicly disassociate themselves from Zionism.[14]

Dr Sami Shawkat, director-general of the Iraqi Ministry of Education, wrote *The Craft of Death* in 1939.[15] But violence by the Muslim Brotherhood was more than the glorification of militarism: suicide terrorism targeted the enemy while offering the martyr fulfilment in the afterlife. It became a sacred religious principle still practised by its Islamist offshoots today.

In June 1939, bombs were planted in a Cairo synagogue and Jewish homes, but this was as nothing compared to the violence to come. In November 1945, just six months after the end of the Third Reich and after sustained radio incitement by the Grand Mufti of Jerusalem in Berlin,[16] the Muslim Brotherhood carried out what Küntzel calls the worst anti-Jewish pogroms in (modern) Egyptian history,[17] when demonstrators penetrated the Jewish quarter of Cairo on the anniversary of the Balfour Declaration. They ransacked houses and shops, attacked non-Muslims and torched the Ashkenazi synagogue. Six people were killed and a hundred more injured. A few weeks later the Islamists' newspapers 'turned into a frontal attack against the Egyptian Jews, slandering them as Zionists, Communists, capitalists and bloodsuckers, as pimps and merchants of war, or in general, as subversive elements within all states and societies.'[18] It was the Muslim Brotherhood which turned the war against the Jews into a cosmic, eternal, religiously-mandated principle.[19]

According to Küntzel, Jihadist Jew-hatred took on Nazi-style tropes, later cemented in the writings of the Muslim Brotherhood's ideologue Sayyid Qutb, who wrote *Our struggle against the Jews*. Its driving idea is that everything Jewish is evil, but also that everything evil is Jewish.[20] This concept marks a departure from the traditional Muslim view of the Jew which held that the Jewish tribes of the Arabian peninsula deserved their seventh century fate of massacre, expulsion and humiliation for spurning the true religion of Muhammad, but that they had been decisively defeated;

unlike the all-controlling and manipulating Jew conjured up by Nazism, Islam considered Jews powerless and relatively insignificant.

'Arabs Paid the Price for the Holocaust'

The myth that Arabs were innocent bystanders to the Holocaust while foreigners committed atrocities against other foreigners in faraway Europe has gained so much traction that it is virtually politically-incorrect to see Arabs as anything but indirect victims of the Holocaust, and the establishment of Israel the 'price paid by the Palestinians'.[21] Yet the Holocaust was, in the words of author Robert Satloff, as much an Arab story as a European one. Persecution did not descend to extermination or even mass killings more 'for lack of time than lack of will'.[22] It is plausible that, had Rommel's Wehrmacht not been decisively defeated at the battle of El-Alamein, Arabs would not have prevented, and may even have supported, the Nazi project to exterminate the Jews.[23]

Scholars like Matthias Küntzel[24] and Jeffrey Herf[25] continue to uncover evidence of Arab sympathy and collaboration with Nazism. While the impact of the war of the Jews in Arab countries was minimal compared to its effects on the Jews of Europe, the impact of pro-Nazi ideology was huge.

The Nazis incorporated the Jews of the French Maghreb in their extermination plans at the January 1942 Wannsee conference. The *statuts des juifs* – stripping Jews of their French citizenship, seizing property and bank accounts and expelling Jews from state schools, universities and the professions – were implemented in Morocco and Algeria under Vichy rule. Tunisia was occupied[26] by the Nazis for six months from November 1942 under the leadership of SS Commandant Walter Rauff, the inventor of the mobile gas van. Rauff had been responsible for the deaths of over 90,000 Jews in Eastern Europe. But Nazi plans for the extermination of the Jews – the Einzatsgruppen Ägypten death squad was standing by in Greece – were thwarted by the Allied victory over General Rommel at El-Alamein in October 1942. Nonetheless, beginning on 9 December 1942, some 5,500 male Jews – some as young as 17 – were rounded up and sent to labour camps. Jewish property was pillaged and hefty fines imposed on the community 'to pay for the damages caused by Allied bombing'.[27] Scores were killed. Jewish eye-witnesses claim that the Germans had begun building gas chambers in Tunisia: had the Americans not recaptured the country in May 1943, the extermination of the Jews would have been underway two months later.[28]

In 1938, Italian racial laws came into force in Libya. Some 600 Libyan Jews died from starvation and typhus in the country's notorious Giado camp. Around 870 Libyan Jews of British nationality were deported to Bergen-Belsen, though the majority are thought to have survived.

The Moroccan Myth

Legend has it that the Moroccan sultan, the future Mohamed V, saved Moroccan Jews from being deported to concentration camps in Europe: but deportation across the Mediterranean was never a realistic possibility. The philo-Semitic sultan famously declared: 'There are no Jews, only Moroccan subjects'. It might be fair to say that he may have prevaricated, but he did not fail to sign every single Vichy anti-Jewish decree: Jews were shunted back into the teeming Jewish ghettoes from the European quarters of Moroccan cities, they were forbidden to employ Muslim maids, and as in Algeria and Tunisia, an inventory of Jewish property was drawn up, quotas were instituted in schools and universities and Jews excluded from public service and the professions. The sultan was branded, in a recent feature, 'just but powerless' by the Moroccan medium *Tel Quel*.[29] Real power lay with the French Resident-General.

Servicemen of the defeated French army, together with political prisoners from Spain, were sent by the Vichy regime to thirty forced labour camps on the Moroccan-Algerian border. They included 2,000 European Jews interned at the Bergent camp.[30] Dozens died from starvation, torture and neglect in the camps, as they built the Trans-Sahara railroad. The Moroccan sultan raised not a single objection.

Wartime labour camps on the Moroccan-Algerian border.

The governments of Egypt and Iraq were pro-British and tens of thousands of Muslims served in the British and Free French armies – but popular feeling was largely pro-Nazi in the Arab world. In his diary Walter Rauff described the Tunisian Arabs as 'depressed', the Jews 'hopeful' at the Allied advance in early 1943. A majority of Egyptians supported the Germans.[31] The Jews of Alexandria fled to Cairo, and the Jews of Cairo moved to the old quarter of Fostat. They watched with trepidation as the front line between Egypt and Libya shifted back and forth during 1941. In Morocco, Jews were subject to mob attacks as soon as General Patton's troops landed in late 1942 (Operation Torch).[32]

Albert Memmi remembers the atmosphere before the Allies recaptured Tunisia from the Nazis in May 1943:

> I have described in *Pillar of Salt* how the French authorities coldly left us to the Germans. But I must add that we were also submerged in a hostile Arab population, which is why so few of us could cross the lines and join the Allies. Some got through in spite of everything, but in most cases they were denounced and caught.[33]

The great mass of Palestinian Arabs supported the Nazis: some 9,000 Arabs enlisted in the British army to fight Hitler but *fifteen* times more Jews (there were half as many Jews as Arabs in Palestine) fought with the British.[34]

Walter Doehle, German Consul in Jerusalem, observed, as early as 1937:

> Palestinian Arabs in all social strata have great sympathies for the new Germany and its Führer … If a person identified himself as a German when faced with threats from an Arab crowd, this alone generally allowed him to pass freely. But when some identified themselves by making the 'Heil Hitler salute, in most cases the Arabs' attitudes became expressions of open enthusiasm.[35]

Demonstrators in Aleppo, Syria chanted, after the 1940 Nazi invasion of France: 'No more monsieur, no more mister/ In heaven Allah, on earth Hitler'.[36]

Three-way Alliance

A three-way alliance developed between Nazi Germany, the Grand Mufti of Jerusalem and the Muslim Brotherhood.[37] The Muslim Brotherhood was founded in Egypt in 1928 by Hassan al-Banna as a millenarian, anti-freedom of thought, anti-women's equality, anti-secularist movement.[38] Al-Banna drew considerable inspiration from Nazism: anti-Semitism was at the movement's core. Al-Banna's movement sought the utopian revival of the caliphate and the submission of non-Muslims to *sharia* law. It broke new ground by glorifying terrorist violence or martyrdom as a religiously-ordained means to an end. From 1936, the Muslim Brotherhood and the Mufti made common cause over Palestine. Only Palestine offered the starting point from which the *Umma*, the community of the world's Muslims, could be united behind one goal.[39]

The German ambassador to Baghdad, Fritz Grobba, a German 'Lawrence of Arabia', serialised Hitler's *Mein Kampf* in Iraqi newspapers.[40] The Nazis financed the Palestinian Mufti's Arab Revolt of 1936 against the British,[41] pro-Nazi youth movements, and a network of pro-German agents, as well as the Muslim Brotherhood in Egypt, which from small beginnings, had, by the end of the war, a million men under arms.[42] The intention was to foment a pro-German uprising in the Middle East and North Africa.

The third force was the Grand Mufti of Jerusalem, Haj Amin al-Husseini, widely regarded as the leader of the Arab world. From the outset, he transformed each November anniversary of the Balfour Declaration, a symbol of British betrayal, into a rallying cry against the Jews, whether they were in Palestine, where he incited the deadly riots of 1920 and 1929, or elsewhere in the Arab world. From Hitler's rise to power in 1933, the Mufti made approaches to the Nazis, who eventually re-classified the Arabs as 'honorary Aryans'. The Mufti made a key speech, '*Islam and the Jews*' in Syria in 1937, later translated into German. It became one of the founding texts of the Islamist tradition, one that defined the religion of Islam as a source of hatred of the Jews.[43]

Wherever the Mufti went in the Arab world, persecution and mayhem followed against the local Jews. In 1921, Yemenite Jews in the *Yishuv* claimed it was due to Palestinian Arab pressure that the decree forcing Jewish orphans to convert to Islam was reinstated.[44] This came about after a Palestinian Arab delegation had visited Yemen to demand that the Imam stop all immigration to Palestine. The Orphans' Decree, argues scholar S.D. Goiten,[45] was the single most important reason why Jews were desperate to flee Yemen. In the 1940s, visits of Palestinian Arabs to Aden (then a British crown colony) became more common, and so did the expression of anti-Jewish sentiments.[46]

For the Palestinian Arab population, the distinction between the Sephardi veterans and the Zionist newcomers lost its significance in 1929 when sixty-seven members of the old-established *Yishuv* were massacred. From December 1931, when he convened a World Islamic Congress in Jerusalem, the Mufti ceased to speak of Zionists but Jews. All Arabs were exhorted to treat the Jews of their countries 'as the Jews treat the Arabs of Palestine'.[47]

The congress was followed by anti-Jewish violence in Morocco – in Casablanca in 1932, Casablanca and Rabat in 1933, Rabat and Meknes in

1937 and Meknes in 1939.[48] In Tunisia, an *entente* between Tunisian nationalists and the Palestinian Arab Higher Committee sparked violence in Sfax in 1932.[49] The Algerian *ulema* declared a boycott of Jews in 1936, obeying the Mufti's instructions.[50] All this took place well before the creation of the state of Israel.

British reports noted the intense propaganda in Yemen. Jewish refugees tried to make for British-controlled Aden. In 1939, a crowd was incited against the British and the Jews when they were shown fabricated photographs of Arab children hanging from telegraph poles. Other newspapers mendaciously reported that thousands of Arabs had been killed and bombs thrown at the Muslim holy places in Jerusalem.[51]

The Pro-Nazi Government in Iraq

But the worst incitement, with the deadliest consequences of all, took place in Iraq. Throughout the 1930s, Palestinian exiles together with the Mufti, along with Syrian and Lebanese emigrés, fanned the flames of Jew-hatred with false propaganda. In April 1939, the first German radio station broadcasting in several languages, including Arabic, was opened in the town of Zeesen south of Berlin. Using the most powerful of short-wave transmitters, Radio Berlin, under the direction of Yunus Bahri, reached the entire Arab Middle East and in North Africa. Arabic broadcasts from the Fascist station at Bari, Italy began in 1934 and are thought to have had a considerable effect on public opinion even before the exiled Mufti's arrival.[52] Arabs gathered in coffee houses to listen to Radio Berlin, while Jews preferred the BBC.

The Mufti himself, expelled to Iraq by the British in 1939, played a leading role in plotting a pro-Nazi military coup, led by Rashid Ali al-Gaylani, to overthrow the pro-British government. The pro-Nazi government lasted two months, and was the only Arab regime to sign a treaty

The shortwave Nazi radio transmitter at Zeesen, south of Berlin.

with Nazi Germany and declare war against the British. Fearful that Iraq's vast oil reserves would fall into Nazi hands, the British sent troops into Iraq. With the British army at the gates of Baghdad, the Mufti was forced again into exile – but not before he had primed the Arabs of the capital, together with defeated, returning troops, to unleash the *Farhud* of 1941. Four days before the *Farhud*, Yunus Bahri made a poisonous broadcast inciting murder of the Jews from the Nazi radio station at Zeesen.[53]

In June 1941, before he too fled, the pro-Nazi, self-styled governor of Baghdad, Yunis al-Sabawi, told the Jews to lock themselves in their homes with enough food for three days. His intention, many believe, was to deport them into detention centres in the desert.[54] The pro-Nazi paramilitary youth group, the Futuwwa, went around daubing Jewish homes with a red handprint.

There is now a respectable body of opinion that the *Farhud* was a Holocaust-related event, caused by Nazi incitement. In December 2015, the Israeli government recognised that survivors of the *Farhud* would be eligible to receive a stipend, as well as discounts on medical care. Finance minister Moshe Kahlon described the move as 'the correction of a historic injustice'.[55]

Genocidal extermination was conceived in the Middle East: the Turks, with the help of German officers subsequently involved in planning Hitler's mass extermination plans, murdered a million Armenians and Thracians in 1915. The Mufti had been an officer in the Ottoman army. It is suggested that the Turkish governor of Jaffa's mass expulsion of Jews from Palestine in April 1917 during the First World War was a prelude to their extermination. According to *Haaretz*, Djemal Pasha threatened the Jews of Palestine with the fate of Armenians subjected to genocide.[56]

One can only speculate what the impact would have been had Iraq's Nazi leadership not been forced to flee in 1941. Although many Jews were saved by their Muslim neighbours, others turned against them. The pogrom claimed the lives of 179 identifiable victims, 1,000 injured, with many mutilated and raped, and many homes and 900 shops looted and wrecked. Jewish patients were poisoned in hospital or left to die untreated. Many more victims were not identified, and at least one historian believes that the death toll may have reached 600.[57] Most of the bodies were buried hurriedly in a loaf-shaped mass grave.

The Mufti's Extermination Plans

The Mufti's collaboration with the Nazis, despite strenuous Arab efforts to downplay it,[58] has been well-documented. He sought Nazi licence to exterminate Jews in Arab countries as well as Palestine 'in the same way as the problem was resolved in the Axis Countries'.[59] When he became the Führer of the Arab world, he intended to implement plans for extermination

MASS GRAVE OF VICTIMS OF THE FARHUD, 1941

The *Farhud* mass grave in Baghdad's old Jewish cemetery was demolished in the late 1950s.

The Palestinian Mufti inspecting SS troops.

camps near Nablus.[60] Taking refuge in Berlin along with sixty other Arabs, the Mufti had a meeting with Hitler, visited Oranienburg concentration camp, hobnobbed with Eichmann and Himmler, and his lavishly-funded Berlin-based Gross Mufti Burö beamed anti-Semitic propaganda radio broadcasts

Palestinian Mufti meeting Adolf Hitler on 28 November 1941.

all over the Middle East and North Africa from the transmitter at Zeesen. 'Kill the Jews wherever you find them', he incited his listeners in 1944. 'This pleases God, history, and religion.' The Mufti introduced the idea that a Muslim who killed a Jew would earn his place in Heaven.[61] Jews were presented as Islam's worst enemies: 'The Jew since the time of Muhammad has never been a friend of the Muslim, the Jew is the enemy and it pleases Allah to kill him.'[62]

The sixty pro-Nazi Arabs who spent the rest of the Second World War in Berlin with the Mufti included Rashid Ali al-Gaylani, Fawzi al-Qawuqji, Abd al-Qadir al-Husseini, Abou Ibrahim al-Kabir, Sheikh Hassan Abu Saud, Hassan Salama, Wasef Kamal, Arif Abd al-Raziq, Abdul Latif and Rasem Khalidi.[63] They spread fear of the Jews as an all-powerful force which wanted to take North Africa from the Arabs:

> Palestine does not satisfy the Jews, because the aim is to take over the rest of the Arab countries, Lebanon, Syria and Iraq and the region of Khaybar in Saudi Arabia, under the pretext that this city was the homeland of the Jewish tribes in the seventh century...The Jews are a threat not just in Palestine, but in every Arab country, since this is where the Allies plan to resettle the millions of Jews who were expelled from Europe. The Arabs must fight with all their strength to put an end to this plot.[64]

By the time the Allies had defeated the Nazis, some 4,000 Jews had died during the Second World War in the Arab world, a tiny fraction of the total murdered by the Nazis in Europe. Most perished in the Allied bombing raids. Hundreds died in labour camps; forty Tunisian Jewish resistance fighters

Tunisian Jews being marched off to Nazi labour camps in December 1942 (Yad Ben Zvi archives).

Libyan Jews on their way back to Tripoli in 1945 after deportation to Bergen-Belsen (Libyan Jewish Heritage Museum, Or Yehuda)

were deported by air to the Nazi death camps in April 1943.[65] Libyan Jews of British nationality were transported to Italy and thence to Bergen-Belsen. Some were exchanged for German PoWs. Most are thought to have survived. But the Nazi legacy endured in the Arab world well beyond the end of the war.

The Mufti was indirectly responsible for the deaths of thousands of European Jews whom he prevented from leaving for Palestine during the Second World War. The Bosnian and Albanian Muslim SS divisions he set up were responsible for unspeakable crimes in Yugoslavia. In spite of all this, the Allies failed to put the Mufti on trial as a war criminal. He was indicted, judged and convicted, however, by Yugoslavia for crimes against humanity, arising from his pivotal role in establishing the Handschar and Skandeberg SS divisions which, among other crimes, deported Balkan Jews from Kosovo, Macedonia and Thrace.

The Nazi Legacy Endures

Six months after the Belsen survivors had returned to Libya, the Jews of Tripoli and outlying villages suffered a vicious three-day pogrom in November 1945, which claimed the lives of 130 and made 10 per cent of the Jews homeless. How was such anti-Jewish violence possible so soon after news of the terrible extermination of the Jews of Europe had reached the Arab world? The 1945 Libyan riots were a spillover from disturbances in

Aftermath of the 1945 Tripoli pogrom.

Egypt in which five Jews were murdered. It is noteworthy that the Egyptian rioters, incited by the Muslim Brotherhood, targeted Coptic, Greek Orthodox and Catholic institutions, as well as Jews, in what has been called the worse pogrom in modern Egypt's history.[66] But one cannot discount the impact of saturation wartime radio propaganda on an illiterate populace. Millions of leaflets dripping with anti-Semitism had been dropped over Arab countries during this period.

While some blame the clash of Zionism and Arab nationalism for the troubles, historians record that the rioters in Libya did not shout anti-Zionist slogans.[67] One Jewish Agency report stated that the mob did not even know what Zionism was. Major-General Duncan Cumming, the British Chief Civil Affairs Officer, also noted that an excited mob took out their anger with the colonial powers on the defenceless Jews – at proposals 'to hand the country back to Italian tutelage or to some other country with suspected Colonial designs'.[68]

Matthias Küntzel has demonstrated the link between the Nazi war against the Jews and the 1948 Arab war against Israel.[69]

What is even more staggering, as we shall see in later chapters, is that, after the Second World War, Arab states passed Nuremberg-style laws to undertake the wholesale eviction of their Jewish citizens and the theft of their property. Arab and Muslim anti-Semitism has since reached stratospheric heights.[70] In fact, the seeds of the epidemic of anti-Semitism we see today in the Arab and Muslim world were sown in the 1930s and 1940s, and as we have seen, the Jews in Arab countries, no less than in Palestine, were its first intended victims.

The Ghost of Bigotry Never Exorcised

In retrospect it is important to consider the longer term effects of Arab sympathy and outright support for Nazism. Failing to indict the Mufti of Jerusalem for his war crimes, the Allies shrank from offending the Arabs. The Mufti remained a hero for tens of thousands. The Arab world never went through a process of 'de-Nazification'. Although Nasser suppressed and persecuted the Muslim Brotherhood, the movement re-emerged in the 1970s; its legacy of Nazi-inspired genocidal anti-Semitism, as set out in the works of its ideologue Sayyid Qutb, endures to this day in the ideology of Islamism. And ironically, Jews originating in Arab lands are, once again, the targets of anti-Semitic terrorism – in their adopted land of France.[71]

Al-Banna's ideas spread from his native Egypt to Palestine, Syria, Sudan and North Africa. They were introduced into Iran in Shi'ite form by the Ayatollah Khomeini and Ali Shariati. They were then exported from Iran to the Shi'a in Lebanon, and then into India and Pakistan by Abul Ala Mawdudi. In Palestine, the Muslim Brotherhood became Hamas.[72] The Muslim

Brotherhood has spawned Islamist splinter groups such as Hamas, Al Nusra, Islamic Jihad, Al-Qaeda, Daesh (ISIS/ISIL). Its fingerprints can be seen in the Iranian regime's philosophy of overt Holocaust denial and its declared intention to annihilate the state of Israel.

The ghost of Nazi-inspired, anti-Jewish bigotry was never exorcised: after the Second World War, the Arab world gave safe haven to Nazi war criminals on the run. They became military advisers and spin-doctors of Jew-hatred. Anti-Semitism soared. Adolph Eichmann, Nazi architect of the 'final solution', hoped his 'Arab friends' would continue his battle against the Jews, who were always the 'principal war criminals' and 'principal aggressors'. 'I have not managed to complete my task of total annihilation but I hope the Muslims will complete it for me', declared Adolph Eichmann in his memoirs.[73]

The Muslim Brotherhood, and its local Palestinian branch Hamas, al-Qaeda, Islamic State (whose leader Abu Bakr al-Baghdadi was a member of the Muslim Brotherhood) and assorted Islamist groups still carry the torch for an ideology born in the Nazi era. (In April 2017 Hamas released a document purporting to show its more 'moderate' face, but it retains its eliminationist anti-Semitic aims, tactically rebranding a religious war as an armed political struggle.)

The theory has been advanced that Nazi anti-Semitism had a lasting influence on the young Ruhollah Khomeini, later the leader of the Islamic fundamentalist revolution in Iran. 'Radio Zeesen was a success not only in Cairo; it made an impact in Tehran as well'. When in the winter of 1938 the thirty-six-year-old Khomeini returned to the Iranian city of Qom from Iraq he 'had brought with him a radio receiver set made by the British company Pye ... The radio proved a good buy... Many mullahs would gather at his home, often on the terrace, in the evenings to listen to Radio Berlin and the BBC', writes his biographer Amir Taheri. Even the German consulate in Tehran was surprised by the success of this propaganda. 'Throughout the country spiritual leaders are coming out and saying "that the twelfth Imam has been sent into the world by God in the form of Adolf Hitler" we learn from a report to Berlin in February 1941 ...'[74]

Khomeini was mentored by the head of a Muslim Brotherhood affiliate called the Devotees of Islam. Khomeini's exile in France prior to assuming power was financed by Francois Genoud, one of the most important figures in the post-War Underground Reich.[75] The links between Iran and the Muslim Brotherhood are long-standing. The first religiously motivated terrorist movement in Iran, Fadayan-e Islam, under the leadership of Navob Safavi, was inspired by the example of the Egyptian Muslim Brotherhood and its leader Sayyid Qutb.[76] In spite of strains created by the Syrian civil war, the Iranian alliance with the avowedly anti-Semitic Hamas, the Gaza branch of the Muslim Brotherhood, remains strong.[77]

The theocracy ruling Iran is committed to a religious war against all Jews, except the cowed and docile minority still living there. The regime proudly proclaims its genocidal aims: the destruction of Israel. [78] As Matthias Küntzel says, Holocaust denial, demonisation of the Jews as the epitomy of evil and the elimination of Israel are the three pillars of Iranian Islamism. Holocaust denial is rampant in the Arab world, but in Iran, the government's Holocaust denial 'contains an appeal to repeat it.'[79]

Every year on 27 January, the West observes Holocaust Memorial Day. Iran states that that the Holocaust may not have happened, and in the next breath, proudly declares its intention to exterminate the Jews of Israel.[80] We are left to wonder when the West will recognise that the demons of totalitarian anti-Semitism unleashed in the first half of the twentieth century across the Middle East are still with us today.

Notes

1. Robert Kaplan, 'The legacy of Islamic antisemitism' *American Thinker*, 18 May 2008, http://www.americanthinker.com/articles/2008/05/the_legacy_of_islamic_antisemi.htm. (Last accessed 26 April 2017).
2. Bernard Lewis, *Semites and Anti-Semites* (New York: Norton, 1986), p.132.
3. Weinstock, *Cha'alu Chelom Yerushalayim* (Demandez des nouvelles de Jérusalem) *Rechoummoth* 1922, (Berlin, 1716), pp.461–93.
4. Bernard Lewis, *Jews of Islam* (Princeton University Press, 1984), p.55.
5. 'Islamism/Nazism: Küntzel and Bostom cross swords', *Point of No Return*, 1 January 2008, http://jewishrefugees.blogspot.co.uk/2008/01/islamism-and-nazism-kuntzel-and-bostom.html. (Last accessed 26 April 2017).
6. Sahih al-Bukhari, Sahi Muslim, cited in *Quoting Islam*, http://quotingislam.blogspot.co.uk/2011/06/muhammad-says-that-one-day-very-trees.html. (Last accessed 26 April 2017).
7. 'Islamism/ Nazism - Küntzel and Bostom cross swords', *Point of No Return* blog, 1 January 2008, http://jewishrefugees.blogspot.co.uk/2008/01/islamism-and-nazism-kuntzel-and-bostom.html. (Last accessed 26 April 2017).
8. Shmuel Moreh, 'Introduction' in Moreh and Yehuda (eds) *Al-Farhud* (Hebrew University Magnes Press, 2010), p.2.
9. Gilbert Achcar, *The Arabs and the Holocaust* (Saqi, 2011), p.112.
10. Daniel Pipes, 'Islam and Islamism', *National Interest*, Spring 2000, http://www.danielpipes.org/366/islam-and-islamism-faith-and-ideology (Last accessed 26 April 2017).
11. M. Küntzel, 'Hitler's legacy of Islamic anti-Semitism in the Middle East', *Articles by Matthias Küntzel*, 30 November 2006, http://www.matthiaskuentzel.de/contents/hitlers-legacy-islamic-antisemitism-in-the-middle-east. (Last accessed 26 April 2017).
12. Jeffrey Herf interviewed in *Masri al-Yom* about his book 'Nazi Propaganda in the Arab World', *Point of No Return*, 14 February 2010, http://jewishrefugees.blogspot.co.uk/2010/02/nazi-propaganda-in-arab-world-by.html. (Last accessed 26 April 2017).
13. Matthias Küntzel, *Jihad and Jew-hatred* (Telos Press Publishing, 2007), p.19.
14. Ibid., p.23.
15. See Moreh and Yehuda (eds), *Al-Farhud*, p.2.

16. Edy Cohen, 'The Mufti, Nazi propaganda and the *Farhud*', London presentation, 7 August 2016.

17. See Küntzel, *Jihad and Jew-hatred*, p.7.

18. Gudrun Krämer, *The Jews in Egypt 1914–1952* (I B Tauris, 1969), p.146.

19. Paul Berman, *The Flight of the intellectuals* (Melville House, 2011), p.187.

20. See Küntzel, *Jihad and Jew-hatred*, p.99.

21. One encounters this theme widely. Just two examples can be found here: Susan Abulhawa, 'Why are Palestinians paying for Germany's sins?' *The Electronic Intifada*, 14 April 2012, and Shlomo Shamir, 'Iranian president: if the Holocaust happened, why must Palestinians pay?' *Haaretz*, 25 September 2007.

22. Satloff, *Among the Righteous* (Public Affairs New York, 2006), p.160.

23. The Cairo-born film-maker Elliot Malki remarks: 'Had Rommel won the war, as we said back in Egypt, *khas ve'khalila* (God forbid), the Jews of Egypt probably would have ended up in Auschwitz.' (Speech at UK premiere of *Starting Over Again*, 11 May 2017.)

24. Irene Lancaster, review of *Jihad and Jew-hatred* by Dr Matthias Küntzel, 1 November 2007, *Point of No Return*, http://jewishrefugees.blogspot.co.uk/2007/11/kuentzel-exposes-links-between-fascism.html. (Last accessed 26 April 2017).

25. Jeffrey Herf, *Nazi propaganda in the Arab world* (US: Yale, 2009).

26. Edith Shaked, *The Nizkor Project*, 2009–12, http://www.nizkor.org/hweb/people/s/shaked-edith/re-examining-wannsee.html. (Last accessed 26 April 2017).

27. Daniel Lee, 'New Generation Thinkers' series, BBC Radio 3, 20 November 2016, http://www.bbc.co.uk/programmes/b0831fpk. (Last accessed 26 April 2017).

28. *Ginette* (2017), film by Nathan Minsberg featuring wartime memories of his Tunis-born grandmother.

29. *Tel quel*, quoted in 'L' histoire secrète des juifs en camps de concentration au Maroc', *Dafina*, 13 May 2014, http://dafina.net/gazette/article/l%C2%B4histoire-secr%C3%A8te-des-juifs-en-camps-de-concentration-au-maroc. (Last accessed 26 April 2017).

30. See Satloff, *Among the Righteous*, p.60.

31. Laskier, *The Jews of Egypt*, p.77.

32. Stillman, *Jews of Arab Lands in Modern Times*, Vol. II, p.134.

33. Memmi, essay: 'Who is an Arab Jew?' February 1975, http://www.sullivan-county.com/x/aj1.htm. (Last accessed 26 April 2017).

34. G. Bensoussan, *Juifs en pays arabes*, p.598.

35. Mallmann & Cüppers, *Nazi Palestine* (English translation: Enigma Books, 2010), p.39.

36. Ibid., p.31. So popular in Iraq was the Führer that my mother's Arab Muslim gardener, who lived at the bottom of the garden with his family, named his newborn son Hitler. My mother was mortified.

37. Karin McQuillan, 'Hitler's Long Shadow over Israel', *American Thinker*, 4 May 2012.

38. See Küntzel, *Jihad and Jew-hatred*, p. 32.

39. Ibid., p.57.

40. Edwin Black, 'In truth, the *Farhud* was Iraq's Shoah', *The Jewish Chronicle*, 28 May 2015.

41. According to records, in 1939 the Grand Mufti had his representative thank the German government for 'the support provided thus far'. (Klaus-Michael Mallmann and Martin Cüppers, *Nazi Palestine* (Enigma Books, 2005), p.49.

42. Paul Berman, *The Flight of the Intellectuals* (Mellville House, 2011), p.102.

43. J. Herf, 'Haj Amin al-Husseini, the Nazis and the Holocaust: the origins, nature and after-effects of collaboration', *Jerusalem Center for Public Affairs*, 5 January 2016, http://jcpa.org/article/haj-amin-al-husseini-the-nazis-and-the-holocaust-the-origins-nature-and-aftereffects-of-collaboration/.(Last accessed 26 April 2017).

44. See Bensoussan, *Juifs en pays arabes*, p.544.

45. S.D. Goiten, *Jews and Arabs*, p.78.

46. R. Ahroni, The Jews of the British Crown Colony of Aden: History, Culture, and Ethnic Relations (Brill, 1994), p.210–11.

47. See Bensoussan, *Juifs en pays arabes*, p.541.

48. Ibid.

49. Ibid.

50. Bat Ye'or, *Islam and Dhimmitude* (USA: Fairleigh Dickinson Press, 2002), p.169.

51. See Bensoussan, *Juifs en pays arabes*, p.544.

52. See Moreh and Yehuda (eds.), *Al-Farhud*, p.123.

53. Dr Edy Cohen, London lecture, 7 August 2016.

54. Edwin Black, *The Farhud* (Washington DC: Dialog Press, 2010), p.298.

55. Applicants would receive an annual grant of 3,600 shekels ($929), as well as discounts on medication. ('Jews from Iraq, Algeria to get Holocaust survivors' benefits', *The Times of Israel*, 4 December 2015.)

56. 'Djemal Pasha threatened Jews of Palestine with the fate of Armenians, subjecting them to genocide', *Gagrule.net*, 29 July 2014, http://www.gagrule.net/according-haartz-djemal-pasha-threatened-jews-palestine-fate-armenians-subjecting-genocide/. (Last accessed 26 April 2017).

57. Elie Kedourie, 'Minorities' essay in *The Chatham House Version* (Chicago: Ivan R Dee, 2004), p.307.

58. See Achcar, *The Arabs and the Holocaust*, p.140.

59. Bernard Lewis quoting German and English documentary sources in *Semites and Anti-Semites*, p.157.

60. *Mufti's memoirs*, p.164, as per Dr Edy Cohen, 'The Mufti, Nazi propaganda and the Farhud', London presentation, 7 August 2016.

61. Ibid.

62. Küntzel, 'Hitler's Legacy: Islamic Anti-Semitism in the Middle East', paper presented at Yale University, 30 November 2006.

63. Rudi Roth, 'Comment Henry Laurens dédouane Amin al-Husseini', *Pardès* 55, p.278.

64. Edy Cohen 'The Grand Mufti's Nazi Connection', *Jerusalem Post*, 4 July 2014, http://www.jpost.com/Opinion/Op-Ed-Contributors/The-Grand-Muftis-Nazi-connection-347823. (Last accessed 26 April 2017).

65. Véronique Chemla, interview with Claude Nataf, 20 May 2016, http://www.veroniquechemla.info/2014/05/les-juifs-dafrique-du-nord-pendant-la.html. (Last accessed 26 April 2017).

66. See Küntzel, *Jihad and Jew-hatred*, p.7.

67. Roumani, *Jews of Libya* (Portland, Oregon: Sussex Academic Press, 2008). p.52.

68. 'The origins of the 1945 Tripoli pogroms', *Wikipedia*, http://yavix.ru/%7B+(%3E%D1%81%D0%B0%D0%B9%D1%82%3C=%3E[%3Ehttp:%E2%95%B1%E2%95%B1en.wikipedia.org%E2%95%B1wiki%E2%95%B11945_Tripoli_pogrom%3C]%3C)+%7D. (Last accessed 26 April 2017).

69. M. Küntzel, 'The aftershock of the Nazi war against the Jews: Could war in the Middle East have been prevented?' *JCPA*, 31 March 2016, http://jcpa.org/article/aftershock-nazi-war-jews-1947-1948-could-war-middle-east-prevented/#sthash.rY6RNjvE.dpuf. (Last accessed 26 April 2017).

70. See Lewis, *Semites and Anti-Semites*, Ch.8: 'The War against the Jews' (New York: Norton, 1986).pp. 192–235.

71. In 2012, Mohammed Merah killed four Jews, including three children, at the Ozar HaTorah Jewish school in Toulouse. Shortly after the *Charlie Hebdo* shooting in 2015 (two Jews of Tunisian extraction were among the victims), Amedy Coulibaly murdered

four Jewish patrons of a Kosher supermarket in Paris. There have been other, less publicised murders.

72. Berman on 'The Nazi origins of Modern militant Islamism', *Beastrabban* blog, 11 January 2016, https://beastrabban.wordpress.com/2016/01/11/berman-on-the-nazi-origins-of-modern-militant-islamism/.(Last accessed 26 April 2017).

73. Douglas Murray, 'Adolph Eichmann believed the Muslim world would complete the task he failed to finish', *Mosaic*, 28 January 2015, http://mosaicmagazine.com/picks/2015/01/adolf-eichmann-believed-the-muslim-world-would-complete-the-task-he-failed-to-finish/.(Last accessed 26 April 2017).

74. Küntzel, 'Hitler's legacy: Islamic anti-Semitism and the impact of the Muslim Brotherhood', *Articles by Matthias Küntzel*, 10 October 2007, http://www.matthiaskuentzel.de/contents/hitlers-legacy-islamic-antisemitism-and-the-impact-of-the-muslim-brotherhood. (Last accessed 26 April 2017).

75. Robert Dreyfuss, 'Cold War, Holy Warrior', *Mother Jones*, Jan/Feb issue 2006, http://www.motherjones.com/politics/2006/01/cold-war-holy-warrior. (Last accessed 26 April 2017).

76. H. Pinsecky and A. Grinberg, 'Iran and the Muslim Brotherhood in the Arabic-speaking world: the best of friends?', Rubin Center, 14 January 2016, http://www.rubincenter.org/wp-content/uploads/2016/02/Pisecky-Grinberg-YC-au2-PDF.pdf (Last accessed 26 April 2017).

77. Hazem Balousha,'Why Hamas resumed ties with Iran', *Al-Monitor*, 29 June 2016.

78. To cite only two of numerous such declarations: Elliott C. McLaughlin, 'Iran's supreme leader: there will be no such thing as Israel in 25 years' CNN, 11 September 2015 and 'Iran's Khamenei calls for Holy Intifada to destroy Israeli 'cancer', *The Tower*, 21 February 2017.

79. Karmel Melamed's Q&A with Matthias Küntzel, 'Küntzel on the roots and development of the Iranian regime's anti-Semitism', *Articles of Matthias Küntzel*, 26 August 2015, http://www.matthiaskuentzel.de/contents/q-a-kuentzel-on-roots-and-develoment-of-the-iranian-regimes-antisemitism.
http://www.rubincenter.org/wp-content/uploads/2016/02/Pisecky-Grinberg-YC-au2-PDF.pdf. (Last accessed 26 April 2017).

80. See Jeffrey Goldberg,'The Iranian regime on Israel's right to Exist', *The Atlantic*, 9 March 2015; Seth Frantzman, 'Iran takes credit for saving Jews and denies Holocaust at the same time', *Jerusalem Post*, 15 May 2015.

5

A Virulent Nationalism

*Three whom God should not have created: Persians,
Jews and Flies*
> (Title of a book published in 1940 by
> Khairallah Talfah)

In the early twentieth century in the Arab world, a virulent nationalism arose
out of the ashes of the Ottoman Empire – a form of nationalism inspired by
totalitarianism. Historian Robert Wistrich describes the emergence of a
Nazified anti-Semitism, grafted on to the pan-Arab vision of a single,
powerful, homogeneous, Arabic-speaking nation:

'Antisemitism cannot be wholly divorced from the rise of modern Arab
nationalism which constructed an ideology of 'Arabism' (al-'uruba) inimical
to the Jewish and foreign presence in the Middle East. This organic
nationalism facilitated a stereotypical way of thinking about all "outsiders"
(including Jews) as "aliens" and enemies.'[1]

Bnot Mitzvah ceremony at the Nebi Daniel Synagogue in Alexandria in the 1940s.

Egypt was, and still is, the most populous of the Arab nations. Enjoying equal rights since the abolition of *dhimmitude*, Jews initially welcomed Egyptian nationalism with enthusiasm: the secretary of the Wafd party was the Zionist Leon Castro. Felix Benzaken, Saad Malki, Vita Sonssino and David Hazan were active members of the party. However, the nationality rules began marginalising non-Muslims well before the Balfour Declaration of 1917. In practice, non-Muslims (Jews, Greeks, Armenians and Syrians) who had settled in Egypt from other Ottoman provinces were denied Egyptian nationality. Egypt became nominally independent from Britain in 1922, but an increasingly racial concept of Egyptian-ness began to be applied from the 1880s onwards.

Article 7 of the 1929 Egyptian Citizenship Law allowed Syrian or Lebanese Jews born in Egypt, for instance, who permanently resided in the country, to claim Egyptian citizenship at the age of majority. Article 6 gave preference to Arab Muslims. However, Jews whose parents or who themselves were born in Egypt had to prove that they had not held any foreign nationality since 1848, which many could not do. A large number, therefore, became 'stateless'.[2] Paradoxically, the most Egyptian of Egyptian Jews had the greatest trouble establishing their status.[3]

One would have expected that 40,000 eligible Jews would have acquired Egyptian nationality, but only 5,000 actually did. The poorer classes could not afford the fee of five Egyptian pounds. It was not compulsory, and some did not actually bother to apply. But, in the main, most Jews 'found it exceedingly difficult to gain nationality after the convention of Montreux in 1937 when Egyptianisation intensified.'[4]

Some 25 per cent of Jews held foreign passports, affording the holders special protection by the Western powers. The abolition of the Capitulations system in 1949 was understandable in a country asserting its independence. But, denied Egyptian nationality, the poor or lower classes – or, like some 75 per cent of Jews either native to Egypt or whose family had moved there from other parts of the Ottoman Empire – found themselves deprived of an elementary civil liberty.

In Iraq, the most virulent nationalism of all took root. Pro-Nazi, anti-British nationalists, some of whom had studied in Germany and had served in the German-allied Ottoman army, moved to Iraq from Syria and Palestine during the 1920s and 1930s and were given senior posts in Iraq's institutions. In the words of Professor Shmuel Moreh, 'Arab nationalist and pro-Nazi propaganda ignited the Muslims and Christians of Iraq to religious and national fanaticism.'[5] Here, ironically, nationality was not an issue: almost all Jews were Iraqi citizens, in spite of vain attempts by the Jewish community leadership to be granted British nationality.[6]

The novelist Naim Kattan describes how, on the eve of Iraq's independence, enthusiastic Jews, who excelled in the Arabic language, rushed to become the first architects of the new Iraqi culture, only to be rebuffed – except where their contribution was indispensable.[7] Public servants were dismissed, quotas were imposed on Jews in law and medicine, and they were excluded from the army and diplomacy. It was a sinister portent of 'Otherisation' and disasters to come. Kattan wrote: 'We lived in the shadow of a beast which preserved a stony silence for years, and then suddenly his giant body was wracked with fever'.[8]

The philo-Semitic Faisal arrived in Iraq with anti-Semitic nationalists like Sati al-Husri.

While the Grand Mufti of Jerusalem, Haj Amin Al-Husseini, was a key factor in causing the *Farhud*, scholars have tended not to pay much attention to the Syrian and Palestinian emigrés who were the driving force behind anti-Semitism in Iraq. By the time the *Farhud* broke out, there were more than 400 such families in the country. They exerted an influence far beyond their numbers. They were doctors, teachers and intellectuals who had mainly been exiled from Palestine with the Mufti after 1936 and were to join him in Berlin as Hitler's guests after 1941.

However, some nationalists had been in Iraq since the 1920s. A contingent of disappointed exiles from Syria and Palestine accompanied Emir Faisal when he arrived in Baghdad to become the British-installed king. Their aspirations to rule a pan-Arab kingdom from Damascus had been thwarted by the French. At their head was the Syrian ultra-nationalist Sati al-Husri, who became Director General of Education of Iraq and turned it into the 'Prussia of Arab nations'. Al-Husri engaged in vicious anti-Semitism, doing his best to undermine Iraq's first finance minister, the Jew Sir Sasson Heskel.[9]

Al-Husri founded the nationalist Muthanna club. From this club sprang the ringleaders of the wartime *Farhud* riot. Al-Husri was later joined by the Syrian Fawzi al-Quwukji (who fought in the 1948 war against Israel) and other virulent anti-Semites. Some took matters into their own hands: the Palestinian Dr Amin Ruwayba was accused of throwing a hand-grenade in 1936 against a Jewish club.[10]

Sati al-Husri promoted Arab nationalism through education. In 1930s Iraq, the strident pan-Arab nationalists who surrounded the king had already ensured that there was really no place for Jews within political parties.[11] In Iraqi schools, the teaching of Hebrew was banned and the school curriculum was 'Nazified'. In 1937, the director-general of the Iraqi Ministry of Education, Fadel Jamali, was warmly welcomed in Germany and invited to send a delegation to the Nuremberg Nazi party congress in 1938.[12]

The Palestinian Darwish al-Miqdadi returned to Iraq from studying in Germany and became leader of the pro-Nazi youth brigade, the Futuwwa. The Futuwwa went around daubing the houses of Jews with a red *khamsa* prior to the *Farhud* in order to indicate to the mob which were the Jewish homes.

No Jewish representative was invited to the National Congress of 1919 in Syria.[13] Throughout the Second World War, anti-Jewish and anti-Zionist demonstrations were common. In 1944, the Jewish quarter of Damascus was twice sacked by mobs.[14] As soon as Syria acquired its independence from France in 1946, a Mossad emissary stationed in the country reported that the prevailing mood in the Syrian nation was an 'overt Nazi spirit'.[15]

Non-Arabs and Non-Muslims Excluded

The rise of Arab nationalism and anti-Zionism are commonly viewed as a reaction to colonialism and the Balfour declaration. But the exclusion of non-Arabs and non-Muslims became a key feature of Arab politics in the twentieth century. According to one theory, Arab nationalists resented influential Jewish communities who constituted 'a state within a state'.[16] Sooner or later, the Jews would constitute an obstacle to the vision of a unitary independent Arab state. The French author Guy de Maupassant wrote in 1909, 'Tunis is neither a French city nor an Arab city. It is a Jewish city'.[17]

Jews had certain skills which nascent Arab states were determined to transfer to their people. In 1924, Imam Yahia in Yemen made Jewish tailors teach their trade to a school of orphans so that they could produce new uniforms for his soldiers.[18] In 1905 an association was set up by a Tunisian of Turkish origin in order to bring over Turkish Muslim artisans to break up the Jewish shoe and clothing monopolies.[19]

Under Fascist control from the 1920s, Libya witnessed a gradual erosion of Jewish community autonomy, together with bursts of anti-Jewish hostility. In Morocco, nationalism fired up Arabs to bully and intimidate Jews so that they could take their places. 'They wanted the public jobs held by Jewish people, Jewish houses and businesses. They succeeded by inflicting fear and persecution', says Penina Elbaz, who grew up in the southern Moroccan town of Safi.[20]

Secular Arab nationalist parties, such as the Ba'ath and the Syrian Socialist National party, founded on the Nazi model, still exist today. They sprang up after Hitler and his party came to power in 1933. 'We were racists', said Sami al-Joundi, of the Syrian Ba'ath party.[21] Paramilitary youth movements, such as Young Egypt, the Iron Shirts in Syria and the Futuwwa in Iraq, also date back to this period.

French police seized pro-Nazi propaganda material in Algeria in 1937.[22] North African nationalists openly collaborated with the Axis powers: the Moroccan Abd-al Khaliq Torres met with Hermann Göring and Heinrich Himmler in January 1941. They promised him arms and money with a view to the planned German invasion of Morocco.[23] The pro-Nazi government under Rashid Ali in Iraq was, however, the only Arab country to cement an official alliance with the Axis powers.

Exclusionary Palestinian nationalism, fathered by the Mufti, was a hybrid creature of racial and religious anti-Semitism. The strands became impossible to disentangle. Almost from the start, the hostility to Jews at the core of Palestinian nationalism spilled over into the Arab world and was aimed at Jewish citizens. Palestinian exiles played a key role in inciting anti-Semitism in the Arab world. The 1941 *Farhud* against the Jews of Iraq could be termed the first deadly skirmish in the Palestinian Arab war against Jews – not Zionists.

The root cause of the post-1948 exodus of over 850,000 Jews from the Middle East and North Africa was pan-Arab racism, itself influenced by Nazism. Before the first Arab-Israeli war broke out, saturation Nazi propaganda[24] on an illiterate and gullible population had already destroyed any prospect of peaceful coexistence between Jews and Arabs.

The Muslim Brotherhood in Egypt played a role in inciting grassroots violence against Jewish citizens in Arab lands, as was discussed in the last chapter, but what sealed the Jews' fate was top-down, state sanctioned measures. Indeed, the Mufti-inspired charter of the Arab League would soon form the basis of the League's declaration of war to destroy the nascent state of Israel in 1948.[25]

Political marginalisation was the first step in a process reminiscent of the Nuremberg laws – stripping Jews of citizenship, exclusion from public service (Jewish public servants were sacked in Egypt, Lebanon, Iraq and Yemen and post-1979 Iran), financial strangulation and restrictions on business and property ownership, arbitrary arrests on spurious grounds for 'Zionism', travel bans, and finally destruction and dispossession. Denationalisation and pauperisation are the preliminary stages of 'ethnic cleansing'. Before a single Palestinian fled what became Israel, the Arab League, founded in 1945, hatched a post-War, coordinated Nuremberg-style plan[26] to persecute their Jewish citizens as enemy aliens – the 'Jewish minority of Palestine'.

The Arab League's decision to launch their ill-fated 1948 war against the fledgling state of Israel came after fierce lobbying by the Palestinian Grand Mufti of Jerusalem, head of the Higher Arab Committee and later, the Palestinian branch of the Muslim Brotherhood. Palestinian Arab leaders were full participants in all the meetings of the Arab League.[27]

All Jewish clerks working in Syria in the pre-independence French civil service were fired and not reinstated. Pedlars, once the mainstay of Syrian-Jewish society, ceased to be protected by the authorities and did not dare leave their villages and towns.[28] In December 1947, to stop Jews from leaving, the government announced that Jews were banned from selling their possessions. It severely restricted the teaching of Hebrew in Jewish schools. Boycotts were called against Jewish businesses. Jews were not allowed to work for the government or banks, could not acquire telephones or driver's licenses, and were barred from buying property.[29]

Between 1950 and 1956, Egypt passed several nationality laws. Nationality was withdrawn from Jews (any person acting on behalf of 'enemy states or states having no relations with Egypt'). The fact that they were members of the 'Israelite' Community aggravated the confusion. Egyptian Jews fleeing the country were stripped of their nationality. It became impossible for a non-Muslim to acquire Egyptian nationality.[30]

On 12 June 1951, Libya passed a law stating that religious tribunals would determine personal status. The Maccabi all-Jewish sports club was forced to accept Arab members after 1954. In 1953, economic boycotts were declared against Jews. Those with relatives in Israel were forced, by a 1957 decree, to register at the Libyan boycott office. By 1960, Jews were not allowed to hold public office, vote or serve in the army or police.[31]

In Lebanon too, Jewish organisations (such as the Maccabi sports club) were prohibited, Jews were discharged from public service and Jewish youth movements were banned. The Jewish population of Lebanon increased after 1948, swollen by Jews seeking refuge from the 1947 Syrian pogroms and Iraqi government persecution.[32] But the stay of these Jews was transitory and they were never granted Lebanese citizenship. Indeed, no Jews born in Lebanon to foreign-born parents could acquire Lebanese citizenship – and any person who married a stateless citizen lost his or her Lebanese citizenship.[33]

At about the same time in Iraq, the law of 9 March 1950 stripped Jews leaving Iraq of their nationality. School certificates issued to Jewish school children in 1960s Iraq bore the words 'not yet denationalised'. [34]

Tunisian nationalists enjoyed a brief honeymoon with their Jews – in 1954, Yom Kippur was even proclaimed a national holiday – but, within three years, the rabbinate had been disbanded, the Tunis Jewish cemetery expropriated and bulldozed into a park and the great synagogue of the Tunis *Hara* was demolished.[35]

In the run-up to Moroccan independence, Muslim merchants and artisans were encouraged by the nationalists to boycott Jewish merchants in order to eliminate '*la concurrence juive*'.[36]

Throughout the Middle East, Jewish schools were arabised. Jews were expelled from Lebanese universities in 1947 and, after 1967, in Iraq. In Syria, in 1967 and after the 1979 revolution in Iran, Muslims were appointed to

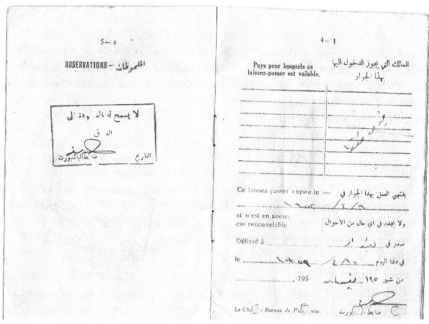

On the top left-hand page of this laissez-passer issued to an Iraqi -Jewish clerk is a stamp stating that the bearer cannot return to Iraq (Laurence Julius collection)

Laissez-passers were issued to Iraqi Jews travelling to Israel in 1950–1. At first they were flown via Cyprus (Laurence Julius collection)

head Jewish schools. In post-independence Morocco, Tunisia and Libya, Jewish charitable and community institutions were arabised or dissolved.[37]

One Algerian nationalist song declared: 'The Algerian people is Muslim, its genealogy is Arab.'[38] Following independence, the nationality code passed by the Algerian parliament in 1963 granted citizenship only to Algerian-born Muslims.[39]

Travel bans operated by denying Jews passports. The bans were in force in Egypt, Syria and Iraq in 1948, Yemen in 1949 and Libya in 1951. Syrian Jews who attempted to flee faced either the death penalty or imprisonment with hard labour.[40] Syrian and Iraqi Jews were restricted in their internal movements and constantly under the surveillance of the secret police. As soon as Morocco became independent in 1956, Jews were prevented from leaving. Postal links with Israel were suspended. Where an individual member of a family was allowed to travel (usually in exchange for a monetary bond), the rest of his family was held hostage.

Economic despoilment during this period consisted of seizures and sequestration of Jewish property, extortion, freezing of bank accounts. Departing Jews had their personal possessions stolen at the port or airport. Nationalisation of banks put Jewish brokers out of business. Laws making Jews go into partnerships with Muslims came into force in Iraq and Egypt from 1947, Tunisia from 1956 and Morocco from 1960. This was not proof of equitable coexistence, but to ensure that profits would not go back exclusively into Jewish pockets.[41] In 1948, Yemenite craftsmen and traders were delayed from leaving the country until they had passed on their skills to local Muslims. Iraqi-Jewish musicians were held back for six months while they taught their Muslim successors the *joza* and the *santur* instruments.[42]

Pogroms, intimidation, the threat of violence and arrests were the backdrop against which these measures were implemented. The government made examples of prominent Jews (the wealthiest and best-connected of all, the Ford Motor Co. agent in Iraq, Shafiq Ades,[43] was executed in September 1948 for allegedly selling scrap metal to the 'Zionist entity'). Synagogues were attacked. The forces of law and order either cooperated with the violence or did not intervene to stop it.

After the end of the Second World War, ex-Nazi war criminals sought refuge in the Arab world, bringing their lethal Jew-hatred with them. They became military advisers and helped spread anti-Semitic propaganda. Not a few converted to Islam.

Several Jewish organisations in the West reported that Egypt had taken anti-Semitic measures – internment, denaturalisation, dispossession, and expulsion – reminiscent of Nazi Germany.[44] However, at least one scholar, Joel Beinin, disputes this, claiming that, so soon after the Holocaust's full horror had become apparent, Jewish organisations such as the American Jewish Committee were projecting their paranoia and obsession with Nazi anti-Semitism onto the Egyptians. Beinin lays the blame for the flight of Egypt's Jews at Zionism's door by dwelling at length on Operation Susannah,[45] the ill-conceived and botched bombing project instigated by the Israeli government in 1954. Operation Susannah revealed the perpetrators to be 'fifth column' Egyptian Jews (see Chapter Six). Two questions arise out of Beinin's interpretation of history, however: why was it legitimate to inflict collective punishment on tens of thousands of Jews in Egypt because of the actions of a few? And why does Beinin not account for measures taken *before* 1954, resulting in the exodus of 20,000 Jews?[46] He infers that detentions, sequestrations, physical attacks and a constriction of Jewish communal life could not have been such a feature of Egyptian-Jewish existence, or the majority of the community would have left before 1956.[47] But the decision to uproot oneself is never easy, and it seems likely that a typical Jewish optimism ('it will blow over') would have held sway. André Aciman writes: 'Until the very end they hoped – and each of their husbands swore he always knew someone in high places who could be bribed when the time came.'[45]

Within a year of the Suez crisis, the end came for 25,000 Jews. Nasser was to exact swift revenge on the Jewish community for Israel's 29 October 1956 invasion of the Sinai. Jews were expelled in two waves: the first (accounting for some 500 Jews who were British and French subjects) were given twenty-four hours to leave. The second were ordered to leave the country within two to seven days with their families.[48] Offices and businesses were sealed and 95 per cent of property sequestered by the government was Jewish-owned.

Lilian Abda, from the city of Suez, was forced to make a most dramatic exit. She was arrested by Egyptian soldiers while she was swimming leisurely in the canal. Abda was charged with trying to relay information to Israeli forces advancing across the Sinai Peninsula. 'I was brought in my bathing suit to the police station, and I was questioned

Y. Rofé Certificate issued for shares sold in a 1922 War Damages Cooperative. Jews accounted for up to 90 percent of all stockbrokers. Most were expelled from Egypt after 1956.

until they extracted a confession from me', she said. 'The next day they expelled me and my entire family from the country. In the 'papers, they called me the Mata Hari of the canal.' [49] Twenty thousand Jews left between November 1956 and June 1957, stripped of their citizenship, their laissez-passer documents bearing the words: ONE WAY – NO RETURN.

At least 900 Jews had been arrested as of 7 December 1956. After the initial expulsions, the regime used intimidation and psychological warfare.[50]Jews were blacklisted at random. Some returned from internment to find Egyptian Muslims had taken their jobs.[51] The regime strangulated Jewish trading businesses by withdrawing export licences from them. It amended its citizenship and nationality laws in order to exclude Jews and other minorities from becoming Egyptian. From 1959, the bearer's religion had to be listed on identity papers: as a result, companies were deterred from employing Jews.[52]

It may be argued that the Egyptian expulsion was an understandable act of decolonisation: all British and French subjects were expelled in retaliation for British and French collusion in the invasion of Egypt. But Egyptian and stateless Jews, heads of families, were also expelled in revenge for Israel's attack, although none were Israeli citizens; almost every Jewish family was, at one point, detained or placed under house arrest.[53] The Egyptian Ministry of Religion issued a decree declaring 'All Jews are Zionists and enemies of the state.'[54]

President Gamal Abdel Nasser's policy had a devastating effect on the economy where Jews were prominent but also trickled down to exclude

The Cicurel department store in Cairo, one of several Jewish-owned stores nationalised after 1956.

Jewish store employees, doctors, lawyers and engineers. Jewish employees were sacked from their jobs in both Jewish-owned and non-Jewish firms, including Jews who were Italian or Greek subjects. Non-Jewish Armenians, Greeks and Italians were not targeted – Greece declared itself on the side of the Egyptians – but felt increasingly unwanted in the xenophobic climate. In July 1957, the US embassy in Cairo reported: 'The Greeks,[55] Armenians, Italians and other Christian groups were affected as well. Still the creation of Israel and the wars that ensued between the young state and Egypt aggravated the position of the Jews *well beyond* [my emphasis] the precarious position of the other minorities.'[56] All but 7,000 Jews vanished from Egypt.

However, Nasser did pursue an indiscriminate policy of agrarian reform and 'socialist' nationalisation in the early 1960s. It was to affect Egypt's 600 wealthiest families – not just Jews but Copts, Muslims and assorted 'foreigners'.

A witness at the time of Suez, George Naldrett-Jays, British Assistant Commandant of the Alexandria City Police, could hardly contain his outrage at the regime's treatment of the Jews who were Egyptian nationals or stateless: 'The full-blown Egyptian Jews conveniently ... labelled Zionists are similarly treated and see [*sic*] the closing down (and re-opening under national auspices), the blocking of funds, the high-handed dismissal of co-religionists, the seizure of goods characterizing the regime's deliberate maltreatment of a constitutionally-protected minority.'[57] The community dwindled further, suffered vicious reprisals in the aftermath of Israel's Six Day War and today numbers thirteen people or fewer.

Anti-Zionism was Not Inevitable

A recent Jewish visitor to Egypt procured a 1941 telephone directory of the city of Alexandria.[58] The offices of the Zionist movement were listed openly. (The 24,000 Jews were disproportionately represented in a country where most residents could barely read or write. The Jewish names comprised 7 per cent of the city's total – merchants, bankers, industrialists, shopkeepers. One was a manufacturer of artificial eyes.)

Anti-Zionism was not inevitable, especially in Egypt, the leader and most populous country of the Arab world. But, as we have seen, the forces of extremism had been unleashed, and had rendered Zionism taboo.

The Balfour Declaration has, since then, been accepted as the starting point for the Jewish-Arab conflict. On 2 November 1917 the British government, through its Foreign Minister, Lord Balfour, announced its support for the establishment in Palestine of a national home for the Jewish people.

Even before the end of the First World War, however, 'the Muslim population of Judea took little or no interest in the Arab national movement',

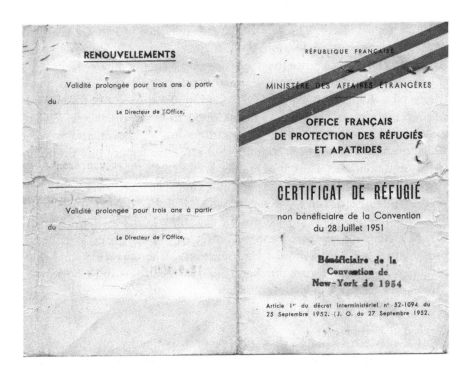

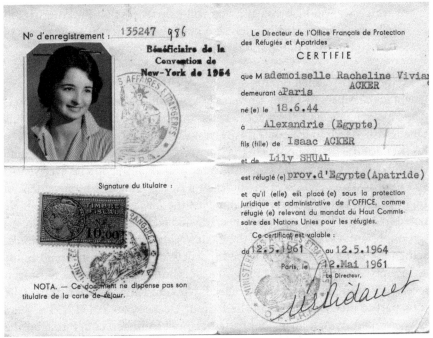

Refugee Certificate issued by the French government to stateless Alexandria-born Jewess Viviane Acker Levy in 1961.

a British report stated. The growing Jewish presence in Palestine met no widespread opposition beyond the odd local dispute.[59] However, pan-Arabism needed to coalesce the masses around a common hatred.

Yet, in spite of increasing Palestinian Arab hostility to Zionism, there were Arabs willing to collaborate with the Zionists throughout this period. According to researcher Hillel Cohen: 'Cooperation and collaboration were prevalent, in a variety of forms ... and among all classes and sectors. Collaboration was not only common but a central feature of Palestinian society and politics.'[60] The editor of the Egyptian daily *al-Ahram* declared in 1913: 'The Zionists are necessary for this region. The money they will bring in, their intelligence and the diligence which is one of their characteristics will, without doubt, bring new life to the country.'[61] Emir Faisal, the British-backed pretender to the Syrian throne, conferred with Dr Chaim Weizmann, president of the World Zionist Organization, in January 1919, and they produced the Faisal-Weizmann Agreement for Arab-Jewish Cooperation. Thereupon, Faisal issued the following statement, which appears quite fantastic in view of all that followed:

> We Arabs ... look with the deepest sympathy on the Zionist movement ... We will wish the Jews a most hearty welcome home... I look forward, and my people with me look forward, to a future in which we will help you and you will help us, so that the countries in which we are mutually interested may once again take their places in the community of the civilised peoples of the world.[62]

Until the 1930s, Zionist groups operated openly in the region, Hebrew was taught in the Alliance Israëlite Universelle school in Baghdad, letters and goods could be exchanged and Jews could come and go between Iraq and Palestine. One Jewish visitor to Iraq, R. Zaslany, wrote a letter dated 3 October 1934 to his friend at the Iraqi Ministry of the Interior, thanking him for his hospitality in Baghdad and expressing the wish to reciprocate if the official ever visited Palestine. Zaslany expressed his shock at a recent anti-Jewish movement in Iraq which saw the *Palestine Post* and even the *Jewish Chronicle* banned. He noted that many Jews had already been dismissed from their posts.[63]

Important representatives of the Arab world of the day supported Zionist settlement in Palestine. They hoped that Jewish immigration would boost economic development, thus bringing the Middle East closer to European levels. For example, Ziwar Pasha, later Egyptian Prime Minister, personally took part in the celebrations of the Balfour Declaration in 1917. Five years later, Ahmed Zaki, a former Egyptian cabinet minister, congratulated the Zionist Executive in Palestine on its progress: 'The victory of the Zionist idea is the turning point for the fulfilment of an ideal which is so dear to me, the revival of the Orient.'[64]

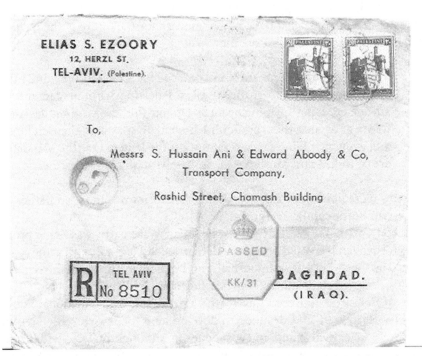

A letter to the famous Zilkha Bank in Baghdad needs no fuller address. Until the mid-1930s there were postal links between Palestine and Iraq (Laurence Julius collection)

Two years later, the Chairman of the Zionist Executive Frederick H. Kisch travelled to Cairo for talks with three high-ranking Egyptian officials on future relations. These officials 'were equally emphatic in their pro-Zionist declarations', noted Kisch in his diary. All three 'recognised that the progress of Zionism might help to secure the development of a new Eastern civilization'.[65] In 1925, the Egyptian Interior Minister Ismail Sidqi took action against a group of Palestinians protesting against the Balfour Declaration in Cairo. He was, at the time, on his way to Jerusalem to take part in the opening of the first Hebrew university.[66]

In 1926, the Egyptian government extended a cordial welcome to a Jewish teachers' association delegation from the British mandate territory. Students from the Egyptian University travelled on an official visit to Tel Aviv to take part in a sports competition there. When the conflict in Palestine escalated in 1929, the Egyptian Interior Ministry ordered its press office to censor all anti-Zionist and anti-Jewish articles. Even in 1933, the Egyptian government allowed 1,000 new Jewish immigrants to land in Port Said on their way to Palestine. No wonder, therefore, that the German Nazi party's Egyptian section was in despair in 1933. 'The level of education of the broad masses is not advanced enough for the understanding of race theory', declared a spokesman for the Cairo Nazis in 1933. 'An understanding of the Jewish threat has not yet been awakened here ...'[67]

In 1936, Syrian Alawite notables sent a letter to the French Foreign Minister in which they expressed their concern for the future of the region. Referring to the Jewish question, they wrote:

> The Jews brought civilisation and peace to the Arab Muslims, and they dispersed gold and prosperity over Palestine without damage to anyone or taking anything by force. Despite this, the Muslims declared holy war against them and didn't hesitate to massacre their children and women ... Thus, a black fate awaits the Jews in case the Mandates are cancelled and Muslim Syria united with Muslim Palestine.

It seems incredible today that one of the signatories was the grandfather of the Syrian President, Bashar al-Assad.[68]

Leon Castro, the secretary of the Egyptian Wafd party, was living proof that an Egyptian Jew could be an Egyptian nationalist and a Zionist at the same time. The Cairo-born Jewish journalist and diplomat Eric Rouleau recalled: 'Zionists enjoyed complete freedom of action in Egypt. The Jewish Agency was well-off in Cairo and Keren Kayemeth LeIsrael, the Jewish National Fund, established in 1901 and destined to develop land for Jewish settlement in Palestine, welcomed grants in synagogues.'[69] Although he later repudiated Zionism as 'narrow nationalism', Rouleau belonged to the *Hashomer Hatzair* movement in Egypt, the 'Youth Guard', a far-leftist Zionist movement: 'The hundreds of adolescents who joined the movement participated in sports competitions, took Jewish history classes, and engaged in philosophical debates where the labour movement ideologists were prominently present.[70]

Not so long ago, Egyptian intellectuals and politicians were not only, *not* anti-Semites, some were philo-Semites and even exhibited pro-Zionist sentiments.[71]

The modernising forces in Egypt did not go down to the forces of extremism without a fight. Religious leaders fought the Muslim Brotherhood's attempts to politicise Friday prayers with false claims that Jews were attacking Al Aqsa and the Qur'an. The rector of Al-Azhar, Sunni Islam's most important university, forbade anti-Jewish propaganda. Ali Mahir, Egyptian King Farouk's top adviser, called for a united Palestinian state based on mutual tolerance and regulated immigration for both Jew and Arab.[72] Until the 1936–9 Arab Revolt in Palestine, Egyptian Zionism was not considered inconsistent with patriotic loyalty to Egypt.[73] Ten years later, almost nothing remained of such benevolence.

Notes

1. Robert S. Wistrich, 'Islamic judeophobia: an existential threat', *Nativ*, Vol. 2, 2004, http://www.acpr.org.il/english-nativ/02-issue/wistrich-2.htm. (Last accessed 26 April 2017).
2. Association Internationale Nebi Daniel – History, http://www.nebidaniel.org/histoire.php?lang=en. (Last accessed 26 April 2017).
3. Ruth Toledano Attias, 'La dénationisation des juifs d' Egypte' in S. Trigano (ed.), *La Fin du Judaïsme en terres d'Islam* (France: Denoël, 2009), p.63.
4. Michael Laskier, *Jews of Egypt* (New York University Press, 1992), p.9.
5. Shmuel Moreh & Zvi Yehuda (eds), *Al-Farhud* (Jerusalem: Hebrew University Magnes Press, 2010), p.120.
6. G. Bensoussan, *Juifs en Pays Arabes: Le Grand Déracinement 1850–1975* (Paris: Tallandier, 2012).p.519.
7. Kattan, *Adieu Babylone* (Montreal: La Presse, 1975), p.82.
8. Ibid., p.83.
9. Shmuel Moreh and Zvi Yehuda, *Al-Farhud*, p.120.
10. Ibid., pp.130–1.
11. Stillman, *The Jews of Arab Lands: A History and Source Book* (Philadelphia, PA: Jewish Publication Society of America, 1979), Vol. II, p.56.
12. See Bensoussan, *Juifs en pays arabes*, p.537.
13. Ibid., p.513.
14. Harold Troper, *The Ransomed of God* (Malcolm Lester, 1999), p.2.
15. Itamar Levin, *Locked doors* (Praeger, 2001), p.170.
16. J-P. Allali, *Les réfugiés échangés* (JIPEA, 2007), p.109.
17. Ibid.
18. See Bensoussan, *Juifs en pays arabes*, p.532.
19. 'How Bourguiba's Tunisia pushed out its Jews', *Point of No Return*, 15 October 2008, http://jewishrefugees.blogspot.co.uk/2008/10/how-bourguibas-tunisia-pushed-out-its.html. (Last accessed 26 April 2017).

20. 'The truth about Morocco: fear made Jews leave', *Point of No Return*, 11 September 2016, http://jewishrefugees.blogspot.co.uk/2016/09/the-truth-about-morocco-fear-made-jews.html. (Last accessed 26 April 2017).

21. Ian Buruma, 'Revolution from Above', *New York Review of Books*, 1 May 2003.

22. See Bensoussan, *Juifs en pays arabes*, p.536.

23. Abitbol, *Le Passé d'une Discorde: Juifs et Arabes depuis le VIIe siècle* (Paris: Perrin, 2003), p.375.

24. Rafael Medoff, 'New Research sheds light on Nazi influence in the Arab world', *JNS*, 30 April 2013, http://www.algemeiner.com/2013/04/30/new-research-sheds-light-on-nazi-influence-in-arab-world/#.(Last accessed 26 April 2017).

25. Shmuel Trigano, 'The expulsion of Jews from Muslim Countries: a history of ongoing cruelty and discrimination', *Jerusalem Centre for Public Affairs*, 4 November 2010, http://jcpa.org/article/the-expulsion-of-the-jews-from-muslim-countries-1920-1970-a-history-of-ongoing-cruelty-and-discrimination/. (Last accessed 26 April 2017).

26. Arab League Draft Law regarding Jews in Arab countries, 1947.

27. Moreh and Yehuda, *Al-Farhud*, p.142.

28. Itamar Levin, *Locked doors* (Praeger, 2001), p.171.

29. 'Jews in Islamic lands: Syria', *Jewish Virtual Library*, February 2016, https://www.jewishvirtuallibrary.org/jsource/anti-semitism/syrianjews.html. (Last accessed 26 April 2017).

30. Laskier, *Jews of Egypt* (New York: New York University Press, 1992), p.264.

31. See Shmuel Trigano, 'The expulsion of Jews from Muslim Countries 1920–70: a history of ongoing cruelty and discrimination', *Jerusalem Centre for Public Affairs*, 4 November 2010, http://jcpa.org/article/the-expulsion-of-the-jews-from-muslim-countries-1920-1970-a-history-of-ongoing-cruelty-and-discrimination/. (Last accessed 26 April 2017).

32. Lyn Julius,'Rewriting Jewish history in Lebanon', *Clash of Cultures* blog, *Jerusalem Post*, 11 April 2016, http://www.jpost.com/Blogs/Clash-of-Cultures/Rewriting-Jewish-history-in-Lebanon-450703. (Last accessed 26 April 2017).

33. *Une petite histoire des juifs du Liban*', Review of Yves Turquier's eponymous film, *Point of No Return*, 25 September 2008, http://jewishrefugees.blogspot.co.uk/2008/09/jews-of-lebanon-joie-de-vivre-in-exile.html. (Last accessed 26 April 2017).

34. 'Three little words that say apartheid', *Point of No Return*, 10 January 2014, http://jewishrefugees.blogspot.co.uk/2014/01/three-little-words-that-say-apartheid.html. (Last accessed 26 April 2017)

35. Jacques Taïeb, 'L' échec de l'intégration des juifs de Tunisie' in S. Trigano (ed.), *La fin du judaïsme en terres d'Islam* (France: Denoël, 2009), p.368.

36. M. Laskier, *North African Jewry in the 20th Century* (NYU Press, 1994), p.171.

37. See Trigano, 'The Expulsion of Jews', *JCPA*, 4 November 2010.

38. See Bensoussan, *Juifs en pays arabes*, p.522.

39. Richard Ayoun,'De l' émancipation à l'éxode brutale des juifs d'Algerie' in S. Trigano (ed.), *La fin du judaïsme en terres d'Islam* (France: Denoël, 2009), p.224.

40. 'Jews in Islamic lands: Syria', *Jewish Virtual Library*, February 2016, https://www.jewishvirtuallibrary.org/jsource/anti-semitism/syrianjews.html. (Last accessed 26 April 2017).

41. See Allali, *Les réfugiés échangés*, p.106.

42. Shlomo El-Kivity interviewed in T. Morad, D. Shasha and R. Shasha (eds), *Iraq's last Jews* (US: Palgrave Macmillan, 2008), p.22.

43. For more about the Shafiq Ades case, see Charles Tripp, *A History of Iraq* (Cambridge University Press, 2000), p.123.

44. Beinin, *The Dispersion of Egyptian Jewry: Culture, Politics, and the Formation of a Modern Diaspora* (Berkeley, CA: University of California Press, 1998), p.108.
45. Also known as the Lavon Affair, the Mishap, or the Unfortunate Business.
46. See Laskier, *Jews of Egypt*, p.144.
47. See Beinin, *The Dispersion of Egyptian Jewry*, p.209.
48. Mina Thabet, 'Approaching end of Egypt's Jewish community', *Mada Masr*, 4 May 2015, http://www.madamasr.com/opinion/approaching-end-egypts-jewish-community. (Last accessed 26 April 2017).
49. Amiram Barkat, 'Remembering the "Second Exodus" from Egypt', *Haaretz*, 11 July 2006.
50. Laskier, *Jews of Egypt*, p.256.
51. Albert Tam, who held a senior position in an advertising agency, returned to find Anwar Sadat had taken over his post. (His son's testimony, 9 January 2017, Centre for Egyptian Jews, Tel Aviv).
52. Levin, *Locked Doors*, p.143.
53. Laskier, *Jews of Egypt*, p.254.
54. Josh Weil, 'The last Jews of Cairo', *Guernica*, 8 November 2006.
55. Alexander Kazamias argues in 'The Purge of Greeks from Nasserite Egypt' (*Journal of the Hellenic Diaspora*, 35, February 2009) that the Greek community was not expelled in the wake of the 1957 nationalisations and that 15,000 Greeks stayed on until the early 1960s. The Greek foreign minister Evangelos Averoff struck a deal for the compensation of Greek nationals leaving Egypt: the Greek government would compensate them while the Egyptian government would grant equivalent compensation to Greece by allowing free imports for several years.
56. Michael R. Fischbach, *Jewish Property Claims against Arab Countries* (Columbia University Press, 2008), p.47.
57. FO 371/125602. UK National Archives, Kew.
58. 'Post-Weinstein Egyptian heritage at risk', *Point of No Return*, 7 February 2014, http://jewishrefugees.blogspot.co.uk/2014/02/post-weinstein-egypts-heritage-at-risk.html. (Last accessed 26 April 2017).
59. E. Karsh *Islamic Imperialism* (Yale, 2006), p.137.
60. Hillel Cohen, *Army of Shadows* (University of California Press, 2008), p.259.
61. Mark Tessler, *A History of the Israel-Palestinian Conflict* (Indiana University Press, 1994), p.142.
62. *The Syrian Times*,17 July 2014, http://thesyriantimes.com/2014/07/17/faisal-weizmann-agreement-between-%D9%90arabs-and-jews-about-palestine-3-jan1919/. (Last accessed 26 April 2017).
63. Mayor Meir Dizengoff archive.
64. Matthias Küntzel, *Jihad and Jew-hatred*, p.6.
65. Ibid.
66. Ibid., p.7.
67. G. Krämer, *The Jews in Modern Egypt 1914–52* (IB Tauris, 1989), p.278.
68. Ben-Dror Yemini, 'The Jewish Nakba – far worse than the Arab', *Maariv* (translated into English by *Iraqijews* for *Point of No Return*), 20 May 2009, http://jewishrefugees. blogspot.co.uk/2009/05/jewish-nakba-more-serious-than.html. (Last accessed 26 April 2017).
69. Alain Gresh, tribute to Rouleau, *Cairo Review of Global Affairs*, quoted in *Point of no Return*, 13 October 2015, http://jewishrefugees.blogspot.co.uk/2015/10/cairo-holds-tribute-to-journalist-eric.html. (Last accessed 26 April 2017).
70. 'My Egyptian-Jewish childhood', *Point of No Return*, 29 August 2012, http:// jewishrefugees.blogspot.co.uk/2012/08/eric-rouleaus-egyptian-years.html. (Last accessed 26 April 2017).

71. Samuel Tadros, 'The sources of Egyptian anti-Semitism', *American Thinker*, 13 October 2015, http://www.the-american-interest.com/2014/04/21/the-sources-of-egyptian-anti-semitism/. (Last accessed 26 April 2017).

72. Karen McQuillan, 'Hitler's Long Shadow over Israel', *American Thinker*, 4 May 2012, http://www.americanthinker.com/articles/2012/05/hitlers_long_shadow_over_israel.ht ml#ixzz1uAJjQK. (Last accessed 26 April 2017).

73. See Beinin, *The Dispersion of Egyptian Jewry*, p.121.

6

What Came First: Anti-Semitism or Anti-Zionism?

In the autumn of 2012, the then deputy foreign minister of Israel, Danny Ayalon, launched the first ever governmental campaign for Justice for Jewish refugees from Arab countries. A frenetic stream of critical articles by Palestinians and pro-Palestinians followed, in order to argue why the campaign was a bad idea.

Senior Palestinian Liberation Organization (PLO) official Hanan Ashrawi claimed that Jews from Arab lands are not refugees at all and that Israel is using their claims in order to throw a spanner in the works of the peace process. The Israeli government stands accused of 'refugee-washing' (like 'pinkwashing' – a word used to suggest that Israel promotes its tolerance of and protection for lesbians and gays in order to obscure its oppressive treatment of Palestinians), its latest tactic for neutralising the claims of Palestinian refugees. Sounding remarkably like a Zionist, Hanan Ashrawi rebuked the Israeli government for its campaign to designate Jewish immigrants to Israel as Jewish refugees from Arab lands. She wrote:[1]

> At the very core of Zionist ideology is the idea that Israel is the homeland of the Jewish people. If this is the case, and Jews living in Israel are citizens of their singular national homeland, then the state cannot consider them refugees – they cannot be returnees to Israel and refugees from another homeland at the same time.
>
> If Israel is their homeland, then they are not 'refugees'; they are emigrants who returned either voluntarily or due to a political decision. [2]

In other words, Arab states have no responsibility for the exodus of their Jews. It seems to be the case that many Arabs even remain convinced that Jews never lived in their countries. 'You're lying', Egyptians accused Ellis Douek when he told them he had been ejected from his native Cairo to Britain.[3] Furthermore, Arab regimes have a vested interest in denying that Jews were refugees. In his memoirs, even the Iraqi prime minister Tawfiq al-Suwaydi 'does not recall' the mass departure of Jews over which he presided.[4] To do otherwise would be to recognise that Jews are victims. It would open the door to an apology, substantial demands for compensation, and drive a coach and horses through the Palestinian narrative.

By the universally-accepted UNHCR definition, however, Jews fleeing Arab countries *are* refugees: 'A refugee is someone who has been forced to flee his or her country because of persecution, war or violence. A refugee has a well-founded fear of persecution for reasons of race, religion, nationality, political opinion, or membership in a particular social group. Most likely, they cannot return home or are afraid to do so.'[5]

On two occasions, the UN recognised Jews as refugees. August Lindt, the UNHCR High Commissioner for Refugees, recognised Jews fleeing Egypt as *bona fide* refugees.[6] On a second occasion, the UNHCR recognised Jews fleeing Libya as refugees under the UNHCR mandate.

Contrary to Ashrawi's claim, the Jewish refugees had no choice but to leave their countries of birth owing to irresistible 'push' factors: persecution and expulsion. They were, by any definition, refugees at the time. They no longer *are* refugees because their adopted countries gave them full citizenship. In other words, a humanitarian solution was applied. Although they are no longer refugees, they do not want to return because they *cannot*: their countries of birth remain as hostile and dangerous to Jews as the day they left. The UNHCR definition, which says that the refugee cannot go back to his country of birth because he has a well-founded fear of persecution, certainly applies to Jews from Arab countries, including those which were still under colonial rule at the time they left.

Critics have charged that the Jews could not possibly be refugees, because they did not all leave their countries at once (although 90 per cent of Jews who fled Iraq, Syria, Libya and Yemen departed within three years of 1948).[7] The departure of Jews from the Arab world was spread out over thirty years, between 1948 and 1972. The population had halved by 1958, and by 1968 had dwindled to less than 9 per cent.[8] The reason for this extended period of departure is because the remaining Jews were, for the most part, hostages – trapped by emigration bans. This was the case in Syria, in Iraq from the time of the rise of the Ba'ath party to power, in Yemen until the 1990s and in Morocco, where a travel ban operated from 1956 to 1961.

Not only did Jewish refugees find themselves outside their countries of origin, as the UNHCR stipulates, but they were unable to receive protection from them, having been declared enemy aliens. They continue to fit the UNHCR definition because, for the most part, returning to their countries of birth would put their lives at risk.

Another favoured allegation is that, given that the Holocaust had decimated a third of the Jewish people, Israel was relying on Jews from Arab lands to populate the land, and as a source of cheap labour. However, so desperate to escape annihilation were the Yemenite, Iraqi and Libyan *aliyot* that Israel could not afford the luxury of operating a selection policy to pick the healthiest and most able-bodied. This it did, for a short period only[9] with immigrants arriving from pre-independence Morocco. When Israel took in the very young, the sick, the elderly and those with no transferable skills, it also took on a heavy burden at a time when the young Jewish state was least able to cope with it.

The Non-Zionist Majority

The 650,000 Jews driven from Arab countries to Israel did not all come out of choice – far from it. They arrived in a country which had just sacrificed 1 per cent of its population in war and suffered every kind of shortage. There is every reason to believe that Jewish communities would have continued to live in most Arab countries had they not been scapegoated as Zionists. Said the Egyptian-born journalist and diplomat Eric Rouleau: 'Egypt's Jews felt they were Egyptian, and the Zionist siren song never bewitched them.'[10] Apart from the Zionist minority, no one felt the need for a Jewish state or the urge to chant "*L' an prochain à Jérusalem*" when it was enough to take the 9:45 am train to get there', the French author Gilles Perrault wrote in *Un Homme Apart*, his biography of the Egyptian-Jewish communist Henri Curiel.

Nonetheless, wealthy Jews who had no intention of leaving their countries of birth felt the need to support the Zionist enterprise in Palestine. In the early twentieth century, Persian, Egyptian and Iraqi Jews bought plots of land in *Eretz Yisrael*.

All Jews, despite their leadership's increasingly shrill protestations of loyalty, were eventually branded as enemy aliens by Arab and Muslim anti-Semitism. It was but a short step to criminalising Judaism. Arab xenophobia ostracised all Jews, even the communists, the anti-colonialists and the ideological anti-Zionists among them. Absent the big 'push', one would have expected that *aliyah* (immigration to Israel) would have been confined to 'ideological' Zionists. It is perhaps safe to assume that those who moved to Israel for ideological reasons would not have exceeded 10 per cent of the Jewish community, mirroring the level in the 'secure and comfortable' West.

The myth that the Jews from Arab countries came as Zionist immigrants has been fuelled by the Israeli government. For ethnocentric reasons, Israel discouraged the Jews from seeing themselves as 'refugees', but rather as immigrants returning to their ancestral homeland. Danny Ayalon's own father came as a Zionist, and until his own epiphany, Danny was brought up with no interest or knowledge of his Algerian roots.[11] Critics of Ayalon's policy initiative to highlight the imperative for Justice for Jewish refugees from Arab countries gleefully point to the declarations of prominent self-declared Zionist Israelis such as Ran Cohen (who, in fact, arrived in 1950 as a thirteen-year-old refugee), Yisrael Yeshayahu and Shlomo Hillel, who arrived before Israel was born. All are on record as saying they came as Zionists, not refugees.

From their testimonies, it is extrapolated that Jews left their Arab countries out of Zionist idealism. However, Cohen, Hillel and Yeshayahu are not representative of the experience of the great mass of refugees, and do not account for push factors. Nor do they explain how 200,000 Jews ended up in Europe, Canada, the US, Central and South America or Australia.

'Zionism caused the Exodus'

A favoured myth – but one which contradicts the claim that the Jews left of 'their own free will' – is that Zionism caused Jews to leave Arab lands. It has been suggested that Zionist agents set off the 1950–1 bombs to scare Iraqi Jews into leaving. In his book *The Gun & the Olive Branch*, David Hirst describes in detail covert Israeli operations to scare Iraqi and Egyptian Jews into fleeing their homes for the 'sanctuary' of Israel. Wilbur Crane Eveland, a former CIA operative, wrote about the 'Zionist crimes' against 'Arab' Jews in Iraq.[12] The writings of the disaffected Iraqi Jew Naiem Giladi[13] are frequently invoked to support this myth.

In the Iraqi case no one will ever know for certain who planted bombs in 1950–1, but three of the five episodes occurred after 80,000 – the vast majority of the Jews – had already left or had given up their nationality in readiness to leave;[14] these bombs caused no casualties. The only fatal bombing occurred in a synagogue which was being used as a registration centre for departing Jews, just six weeks before Iraq again banned emigration. The Israeli 'new' historian Tom Segev[15] has produced evidence blaming the Messouda Shemtob synagogue attack on Iraqi nationalists. According to Yehuda Tager, an Israeli agent who operated in Baghdad and spent ten years in prison there, the bombing of the synagogue was not carried out by Jews but by members of the Muslim Brotherhood. Historian Benny Morris discovered that a secret investigation, conducted in Israel in 1960, to which Tager gave evidence, found no proof that Mossad was involved in the Messouda Shemtob bombing. 'In any case, Israelis don't bomb synagogues', Morris said.[16] He might have added that bombs were aimed at Jewish targets throughout the 1930s in Iraq and Egypt, and that a bomb planted at a Syrian synagogue had killed fourteen – yet nobody accuses the Mossad of these bombings.

Others blame members of the ultra-nationalist Istiqal party[17] or the police. (Only the Iraqi authorities possessed the no.36 high potential grenades used in the bombings.) Besides, the two Zionist 'culprits' executed in January 1952, whose confessions were extracted under torture, were never accused of the fatal bombing of 14 January 1951.[18]

Mordechai Ben-Porat, Mossad's leading operative in Baghdad, had his name cleared in an Israeli court when he sued an Israeli magazine for libel. The court heard evidence[19] in support of the theory that non-Jews threw the January 1951 bombs; Muslim pedlars were tipped off to clear the scene just before grenades were thrown at the Messouda Shemtob synagogue.

The Egyptian bombs of 1954, known as Operation Susannah or the Lavon Affair, were indeed the work of a pro-Zionist group: Egyptian Jews were recruited by Israeli military intelligence to plant bombs inside Egyptian, US and British-owned cinemas, libraries and American educational centres. The bombs failed to detonate. The attacks were to be blamed on local Islamists, communists or nationalists with the aim of creating enough instability to induce the British government to keep its occupying troops in Egypt's Suez Canal zone. The operation caused no casualties, except for injuring operative Philip Natanson: a bomb he was taking to a cinema ignited prematurely in his pocket. Two members of the cell committed suicide after being captured; two operatives, Moshe Marzouk and Samuel Azar, were tried, convicted and executed by Egypt.

Although the episode must have increased suspicions of the Jewish community, 'no drastic measures were then adopted by the new officers' regime in relation to the overwhelming majority of Jews':[20] there is no causal link with Nasser's expulsion of 25,000 Jews two years later after his nationalisation of the Suez Canal.

'The Jews Experienced Blowback'

Some sceptics concede that the vast majority of Jews did arrive in Israel as refugees, but argue that if Israel had not been established, these Jews would not have been forced to leave their home countries. In other words, they assert that these Jews experienced 'blowback'. They paid the price for the creation of Israel – supposedly a terrible mistake. In revenge for the mass exodus of Palestinian Arab refugees, Arab mobs and governments turned on their defenceless Jewish citizens. Indeed, Jews felt the repercussions of the Arab reaction to the Balfour Declaration – and subsequently, the Arab-Israeli conflict. With every war, tensions rose in Arab countries and more Jews sought to leave. The implication is that Israel is to blame for a perfectly-understandable Arab backlash leading to the uprooting of 850,000 Jewish refugees from Arab countries. By extension, the assertion is that Jews are to blame for their own misfortune.

The 'understandable backlash' argument is flawed, however. It does not, for example, explain why some 1,000 Jews were murdered in the Arab world in the decade before the creation of Israel, nor indeed why anti-Semitic violence broke out sporadically in the fourteen centuries of Judeo-Muslim coexistence. If Zionism is justification enough for 'collective punishment' of communities which were largely non-Zionist how does one explain why Jews suffered persecution, massacres and riots well before the Zionist movement was founded, and well before the creation of Israel: the Damascus blood libel of 1840, a succession of massacres in the nineteenth century in North Africa: the destruction of synagogues in Libya in the 1860s; the Casablanca massacre of 1907; the 1912 Fez pogrom (The *Tritl*); anti-Jewish riots in Tunisia in 1917; the Constantine (Algeria) pogrom of 1934; disturbances in Rabat and Oujda (Morocco) in 1933, 1934 and 1938; the Gabès pogrom and pro-Nazi *Farhud* in Iraq in 1941; and riots in Sefrou, Morocco in 1944? The 1945 riots in Egypt and Libya (resulting in the deaths of 140 Jews) appeared to have more to do with xenophobia and the anti-Jewish incitement generated by Nazi propaganda, than with resentment of Zionism.[21]

Postcard showing the aftermath of the 1912 Fez pogrom (Laurence Julius collection)

Jews sheltering in the Sultan's menagerie after the 1912 Fez pogrom.

Zionism did not cause the Jewish exodus. 'The Palestine question did not invent a situation heavy with violence', writes the French historian Georges Bensoussan.[22] 'It brought it to the surface.' 'The real causes are to be found', he writes, 'in the latent mutual hatred between two communities, peaking into violence when it finds the right pretext.' [23]

Penina Elbaz, a Moroccan-born Canadian psychologist, witnessing the bullying and intimidation to which Jews living in Muslim areas were exposed, saw Zionism as the solution to anti-Semitism. She writes: 'Those Zionists were delegated by the Messiah. They saved thousands of lives.'[24]

The mob, impressionable and illiterate, had a unique role to play in the intemperate Arab reaction to Zionism. However, slogans shouted in every anti-Jewish riot, *Itbach al Yahud* and *Yahud klib-al Arab*, suggest that the incited mobs were not interested in making the distinction between Zionists and Jews. The word 'Jew' became elided with 'Zionist' and 'enemy of the state'.

The entire Jewish citizenry in Arab countries became hostages to the conflict with Zionism. Inflicting 'collective punishment' on non-combatant Jews for what their co-religionists did or were thought to have done, thousands of miles away in Palestine, was seen in the Arab world as legitimate, although it entailed mass violations of human and civil rights. The most egregious example was the mass round-up of all Jewish males living in Egypt after the Arab defeat in the Six Day War. All were arrested and imprisoned as Israeli PoWs. Some were tortured and sodomised and remained in jail for years.[25] 'Collective punishment' is still seen as legitimate today: terrorist attacks on Jewish targets in Europe are often rationalised as a reaction to 'what Israel is doing to our Palestinian brothers'. One explanation favoured by anthropologists is that the '*hamula*'[26] clan mentality legitimises collective punishment because it is incapable of ascribing responsibility for a crime to an individual, but tars the entire tribe with the same guilty brush.[27]

'Anti-Semitism happens when groups feel their world is spinning out of control', ex-UK Chief Rabbi Jonathan Sacks once said.[28] It peaks at times of maximum fear and uncertainty. Clearly, violence by mob rule was a time-honoured means of getting the majority to vent their fears and frustrations on the scapegoated minority, with the added potential attraction of gains from looted possessions.

It was the anti-Semitic adviser to the sultan of Morocco, al-Mokri, who explained to Paul Baudoin, Marshall Pétain's foreign minister in 1940, how the Jewish problem was handled in Morocco:

> Before the protectorate, the Jews took twenty years to make large amounts of money. They spent ten years enjoying it. Then a small

revolution broke out to make them lose it all. The Jews began enriching themselves all over again over the next thirty years, leading to the eventual confiscation of their excessive wealth. Now that there is a Protectorate, we fear that this thirty-year rhythm be disrupted. The Protectorate has lasted just twenty-eight years. We therefore have two years left until we confiscate the Israelites' fortune, according to this centuries-old rule, which seems very wise to me.[29]

A mob incited to hatred against a victim group does not find it necessary to react to what a victim has done. The mere fantasy that the victim has done a provocative deed or intends to do it provides pretext enough. Thus many acts of violence against Jews originated with false accusations. A favourite pretext was connected to the Jewish use of alcohol. Others are classic Christian tropes: the 1840 Damascus Blood libel, for instance – alleging that Jews murdered children in order to use their blood to bake *Matza*. Charges that Jews have defiled the Qur'an or Muslim holy sites, committed blasphemy, or fabricated Jewish designs on the Al-Aqsa mosque on Jerusalem's Temple Mount have fuelled anti-Jewish violence for decades and still do today.

In societies where no checks and balances exist to protect against hate speech, the Other becomes a proxy for the enemy *du jour*. Christians in the Middle East are proxies for the West. Hindus in Pakistan are proxies for India. Jews in the Muslim world are proxies for Israel. Arab autocracies used the conflict with Zionism as a means to unite the masses and distract them from their own domestic failings.

Under cover of such grievances, a vulnerable minority becomes a scapegoat for the majority's ills and a vehicle, not just for enriching opportunists at the minority's expense, but for settling scores.

The final ingredient in this toxic mix is the inability – or unwillingness – of the forces of law and order to protect the targeted minority. In the early twentieth century, as explained in Chapter Three, Western colonial powers encouraged rifts between communities as part of a policy of 'divide and rule' and frequently failed to prevent the loss of Jewish life. Examples abound of the police or army arriving too late to prevent an incident spiralling out of control. In many cases policemen joined the rioters. Much to the embarrassment of the British, the colonial power in Aden, the 'trigger-happy' British-armed and officered Aden Protectorate Levies were blamed for many of the eighty-seven deaths resulting from the anti-Jewish riots in 1947.[30] For fear of confronting the Muslim Brotherhood, the Egyptian authorities did little to protect Egyptian Jews and their property from bombings during the summer of 1948.[31]

All Minorities were Persecuted

Those who claim that if Israel had not existed, the Jews would have continued to live in relative security as just another minority must explain why Jews were not the only minority who could not depend on governmental protection, and why minorities who have no Israel of their own have suffered persecution and violence: some 5,000 Christians were massacred in Damascus in the late nineteenth century;[32] around 20,000 Christians were killed by the Druze in the Mount Lebanon civil war in 1860, and 380 Christian villages and 560 churches were destroyed. Massacres were perpetrated against Armenian Christians, Assyrian Christians, Thraceans, other Greeks living in Turkey and other non-Muslim groups in the early twentieth century. The Ottoman Turks began to harass Armenians in the 1880s, leading eventually to the extermination and dispersal of the Armenian communities of Turkey.[33] Massacres of Armenians prefigured the great Armenian and Assyrian 'genocide' of 1915: they began in 1894 and continued until 1923.[34] Not all the victims were non-Muslims – there were mass killings of Kurds, Circassians, Crimean Tatars – and it has to be said that non-Muslims too committed killings of Muslims during the wars that erupted during the break-up of the Ottoman Empire and the First World War. (In 1919 there was even a massacre of Jews in the city of Guba – by Armenians.)[35]

The mistreatment of minorities in police states, well into the twenty-first century, speaks for itself. Iraq's first act since becoming independent, in violation of its commitment to protect its minorities, was to massacre 600 Assyrian Christians at Simele in 1933, an episode that rang alarm bells with the Iraqi-Jewish family of Zionist agent Shlomo Hillel: 'In the strife-torn Middle East, the action was in itself not a particular cause for surprise. But the response to it spelled more evil to come. Not only were the perpetrators of the crime never brought to justice, they were actually decorated by Crown Prince Ghazi.'[36] When Ghazi ascended the throne of Iraq, Hillel's father became determined to leave Iraq for Palestine.

In *Jewish Property Claims against Arab Countries*,[37] Professor Michael Fischbach argues that the measures taken against Jews in Arab countries were in retaliation for the 'expulsion' and dispossession of Palestinian Arab refugees. Another theory is that the exchange was encouraged by manipulative colonial powers. Both Britain and the USA were thought to have 'pressed the Iraqi government to facilitate Jewish emigration' and to be 'toying with various schemes to exchange refugee populations'.[38] Such exchange schemes collapsed in Iraq when Nuri al-Said replaced Tawfiq al-Suwaydi as Prime Minister in September 1950. Al-Said was 'determined to drive Jews out of his country as quickly as possible'.[39]

However, even before the establishment of the Jewish state and before the great mass of Arab refugees had fled, the first refugees to be expelled in the first Arab-Israeli war were Jews from the Shimon Hatsaddik quarter in Jerusalem. Moreover, as we shall see, there is pre-existing evidence that Arab governments were conspiring to victimise their Jews and dispossess them of their land and property before the 1947 UN Partition Plan was passed.[40] To argue otherwise is, in the words of the Israeli columnist Ben-Dror Yemini, 'to erase the natural order of things'. [41]

Clearly there is a difference between discrimination and persecution. The former is more often social prejudice. The latter can be official and state-sanctioned, or it can be practised by powerful groups in society to make life hell for the targeted minority. There is a point, however, when discrimination can become persecution, and persecution a threat to life and limb. Whether state-sanctioned or not, discrimination can degenerate into intimidation, psychological warfare and violence. It can put lives at risk.

The *Farhud* (Arabic for 'violent dispossession') of 1941 in Iraq was followed by other *Farhuds*: in Syria, Aden, Bahrain, Morocco, Libya and Egypt in 1947–8 murderous riots in Morocco, Libya and Aden and the destruction of Jewish property had the net effect also of dispossessing Jews, even though those countries were still under colonial rule and had not yet passed any anti-Jewish legislation. Those new Arab states without Jews, like Jordan, made sure not to acquire any.

Scapegoating the Jews

Whereas many Palestinian Arabs took up arms against the Zionists in a war declared by their leaders, or fled the dangerous chaos of a war zone in Israel, Jews in Arab lands did not engage in subversion and were non-combatants – hundreds, if not thousands, of miles from the theatre of war. The Jews in Arab lands were victimised purely for sharing the same religion and ethnicity as the Israelis.

The Balfour Declaration of 1917 demanded of the Zionists that a Jewish homeland in Palestine should not prejudice the rights and status of non-Jewish communities in Palestine. What is often forgotten, however, is the tail-end of Lord Balfour's letter: '… or of Jews in any other country'. [42] Clearly nothing was demanded of Arab states that were created out of the ruins of the Ottoman Empire: they violated any constitutional obligation they may have had towards their own Jewish citizens. The Arab League even met in Syria as late as 1946 and Lebanon in 1947, and agreed a draft plan to rob the Jews, threaten them with imprisonment and expel them, having first dispossessed them.[43] The war against the Jews was ongoing. In 1947, anti-Jewish tensions reached new peaks in Palestine and the Arab world as Arab delegates ramped up their rhetoric at the UN, which was due to vote on the Partition of Palestine. The Egyptian delegate, Heykal Pasha, was already warning of the consequences of establishing a Jewish state on Jews living in Arab countries:

> The United Nations ... should not lose sight of the fact that the proposed solution might endanger a million Jews living in Muslim countries ... creating anti-Semitism in those countries even more difficult to root out than the anti-Semitism which the Allies tried to eradicate in Germany ... making the UN ... responsible for very grave disorders and for the massacre of a large number of Jews.

Heykal Pasha's words were prefaced with talk of 'massacre', 'riots' and 'war between two races'. His threats were, according to Yaakov Meron, 'the outcome of prior coordination between Arab states then represented at the UN and the Arab League'.[44] The Palestinian delegate, Jamal Al-Hussayni, said the Jews' situation in the Arab world 'will become very precarious. Governments in general have always been unable to prevent mob excitement and violence.' The *New York Times* of 19 February 1947 quoted Syrian UN representative Faris Al-Khuri: 'Unless the Palestinian problem is settled, we shall have difficulty in protecting the Jews in the Arab world.'[45]

In Iraq the threats were made publicly, and its Foreign Minister Fadel Jamali stated at the UN:

> The masses in the Arab world cannot be restrained. The Arab-Jewish relationship in the Arab world will greatly deteriorate. There are more Jews in the Arab world outside Palestine than there are in Palestine. In Iraq alone we have about 150,000 Jews who share with Muslims and Christians all the advantages of political and economic rights. But any injustice imposed on the Arabs of Palestine will disturb the harmony among Jews and non-Jews in Iraq. It will breed interreligious prejudice and hatred.[46]

The outbreak, on 30 November and in December 1947, of riots in Aden, Syria and Bahrain as soon as the Partition Plan was passed, suggests a degree of collusion. Just two days after the State of Israel was proclaimed, a *New York Times* headline on 16 May 1948 declared: '*Jews in Grave Danger in All Moslem Lands, Nine hundred thousand in Africa and Asia face wrath of their foes.*' The article, written by Mallory Browne, reported on a series of discriminatory measures taken by the Arab League against the Jewish residents of Arab League member states (at that time, Egypt, Iraq, Jordan, Lebanon, Saudi Arabia, Syria and Yemen). The article cited the text of a law drafted by the Political Committee of the Arab League which was intended to govern the legal status of Jewish residents of Arab League countries. It provided that, beginning on an unspecified date, all Jews, except citizens of non-Arab states, would be considered 'members of the Jewish minority state of Palestine'. Their bank accounts would be frozen and used to finance resistance to 'Zionist ambitions in Palestine'. Jews believed to be active

The George V Jewish Boys' School was burnt down in the 1947 Aden riots.

Jews in Grave Danger in all Moslem Lands was the headline n the New York Times of 16 May 1948. The article cited a coordinated Arab plan to persecute and rob Jews.

Text of Law drafted by Political Committee of Arab League

1. Beginning with (date), all Jewish citizens of (name of country) will be considered as members of the Jewish minority State of Palestine and will have to register with the authorities of the region wherein they reside, giving their names, the exact number of members in their families, their addresses, the names of their banks and the amounts of their deposits in these banks. This formality is to be accomplished within seven days.

2. Beginning with (date), bank accounts of Jews will be frozen. These funds will be utilized in part or in full to finance the movement of resistance to Zionist ambitions in Palestine.

3. Beginning with (date), only Jews who are subjects of foreign countries will be considered as "neutrals". These will be compelled either to return to their countries, with a minimum of delay, or be considered as Arabs and obliged to accept active service with the Arab army.

4. Jews who accept active service in Arab armies or place themselves at the disposal of those armies, will be considered as "Arabs".

5. Every Jew whose activities reveal that he is an active Zionist will be considered as a political prisoner and will be interned in places specifically designated for. that purpose by police authorities or by the Government. His financial resources, instead of being frozen, will be confiscated.

6. Any Jew who will be able to prove that his activities are anti-Zionist will be free to act as he likes, provided that he declares his readiness to join the Arab armies.

7. The foregoing (para. 6), does not mean that those Jews will not be submitted to paragraphs 1 and 2 of this law.

Arab League Plan for state-sanctioned measures against their Jewish citizens, 1947.

Zionists would be interned and their assets confiscated. This policy was not announced in retaliation for Israel's actions against the Palestinians Arabs, but was formulated *before* a single Arab refugee had left Israel.

The Arab League, in its Council Session on 17 February 1948, in Cairo, approved a plan for 'political, military, and economic measures to be taken in response to the Palestine crisis'. One report stated that: 'The Council of the Arab League unanimously adopted the recommendations of its Political Committee concerning Palestine', confirming the collusion among the seven Arab League member states to violate the rights of their Jews.[47]

There is more evidence that Arab countries were collaborating in the forced displacement of Jews from their territories in the form of a Beirut meeting of senior diplomats from all the Arab States in late March 1949. By this time, the Arab states had already lost the first Arab-Israeli war. As reported in a Syrian newspaper, participants at this meeting concluded that:

'If Israel should oppose the return of the Arab refugees to their homes, the Arab governments will expel the Jews living in their countries.'[48]

Once Zionism had been outlawed it was easy for Arab governments to scapegoat their Jewish citizens – even the sworn anti-Zionists among them – as spies or traitors.

In summary:

Stripping Jews of citizenship happened in all countries except Lebanon and Tunisia.

Arrests and detentions occurred in all countries except Lebanon and Tunisia.

Islamic religious restrictions were in force in Algeria, Egypt, Morocco, Tunisia and Yemen.

Zionism became a crime by law in Egypt, Iraq, Lebanon, Libya, Morocco and Syria. (To confuse the issue, Israelite (the genteel term for Jew, preferred by many Jewish communities in the Arab world) and Israeli were used interchangeably, so much so that one lawmaker has, relatively recently, proposed to amend the law in Lebanon.)[49]

Freedom of movement was curtailed in Iraq, Libya, Morocco, Syria and Yemen.

Loss of work and employment discrimination resulted in Jews being dismissed and/or banned from certain careers (*eg* government service) in Egypt, Iraq, Lebanon, Morocco, Syria and Yemen. They were forced to take Muslim business partners. In Egypt, 75 per cent of employees had to be Arabs or Muslims.

Freezing of assets occurred in all countries except Morocco.

Confiscation of property occurred in all countries except Morocco.[50]

A Blueprint for Persecution

The Arab League plan of 1947 became a blueprint, in country after country, for the actions that devastated the Jewish communities in Arab lands; and for the forced exodus that was to follow. Some 90 per cent of Jews had fled the Arab world by 1972. According to the Egyptian-Jewish journalist Victor Nahmias, the Arab League followed up the plan by adopting secret recommendations from 1950–5 designed to put pressure on the Jews remaining in Arab countries to leave their homes 'without giving the impression of expelling them.'[51]

For Canadian ex-justice minister Irwin Cotler, the persecution was also far more systematic and accompanied by what he brands 'mass human rights violations ... including Nuremberg-type laws against their Jewish citizens' – acts that Cotler, a lifelong human rights activist, brands evidence of 'criminal intention if not criminal conspiracy': 'If we look at the concerted pattern of state sanctioning of repression, and of systematic legislation which criminalized and disenfranchised Jews and sequestered their property, then what happened belongs in the annals of ethnic cleansing.'[52]

On 19 January 1948, the World Jewish Congress sent a memorandum appended to the Arab League draft law to the United Nations Economic and Social Council to protest against it and the anti-Jewish unrest it had generated in the Arab world. Unfortunately, the fate of this memorandum rested in the hands of the President of the Council, Dr Charles H. Malik, the representative of Lebanon to the United Nations, designated by Arab states to be their Council representative. Lebanon was one of the founding members of the Arab League, one of the states which had deliberated upon the anti-Semitic draft law. Mr Malik used a procedural manoeuvre to ensure that nothing was done in response to the World Jewish Congress memorandum.

One theory is that the Arab League stopped short of passing the Nuremberg-style draft law because newly-independent Arab states wanted to be part of the new post-War order. They wanted seats at the United Nations, which was set up to prevent regimes such as Nazi Germany, with its Nuremberg laws, from ever emerging again.[53] But, in practice, Arab states passed their own anti-Jewish measures, did not fail to incite their people to violence, enact legal decrees, denationalise their Jews and engage in economic despoilment and expulsions.

Years later, in 1984, sitting in the garden of his house with other Arab Affairs journalists, the Israeli columnist Dr Guy Bechor challenged Charles Malik.[54] He asked him why he did nothing to block an anti-Zionist –indeed anti-Semitic – plan. Charles Malik responded: 'Lebanon had no choice but to toe the Arab line'. As a Christian, Malik asserted, he had to prove loyalty to the Arab/Palestinian cause, and was even required to be more anti-Israel than the Muslims.

Two Case Studies

At opposing ends of the spectrum: Iraq and Morocco

In some countries the departure of the Jews was precipitous. In others, they were ushered gradually towards the exit.

Iraq was possibly the harshest of all the Arab countries, being the only one to hang its Jews for being 'Zionists'.

Iraqi Jews such as these merchants (back row, with handlebar moustaches) were prominent in the economy. The photo was taken in Baghdad circa 1910.

Comprising up to 40 per cent to a third of Baghdad's population, Jews enjoyed their golden era under the British mandate, which began in 1917. They dominated trade and the civil service, while taking a full part in the country's cultural renaissance or *Nahda*. One in five Iraqi writers was Jewish. The first novel of prose fiction was written by a Jew, Yaqub Balbul, and Jews pioneered popular Iraqi music.

The rot began to set in in the 1930s, as Nazi influence penetrated society. The influential German ambassador in Baghdad Fritz Grobba built up a network of pro-Nazi sympathisers. He financed pro-Nazi newspapers, and serialised *Mein Kampf*. The school curriculum abandoned the British model in favour of the German one. In 1934, dozens of Jewish clerks were dismissed.[55] The Arab Revolt in Palestine marked the onset of physical attacks on Iraqi Jews in 1936. Ten were killed and eight bombs were thrown at synagogues. Community leaders rushed to disassociate themselves from Zionism. Then came the build-up to the *Farhud* pogrom, which totally undermined Jewish confidence and shattered the idea that

In the 1930s in Iraq, Hitler's *Mein Kampf* was translated and serialised in Iraqi newspapers. Today it is a bestseller in the Arab world.

Jews could ever be integrated into Iraqi society. Young Jews thereafter looked
to Zionism or communism for salvation.

After the Partition Plan for Palestine passed in 1947, Iraq sent volunteers
to take part in the Arab war against the Zionists. The government sought to
divert popular attention from pressing domestic issues:[56] the Jews were the
perfect scapegoat. The Jews of Iraq were forced to donate to the Palestinian
cause. As Iraq's defeated soldiers trudged home, the Jews were gripped by
fear of another *Farhud*. In July 1948, Zionism was added to the Penal Code.
Iraq imposed martial law and Jewish freedom of movement was restricted.
Jews were prohibited from leaving the country. They were detained by the
secret police for questioning and only released on payment of large bribes.
The entire community was traumatised by the hanging, in September 1948,

Shortly after this Baghdad wedding photograph was taken in 1948, the Jewish bridegroom
and best man were interrogated by police and only released after a large bribe was paid.

of the wealthiest and best-connected Jew of all, Shafiq Ades – on trumped up charges. In 1949, Zionists and communists were sentenced to death.[57] For the great mass of Jews, any evidence of contact with Palestine could be a pretext for arrest: letters to relatives – but also stars of David on prayer shawls, even Bibles and *haggadot*.

The conflation of the terms 'Jew' with 'Zionist' was taken to absurd levels. A decree issued in 1948 related not just to religion and political beliefs but to wristwatches:

> With very few exceptions, only Jews wore watches. On spotting one that looked expensive, a policeman had approached the owner as if to ask the hour. Once assured that the man was Jewish, he relieved him of the timepiece and took him into custody. The watch, he told the judge, contained a wireless; he'd caught the Jew sending military secrets to the Zionists in Palestine. Without examining the 'evidence' or asking any questions, the judge pronounced his sentence. The 'traitor' went to prison, the watch to the policeman as reward.[58]

Until Iraq permitted legal emigration, Jews, especially the youth, were being smuggled out through the south of the country to Iran at a rate of a thousand a month –because the Zionists among them were being hounded. Jews were banned from higher education, could not travel abroad, sell property, were denied work and suffered restrictions in employment. 'But for these severe handicaps, Iraqi Jews would not have gone so far as to attempt large-scale flight from the country',[59] the Jewish senator Ezra Menahem Daniel said, making his last futile appeal against the Denaturalisation Bill in March 1950.

By the time the gates slammed shut on Jewish emigration in March 1951, some 119,000 out of some 140,000 Jews had registered to go, confounding the Mossad's prediction that only 10,000 would leave.[60] The world's oldest diaspora was transplanted to Israel, with no prospect of return. Then, on 1 March 1951, came the final twist of the knife – the Iraqi parliament passed a law

This School Certificate, issued to Edwin Shuker in the 1960s, bears the discriminatory words *Hawiyat adam al-Iskat* (Not Yet Denaturalised). On leaving Iraq, Jews were stripped of their citizenship.

freezing all Jewish property. All those who had registered to leave were, at once, left destitute.

That was not the end of the story, however. Some 6,000 Jews – mainly the wealthier families – remained in Iraq. The royal family was deposed in 1958 in a bloodbath; conditions momentarily improved for the Jews, who were free to come and go during the 'golden years' of General Kassam's rule, but after the Ba'ath party temporarily seized power in 1963, Jews were made to carry yellow ID cards, they were restricted in their movements and banned from foreign travel. Following the Arab defeat in the 1967 war with Israel, Jews were sacked from their jobs and banned from places of higher education, telephones cut off, their homes placed under constant surveillance and their bank accounts frozen. The nadir was reached when nine Jews were executed on trumped-up spying charges on 27 January 1969. Half a million Iraqis came to sing and dance under their corpses hanging in Liberation Square. During these years of terror, around fifty Jews disappeared without trace. Denied a passport to leave, some 2,000 Jews escaped through the northern border into Iran.[61] The community dwindled further through the eighties and nineties – the invading US troops found only thirty Jews still living in Baghdad in 2003. In 2016, there were just five.

Royal Protection, Popular Hostility

At the other end of the spectrum is Morocco with its 265,000 Jews in 1948,[62] the largest community in the Arab world. Morocco has never severed its links

10 'Prayer sculpture' in Ramat Gan, Israel, memorialising the victims of the 1941 *Farhud* and the Jews executed in Baghdad's main square in January 1969 (David Shai).

with its Jews, nor they with Morocco, and thousands of Israelis of Moroccan origin visit the country every year. The Moroccan monarchy has had a symbiotic relationship with its Jewish subjects. In the twentieth century, the King generally assured a certain degree of Western-oriented stability and continuity, and even sympathy towards his Jews. Historically, a privileged few Jewish financiers and traders were his mainstay and contact with the outside world. (It is telling that these seem to have preferred to live in the Portuguese-held coastal towns rather than the Islamic interior.) [63] On the other hand, popular feeling was very often anti-Jewish, leading to Jews being locked into ghettoes for their own safety and to more pogroms than in other parts of the Arab world, especially in the interregnum between rulers.

Ask the Moroccan Jews themselves and they profess fierce loyalty and undying affection for the King. Did the wartime sultan, the future Mohammed V, they claim, not save the Jews of Morocco from being deported to concentration camps? Did he not ask the Vichy regime which imposed itself on the Moroccan protectorate to let him wear the Nazi yellow star? And even ask for twenty more for the royal family?

Yet historians affirm that the Sultan's philo-Semitism is the stuff of legend. Even if he prevaricated and locked anti-Jewish Vichy decrees away in a drawer, the Sultan did not fail eventually to sign every one of them. He never uttered a word of protest at the atrocious conditions in the thirty labour camps (a quarter of the prisoners were European Jews) established on

Jews have a special affection for the wartime sultan of Morocco, the future Mohamed V, whom they believe saved them from the Nazis.

Moroccan and Algerian soil to build the Trans-Saharan railway.[64] In his kingdom anti-Semitism came from the bottom up, and had its roots in centuries of contempt for the *dhimmi*, resulting in Jewish degradation and insecurity. *Dhimmi* rules were applied to the letter according to the ultra-conservative Maliki school of jurisprudence prevalent in Morocco and owing to the influence of fanatical theologians such as the fifteenth century Al Maghili, who ordered the destruction of the Jewish community of Touat.

The twelfth century Moroccan Berber, fanatical, Muslim Almohad dynasty devastated the Iberian peninsula when it was at its apex of social development and integration, and almost put an end to Judaism in Morocco. Christianity died out and thousands of Jews were forcibly converted in Morocco itself. But matters were even worse in Spain under Almohad rule. The illustrious rabbi and thinker Maimonides and his family and countless others did seek refuge there from his native Córdoba, even appearing to convert temporarily to Islam. Conditions improved under the Merinids, and Jews reverted to their faith. On the other hand, a quarter of the inhabitants of Fez are thought to be descended from *Bildiyyin*, Jews converted in the fifteenth century.

Revd J.W. Brooks visited several Jewish communities in Muslim lands, including Morocco, in the nineteenth century:

> In Morocco they are equally ground down by a barbarous despotism. The Moors consider that the object of a Jew's birth is to serve Musselmen, and he is consequently subject to the most wanton insults. The boys for their pastime beat and torment the Jewish children: the men kick and buffet the adults. They walk into their houses at all hours, and take the grossest freedoms with their wives and daughters, the Jews invariably coming off with a sound beating if they venture to resist.[65]

There were bad and good periods, but Jews were so desperate to escape their *dhimmi* condition of precarious subjugation that, centuries before the establishment of Israel, they were already seeking to leave for Palestine, Britain and Latin America. Even if conditions were not much better in the Holy Land –it was the Jewish spiritual home. In 1846, the Moroccan sultan Moulay Abd al-Rahman cautioned the governor of Tangier:

> Wealthy Jews, may God curse them, have been increasing their trips [abroad], claiming they are going on a pilgrimage to Jerusalem. But they are not returning. Consequently Islam is harmed in two ways, first, in their diminishing revenue from *jizya*, and second they are becoming reconnoiterers, directing the enemy to the weak spots of the Muslims. Prevent all of them from travelling from the ports of

Larache and Tangier, be indefatigable in your efforts with them. May God destroy them.[66]

David Littman and Paul Fenton in their book *L'Éxil au Maghreb*[67] describe the appalling conditions Jews endured in the eighteenth and nineteenth centuries. As the European powers extended their influence on the Moroccan coast, Jews tried everything they could to obtain European passports. (Gibraltar's Jews, British since the eighteenth century, have hailed mainly from Morocco.)

The *dhimmi* status, with its ritual humiliations and exactions, was still being applied to Maghrebi Jews into the twentieth century, long after it had been abrogated in the Ottoman Levant. Morocco had a dismal record of forced conversions and abductions of Jewish women. To escape famine in Fez, Muslims were given priority at grain stores,[68] something which may help to account for successive waves of Jews converting to Islam.

Of all the Arab countries, Morocco probably has the worst record of massacres and pogroms: to name but a few in the twentieth century - Taza (1903), Settat (1903), Casablanca (1907), Fez (1912), Sefrou (1944), Oujda and Jerrada (1948). Jews in pre-colonial North Africa had neither material nor physical security. The era of the French protectorate ushered in a more stable period, but few Moroccan Jews managed to acquire French citizenship; after the Fez pogrom of 1912, 340 Jews were reported to have left for Palestine in 1922 alone. There would have been more if each emigrant had not been forced to deposit a guarantee of 1,000 francs.[69]

During the protectorate, Jews could not expect to be treated fairly by the antiquated judicial process, which still followed Islamic law.[70]

In his book *Les Juifs vont en enfer* ('The Jews are going to Hell') the Moroccan Saïd Ghallab corroborates the existence of popular anti-Jewish prejudice:[71] 'The worst insult that a Moroccan could possibly offer was to treat someone as a Jew ... my childhood friends have remained anti-Jewish. They hid their virulent anti-Semitism by contending that the state of Israel was the creation of European imperialism.'[72]

On the other hand, the Jewish population was not immune from French colonial anti-Semitism. During the Second World War, the pro-Nazi Vichy regime brought in a raft of anti-Jewish measures, from quotas to laws excluding Jews from public parks, banning them from employing Muslim maids and shunting them back from the European quarters into the overcrowded and disease-ridden city *mellahs*.

As Morocco strove for independence from France, Arab resentment of Jews as economic competitors and collaborators with the French colonisers led to outbreaks of violence that had little to do with the Arab-Israeli conflict. Jews were the helpless victims of the Petit-Jean massacre of 1954, which can only be described as anti-colonialist violence. When France sent the sultan

(Mohammed V) into exile, a million rioters vented their frustration 'for no reason'[73] on the Jews – torturing, eviscerating and then dousing with petrol and burning their six victims.[74]

Maurice Harris, the son of a Jewish refugee from Morocco, wrote:

> My relatives were subjected to repeated episodes of intimidation and violence living as Jews during the upheavals of Morocco in the 1950s. They were expected to show deference to Muslims in public, and while they generally speak of good historic relations between Moroccan Jews and Muslims, they also speak of how quickly all of that unravelled as soon as Jews became a suspected wedge group in the fighting between the French colonizers and the Arab independence fighters. My grandfather, who had worked his whole life to build a furniture factory in Casablanca, first had his business seized and assets frozen. The family was large – lots of kids – and they began to struggle with hunger and fear for their future. Eventually, my grandfather was targeted to be killed by the al-Fatah movement, and a Muslim friend of his gave him the warning. My family had to flee in the middle of the night, leaving behind their home (which now belongs to a Moroccan Arab family), traumatized and in panic, smuggling themselves aboard a boat that carried them to a refugee camp in southern France, while they waited for passage to Israel.[75]

Dina Gabay, whose family left Morocco in the 1950s[76] describes insults and ceaseless intimidation. Her father, who owned a large and successful butcher's shop, was at the mercy of local thieves, who sometimes simply walked into his business and demanded that he give them whatever they wanted – at no cost. Her father knew better than to argue.

Before independence in 1956, a third of Moroccan Jewry had fled the country. After 1956, Jewish ministers were appointed to the government. Any idea that Jews and Arabs shared a common destiny in the new Morocco died a death after the emergence of Gamal Abdel Nasser, Egypt's president. Morocco became a member of the Arab League in 1958. It promptly cut all postal links with Israel. Moroccan Jews began to withdraw from the national public sphere.[77] The distinction between Zionism and Judaism became blurred, causing rising insecurity. 'Many left because we failed as nationalists to incorporate them even though we claim the contrary … Did we acknowledge them after independence? No', confessed a Muslim anti-French fighter to Aomar Boum.[78]

In an atmosphere of nationalist and forced arabisation, Jews were increasingly pushed to the political margins. However, threats to strip Moroccan Jews of their passports were never carried out, according to the historian Robert Assaraf. There was no concerted effort to dispossess Jews.[79]

Nonetheless, as in other Arab states, Zionism became a crime. After the humiliation of the Arab defeat in the Six Day War, Moroccan Jews were scapegoated as a fifth column and a boycott was declared against Jewish businesses.[80] Jews were arrested and jailed for so-called 'Zionism'. From the 1960s, Morocco began importing Egyptian and Syrian teachers in order to 'arabise' the school curriculum. It was then that Wahabism and the thoughts of the Muslim Brotherhood penetrated the kingdom.[81]

Morocco formally violated civil rights by preventing its Jews from leaving after 1956. The ban came into force as soon as Morocco became independent and provoked increasingly desperate attempts by Jews to flee, culminating in the 1961 *Pisces* (*Egoz*) disaster, in which forty-two Jews and their Spanish machine operator drowned. Thereafter, the emigration ban was lifted and Israel's Operation Yakhin[82] ransomed each Jew from the Moroccan government for up to $250 per head. (Jews studying abroad and not planning to go to Israel were also stymied by Morocco's refusal to issue new travel documents or to extend passports.)

In sum, the idea that one fine day the Zionists scooped the Jews of Morocco up and shipped them off to Israel overnight does not stand up to scrutiny.

Yet, unlike Iraq, Morocco has maintained links with its Jews. It is the only Arab country to have recognised its Jewish roots in the 2011 Constitution. Hardly a week goes by without a favourable report in the press concerning Morocco's laudable treatment of the Jews. Here, an announcement that Morocco is renovating this synagogue, there the news

Berber Jews of southern Morocco (Alliance Israélite Universelle Photolibrary, Paris)

Jewish bride from Casablanca, 1940s (Courtesy Danielle Jones).

that the Moroccan government is restoring that Jewish cemetery. The King has also supported the creation of internet sites on Moroccan-Jewish heritage.[83]

Indeed, since the late 1970s, the King of Morocco has been pursuing a public relations strategy to project a positive image in which the Jews have played a salient part. Moroccan Jews outside the country, wherever they now live, would be considered to be in exile from their true homeland. Jews returning to Morocco would be entitled instantly to a Moroccan passport.

In 1990, the French left-wing author Gilles Perrault published a damning indictment of King Hassan II's human rights abuses, *Notre ami le roi*. The book had a disastrous effect on Morocco's image. Enter André Azoulay to stage-manage the King's public relations. A former communist, Azoulay had lived away from Morocco for twenty-eight years. He worked in Paris for the bank Paribas before becoming the royal adviser on Jewish affairs. The strategy worked. Liberal US Jews have played their part in spreading the myth that the wartime Moroccan sultan 'protected' his Jewish citizens against the Nazis.[84]

Interfaith projects, Andalusian music festivals and films made with the support of the government cultivate an image of coexistence between Jews and Arabs for external consumption. The only Jewish museum in the Arab world exists in a Casablanca suburb, but it is almost unknown amongst Moroccans themselves, being used as vehicle to project a tolerant image towards the outside world.[85]

There is another good reason why the King first began to harness the goodwill and loyalty of the Moroccan Jewish communities to boost himself with the West. Morocco was engaged in a long-term dispute with its neighbour Algeria over Western Sahara. Morocco needs US support for its territorial claims and military struggle against the terrorist raids by the Polisario Liberation Front, and US Jews are thought to have great influence on US foreign policy.

Besides *realpolitik*, a third reason why Morocco wants to be seen as 'good to the Jews' is the country's reliance on tourism, its second largest currency earner. Morocco attracts some 40,000 Jewish tourists every year[86] – of which some 3,000 are Israelis. Jewish culture is a key attraction for all tourists – synagogues, yearly pilgrimages or *hilulot* to famous rabbis' tombs and the Jewish quarters or *mellah* of Moroccan towns. It is no coincidence that the head of the Jewish community Serge Berdugo has also held the portfolio of Minister of Tourism.[87]

The King of Morocco, it must be recognised, has exerted a stabilising, moderating and normalising influence: he has been able to play a part in mediating in the peace process between Israel and the Arab states. He has been one of the rare Muslim leaders to recognise the Holocaust.[88] Certain Moroccan intellectuals have been able to express their sympathy for Jews and

Israel. They are free to visit the Jewish state. The Amazigh national movement is particularly sympathetic and there even exists an Amazigh-Israel friendship association.[89]

However, two attempted *coups d'état* against the King, in 1971 and 1972, show that the Jews of Morocco walk a tightrope. If the King goes down, they will almost certainly go with him. The 2,500 Jews in Morocco, 1 per cent of their 1948 numbers, hedge their bets, their children leave to study abroad and do not return.[90] It is doubtful whether a Moroccan-Jewish community will exist in another generation. 'The King protects us', a Moroccan Jew loudly told US author Robert Satloff at a lavish Hanucah party. In hushed tones, he added, 'and everyone here has a packed suitcase'.[91]

Notes

1. Khaled Abu Toameh, 'PLO's Ashrawi: no such thing as Jewish refugees', *Jerusalem Post*, 1 September 2012, http://www.jpost.com/Middle-East/PLOs-Ashrawi-No-such-thing-as-Jewish-refugees (Last accessed 26 April 2017).
2. Ibid.
3. Interview of Ellis Douek with *Sephardi Voices UK*, 2016.
4. Y. Meron, 'Why Jews left Arab countries', *Middle East Quarterly*, September1995.
5. UN Definition, 'What is a refugee?', http://www.unrefugees.org/what-is-a-refugee/. (Last accessed 26 April 2017).
6. UNHCR Fourth Session – Geneva, 29 January to 4 February 1957, quoted in JJAC report. Urman, Cotler, Matas, 'Jewish refugees from Arab countries: the case for rights and redress (JJAC, 2007), p.37.
7. See Table showing statistics of mass displacement: ibid.
8. Ibid.
9. Yehuda Dominitz, 'Immigration and Absorption of Jews from Arab Countries' in Malka Hillel Shulewitz (ed.) (Continuum, 1999), p.178.
10. Alain Gresh, 'Eric Rouleau, ambassador of the World', *The Cairo Review*, 11 October 2015, http://www.thecairoreview.com/tahrir-forum/eric-rouleau-ambassador-of-the-world. Last accessed 26 April 2017).
11. Interview with *Sephardi Voices UK*.
12. Feuerlicht, *The Fate of the Jews* (Quartet, 1988), p.231.
13. 'Challenging Naiem Giladi's farrago of lies', *Point of No Return*, 15 June 2010, http://jewishrefugees.blogspot.co.uk/2010/06/challenging-naieem-giladis-farrago-of.html. (Last accessed 26 April 2017).
14. Elie Kedourie, (Cohen and Udovitch (eds)), *The Break between Muslims and Jews in Iraq* (Darwin, 1989), p.55.
15. Tom Segev, 'Now it can be told', *Haaretz*, 6 April 2006, http://www.haaretz.com/now-it-can-be-told-1.184724. (Last accessed 26 April 2017).
16. Benny Morris video lecture, 27 August 2009.
17. Yaacov Meron, 'Why Jews fled Arab Countries', *Middle East Quarterly*, Vol. 2. No. 3, 1995, pp.47–55, http://www.meforum.org/263/why-jews-fled-the-arab-countries. (Last accessed 26 April 2017).
18. N. Weinstock, *Une si longue présence* (Plon, 2008), p.314.
19. M. Ben-Porat, *To Baghdad and Back* (Gefen, 1998), p.180.
20. Laskier, *Jews of Egypt* (NY University, 1992), p.188.

21. Roumani, *Jews of Libya* (Sussex Academic Press, 2008), p.52.

22. Bensoussan, *Juifs en pays arabes: Le grand déracinement 1850–1975* (Paris: Tallandier, 2012), p.235.

23. Georges Bensoussan, *Juifs du monde arabe* (Paris: Odile Jacob, 2017), p.39.

24. 'The truth about Morocco: fear made Jews leave', *Point of No Return*, 11 September 2016, http://jewishrefugees.blogspot.co.uk/2016/09/the-truth-about-morocco-fear-made-jews.html. (Last accessed 26 April 2017).

25. See 'The longest ten minutes' by Rami Mangoubi, *Jerusalem Post*, Appendices.

26. For more information on Arab familism see Raphael Patai, *The Arab Mind* (Hatherleigh, NY, 2002), p.300.

27. Mark Cohen asserts that stricter schools of Islam such as the Malikite hold the view that Muslims should not impose collective retribution for one person's violation of the (*Dhimmi*) Pact if the other non-Muslims repudiate the act or are found to have transgressed under compulsion. Cohen argues that mob assaults on an entire Jewish community are extremely rare (*Under Crescent and Cross* (Princeton 1994), p.74). Nowadays this view does seem questionable.

28. Address to European Parliament, October 2016, https://www.youtube.com/watch?v=uwN1WuDwIf0. (Last accessed 26 April 2017).

29. Abitbol, *Le passé d'une discorde Juifs et arabes depuis le VIIe siècle* (Paris: Perrin, 2003), p.37.

30. '1947 Aden Riots', *Wikipedia* (Russian), (http://yavix.ru/%7B+(%3E%D1%81%D0%B0%D0%B9%D1%82%3C=%3E[%3Ehttp:%E2%95%B1%E2%95%B1en.wikipedia.org%E2%95%B1wiki%E2%95%B11947_Aden_riots%3C]%3C)+%7D. (Last accessed 26 April 2017).

31. J. Beinin, *The Dispersion of Egyptian Jewry: Culture, Politics, and the Formation of a Modern Diaspora* (Berkeley, CA: University of California Press, 1998), p.35.

32. N. Stillman. *Jews of Arab Lands in Modern Times* (Philadelphia, PA: Jewish Publication Society of America, 1979), Vol. II, p.46.

33. Elie Kedourie, *The Chatham House Version* (New York: Praeger, 1970), p.295.

34. Margaret Brearley, 'The forgotten Genocide', *Jewish Quarterly*, Summer 2006, no. 202, p.29.

35. 'Armenians massacred Azeri Jews', *Point of No Return*, 24 May 2006, http://jewishrefugees.blogspot.co.uk/2006/05/armenians-massacred-azeri-mountain.html. (Last accessed 26 April 2017).

36. Shlomo Hillel, *Operation Babylon* (London: Collins, 1988), p.148.

37. M. Fischbach, *Jewish Property Claims against Arabs* (Columbia University Press, 2008).

38. Abbas Shiblak, *Iraqi Jews* (Saqi, 2005), p.25.

39. Meir-Glitzenstein, *Zionism in an Arab Country* (Routledge, 2004), p.253.

40. See full text of Arab League draft law p.131.

41. Ben-Dror Yemini, *Maariv*, 2 February 2014.

42. The full text of the Balfour Declaration can be read here: http://www.jewishvirtuallibrary.org/text-of-the-balfour-declaration. (Last accessed 26 April 2017).

43. Richard Mather, 'Expulsion: Islam's solution. The forgotten Nakba', *Jewish Media Agency*, 16 May 2015.

44. Yaakov Meron, 'Why Jews fled the Arab countries', *Middle East Quarterly*, September 1995, pp.47–55, http://www.meforum.org/263/why-jews-fled-the-arab-countries. (Last accessed 26 April 2017).

45. Ibid.

46. Ibid.

47. Dr Stanley A. Urman, 'The United Nations and Middle East refugees: the differing treatment of Palestinians and Jews', excerpt from unpublished PhD dissertation (Rutgers University). The draft of the *Text of Law Drafted by the Political Committee of the Arab League* was discovered affixed to a 19 January 1948 Memorandum submitted by the World Jewish Congress to the UN Economic and Social Council (ECOSOC) warning that, 'all Jews residing in the Near and Middle East face extreme and imminent danger'.

48. *Al-Kifah*, 28 March 1949, today a weekly magazine in Lebanon.

49. 'Baroud proposes amending law for Jewish Lebanese', *Daily Star*, 28 April 2009, http://www.dailystar.com.lb/News/Lebanon-News/2009/Apr-28/53032-baroud-proposes-amending-law-for-jewish-lebanese.ashx. (Last accessed 26 April 2017).

50. I. Cotler, D. Matas, S. Urman, 'Jewish Refugees from Arab Countries: the Case for Rights and Redress', *Justice for Jews from Arab Countries* (JJAC, 2007).

51. Moreh, *Al-Farhud*, p.143.

52. I. Cotler, D. Matas, S. Urman, 'Jewish Refugees from Arab Countries: the Case for Rights and Redress', p.16, http://web.archive.org/web/20110716153155/http://www.justiceforjews.com/jjac.pdf. (Last accessed 26 April 2017).

53. G. Bensoussan, *Akadem*, June 2012.

54. Dr G. Bechor, *G Planet*, 29 April 2012, http://www.gplanet.co.il/prodetailsamewin.asp?pro_id=1670. (Last accessed 26 April 2017).

55. Moshe Gat, *The Jewish Exodus from Iraq* (London: Frank Cass, 1997), p.18.

56. These included riots and protests over the Anglo-Iraqi Portsmouth Treaty.

57. See Moshe Gat, *The Jewish Exodus from Iraq*, p. 41.

58. Heskel Haddad, *Flight from Babylon* (Mcgraw-Hill, 1986), p.176.

59. N Stillman, Summary by British Ambassador of this decisive parliamentary debate, in *The Jews of Arab Lands in Modern Times*, Vol II, p.522.

60. Mordechai Ben-Porat, *To Baghdad and Back* (Jerusalem, 1998), p.80.

61. See, for example, 'The last Jews of Iraq', Morad Shasha and Shasha (eds) for personal testimonies of this era.

62. JJAC. See Appendix.

63. N. Stillman, ' The Moroccan Jewish Experience', in *The Legacy of Islamic Antisemitism*, Andrew G Bostom (ed.) (Prometheus, 2008), p.551.

64. Robert Satloff, *Among the Righteous* (New York: Public Affairs, 2006), p.61.

65. Revd J.W. Brooks, *History of the Hebrew Nation (1841)*.

66. Ibid., p.98.

67. The book was published in an English version as *Exile in the Maghreb: Jews under Islam, Sources and Documents 997–1912* (Rowan and Littlefield, 2016).

68. Professor Paul Fenton, London lecture, 'Exile in the Maghreb', 13 December 2015. Summary in *Point of No Return*, http://jewishrefugees.blogspot.co.uk/2014/10/the-curious-case-of-moroccan-marranos.html. (Last accessed 26 April 2017).

69. Lyn Julius, 'When the Jews sheltered with the sultan's lions', *Times of Israel*, April 2012, http://blogs.timesofisrael.com/when-the-jews-sheltered-with-the-sultans-lions/. (Last accessed 26 April 2017).

70. Assaraf, *Une certaine histoire des juifs du Maroc* (Gawsewitch, 1998), p.352.

71. Saïd Ghallab, *Les juifs vont en enfer* (1965).

72. Boum, *Memories of Absence*, p.148.

73. Weinstock, *Une si longue présence* (Paris: Mille et Une Nuits, 2004), p.147.

74. See Assaraf, *Une Certaine histoire des juifs du Maroc*, (Paris: Gawsewitch, 2005), pp.578–82.

75. Comment at Ron Gerlitz,'Why Morocco can be a model for Jewish-Arab partnership', *+972 magazine*, 18 April 2016, http://972mag.com/morocco-a-model-for-jewish-arab-

partnership/118649/?fb_comment_id=fbc_1064561640267830_1064868626903798_106
4868626903798#f15c2f240fac626. (Last accessed 26 April 2017).

76. Lela Gilbert, 'The Nakba of Morocco's Jews', *Jerusalem Post*, 28 April 2010,
http://www.jpost.com/Features/In-Thespotlight/The-Nakba-of-Moroccos-Jews. (Last
accessed 26 April 2017).

77. See Boum, *Memories of Absence* (Stanford, CA: Stanford University Press, 2013), p.107.

78. Ibid., p.90.

79. Nonetheless, Jews desperate to leave at times abandoned their assets, put them in the
hands of less-than-honest lawyers, or sold property at rock bottom prices. (Indeed, a
film by Moroccan Muslim Younes Laghrari and produced by Simon Skira, *Les destins
contrariés*, (http://lavieeco.com/news/culture/les-destins-contraries-des-juifs-marocains-
33170.html) interviews a Jewish man who got rich on the back of fleeing Jews.) (Last
accessed 26 April 2017).

80. See Assaraf, *Une certaine histoire des juifs du Maroc*, p.737.

81. 'Le Maroc enterre trente ans d'arabisation pour retourner au français', *Le Monde Afrique*,
19 February 2016, http://www.lemonde.fr/afrique/article/2016/02/19/maroc-le-roi-
mohamed-vi-enterre-trente-ans-d-arabisation-pour-retourner-au-francais_4868524_32
12.html#jwAu2xsWxhcgWpSf.99. (Last accessed 26 April 2017).

82. Xavier Cornut, 'The Moroccan Connection' *Jerusalem Post*, 22 June 2009, http://
www.jpost.com/Features/The-Moroccan-connection. (Last accessed 26 April 2017).

83. See Boum, *Memories of Absence*, p.155.

84. Anne Cohen, 'Honoring the Moroccan king who saved Jews', *The Forward*, 22 December
2015, http://forward.com/news/breaking-news/327772/honoring-the-moroccan-king-
who-saved-the-jews/. (Last accessed 26 April 2017).

85. See Boum, *Memories of Absence*, p.164.

86. Ibid., p.126.

87. Marc Perelman, 'From royal advisors to far-left militants, Moroccan Jews embody
coexistence', *The Forward*, 10 October 2007, http://forward.com/news/11792/from-royal-
advisers-to-far-left-militants-morocca-00611/. (Last accessed 26 April 2017).

88. 'Morocco's Holocaust recognition rare in Islam', AP, 25 July 2009, http://www.
nbcnews.com/id/32147263/ns/world_news-mideast_n_africa/t/moroccos-holocaust-
recognition-rare-islam/#.WPoljlOGNE5. (Last accessed 26 April 2017).

89. See Arie Tepper, 'Toward a pluralistic Middle East', *Jewish Ideas Daily*, 17 March 2011,
http://www.jewishideasdaily.com/844/features/toward-a-pluralistic-middle-east/.(Last
accessed 26 April 2017).

90. 'Three-quarters of Jews are thinking of leaving Morocco', *Point of No Return*, 12 June
2011, http://jewishrefugees.blogspot.co.il/2011/06/three-quarters-of-moroccan-jews-
think.html, (Last accessed 26 April 2017).

91. See Satloff, *Among the Righteous*, p.177.

7

Jewish Refugees: Forgotten No More?

If there have been more Jewish refugees from Arab countries since 1948 than Palestinian Arab refugees from Israel[1] how does one explain the almost complete absence of the Jewish refugee issue from the international peace agenda?

One reason is that Jewish refugees have never been on the radar of the United Nations – the international body charged with protecting, resettling and rehabilitating refugees since the Second World War. Of 289 Security Council resolutions, ten have dealt with Palestinian refugees, none with Jewish refugees. Of 1,088 UN General Assembly resolutions dealing with the Arab-Israeli conflict, 172 mention Palestinian refugees. None mentions Jewish refugees.[2]

Why is this? To quote the organisation Justice for Jews from Arab Countries, the UN has played a 'pernicious and prejudicial' role by systematically excluding the narrative of Jewish refugees or by exclusively identifying only Palestinian refugee rights and redress.[3]

Yemeni Jews bound for Israel walked to Aden to join the 'Operation Wings of Eagles' airlift in 1949.

From an early stage in the conflict, the UN was co-opted by the powerful Arab-Muslim voting bloc to skew its mandate and defend the rights of only one refugee population – the Palestinians. The UN dedicated an agency, UNWRA, to the exclusive care of Palestinian refugees.[4] There are ten UN agencies solely concerned with Palestinian refugees. These even define refugee status for the Palestinians explicitly: one that stipulates that status depends on 'two years' residence' in Palestine.[5] The definition makes no mention of 'fear of persecution' nor of resettlement. Palestinian refugees are the only refugee population in the world, out of 65 million recognised refugees,[6] permitted to pass on their refugee status to succeeding generations, even if they enjoy citizenship in their adoptive countries. It is estimated that the current population of Palestinian 'refugees' is 5,493, million. Instead of resettlement, they demand 'repatriation', an Israeli red line.[7] This evidence clearly implies that the UN mandate is to perpetuate, not resolve the Palestinian refugee problem.

In contrast to the $17.7 billion allocated to the Palestinian refugees, no international aid has been earmarked for Jewish refugees. The exception was a $30,000 grant in 1957 which the UN, fearing protests from its Muslim members, did not want publicised. The grant was eventually converted into a loan and paid back by the American Joint Distribution Committee, the main agency caring for Jews in distress.[8]

Yet on two occasions the UN did determine that Jews fleeing Egypt and North Africa were *bona fide* refugees. In 1957, the UN High Commissioner for Refugees, August Lindt, declared that the Jews of Egypt who were 'unable or unwilling to avail themselves of the protection of the government of their nationality' fell within his remit. In July 1967,-the UNHCR recognised Jews fleeing Libya as refugees under the UNHCR mandate.[9]

For any peace process to be credible and enduring, the international community would be expected to address the rights of all Middle East refugees, including Jewish refugees displaced from Arab countries. Two victim populations arose out of the Arab-Israeli conflict, and the Arab leadership bears responsibility for needlessly causing both *Nakbas* – the Jewish and the Arab. As the human rights lawyer Irwin Cotler observes: 'Put simply, if the Arab leadership had accepted the UN Partition Resolution of 1947, there would have been no refugees, Arab or Jewish.'[10]

Following the Six Day War, Resolution 242, adopted by the UN Security Council in November 1967, stated that a comprehensive agreement would be necessary for achieving 'a just settlement of the refugee problem'.[11] Arthur Goldberg, the US ambassador to the UN, and architect of the resolution, wrote that 'this language presumably refers both to Arab and Jewish refugees, for about an equal number of each abandoned their homes as a result of the several wars'.

Children celebrating the festival of TuB'shvat at the Rosh Ha'yayin transit camp, 1950 (Zoltan-Kluger/Israel Government Press Office)

Refugees collect their new Israeli passports.

The Pardes Hana transit camp (Teddy Brauner/Israel Government Press Office)

UNSC 2334 of December 2016 departs from this balanced position by evoking the Arab Peace Initiative as a basis for a peace settlement. This document has a one-sided agenda calling only for a resolution of the Palestinian refugee problem, thus negating Jewish rights. On 27 October 1977, US President Carter stated that the Jewish refugees 'have the same rights as others do'. And, on 3 June 2005, Canadian Prime Minister Paul Martin declared that 'a refugee is a refugee and that the situation of Jewish refugees from Arab lands must be recognised'.[12]

The Failed Iraqi Exchange

In July 1949, in an early attempt to tie the plight of both sets of refugees together, Iraqi Prime Minister Nuri al-Said suggested a 'voluntary exchange' between the Jewish and Palestinian Arab populations. Although transfers were common in conflicts of the latter twentieth century, this was the only scheme proposed for the Arab-Israeli conflict.[13] From the end of the first Arab-Israeli war in 1949, Iraq suggested to the United Nations and American and British officials that more than 100,000 Iraqi Jews could be transferred to Israel in exchange for the same number of Arab Palestinians. Al-Said backed up his words with a scarcely-veiled threat. If Iraqi Jews were not shipped out, he said, 'firebrand Iraqis', incensed by the creation of a Zionist state, 'might take matters into their own hands and cause untold misery to thousands of innocent persons'.[14] Nuri al-Said's threat generated an unstoppable momentum.[15]

The Jews of Iraq – settled in the country since Biblical times but increasingly being driven from their jobs and treated as if they had no right to be there – were now seen as 'pawns and hostages to ... allow Nuri to appear as champion of the Palestinian Arabs'.[16] The outside powers, too, cynically viewed the Iraqi Jews as useful pawns for resolving the Israeli-Arab conflict.

The Israeli foreign minister, Moshe Sharrett, initially refused any possible linkage between the two sets of refugees. And, as the Jewish exodus got underway, Levi Eshkol, treasurer of the Jewish Agency, told the Zionist Underground in Baghdad that they must not rush: Israel did not have enough tents. 'If they come, they'd have to live on the street', he said.[17] As it happened, the airlifts did not begin until May 1950[18] and could not cope with the volume of de-nationalised, would-be emigrants, many of whom were still waiting to leave Iraq more than one year later.

In 1950, Israel toyed with the idea of exchanging Palestinians for Libyan Jews. This came to nothing. By 1956, Israel was close to buying 100,000 *dunums* of land in Libya for resettling 17,000 Palestinian refugees. In return, the refugees would drop all compensation claims against Israel.[19] Nothing came of this either.

Meanwhile, it was with more than a hint of malice that the Iraqi government permitted the mass denationalisation – or *Taskeet* – of stateless Iraqi Jews. The plan had originally been to dump the Jews on struggling Israel's borders, in the knowledge that the fledgling state would be brought to the brink of economic collapse. The Iraqis were persuaded by the British to drop the plan.[20]

The transfer proved incomplete – almost 120,000 Iraqi Jews went to Israel when the immigration ban was lifted in March 1950. But it was re-imposed one year later. Only 14,000 Palestinian Arabs arrived in Iraq. The Iraqi Parliament delivered the last twist of the knife on 10 March 1951 by freezing Iraqi-Jewish property and assets: 70,000 Jews, stranded in Iraq, were left destitute.[21] Just before the law came into force, the banks shut for three days to prevent Jews from doing any last-minute selling. In the end, after attempts to salvage the property of the Jewish community in Iraq failed, Israel's Foreign Minister Moshe Sharett announced in the Knesset on 19 March 1951: 'By freezing the property of tens of thousands of Jewish immigrants to Israel ... the government of Iraq invited a reckoning between itself and the State of Israel. An account already existed between us and the Arabs regarding compensation due to Arabs who left the territory of Israel ...'[22]

Offsetting Losses on Both Sides

At first, Israel refused to compare the two sets of refugees, viewing them as morally distinct. In a letter sent to the UN's Reconciliation Commission in 1951, Foreign Ministry Director General Walter Eytan stated that:

> the Palestinian Arabs who left the country and abandoned their property in 1948 joined hands with the neighbouring Arab countries

in attacking the Jewish state, with the declared objective of destroying the Jewish community and preventing the establishment of the state. The case of Iraqi Jews is entirely different: They were not involved in any act of aggression against the government or the Iraqi people.[23]

Contrary to popular belief, Israel did not ignore the exodus. The fact that there is not one recorded UN resolution on Jewish refugees is 'not for lack of trying'.[24] Israel tried to incorporate the issue of Jewish refugees into its foreign policy in order to neutralise pressure brought to bear on the issue of the Arab refugees. Several proposals were advanced but never got off the ground, including an audacious plan for parity to be achieved on the basis of population density. The plan proposed that Iraqi Jewry was entitled to a 'share' of Iraq's national patrimony based on its percentage within the population.[25]

Later, Israel developed a policy of *kizzuz* – offsetting lost Jewish assets against Palestinian losses. *Kizzuz* was the dark cloud hovering over any concerted efforts by Jewish refugees to seek compensation. *Kizzuz* meant that, if losses cancelled each other out, individual Jewish refugees would get nothing.

Some warned that simmering ethnic tensions would explode if the Sephardi/Mizrahi Jews – whom the Ashkenazi establishment had dispatched to transit camps, and then the development towns of the periphery – were left empty-handed. Officials countered that, since Israel had spent millions absorbing the Mizrahi and Sephardi Jews, they could hardly consider themselves short-changed by Israel. But this argument could hardly wash with Jewish refugees who settled outside the Jewish state. 'What has the Israeli government got to do with me?' snorted Naim Dangoor, the businessman and philanthropist who fled Iraq for Britain as a refugee.[26]

One of the first to highlight the injustice of such a policy was Yehouda Shenhav, a sociology professor of Iraqi descent at Tel Aviv University. 'The property of the Jews of the Middle East is not a matter for the State of Israel. They are manipulating me for an ulterior motive', he argued.[27] Shenhav's answer to the problem was for individual refugees to take legal action against Arab governments. There was one major flaw with this approach, however. It was difficult, but not unknown, for Jews now resident in Britain or France to sue the government of Egypt, for example. But not a single Jewish refugee from an Arab country now living in Israel has managed to bring a court case against an Arab government, although David Nawi, an Israeli lawyer, attempted to bring a class action against Iraq in the aftermath of the US invasion.[28] And so individuals suspended their claims in order to allow the Israel government to handle the matter of confiscated or stolen properties on their behalf.

For some fifty years the Israeli government dithered, ducked and dived on the Jewish refugee issue, saying it was not the right time to deal with it.[29] The Palestinians made exorbitant demands for compensation by Israel.[30] They denied any linkage between Jewish and Palestinian assets. On the claims of Jewish refugees from Arab countries, Israel had to negotiate directly with the Arab states, they declared. With the prospect of final status talks looming after the signing of the Oslo accords, the Israeli government undertook a campaign in 1999 to persuade Jewish refugees from Arab countries to register their property claims.

The International Fund

In 2000, however, the *kizzuz* approach appeared dead in the water, superseded by the notion of actual compensation to individual refugees. The catalyst was the Camp David talks brokered by the US between Israel and the Palestinians, when President Bill Clinton hosted a summit attended by Prime Minister Ehud Barak and Palestinian Authority Chairman Yasser Arafat. Clinton was asked by an Israeli interviewer about the matter of Jewish refugees. 'If there is an agreement ... there will have to be some sort of international fund set up for the refugees', he said, adding, 'There is, I think, some interest, interestingly enough, on both sides, in also having a fund which compensates the Israelis who were made refugees by the war, which occurred after the birth of the State of Israel. Israel is full of people, Jewish people, who lived in predominantly Arab countries who came to Israel because they were made refugees in their own lands.'[31] The principle was that both Israel and the Arab states would contribute to a fund of perhaps $10 billion, but the lion's share would come from the international community – namely the US. The Clinton proposal had a precedent: in 1991, Kuwaiti, Iraqi and Israeli victims of SCUD missile attacks were compensated from an international fund.[32]

The proposed Clinton international fund has injected new life into the campaign for Justice for Jewish refugees. Organisations representing Jewish refugees have embraced, with enthusiasm, the prospect of individual refugees receiving compensation payments, just as Holocaust survivors have done. The fund has the advantage of promising compensation to the hundreds of thousands of Jewish refugees from Arab countries now resident outside Israel. However, it remains to be seen whether descendants of refugees will be able to benefit.

Israel's Greatest Blunder

Until recently, the Israeli government could be accused of doing the bare minimum for Jewish refugees from Arab and Muslim countries. When the

1979 peace treaty between Israel and Egypt incorporated the idea of a Claims Commission (Article VIII) so that both sides could settle their claims, Israel passed up on the opportunity. The issue became entangled in fears that the Egyptians would demand compensation for Israel's exploitation of the Abu Rudeis oil fields in Sinai.

Given the centrality of the refugee issue to the Arab-Israeli conflict, the journalist and writer Adi Schwartz has labelled Israel's prolonged silence 'incomprehensible'. Tommy Lapid, who served as Justice Minister, recognised the long-term damage from Israel's failure to make an issue of Jewish refugees; it has helped perpetuate the myth that the Jews were the aggressors and dispossessors, and not the other way around, with all that this implies for Israel's legitimacy. He has described the failure 'to play the refugee card' as 'one of the greatest blunders made in the state's history'.[33]

The reasons why a major national trauma affecting over 50 per cent of Israel's Jews has been swept under the carpet are many and complex. Firstly, Israel has a fundamental difference in approach to the Arabs – one of, 'We'll discuss this issue when we come to it.' The Arabs, in contrast, talk about rights and justice while the Israeli approach has always been pragmatic – a flexible one signalling that they are prepared to make 'painful concessions'. To the outside observer this approach has always made Israel seem on the defensive and given the impression that the Palestinians hold the moral high ground. This perception has been aggravated by the fact many Israeli media and intellectuals have embraced the Arab narrative. This narrative has narrowed the conflict to the Israel-Palestinian dispute and excluded the larger Arab context in which the expulsion of the Jewish refugees from Arab countries is central. It also casts the Palestinians as innocent victims who are able to ask the question, 'What did we have to do with the expulsion of Jews from Arab lands?'

Secondly, the Israeli Foreign Ministry has balked at raising the topic of Jewish refugees since it has feared bringing the Palestinian refugee issue to the fore. But even as Israel has remained silent, the Arab side has never ceased to raise the issue of the 'catastrophic' *Nakba*.[34]

Thirdly, the problem was essentially solved: Jewish refugees were successfully absorbed. No Jew still considers himself a refugee. The very act of calling the Jews from Arab countries 'refugees' is somewhat at variance with the core of Israel's national ethos. Despite all the *push* factors, from a Zionist perspective, these Jews were coming home. Former Knesset member Ran Cohen, who was born in Iraq, was quoted as saying: 'No one is going to define me as a refugee ... I came at the behest of Zionism, due to the pull that [Israel] exerts.'[35] In 2001, the organisation Justice for Jews from Arab Countries (JJAC) sent a delegation to the US state department to lobby for Jewish refugee rights, only to be told: they are no longer refugees – they went to Israel.[36] But under international human rights law, JJAC affirms, there is no statute of limitations on Jewish refugee rights.

Arab Responses

Paradoxically, some of the voices that called for recognition of the injustice done to Jewish refugees came from within the Arab world itself. Leading Palestine Liberation Organisation (PLO) official Sabri Jiryis pointedly criticised the Arab states for expelling the Jews 'in a most ugly fashion, and after confiscating their possessions or taking control thereof at the lowest price.'[37] He added that 'clearly, Israel will raise the question in all serious negotiations that may in time be conducted over the rights of the Palestinians'. Egyptian journalist Nabil Sharaf Eldin wrote:[38] 'we owe our Egyptian Jewish brothers a historic apology for the injustice we caused them, for causing a community, whose roots in the land of Egypt go back to the prophet Musa [Moses] ... to disappear.'

In other words, Jiryis was endorsing the concept of the 'exchange of populations'. Not many agreed with him. An exchange would undermine the Palestinian's immutable objective of a Right of Return to Israel, a principle on which they have consistently said they will never compromise. Realising that the existence of Jewish refugees would expose the weakness in their argument for a Right of Return, the Palestinian national covenant of 1964 (amended in 1968) expressed the idea of sending Jews back to their lands of origin.[39]

In all international blueprints for peace, the two refugee populations are inextricably linked. From 1967, the parameters of a peace settlement have been outlined in UN Security Council 242. The resolution refers to a just solution to the 'refugee problem' without specifying whether the refugees are Arab or Jewish. One of the resolution's drafters, US ambassador to the UN Arthur Goldberg, fought a Russian move to insert the word 'Palestinian' before 'refugees'.

The 1991 Madrid Peace Conference created a Working Group on Refugees whose mandate was to 'consider practical ways of improving the lot of people throughout the region who have been displaced from their homes' – generic language applicable to both Palestinian and Jewish refugees. The 2002 Road Map to Middle East Peace also refers in Phase III to an 'agreed, just, fair and realistic solution to the refugee issue', language applicable both to Palestinian and Jewish refugees.[40]

In 2002, the Saudi Peace Initiative offered 'normalisation' to Israel but demanded that the Palestinian refugee problem be resolved in accordance with UN General Assembly Resolution 194. UN Resolution 194 called for a diplomatic resolution to the conflict and resolves that any refugees 'wishing to return to their homes and live at peace with their neighbours' should be able to do so or, if they otherwise wish, should be provided with compensation.' The initiative is understood to refer exclusively to Palestinian refugees. The Israeli response has been to take 'a return to their homes' to mean 'a Palestinian Right of Return', historically an Israeli red line.[41]

When, in the 1970s, the Arab countries realised they could not demand a unilateral Right of Return without offering the same to their ex-Jews, one Arab country after another invited back their former Jewish citizens (except the Zionists among them).[42] In 1975, Farouk Kaddoumi of the PLO said the Jews were 'welcome to return to exercise their full rights'. An Iraqi broadcast followed the next day and, two weeks later, advertisements appeared in major Western newspapers. Libya in 1970 and again in 1973, along with Sudan and Egypt in 1975, all issued invitations. The Jews dismissed the invitations as a 'propaganda move.'[43]

Israel: 'They were Zionist immigrants'

In addition to the reasons given above for minimal recognition of Jewish refugee status, Israel thought that to raise the Jewish refugee issue would be socially divisive. The country's main task was to integrate refugees from 120 countries, and not to privilege one particular group over another. This explains why it painted all refugees as 'Zionist immigrants'. Israel did not want to drive a wedge between arrivals from different ethnic groups, *ie* unleash 'an ethnic demon' – it wanted to create a new Israeli citizen. The country wanted its new citizens not to be obsessed with the past, but engaged in building a new future in their ancestral homeland. The submissive and apologetic diaspora Jew would be transformed into a proud and virile, Hebrew-speaking Israeli. This policy broadly paid off – intermarriage between Ashkenazim and Mizrahim is over 25 per cent and barriers between ethnic groups are rapidly breaking down – but Israel has paid a high price for integration in terms of justice for the aggrieved refugees, world public opinion and public diplomacy. Ultimately, its policy can be said to have set back the cause of peace and justice, by allowing distortions and misconceptions to go unchallenged.

Moreover, it is often said that the Jewish refugees from Arab lands themselves found that their story had to take a back seat to that of the Holocaust survivors. After all, the Mizrahim had suffered, but at least they had got out alive. Others thought it was beneath their dignity to re-visit the humiliation they had been through. They had a sense that they were victims, but no longer refugees. Besides, they were busy building new lives for themselves. Why dredge up the past?

This was also the reaction among refugees who did not go to Israel. The French author Colette Fellous writes about her parents, who left Tunis in 1967:

> My father never spoke about our break with the past. He arrived in Paris aged 61, a few months after my mother, abandoning a country

where his ancestors had lived for centuries. In a few months, he was compelled to join his children in France, he had had to abandon his lifestyle, his job, his home, his habits, his music, his landscape, and most importantly, his shop, his 'whole life' – as he put it. Neither he nor my mother ever uttered a word about the great uprooting; they never complained. They always wore that same embarrassed smile, as if they sought not to disturb anyone, not to burden anyone, even when things were going really badly. It was a disarming smile which still makes me shudder.[44]

With the passage of time, however, suppression of their story has given way to frustration and a desire for recognition, particularly among the children and grandchildren of refugees. There has been a maturation process similar to that experienced by Holocaust survivors, and the refugees are now ready to tell their stories.

Interviewed for the *Jerusalem Post*, 'Meir from Tunis' says:

My father had been a jeweller. He had two stores and we lived well … My parents hadn't wanted to leave Tunis. They had no choice. They were afraid, like all the Jews were … We went from wealth to nothing … After a few years [in France] we came to Israel.

[My parents] never talked about their fears, and they never talked about how bitter and sad their lives were. But as a child, I could tell. We were refugees … and when we came to Israel, we tried to hide how poor we were. But now I understand, and even though my parents wouldn't talk about it, I want our story told.[45]

Another factor which has contributed to Israel's silence is that efforts were still going on until the 1990s (for example, in Syria) to rescue the beleaguered remnants of various Jewish communities. There were delicate negotiations going on behind the scenes to rescue these hostage Jews and any publicity would have made their plight worse.

During the Oslo years in the 1990s, the parties on the Israeli left in particular believed that the issue of Jewish refugees was a needless spanner in the peace works between Israel and the Palestinians, which they genuinely thought was just around the corner. Hence, Justice Minister Yossi Beilin of the Meretz party closed down the department dealing with property claims for Jews from Arab countries and ordered a room containing files to be moved to the basement. Subsequent justice ministers have realised that this was a serious mistake and re-opened the department, but the damage was done. Israel's state comptroller Joseph Shapira, investigating during the period of August 2012 to May 2013, found 'severe' deficiencies regarding the 'research, compiling, recording and gathering of information with regard to the rights of the Jewish refugees from Arab countries and Iran.'[46]

The scrappy and inadequate effort to collect claims has been compounded by the inability to access property records and documentation in Arab countries and Iran. Important documents and primary sources concerning decisions of the Arab League and the activities of Arab states in the 1940s and 1950s, as well as the precise registration of personal and communal property, are extremely difficult to come by –if not completely inaccessible.[47]

Over the years, immigrants from Iran and Arab states were instructed to fill in and submit forms aimed at enabling the coordination of both individual and communal claims. Between 1969 and 2009, the Justice Ministry collected around 14,000 forms, but they were never digitised. Some of the records are still in the Ministry's archive, waiting to be scanned digitally, but thousands have deteriorated so badly as to be worthless. The retirement of a single clerk who was in charge of the material at one point but did not train her successor is thought to have led to the disappearance of still more documents connected to the issue.[48]

A Question of Human Rights

Why, after years of neglect, has Israel now decided to dust off the cobwebs? The impetus can be said to have come from outside Israel. In 1975, The World Organisation for Jews from Arab Countries (WOJAC) was established to raise the banner for Jewish refugees.[49] WOJAC was an umbrella body founded by the leaders of organisations of Jews from Arab countries in Israel and overseas. It was headed by Mordechai Ben-Porat, an Israeli cabinet minister of Iraqi origin, and other Sephardi leaders.

In the early to mid-1970s, Israel witnessed a proliferation of organisations of Jewish immigrants from Arab and Islamic countries demanding proportionate representation in public and governmental institutions. WOJAC collected claims and documentation, but by 1999, its efforts were stagnating. The Israeli government withdrew its funding.

The case for Jewish refugees needed to be elaborated in the context of the post-Second World War emergence of human rights law. In 2001, Justice for Jews from Arab Countries (JJAC) was established, a coalition of nearly two-dozen North American and worldwide Jewish organisations, with its headquarters in the US. Its honorary vice-presidents were prominent figures in the Sephardi and diaspora Jewish community. With the help of a group of Canadian lawyers, led by ex-justice minister and international human rights lawyer Irwin Cotler, JJAC set out the legal case for Jewish refugees.[50] In 2003, a round of conferences, held worldwide in conjunction with the World Jewish Congress, introduced the predominantly Ashkenazi diaspora, hitherto unaware of the plight of Jewish refugees from Arab lands, to the cause. New bodies were founded to advocate for Jewish refugees – JIMENA in California and Harif in the UK. On 3 June 2005, Canadian Prime Minister Paul Martin declared that 'a refugee is a refugee and that the situation of Jewish refugees from Arab lands must be recognised'.[51]

In 2008, JJAC saw the first fruits of its lobbying efforts: the US Congress passed resolution 185, instructing the US government to ensure that official documents referring to Palestinian refugees include a 'similarly explicit reference' to Jewish refugees'.[52] In 2016, four congressmen introduced a bill to build on resolution 185: 'The Jewish Refugees Act'. This piece of legislation would call on the US President to report back on what progress had been made on the issue.

In March 2014,[53] Canadian Foreign Affairs Minister John Baird issued a statement after the House of Commons concurred with the recommendations in the report by the Standing Committee on Foreign Affairs and International Development to recognise the experience of Jewish refugees from the Middle East and North Africa after 1948: 'Fair and equal acknowledgement of all refugee populations arising out of the Arab-Israeli conflict requires the recognition of Jewish refugees. Such recognition does not diminish or compete with the situation of Palestinian refugees.' But Canada stopped short of calling for the Jewish refugees to be included in peace talks. 'The Government of Canada agrees in principle with the committee's second recommendation, that the experience of Jewish refugees should be taken into consideration as a part of any just and comprehensive

Harif, an association founded in the UK in 2005 to represent Middle Eastern and North African Jews, hold a demonstration in central London for minority rights.

peace deal, however, we believe that the peace process as it is currently structured offers the best hope for a positive solution.'

The Oslo Accords termed the issue of refugees a 'final status issue'. On 22 February 2010, the Israeli Knesset had passed a law unanimously stating that no Middle East peace agreement could be signed unless the issue of compensation for Jewish refugees from Arab countries and Iran for the loss of property, specifically the assets owned by the Jewish community in these countries, was addressed. The law was proposed by Nissim Zeev, MK for the Shas party, whose constituency is mostly Mizrahi ultra-orthodox. This was not the first law affirming Jewish rights – since 1957, the Knesset has passed sixteen laws and resolutions[54] – but it was the first to make a peace deal conditional on compensation for Jewish refugees.

Jewish Refugees: A Core Issue

The turning point in Israeli government thinking came with Prime Minister Benjamin Netanyahu's speech at Bar-Ilan University in June 2009, in which he accepted the two-state model as a basis for negotiations with the Palestinians. But in a rebuttal to President Obama's Cairo speech ten days earlier, linking the Holocaust to the Palestinian *Nakba*, Netanyahu pointedly mentioned that 'tiny Israel took in of hundreds of thousands of Jewish refugees who were uprooted from Arab countries.'[55]

Netanyahu's then-national security adviser Uzi Arad set up a task force of academics and government officials to formulate a new Israeli position

Prime minister Benjamin Netanyahu celebrates the Mimouna festival with Moroccan Jews in Kiryat Ata (Moshe Milner/Israel Government Press Office)

on the Jewish refugee issue. On 24 May 2011, the panel submitted its 'groundbreaking' recommendation that Jewish refugees be made a core issue in future talks with the Palestinians: Israeli negotiating strategy would be best served by linking the two refugee populations. The task force proposed that 'compensation for Jewish refugees be made an integral part of negotiations'; that Israel insist that both sets of refugees waive the right of return and accept compensation instead; and that it demand a 3:2 ratio in compensation to a 'higher number of Jewish refugees and greater assets lost.'[56] One journalist commented: 'The underlying idea was to take the sting out of the emotion-laden refugee issue by reducing it from unrealistic Palestinian demands for return to Israel proper, to pragmatic questions of financial compensation for both sets of refugees. So far no Palestinian leader has indicated the slightest readiness to accept a formula of this kind.'[57]

In 2012, the deputy foreign minister Danny Ayalon, whose father was born in Algeria, broke with the Israel Ministry of Foreign Affairs' customary mealy-mouthedness and convened a conference in Jerusalem entitled 'Justice for Jewish Refugees from Arab countries'. Ayalon's initiative was greeted with an almost daily stream of critical pieces in the press. He went on to arrange the 21 September 2012 UN conference to highlight the issue of Jewish refugees from Arab countries. It was criticised by Hamas spokesman, Sami Abu Zuhri, who stated that the Jewish refugees from Arab countries were, in fact, responsible for the Palestinian displacement and that 'those Jews are criminals rather than refugees'.[58]

Nonetheless, the campaign proceeded apace: Israel has held meetings to remember the plight of Jewish refugees at the UN every year since. The 2015 Knesset inaugurated a new Lobby for the recovery of Jewish property in Arab lands and one for the preservation of Jewish heritage.

In 2014, *The Economist*[59] carried its first piece about Jewish refugees; the films *Shadow in Baghdad* and the *Dove Flyer* brought home to mass audiences the tribulations suffered by Iraqi Jews. On 23 June 2014, the Knesset passed a law designating a new national commemoration day in the calendar – 30 November.[60] On or around this date in the calendar, Jewish organisations worldwide supplement the official commemorations in Israel with events of their own. The bill was proposed by Nissim Ze'ev of the Shas party, and shepherded through the Knesset by Shimon Ohayon of Yisrael Beteinu. In the summer of 2016, the Biton Committee, headed by the blind poet of North African descent Erez Biton, submitted its recommendations[61] for a greater focus on Mizrahi history, culture and heritage in the Israeli school curriculum.

In December 2016, the campaign reached a watershed when the Israeli minister for Social Equality, Gila Gamliel – of Libyan and Yemeni origin – allocated $2.6 million to a project to record the oral histories of Jews from the Middle East and North Africa. (There is also talk of establishing a national heritage centre.) Gamliel declared: 'This is not a uniquely Mizrahi interest but a national, Jewish and Zionist interest. From now on, the Jewish story will be more complete and Israeli citizens young and old will get to hear, study and become familiar with both the Eastern and Western sides of the glorious heritage of the Jewish people.'[62]

In March 2017, Hillel Neuer of NGO Watch rebuked the Arab states of the UN Human Rights Council in Geneva at a debate on 'Israeli apartheid': 'Where are your Jews?' he asked. The chamber sat in stunned silence.[63]

The Key to Peace?

Are the Jewish refugees an obstacle to peace – or the key to peace? It has been argued that the two refugee situations are asymmetrical in character, and that this must also be recognised.

Analysis, however, shows that they are only asymmetrical in the following way: one group of refugees has been resettled and is now made up of fully-fledged citizens of Israel and the West. The other group is, uniquely among the world's refugees, still confined sixty years later to camps (although these are now more like small towns). Its members depend on the UN agency UNWRA for support and, except in Jordan, are deprived of civil rights and the right to own property and to do certain jobs.

In 1959, the Arab League passed Resolution 1457: 'The Arab countries will not grant citizenship to applicants of Palestinian origin in order to prevent their assimilation into the host countries.'[64] Under the Refugee Convention, stateless people are technically refugees. However, this situation can be easily remedied by host Arab countries. Indeed, Palestinian refugees in Jordan have been granted Jordanian citizenship, Christian Palestinians have been granted Lebanese citizenship and Egyptian nationality has been granted to individuals with a Palestinian father and an Egyptian mother.[65] That is exactly why Jewish and Arab refugees should be compared: in the former case, Jews were absorbed, resettled and built new lives, making a vital contribution to Israeli culture and society. In the second case, the Palestinian refugees were allowed by the UN to pass on their refugee status in perpetuity, to the extent that the number of 'refugees' has ballooned from about 700,000 to over five million, only 30,000 of whom were born in Palestine. Not only does the existence of these Palestinians in a perpetual refugee limbo create an obstacle to peace, but to leave them in that state seems both supremely unnatural and an obscene abuse of their human rights for political purposes. Arab states need to be held to account for failing to do their humanitarian duty towards Palestinian refugees. They are not entitled to extract a political cost –a Right of Return to Israel. In that sense, the resettlement of the Jewish refugees is an object lesson to the Arab side. Granting citizenship to

Palestinian refugees would provide one of the building blocks of an independent Palestinian state.

According to Justice for Jews from Arab Countries, in international law, any human rights violation gives rise to a right to redress. The right belongs both to the victim and the beneficiaries of the victim. Even where the regimes are not those in place at the time the violations occurred, JJAC argues[66] that successor regimes should provide reparation to the victims. Arbitrary deprivation of property is itself a violation of a fundamental human right, forbidden by the Universal Declaration of Human Rights.

The Palestinian refugee problem was deliberately left unsolved. At the very least, a future Palestinian state in the West Bank and Gaza would be expected to welcome Palestinian refugees home and give them full civil rights. So far, the Palestinian leadership has refused to do this.[67] In 2014, the Palestinian president Mahmoud Abbas turned down an offer by Egyptian president el-Sisi to allocate a 618-square-mile area of Sinai for the absorption of Palestinian refugees.[68] Objectively-speaking, Palestinian Arabs ought to be easily integrated in host countries where people speak the same language, share the same culture and religion, and where their children were born.

The massive Syrian refugee crisis contrasts with the Palestinian anomaly. Whereas the international community has mobilised, not only to give refuge to fleeing civilians, but to provide education and jobs in order to ensure their long-term settlement is successful, the Palestinian refugees are still treated as Israel's issue, to be resolved politically.

If anything, the current campaign demanding equivalence between the two sets of refugees does a disservice to the uprooted Jews. There is a difference between Palestinian Arabs fleeing a war zone and Jewish civilians forced to flee as a result of being specifically targeted by the threat of violence and state-sanctioned persecution. Apart from enduring dispossession, humiliation, arrest, torture and murder, the Jews lost their entire civilisation, their Judeo-Arabic language and much of their culture. Their displacement was on a larger scale than that of the Palestinians, and their material losses were greater. Whereas Arab refugees fled a war which Arab leaders had instigated, the Jews were victims of unpredictable violence and a deliberate legislative policy scapegoating them for being Jews. The proof is in the pudding: 1.4 million Arabs[69] live in Israel today, whereas fewer than 4,500 Jews from a 1948 population of one million live in Arab countries. [70]

So why did the 2008 US Congressional bill 185 demand equivalence for the two sets of refugees if it's not fair to the Jews? The answer is that the Palestinian issue has held unchallenged sway on the agenda for so long that the Jews are forced to 'play catch-up'.

Advocates for Jewish rights do not seek to delegitimise Palestinian claims, but it is a feature of the prevailing discourse that Jewish refugee rights are dismissed as an impediment to peace, denigrated or ignored, while Arab rights – including the much-vaunted Right of Return – are put on a pedestal. There is no reason for well-meaning but fundamentally ill-informed commentators to privilege Palestinian rights, while dismissing the rights of Jewish refugees.

Notes

1. According to UN figures, there were 726,000 Palestinian refugees, http://web. archive.org/web/20110716153155/http://www.justiceforjews.com/jjac.pdf. (Last accessed 26 April 2017).
2. Stanley Urman PhD, 'The United Nations and Middle Eastern Refugees: the differing treatment of Palestinians and Jews', http://www.justiceforjews.com/stan_phd.pdf. (Last accessed 26 April 2017).
3. Cotler, Matas, Urman 'The case for rights and redress' (JJAC report, 2004), p.7.
4. According to Don Peretz ('Who is a refugee?', *The Palestine – Israel Journal*, Vol. 2 no. 4, 1995, http://www.pij.org/details.php?id=592) initially UNRWA defined a refugee 'as a needy person who, as a result of the war in Palestine, has lost his home and his means of livelihood'. This definition included some 17,000 Jews who had lived in areas of Palestine taken over by Arab forces during the 1948 war and about 50,000 Arabs living within Israel's armistice frontiers. Israel took responsibility for these individuals, and by 1950 they were removed from the UNRWA rolls leaving only Palestine Arabs and a few hundred non-Arab Christian Palestinians outside Israel in UNRWA's refugee category.
5. UNWRA, 'Who is a Palestinian refugee?', https://www.unrwa.org/palestine-refugees. (Last accessed 26 April 2017).
6. 'UNHCR displaced peoples' report, 20 June 2016, http://edition.cnn.com/2016/06/20/ world/unhcr-displaced-peoples-report/. (Last accessed 26 April 2017).
7. See Peretz, 'Who is a refugee?'
8. Stan Urman of JJAC, transcript of speech at House of Commons, March 2014, http://jewishrefugees.blogspot.co.uk/2014/03/peace-without-refugee-recognition-wont.html. (Last accessed 26 April 2017).
9. Cotler, Matas, Urman, 'Jewish Refugees from Arab Countries: the case for rights and redress', *JJAC report*, 5 November 2004, p.3, http://web.archive.org/web/20110716153155/ http://www.justiceforjews.com/jjac.pdf. (Last accessed 26 April 2017).
10. Ibid., p.21.
11. For full text of UNSC 242, see http://www.un.org/Depts/dpi/palestine/ch3.pdf. (Last accessed 26 April 2017).
12. Adi Schwartz, 'A tragedy shrouded in silence: the destruction of the Arab world's Jews', *Azure*, no. 45, Summer 2011, http://azure.org.il/include/print.php?id=581. (Last accessed 26 April 2017).
13. Ibid.
14. Telegram from the American embassy in Baghdad to Washington D.C., 9 May 1949, cited in Y. Meron, 'Why Jews fled Arab Countries', *Middle East Quarterly*, September 1995; http://www.meforum.org/263/why-jews-fled-the-arab-countries. (Last accessed 26 April 2017).
15. Elie Kedourie, 'The break between Muslims and Jews in Iraq' in Cohen and Udovitch (eds) *Jews among Arabs* (US: Darwin, 1989), pp.21–63.
16. Elie Kedourie, 'The Break between Muslims and Jews in Iraq'; p.47'
17. Ibid., p.54.

18. Edwin Black, 'When Iraq expelled its Jews', *Front Page Magazine*, 6 June 2016, http://www.frontpagemag.com/fpm/263069/when-iraq-expelled-its-jews-israel%E2%80%94-inside-story-edwin-black. (Last accessed 26 April 2017).

19. Michael R. Fischbach, *Jewish Property Claims against Arab Countries* (NY: Columbia University Press, 2008), p.117.

20. See Kedourie, 'The Break between Muslims and Jews in Iraq' p.55.

21. Gat, *The Jewish Exodus from Iraq 1948–1951* (London: Cass, 1997), p.151.

22. Levin, *Locked Doors*, p.302.

23. See Adi Schwartz, 'A tragedy shrouded in silence'.

24. Cotler, Matas, Urman, 'Jewish Refugees from Arab Countries: the case for rights and redress', p.39.

25. '15,000 square kilometres of land, compared to 5,200 square kilometres for the Arabs who left the smaller Israel': Eylon Aslan-Levy, 'The Forgotten Refugees', *The Tower*, No. 41, August 2016, http://www.thetower.org/article/the-forgotten-jewish-refugees-of-iraq/. (Last accessed 26 April 2017).
    According to an alternative proposal, Aslan-Levy writes, Jews were 'entitled to 80,000 square kilometers [four times the size of Israel] on an Arab reading of a fair post-World War settlement' as a 'successor element' of the Ottoman Empire.

26. *The Scribe*, abridged from article in the *Jerusalem Post*, September 1999, p.72, http://www.dangoor.com/73page72.html. (Last accessed 26 April 2017).

27. Yehouda Shenhav, 'Spineless book-keeping: the use of Mizrahi Jews as pawns against Palestinian refugees', +*972magazine*, 25 September 2012, http://972mag.com/spineless-bookkeeping-the-use-of-mizrahi-jews-as-pawns-against-palestinian-refugees/56472/. (Last accessed 26 April 2017). Reprinted from 'Hitching a ride on the magic carpet', *Haaretz*, 15 August 2003.

28. Ronen Tal, 'Claiming Babylon's stolen treasures', *YNet News*, 29 May 2006, http://www.ynetnews.com/articles/0,7340,L-3256437,00.html. (Last accessed 26 April 2017).

29. Bobby Brown quoted in Isabel Kershner 'The Other Refugees', *Jerusalem Report*, 12 January 2004.

30. See Levin, *Locked doors*, p.223.

31. See Schwartz, 'A tragedy shrouded in silence'.

32. See Urman, 'The United Nations and Middle Eastern Refugees'.

33. See Fischbach, *Jewish Property Claims against Arab Countries*, p.232.

34. See Schwartz, 'A tragedy shrouded in silence'.

35. 'Girls discriminated on grounds of culture, not skin, *Point of No Return*, 4 May 2010, http://jewishrefugees.blogspot.co.uk/2010/05/girls-discriminated-on-grounds-of.html. (Last accessed 26 April 2017).

36. See Urman, 'The United Nations and Middle Eastern Refugees'.

37. *An-Nahar*, May 1975.

38. *Al-Masry Al-Youm*, 2008.

39. Y. Meron, *Why Jews fled Arab Countries*, p.96.

40. L. Julius/ S. Urman, 'Arab refugees and Jewish refugees: the inextricable link', *Jerusalem Post*, 9 March 2014, http://www.jpost.com/Opinion/Op-Ed-Contributors/Arab-refugees-and-Jewish-refugees-the-inextricable-link-344808. (Last accessed 26 April 2017).

41. 'Arabs offer Israelis peace plan', BBC News, 9 March 2014, http://news.bbc.co.uk/1/hi/world/middle_east/1898736.stm. (Last accessed 26 April 2017). Arab insistence on using UNGA 194 as a template for the resolution of the refugee problem is ironic, given that Arab states voted against the resolution at the time, lest it infer Arab recognition of Israel.

42. Others characterise the initiative as a plan to bring about Israel's collapse through the emigration of Jews from Israel (Moreh, *Al-Farhud*, p.145).

43. J.E. Katz, 'Discrediting Jewish refugees from Arab Countries, official Arab "invitation" to return', *Eretz Yisroel* website, 2001, http://www.eretzyisroel.org/~jkatz/discredit.html. (Last accessed 26 April 2017).

44. Colette Fellous,'*Pièces détachées*' (Gallimard: Paris, 2007), p.156.

45. Eetta Prince-Gibson, 'Right of return', *Jerusalem Post*, 7 August 2003.

46. 'Report condemns Israel's refugee policy', *Point of No Return*, 5 February 2014, http://jewishrefugees.blogspot.co.uk/2014/02/report-condemns-israels-refugee-policy.html. (Last accessed 26 April 2017).

47. See Schwartz, 'A Tragedy Shrouded in Silence'.

48. Ofer Aderet, 'Comptroller blasts state for neglecting Jewish property restitution in Arab states',*Haaretz*, 6 February 2014, http://www.haaretz.com/israel-news/.premium-1.572665. (Last accessed 26 April 2017).

49. Roumani, *Jewish refugees from Arab countries: a neglected issue* (WOJAC, 1983).

50. See Cotler, Matas and Urman, 'Jewish refugees from Arab Countries'.

51. Ibid.

52. See Appendices.

53. 'Government accepts Canadian refugee report', *Point of No Return* 4 March 2014, http://jewishrefugees.blogspot.co.uk/2014/03/government-accepts-canadian-refugee.html.(Last accessed 26 April 2017).

54. Figure produced by Levana Zamir, head of the Merkaz Irgunim, the umbrella organization of associations of Jews from Arab Countries in Israel.

55. Full text of Netanyahu's Bar Ilan speech, *Haaretz*, 14 June 2009 http://www.haaretz.com/news/full-text-of-netanyahu-s-foreign-policy-speech-at-bar-ilan-1.277922. (Last accessed 26 April 2017).

56. *Haaretz* article by Adi Schwartz, quoted in 'Jews were also refugees in 1948', *Point of No Return*, 6 February 2014, http://jewishrefugees.blogspot.co.uk/search?q=adi+schwartz&updated-max=2014-05-12T12:38:00%2B01:00&max-results=20&start=11&by-date=false. (Last accessed 26 April 2017).

57. Leslie Susser, 'Changing the Refugee Paradigm', *Jerusalem Post*, 31 October 2012, http://www.jpost.com/Jerusalem-Report/Israel/Changing-the-refugee-paradigm. (Last accessed 26 April 2017).

58. 'Hamas: "Arab Jews" are not refugees but criminals', *Jerusalem Post*, 23 September 2012, http://www.jpost.com/Middle-East/Hamas-Arab-Jews-are-not-refugees-but-criminals. (Last accessed 26 April 2017).

59. 'Don't forget what we lost, too', *The Economist*, 15 February 2014.

60. 'Knesset confirms 30 November as Refugee Day', *Point of No Return*, http://jewishrefugees.blogspot.co.uk/2014/06/knesset-confirms-30-november-as-refugee.html. (Last accessed 26 April 2017).

61. 'Key Committee recommends recognition of Mizrahi culture', *New Israel Fund*, 14 July 2016, http://www.nif.org/stories/social-and-economic-justice/key-committee-recommends-recognition-mizrahi-culture/. (Last accessed 26 April 2017).

62. Ofer Aderet, 'Israel Launches $2.6m Project to Document Lives of Mizrahi, Sephardi Jews', *Haaretz*, 13 December 2016, http://www.haaretz.com/israel-news/.premium-1.758554. (Last accessed 26 April 2017).

63. Hillel Neuer, 'Algeria, where are your Jews? UNHRC's Israel apartheid debate, *Times of Israel* blogs, 22 March 2017.

64. Fateh Azzam in a 'Bold Proposal: Palestine should give its Refugees Citizenship' (*Al-Shabaka*, 5 May 2015), tried to break with orthodox Arab thinking by advocating that

an internationally-recognised state of Palestine should 'create facts on the ground' and give refugees citizenship.

65.   'Palestinians born of an Egyptian mother get Egyptian nationality', *Egypt Independent*, 8 May 2011, http://www.egyptindependent.com/news/palestinians-born-egyptian-mother-get-egyptian-nationality. (Last accessed 26 April 2017).

66.   JJAC.

67.   Annie Slemrod, 'Interview: refugees will not be citizens of Palestinian state', *Beirut Daily Star*, 15 September 2011, http://www.dailystar.com.lb/News/Politics/2011/Sep-15/148791-interview-refugees-will-not-be-citizens-of-new-state.ashx. (Last accessed 26 April 2017).

68.   Jonathan Tobin, 'Egypt offers to absorb Palestinians. Why did Abbas refuse?' *Jewish World Review*, 5 September 2014, http://www.jewishworldreview.com/0914/tobin 090514.php3. (Last accessed 26 April 2017).

69.   Israel Central Bureau of Statistics, 2012.

70.   See Appendix.

8

'My House is Your House'

Some years ago, a daughter of the wealthy Jewish Castro family from Egypt heard ex-President Anwar Sadat's widow Jehan deliver a talk in New York. Congratulating her afterwards, the Egyptian Jewess exchanged pleasantries with Mrs Sadat. 'But you must come back to visit [Egypt] and to show it to your children', Mrs Sadat said, adding the traditional Egyptian courtesy, *beti betak* –'my house is your house'.[1]

Little did she appreciate the irony, but Jehan Sadat's presidential villa had literally belonged to the Castro family, expelled by Gamal Abdel Nasser in 1956. Observers of the Middle East conflict frequently talk of trampled Palestinian rights, but suffer from a blind spot when it comes to the mass dispossession of a greater number of Jews across ten Arab countries. Few Jews lived as opulently as the Castros, but all over the Middle East and North Africa, Jewish land, homes, shops and businesses were seized or sold for well under market value as fearful Jews fled or were forced out.

Contradicting the impression that Jews in Arab countries lost their assets and properties in retaliation for Palestinian Arab losses, the Political Committee of the Arab League drafted a law in 1947 that was to govern the legal status of Jewish residents in all Arab League countries. Entitled 'Text of Law drafted by the Political Committee of the Arab League', it provided that 'all Jews … were to be considered 'members of the Jewish 'minority of Palestine'. The plan demanded that they register the names of their banks and the amounts of deposits in these banks. Bank accounts would be frozen and the funds used in part or full to 'finance the movement of resistance to Zionist ambitions in Palestine'. There is some evidence that the draft may have been adopted. It certainly provided a blueprint for Iraq, Syria and Egypt to implement harsh measures against their Jewish citizens.[2]

A key demand by groups campaigning on behalf of Jews from Arab countries is for Jewish refugees to be compensated for lost or abandoned property and assets. The Israeli government began collecting claims in the early 1950s and thereafter, in fits and starts, has undertaken subsequent drives to encourage claimants to register their lost assets. Other bodies, like the World Organization of Jews from Arab Countries (WOJAC), the American Sephardi Federation and Justice for Jews from Arab Countries (JJAC) have also registered claims, lodged with the Israeli Ministry of Justice. More recently, the Israeli Ministry for Social Equality (previously the

Iraqi Jews being transported to Israel on Operation Ezra and Nehemiah.

Ministry of Pensioners' Affairs) became the address for claims registration. But it has taken an investigative documentary by film-maker Emanuel Rosen to uncover just how confused, chaotic and inaccessible the system is to claimants themselves.

Rosen's 2011 film *Secrets of the lost Treasures* (Hebrew)[3] follows two Israeli claimants, Lucy Calamaro of Egypt and Samir Muallem of Iraq, in their quest for compensation. Muallem's family business, a brickworks, could be worth thirty-eight million dollars alone. Lucy, who left Egypt in the 1960s, promised her father she would not rest until she obtained justice.

The two claimants soon find themselves shunted from pillar to post. Important documents are stored in the bowels of the Israeli Ministry of Justice, in a garden shed or in an underground car park. The claimants are not allowed to inspect the documents in the Ministry of Justice 'for security reasons'.

The word *kizzuz* is the dark cloud hovering over the issue of reparations for Jewish refugees, and the film's protagonists are met with a wall of secrecy. For years, Israeli government policy was to 'offset' Jewish losses with Palestinian losses when this 'final issue' reached the negotiating table. The Jews would get nothing.

Many refugees fled with no deeds or other documents. Instead, Samir Muallem has a home movie[4] of his family's brickworks. However, Lucy has documents of her own recording her family's assets in Egypt; these are so precious to her that she pleaded with burglars not to take them from her home.

Very few, if any, Israelis have ever received compensation from an Arab government And so Lucy approaches the Italian government (she has an Italian passport); her efforts come to nought. Even Jews now resident outside Israel who have won cases in the Egyptian court, find that the compensation is worthless. One Egyptian lawyer advises Lucy to get together with other claimants and file a class action.

The Iraqi trail ends with a furtive interview with Mordechai Ben-Porat, Israeli Mossad agent, who is alleged to hold thousands of documents. Is he also an agent of *Kizzuz*, jealously guarding information for the Israeli government? He claims only to have communal property records. While the camera is still rolling, he admits to having 5,000 private property deeds. The film ends with a big question mark. Where are these deeds? Why is their existence secret? Will these claimants ever see one *grush* of their lost assets? Evidence presented by Rosen makes it look highly unlikely that they will.

Inverted Reality

Researchers and organisations are at odds over the scope of the lost property. Economist Sidney Zabludoff [5] estimates that there were 50 per cent more Jewish refugees than Palestinian Arab refugees, and that they almost certainly lost 50 percent more in terms of assets and property. While the world is fixated on Israeli building in a Jerusalem suburb, nobody reproaches Arab states for seizing Jewish land and property in Baghdad, Cairo, Tripoli and Damascus, estimated by WOJAC at five times the size of Israel itself.[6]

The concept of Jews 'stealing Arab land' is an offensive inversion of reality. Across the Arab world, Jewish property has been abandoned, confiscated, sequestered or sold well below market value as Jews left in haste or were driven out. The takeover of millions of dollars' worth of Jewish homes, land, bank accounts, pensions, shops, offices and communal property by Arabs has never been considered provocative or an 'obstacle to peace'.

How much did the Jews lose? No official figures exist. The property and belongings of the Jewish refugees, confiscated by Arab governments, has been conservatively estimated at about $2.5 billion in 1948 dollars.[7]

In an interview,[8] Dr Heskel Haddad of WOJAC estimated that the value of Jewish property seized at today's prices is between $200 and 300 billion.

How do Jewish losses compare to Palestinian? In the early 1950s, the UN Conciliation Commission[9] for Palestine estimated the value of lost Palestinian property at £122 million, or approximately $1.85 billion 1990 US dollars. This was the only independent study ever done of Palestinian losses until the Aix Group, comprised of Israeli, Palestinian and international experts, estimated, in 2007, that the cost of resolving the issue of the 'Right of Return' would run to between $55 billion and $85 billion.[10]

The scope of Palestinian property is also a matter of controversy. In 1999, the Palestinians presented a $670 billion compensation claim before the European Union Commission for lost assets, use of those assets and emotional distress.[11] Economist John Barncastle evaluated the Palestinian property of the 1950s at some $450 million. According to Sidney Zabludoff, it stands at some $4 billion. The Camp David peace talks discussed $20 billion, while Arab organisations spoke of some $200 billion.[12] The disagreement stems from the re-evaluation method. Questions of whether the Jews will be compensated for the looted property and whether or not their compensation can and should be deducted from the property Israel took from the Palestinians are all issues which serve to muddy the waters.[13] As Israeli house prices have soared in relation to property in the Arab world, lost Palestinian property is worth much more than its original value. Property should be compensated on its value at the time plus a notional rent for lost income, and revalued for inflation.

For years, the Israeli government was afraid that it would have to pay the Palestinians more than was owed to Jews who lost property in Arab lands.[14]

A partial exchange of property occurred – Jewish refugees from Arab lands were resettled in abandoned Palestinian homes and villages. In Iraq, some Palestinian refugees were rehoused in the upmarket district of Baghdad known as Batacween, Jewish social clubs and the Alliance Israëlite Laura Kadoorie girls' school.[15] In Damascus, Sidon and Beirut, and in Libya[16] Palestinian refugees were moved into synagogues and the abandoned Jewish homes in the Jewish quarter. The Alliance Israëlite School in Beirut was requisitioned for a time in 1948. The Syrian government took over the Alliance school in Damascus for Palestinian refugee children.[17] The Jordanian Custodian [of Enemy Property] held and administered Jewish-owned property in the West Bank until 1967. Some of these assets were used, in violation of international law, by the Custodian to establish refugee camps, army camps and marketplaces. In other cases, the property was leased to private individuals, who used the land for agricultural, commercial or residential purposes.[18]

Egypt appointed a Director General to administer property owned by Jews who fled in 1948. The Director General used the parcels for public projects, including refugee camps for Palestine Arabs, or leased them for private uses.[19]

In 1951 the Iraqi government confiscated Jewish property 'to compensate the Palestinian refugees'. According to Zvi Yehuda: 'Government workers would arrive at a business and ask the Jewish owner how much he would like to "donate" to the refugees. If he wouldn't – that was the end of the business. Most of the property reached people with ties to the government."[20]

In 1950, the Iraqi government quietly agreed to let Jews emigrate to Israel, and almost all of them did. As the law permitting emigration expired, Iraq enacted Law no. 5 in March 1951. All Jewish assets – houses, factories, goods, jewellery and bank accounts would be nationalised. Shops were sealed, vehicles seized and Jews arrested on the street, their belongings confiscated.[21] The law was even extended to cover the property of Iraqi-Jewish nationals resident abroad.[22]

Following the US invasion in 2003, it was hoped that the new democratic Iraq would turn over a new leaf in relation to its minorities. A Claims Commission (IPCC) was set up, but it only dealt with those who were dispossessed after 1968 under the Ba'ath regime. As far as is known not a single Jewish claimant has been compensated. In addition, the 1950 and 1951 nationalisation laws remain in force so that no claims would be considered from Jews who left during the *Taskeet* (Denaturalisation) of the 1950s.

Egyptian leader Gamal Abdel Nasser enacted similar laws after the Lavon Affair and the Sinai war: 95 per cent of property sequestered in 1956–7 belonged to Jews. The property of Libya's Jews who left for Israel was sequestered by Law no. 6 of 1961.[23] Libyan leader Muammar Gaddafi enacted Law no. 57 of 1970 which sequestered the property of all those who had left Libya permanently.[24] 'He promised to return everything within thirty years. He never did', says a Jewish refugee from Libya, Yaakov Hajaj, director of the Institute for the Research and Study of Libyan Jewry: 'My father was one of Libya's biggest billionaires and immigrated with a suitcase weighing twenty kilos.'[25]

Tunisia and Algeria did not nationalise property, but the Jews fled those countries when they gained independence (in 1956 and 1962, respectively), leaving their property – often in central and prime locations – in the care of domestic staff, middlemen or at the mercy of dishonest lawyers and racketeers. A similar fate befell the property of Yemeni Jews who fled to Israel on Operation Magic Carpet (*aka* Operation Wings of Eagles). Deeds have been falsified, squatters have moved in, looters have stripped the properties bare. The restitution process and recovery of property and abandoned bank accounts is tortuous and seemingly interminable, but not impossible. One Sousse-based (Tunisia) French lawyer reassures dispossessed Jews: 'You will get your property back – If you don't die first!'[26]

'Some of Morocco's Jews "got off easy": they immigrated with the money and "only" left the homes',[27] says Yaakov Hajaj. Although the Jews of Morocco were never dispossessed by the state, their empty city properties have fallen prey to Mafia-style gangs, aided and abetted by well-placed accomplices with the authority to falsify documents. Private sales contracts have been put in false names. Anyone wishing to check property deeds is often given the run-around by corrupt clerks. The government, which recently took steps to prevent organised real estate crime, estimates that a third of the empty properties are Jewish-owned and are worth almost 500 million dirhams.[28]

Mass Dispossession

Many cities in the 'Arab' Middle East and North Africa had large Jewish populations. Baghdad was between a third and a fifth Jewish. When over 90 per cent of Iraq's Jews left for Israel in 1950–1, property seized by the Iraqi government included three hospitals, nineteen Jewish schools, thirty-one synagogues and two cemeteries. The claim by Dr Heskel Haddad of WOJAC that Jews owned 100,000 square kilometres of deeded property, four or five times the size of Israel, is not as outlandish as it may sound.

In Egypt mansions belonging to wealthy Jewish families became embassies, residences and public institutions. Jehan Sadat still lives in a mansion once owned by the Castro family, and Egyptian presidents have had the use of a villa owned by the Smouha family.

Tahrir Square has been in the news as the focal point for Egypt's 'Arab Spring' revolutions. But how many people know that the imposing buildings around it were once home to Cairo's wealthy Jews? In an extraordinary five-page feature published on 12 July 2013 in the Weekend Supplement of the Hebrew newspaper *Yediot Ahronot*, entitled 'That was my house', Ronen Bergman explored the highly sensitive question of property and assets seized without compensation, or sold for peanuts, from Jews in Egypt. The list below is not exhaustive but gives a good idea of the extent of the confiscations.

- Joseph Nissim's home on the banks of the Nile is now the residence of the Russian ambassador. The site houses the modern Russian embassy.
- Victor Castro's palace is now Jehan Sadat's residence; it is Egyptian government property.
- Emile Zikov's house is now the Pakistani embassy.
- The house of Isaac Abdo, the merchant, is now the South Korean embassy.
- The home of the Zuckerman family is now the Swiss embassy.
- Maurice Cattaoui's home is now the German embassy.
- The home of Ovadia Salem, the manager of the Chemla department store, is today the Canadian embassy.
- Guido Levy's house is the Dutch embassy today.
- Moise Cattaoui's house is now the Great Library of Cairo.
- Henri Curiel's house is now the Algerian embassy.

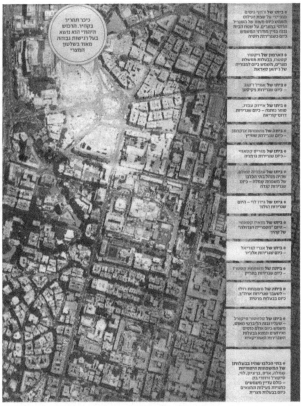

Page from *Yediot Aharonot* showing some of the Jewish properties seized or abandoned around Tahrir Square in Cairo.

Villa confiscated from the Curiel family, now the Algerian embassy.

- A house owned by the Castro family is, today, the embassy of Bahrain.
- The Rollo family house was formerly the US embassy and is now in private hands.
- Salvatore Cicurel's house became a stock exchange and events hall. It is now part of the US embassy.
- The Chemla, Ades, Benzion, Levy, Cicurel and Orosdi Bak department stores still exist, but are owned by the Egyptian government.

Some twenty kilometers from the centre of Cairo, in the prosperous suburb of Maadi, opulent villas and gardens once belonged to Jewish families. Many are now ambassadors' residences.

The Smouha family, British subjects, lodged the largest of Jewish claims for compensation after an Anglo-Egyptian financial agreement was signed – for twelve and a half million pounds.[29] Smouha City, an upscale suburb of Alexandria, built around a sports club, golf course and race track, was sequestered from Jewish businessman Joseph Smouha in 1957. In 1961, the family was finally granted three million pounds sterling in compensation, the sum representing Egyptian government funds held by the UK. (The Egyptian government argued the land was 'agricultural' land.) In 2016, individual units were selling for over a million US dollars (600,000 Egyptian pounds). Joseph's grandson Brian Smouha estimates that compensation represented one-hundredth of what was due the family.[30]

Smouha Sporting Club, Alexandria. The Smouha family obtained inadequate compensation for the loss of Smouha City, which Joseph Smouha reclaimed from marshland (Alexandria Governorate).

However, the Smouha family home in Alexandria,[31] with its rare carpets, fine furniture and ornaments, was never sequestered or sold. Successive Egyptian presidents lived there. Following a 1986 Egyptian court ruling that owners had a right to reclaim properties that had not been sold to a third party, Joseph Smouha's grandsons Richard and Brian embarked on a long and tortuous lawsuit in the Egyptian courts. The case dragged on until 2007: embarrassed to be in confrontation with the President himself, the Court's officials threw all sorts of delays and obstacles in Richard and Brian's path. It was argued that compensation had already been paid, that the brothers did not have the correct documentation, that the grandchildren were not entitled to inherit, that the case was bound by a statute of limitations. Faced with such pressure the brothers decided to give up, but they resumed their struggle when President Mubarak was deposed in 2011. 'I can't let go', says Brian.[32] 'We are back in the fray', writes Richard in his book.[33]

Between 1956 and 1976, Jewish refugees from Egypt, most now living in Israel, filed some 7,000 claims, as requested by the Israeli Ministry of Justice – a quarter of all claims registered by Jews from Arab Countries. These claims are worth billions of dollars in private property alone. Individuals suspended their claims in order to allow the Israeli government to handle the matter of confiscated or stolen properties on their behalf.

The 1979 Camp David Treaty declared: 'Egypt and Israel will work with each other and with other interested parties to establish agreed procedures for a prompt implementation of the resolution of the refugee problem', without specifying if the refugees were Jewish or Arab. Under Article VIII of the Treaty, the two sides agreed to establish a Claims Commission for the mutual return of financial claims. But the Claims Commission was never established.

In 1980, an Egyptian Jew, Shlomo Kohen-Tsidon, wrote to Menahem Begin suggesting that, in the absence of a Claims Commission, the state of Israel was now responsible for meeting Egyptian-Jewish compensation claims. But Kohen-Tsidon's interpretation was rejected by Israel's foreign ministry.

Why was the Claims Commission never established? Egypt has never pressed for it. The Egyptians initially realised that Israeli claims could leave Egypt 'stripped bare', as one Israeli source put it.[34] Israel, for its part, feared that Egypt might file a massive claim for oil pumped from the Abu Rudeis fields in western Sinai between 1967 and 1975. In anticipation, Egyptian Jews formally asked the Israeli government in 1975 not to return the oilfields without claiming compensation for Jewish property claims.[35] Israel did not do so, and the Organization of Jews from Egypt sued the state of Israel before the High Court of Justice in September 1975. They lost the case, however: the Attorney-General Gabriel Bach concluded that it was too late. The agreement returning Abu Rudeis to Egypt had just been signed.

Levana Zamir, then head of the Israel-Egypt Friendship Association, argued that the UN Charter on Wars between countries stipulates that no natural resources need be returned in peacetime. Therefore, the oil pumped by Israel from Abu Rudeis should not have been taken into account.

The government of Israel produced a variety of excuses for not pursuing Egyptian-Jewish claims. In the end they claimed that, at the time their property was taken from the Jewish refugees, they were not Israeli citizens. As one Egyptian Jew ruefully remarked, this argument never stopped Israel from claiming from Germany on behalf of Holocaust victims.

The late Israeli minister of Justice, Yosef 'Tommy' Lapid, declared in 2003 that the failure to resolve Egyptian-Jewish claims was a severe omission by Israel – and its reticence on the question of Jewish refugees 'one of the greatest blunders in the state's history'.[36] Meanwhile, JJAC has given a renewed impetus to the collection of claims, although they now declare recognition of refugee rights, not redress, is their top priority.

In the 1990s, the United States was the first country to recognise Jews' right for compensation from Arab states. Former justice minister Meir Sheetrit stated, in 2006, that Israel would demand compensation. In 2010, the Knesset enacted the 'Law for compensating Jewish refugees from Arab countries', which obligates the government to demand compensation as part of any future peace negotiations. The law states that 'as part of negotiations for peace in the Middle East, the government will include the issue of compensating Jewish refugees from Arab states and Iran for the property they lost, including property which was owned by a Jewish community in those countries.'[37]

The compensation issue has taken a dramatic new turn since 28 July 2000: immediately after Camp David II, when President Clinton introduced the idea of an international fund. He was interviewed on Israeli television and stated: 'There will have to be some international fund set up for the refugees. There is, I think, some interest, interestingly enough, on both sides, in also having a fund which compensates the Israelis, who were made refugees by the war, which occurred after the birth of Israel.'

The international fund might well be the solution that thousands of frustrated claimants have been waiting for. It is thought that hundreds, if not thousands of non-Israeli dispossessed Egyptian Jews have tried unsuccessfully to sue for compensation. Sometimes the lawyers representing them have betrayed them or the process has been so protracted that the family have abandoned the case. If they win the case, it is a Pyrrhic victory. The compensation may be worth little in Egyptian piasters.

In his book *Jewish property claims against Arab countries* Michael Fischbach writes that Israel did not press the claims of Egyptian-Jewish refugees because it was 'saving' them for political linkage with the claims of Palestinian refugees in a final peace settlement. If Jewish refugees were really

The Ba'ath Party in Iraq seized the Coca Coca bottling franchise from businessman Naim Dangoor, who fixed the price at 14 *Fils* a bottle. Dangoor demanded that Iraq pay its dispossessed Jews £12 billion in compensation (Courtesy David Dangoor)

The Talisman Hotel in 2008. This Damascus property owned by the Farhi family was converted into a luxury hotel (Lucien Gubbay).

aggrieved, he suggests, they should not let others speak for them but rather take matters into their own hands. The rejoinder to this advice is that most Jews who lost property also lost the hope that they would ever see a *fils* in compensation from the Arab countries. Those who have tried the legal route to restitution and compensation, have, with few exceptions, failed to get justice. The rest are content to sit back and let their representative bodies and the government of Israel make the running for them. To-date, no progress has been made with this approach. The 2005 Shemesh-Shilushim initiative by David Nawi, an Israeli-Iraqi lawyer, to bring a class action in the Israeli courts to force the Israeli government to seek compensation from the Iraqi government came to nought.[38]

The Cecil Hotel is the only known example of property restituted to its Jewish owners. In 1956, the Jewish owners of Cecil Hotel in Alexandria were expelled from Egypt. They left with one suitcase. Nationalised five years before the family was expelled, the eighty-six-room hotel was resold to Egypt after its return.[39] In its heyday the Cecil hosted such figures as Winston Churchill and Al Capone. In 1996, an Egyptian court ruled that the hotel should be returned to its owners, but the ruling wasn't implemented for fear it would establish a precedent for the restitution of nationalised Jewish property.

After a fifty-year struggle, the Egyptian government agreed to compensate the Metzgers. The hotel's owner, Albert Metzger, died in Tanzania in the 1960s and his son Chris continued the struggle to recover the hotel. In 1996, the Egyptian Supreme Court in Cairo ruled that the hotel and all revenues accruing over the years belong to the Metzgers. But only in June 2007 did the Egyptian government propose a deal whereby the government would agree to implement the court ruling but would immediately buy back the hotel from the Metzgers.

Now living in Canada, the Bigio family have been engaged in a long-running battle for justice against the giant multinational corporation Coca-Cola. The Bigios are among the many Egyptian Jews from whom the Egyptian authorities under Nasser's 'Arab socialist' regime expropriated and nationalised land and property. In November 1961, the Beirut newspaper *al-Hayat* printed the text of a Nasser decree, which stated that 'all Jews included in the list of sequestrations are deprived of their civic rights and cannot serve as guardians, caretakers or proxies in any business association or club'.

After Nasser's regime expropriated the Bigios' Heliopolis plants, producing Coca-Cola under licence and bottle caps, the family fled Egypt and the UN classified them as refugees. They made their way to France, where they were granted asylum. Determined to obtain compensation for the family's assets, the Bigios undertook several trips to Egypt. In 1979, the Egyptian government finally issued an official decree returning their real

The Bigio family, fighting for restitution of their bottling plant in Egypt (Wikimedia Commons)

estate assets. But when the time came to receive these assets, a state-owned insurance company, which was holding the property, refused to return them. The Bigios took their legal fight to the US when they learnt that their assets had been acquired by Coca-Cola International. In 2011, in the US federal court, the Bigio family lost their case for justice against the Coca-Cola Company: the latter had managed to avoid presenting detailed factual evidence of their direct involvement in the acquisition of the Bigio family's real estate assets and factories. Instead, the US court, upholding (together with the Egyptian government) the family's right to compensation, pointed to the liability of a subsidiary of Coca-Cola.[40]

No Closure

The late Libyan leader Colonel Gaddafi's initiative to gain Western support by compensating Libyan Jews, beginning in 2003, broke down[41] after Gaddafi refused to have any dealings with Libyan Jews now living in Israel – 90 per cent of the community.

So far dispossessed Jewish exiles have not managed to achieve closure with the Iraqi government. The same year, following the US invasion of Iraq, the Iraqi Property Claims Commission specifically excluded the vast majority of potential claimants – the 130,000 Jews whose property was frozen when they were airlifted to Israel in the 1950s. The commission set up to compensate victims of Saddam's post-1968 Ba'athist regime has yet, as far as is known, to compensate a single Jewish claimant. Jews of Iraqi origin were allowed to vote in Iraq's elections, but Jews in general are a 'sensitive and dangerous'[42] issue.

For its part, Egypt has reacted with paranoia to Jewish property claims. Media hysteria caused a roots trip from Israel to be cancelled in 2008[43] on the grounds that elderly Egyptian-born Jewish tourists were coming back to reclaim their property. From time to time, the press scaremongers about 'Jewish documents'[44] which it alleges Jews are attempting to steal and smuggle out of the country to support their claims for property restitution. But the vultures – unscrupulous lawyers and property developers – are circling: the Jewish community has untold assets in real estate. Its synagogues may be crumbling but they stand on prime property in Cairo and Alexandria. The sprawling Bassatine cemetery, where community leader Carmen Weinstein was buried and which she fought to salvage from squatters and vandals, used to be on the outskirts of Cairo; now it occupies precious acreage virtually in the centre. Then there are the thousands of homes and businesses seized from or abandoned by Egypt's 80,000 Jews in their mass exodus. Egypt's worst nightmare is that the Jews should return and claim it all back.[45] In the meantime, property deeds are being forged and false ownership claims made.[46]

In an ironic reversal of roles, an Egyptian bank is even suing the Israeli government for the return of shares in the King David Hotel, Jerusalem.[47]

Cheque from the Palestine Hotels Ltd account with Banque Mosseri. Egyptian Jews held shares in hotels such as the King David in Jerusalem.

The Jewish-run Bank Zilkha, which held 1,000 shares in the hotel, was taken over by the huge Egyptian Banque Misr. Clearly, the sums owed to Banque Misr would be dwarfed if the Israeli Administrator General were to sue for the billions owed to Jewish refugees from Egypt.

In 2009, the Prime Minister of Iraq Nouri al-Maliki demanded that Israel compensate Iraq for the destruction of the Osirak nuclear reactor – a demand reiterated on the thirty-fifth anniversary of Israel's bombing raid by the Iraqis in 2016.[48] The academic and activist Edy Cohen called the Iraqi claim 'absurd' in the light of the millions owed by Iraq to its dispossessed Jews.[49] Every so often the Iraqi press runs scare-mongering stories (possibly planted by the Iranians) that the Jews are about to return to Iraq to reclaim their property.[50]

Communal property – hospitals, synagogues, schools, cemeteries and the movable heritage of Torah scrolls, libraries and ritual items – are a different story. The World Organisation of Jews from Iraq was set up in 2008 to lay claim to Iraq's Jewish communal assets when the last Jew has died. The Iraqi and Egyptian governments have possibly benefited from cheap leasing privileges, but communal property rights are understood to have been respected and protected. As for Iraq's Jewish heritage, the community has been waging a bitter battle to recover the so-called 'Iraqi-Jewish archive' of random documents, books and precious artefacts found by US servicemen in the flooded basement of the secret police headquarters. The Americans shipped the archive to Washington DC in 2003 for restoration and signed an agreement promising to return it. Although tens of thousands of Iraqi documents have been shipped out to the US, Iraq has only formalised its claim to the 30,000 documents of the water-stained Jewish archive as its national heritage. Like a 'giant hand ripping out the heart' of a community',[51] Saddam Hussein's regime seized the archive from Jewish homes, offices and

Waterlogged Jewish books and papers drying out at the Iraqi secret police headquarters before shipment for restoration to the US (Harold Rhode)

The oldest item in the Iraqi-Jewish archive is this Venice Bible from 1568 (US National Archives and Records Administration)

synagogues in the l960s and 1970s. By rights, it should be restored to the Iraqi-Jewish community, now transplanted to Israel and the West. The fate of 365 Torah scrolls discovered in the rat-infested basement of the Iraq National Museum is also uncertain.[52]

International law – for example the Hague Convention of 1954 governing a state's cultural property – needs updating, specifically to address situations in which cultural and religious property belonging to a particular ethnic or religious group – now in exile, or within a country under occupation – has been looted by previous national authorities.[53] It needs to resolve the tug-of-war between communal and national heritage, where the community in question has been displaced.

Supported by the tiny local Jewish community, Egypt too claims that the Jewish community's Torah scrolls, archives, libraries and communal registers, and any movable property over a hundred years old constitutes part of its national heritage. Jews of Egyptian origin living abroad are particularly frustrated[54] that they cannot even obtain photocopies of *brit mila* (circumcision), marriage and death certificates from the communal records to prove their lineage or identity. Repeated efforts since 2005 to intercede with the Egyptian authorities have come to nought: the Egyptian government feared that the Jews would use the registers to assert their property rights.

The Ben Ezra Synagogue, Cairo, which housed the medieval Geniza, and is considered part of Egypt's heritage (Seth J Frantzman)

In March 2016, the tiny Jewish community of Cairo 'gave away' its synagogue libraries to the state. A team from the Egyptian National Archives went to seize Jewish libraries in Alexandria.[55] In 2017, a plan was floated to set up a Jewish Museum in a Heliopolis synagogue housing the registers.[56] While this would ensure the preservation of precious historical documents for generations to come, it is not clear at the time of writing whether visitors will be able to consult them.

As far as individual claimants are concerned, the best chance of achieving compensation may well be in Morocco or Egypt. Morocco, which has a relatively stable economy, may be capable of paying compensation if it has to.[57] However, Egypt, which relies on external aid, can barely feed itself, let alone afford to pay out billions in compensation.

The pressure on Egypt to settle individual Jewish claims has slackened since July 2000, when after Camp David II, President Clinton declared that an international fund should be established to compensate both Palestinian refugees and Jewish refugees from Arab Countries. The Fund would certainly ease the burden on an economy that could barely feed its own people, let alone shell out billions in compensation to its former Jewish citizens. At the time of writing, a draft law recommending the establishment of the fund for refugees – but excluding their descendants – has been tabled in the Knesset. Reportedly, talks have even taken place with the Egyptian government.[58] Other states are warzones and collapsing before our very eyes. The possibility that they will ever pay compensation is extremely remote.

US Secretary of State John Kerry broke new ground in early 2014 when he proposed compensation for Jews from Arab countries ahead of a peace agreement between Israel and the Palestinians. The proposal was criticised as a 'sweetener' to win over the Mizrahi hawks of the Israeli electorate, instead of being integral to any peace agreement.[59]

Jewish Property Claims in Palestine

Israel's victory in the Six-Day War, in 1967, opened up the tantalising prospect that Jews who had been expelled from Jerusalem and the West Bank in 1948 might be able to recover their lost property.

To the US government and the European Union, West Jerusalem is 'Jewish', and East Jerusalem, where Israeli sovereignty is not recognised under international law, remains 'Arab'. In truth, this simplistic view ignores the fact that Jerusalem had a Jewish majority since the mid-nineteenth century. The eastern part of Jerusalem only became Jew-free when the thousands of Jewish inhabitants were 'ethnically cleansed' from the Old City in 1948, scores of synagogues destroyed and cemeteries desecrated during nineteen years of Jordanian occupation. The city was reunited when the eastern side of the city was recaptured and annexed in 1967 by Israel.[60]

Destroyed by the Jordanians in 1948, the Hurva Synagogue in the Jewish quarter of Jerusalem's Old City has been rebuilt (Israel Government Press Office)

The issue of land ownership in Jerusalem is far more complex than the western media and governments would have us believe. Mount Scopus – the original site of the Hebrew university campus and the Hadassah hospital – remained a Jewish enclave in Jordanian-controlled territory during the nineteen years that Jordan ruled East Jerusalem. Today, the sale of property to Jews is punishable by death in territory ruled by the Palestinian Authority, which distorts the property market to the advantage of Arab purchasers.[61]

It is estimated that 3,000 Jews were expelled from East Jerusalem in 1948 (17,000 Jews were made refugees from Gaza, the West Bank and Jerusalem). The descendants of those Jews expelled from 100 homes in the Eshel Avraham neighbourhood in East Jerusalem in 1929 still retained their title deeds until April 2014, when they decided to sell the properties.[62]

In 1876, Ashkenazi and Sephardi communities in Jerusalem jointly purchased the site next to Shimon Hatzaddik's tomb.[63] They built dwellings for the pilgrims on part of the site. The Jewish residents of some 100 homes were among the first to be expelled when hostilities broke out at the end of 1947. Arab families moved into the empty Jewish homes. From 1949 to 1967 Jews could not visit the holy sites under Jordanian rule – a violation of the 1949 armistice agreement.

Dozens of families and institutions are pursuing legal action over the ownership of Shimon Hatzaddik, Nahalat Shimon and Jewish neighbourhoods adjoining the Arab neighbourhood of Sheikh Jarrah.[64]

View of Jerusalem from the Mount of Olives. Jewish residents expelled from the eastern section have been seeking restitution since the city's re-unification (Haim Zach, Israel Government Press Office)

The shrine of Shimon Hatsaddik in East Jerusalem was recaptured by Israel in 1967. The quarter's Jewish residents were among the first to be expelled in 1948 (Gideon Julius)

Yemenite Jews, expelled in the 1930s from Silwan (Shiloah), a village on the south side of Jerusalem's city walls,[65] have been attempting to recover their properties. Over the last few years, human rights and left-wing groups have held weekly demonstrations protesting Jewish settlement in 'Arab East Jerusalem.'[66]

'I demand to get my property back', seventy-six-year-old Elisha Ben-Tzur told *Ynet News*.[67] 'My grandfather built this house and the synagogue that was burned down by Arabs in 1948. Before Sheikh Jarrah, we lived in Silwan, but were expelled out of there as well.'

The courts have not always ruled in the Jewish petitioners' favour, recognising that the current inhabitants' rights must also be protected under the law. The only Arab tenant families to be evicted from East Jerusalem and the Old City have been those who have failed to pay rent.[68]

It is also a little-known fact that hundreds of thousands of Arab squatters in 'Arab East Jerusalem' live on land still owned by the Jewish National Fund (JNF). The JNF purchased hundreds of individual parcels of land in and around Jerusalem during the 1920s, 1930s and 1940s. Some ended up under Jordanian control. In 1948, on one of these parcels the UN built the Kalandia refugee camp,[69] seizing the land without permission from the owners, the JNF. The JNF also lost land in the Dheisheh refugee camp in the West Bank. Other parcels of land in 'Arab' East Jerusalem[70] were cut off from their Iraqi and Iranian Jewish owners after they came under Jordanian rule. In total, 145. 976 *dunums*[71] of Jewish land is said to have come under Jordanian control.[72] Another 16. 684.421 *dunums* of Jewish land in the rural West Bank – including the Gush Etzion settlements, land between Nablus, Jenin and Tulkarm, and in Bethlehem and Hebron – were seized by the Jordanians after 1948. Jews also owned land in Gaza. In leaked documents called the 'Palestine Papers', the Palestinian leadership frankly acknowledges former legal Jewish ownership of land in Jerusalem, on its outskirts and in the West Bank, as well as in Gaza.[73]

The Golan Heights are almost universally considered 'Syrian' territory, although a peace treaty has never been signed between Israel and Syria. Yet the JNF lays claim to 73.974 *dunums* in southern Syria.[74] The earliest purchase was made in the 1880s when there were no borders.

Rich Jews from Egypt, Iraq and Iran bought lands in Israel on both sides of the Green Line. The Jordanians nationalised those lands in Judea and Samaria. After the Six Day War and the subsequent end of the Jordanian occupation in 1967, property previously administered by the Jordanian Custodian of Enemy Property was transferred to the administration of the Israeli Custodian of Absentee Property, but the fact that the Jordanian authorities had frequently leased or sold Jewish-owned land to Jordanian citizens further complicated the legal situation.

Land ownership should not be confused with sovereignty, and borders should only be determined in a peace settlement between Israel and its neighbours. Nor should the extent of Arab dispossession in Israel be underestimated. However, there is an asymmetry: Arabs who lost property in Israel are eligible to file for compensation from Israel's Custodian of Absentee Property. The actual formula is the 1949 value, with yearly interest and cost of living (or inflation) adjustments. As of the end of 1993, a total of 14, 692 claims had been filed, claims were settled with respect to more than 200,000 *dunums* of land, more than 10,000,000 NIS (New Israeli Shekels) had been paid in compensation, and more than 54,000 *dunums* of replacement land had been given in compensation. A media watchdog observed:

> Israel has followed this generous policy despite the fact that not a single penny of compensation has ever been paid to any of the more than 500,000 Jewish refugees from Arab countries, who were forced by the Arab governments to abandon their homes, businesses and savings.
>
> In addition, it should not be ignored that many journalists [...] write about Jews living in the Old City's Muslim Quarter as if this violates some unwritten moral or legal code, but they never write about the large number of Arabs living in the nearby Jewish Quarter.[75]

When it comes to lost property on both sides, the *status quo* represents an exchange far more favourable to Arabs than to Jews.[76] There is a fundamental imbalance in so far as Israel is prepared to compensate Arabs who file for compensation, while not a single Arab country is prepared to consider Jewish claims seriously. The situation is aggravated by the tendency of human rights groups and the western media to treat Jews wishing to recover their properties in East Jerusalem as imposters. It is further distorted by the fact that Jews are not allowed to purchase land or property from Palestinian Arabs, while no Israeli restrictions exist for Arabs or foreigners. Arabs who sell to Jews risk the death penalty under the Palestinian Authority.[77]

Lost Cultural Heritage

In theory, individual possessions can be restituted or compensated for; lost heritage is priceless and irreplaceable. Age-old shrines, synagogues and cemeteries in Arab lands have been allowed to decay. In some cases, Jewish heritage has been deliberately destroyed for ideological reasons. Where Jewish shrines have been restored and renovated, there has been nothing to stop them being altered beyond recognition.

The automatic Muslim voting majority has meant that it has been possible for UNESCO to pass resolutions denying any links between Israel and Jerusalem's holy sites.[78] What chance is there that it might speak up for Jewish heritage in Syria and Iraq, where the community has been extinguished? Who will preserve communal property? Who will restore

Tunisian officials inspect a 'rare' Torah scroll which they say they prevented from being smuggled out of the country.

precious synagogues – some real architectural gems – and ensure that, when the time comes to rehabilitate and renovate, traditional Jewish shrines such as the most revered of all, Ezekiel's tomb, are not turned into mosques?

These questions are of very real importance in the light of alterations which have already taken place. The Hebrew inscriptions,[79] for example, have been removed from the renovated tomb of Joshua the High Priest near Baghdad. Loudspeakers are affixed to Ezekiel's tomb, and Qur'anic inscriptions have been hung on the walls. Furthermore, it is incumbent on us to ask if objects stolen from minority communities which are recovered in the West, should be sent back to the Syrian or Iraqi governments who took them. It seems morally right that, for example, in the case of the Iraqi-Jewish archive, the personal possessions and mementos confiscated from their Jewish owners by Saddam Hussein and shipped for restoration to the US should be restituted not to governments, but to the displaced community from whom they were taken.

There is talk of the international community declaring cultural vandalism a 'war crime', and in another important respect, international action might achieve results: at a UNESCO conference in 2014[80] museum chiefs, alarmed at the wholesale destruction and looting of historic sites by Da'esh (Islamic State), declared they would treat with suspicion any artefacts offered to them from the Middle East, and would conduct 'due diligence' checks as far as possible. But private collectors are less likely to be circumspect about the provenance of items. The international art market is a vessel too leaky to render watertight.

It seems that most of the states of western Europe have now realised that there is a limit to how far they can endorse the denial and erasure of Jewish history in the Middle East and mortgage the issue of cultural heritage to their

Tik (Torah case) salvaged by Jews from Aden. Now in the Aden Jewish Heritage Museum, Tel Aviv.

political interests. Jerusalem is, after all, central to Christian, as well as Jewish heritage.[81] Beyond the expression of high-minded sentiments, however, there is little public debate, and the destruction proceeds apace.

Notes

1. Jean Naggar, *Sipping from the Nile* (US: Stony Creek Press, 2008), p.74.
2. Stan A. Urman, excerpt from PhD dissertation, 'The United Nations and Middle East refugees: differing treatment of Palestinians and Jews' (Rutgers University), pp.52–4.
3. E. Rosen and I. Petel (directors), *Sodot HaKsafim HaAvudim* (2011), http://www.israelfilmcenter.org/israeli-film-database/films/secrets-of-the-lost-treasures. (Last accessed 26 April 2017).
4. 'Lost treasure may never be found', *Point of No Return*, 2 January 2015, http://jewishrefugees.blogspot.co.uk/2015/01/lost-treasure-may-never-be-found.html. (Last accessed 26 April 2017).
5. Sidney Zabludoff, 'The Palestinian refugee issue: rhetoric vs reality', Jerusalem Center for Public Affairs, 28 April 2008, http://jcpa.org/article/the-palestinian-refugee-issue-rhetoric-vs-reality/. (Last accessed 26 April 2017).
6. Etgar Lefkovitz interview with Heskel Haddad 'Expelled Jews hold deeds in Arab lands', *Jerusalem Post*, 16 November 2007, http://www.jpost.com/Jewish-World/Jewish-News/Expelled-Jews-hold-deeds-on-Arab-lands. (Last accessed 26 April 2017).
7. See Sidney Zabludoff, 'The Palestinian refugee issue: rhetoric vs reality', JCPA, 28 April 2008, http://jcpa.org/article/the-palestinian-refugee-issue-rhetoric-vs-reality/. (Last accessed 26 April 2017).
8. 'Jews left assets of up to $300 billion', interview with Dr Heskel Haddad of WOJAC in the *Jewish Press*, *Point of No Return* 17 June 2007, http://jewishrefugees.blogspot.co.uk/2007/06/jews-left-assets-of-up-to-300-billion.html.. (Last accessed 26 April 2017).
9. See Zabludoff, 'The Palestinian refugee issue', JCPA, 28 April 2008.
10. Akiva Eldar, 'Refugees and Jerusalem: a question of money', *Haaretz*, 23 November 2007, http://www.haaretz.com/israel-news/refugees-and-jerusalem-a-question-of-money-1.233841. (Last accessed 26 April 2017).
11. Itamar Levin, *Locked Doors: The Seizure of Jewish Property in Arab Countries* (Westport, CT: Praeger, 2001). p.223.
12. See Zabludoff, 'The Palestinian refugee issue', JCPA.
13. Tani Goldstein, 'How Arabs stole Jewish property, *Ynet News*, 15 May 2011, http://www.ynetnews.com/articles/0,7340,L-4068854,00.html. (Last accessed 26 April 2017).
14. See Tani Goldstein, quoting Zvi Yehuda in 'How Arabs stole Jewish property, *Ynet News*.
15. Orly Halpern, *Hadassah magazine* quoted in 'Palestinians evicted from Jewish homes in Baghdad', *Point of No Return*, 19 November 2009, http://jewishrefugees.blogspot.co.uk/2009/11/palestinians-evicted-from-jewish-homes.html. (Last accessed 26 April 2017).
16. M. Fischbach, *Jewish Property Claims against Arab Countries* (New York: Columbia University Press, 2008), p.119.
17. Ibid., p.31.
18. 'Palestine Papers: Jews legally owned land', *Elder of Ziyon* blog, 9 February 2011, http://elderofziyon.blogspot.com/2011/02/palestine-papers-jews-legally-own-land.html. (Last accessed 26 April 2017).
19. Ibid.
20. See Goldstein, 'How Arabs stole Jewish property', *Ynet News*.
21. Moshe Gat, *The Jewish Exodus from Iraq,1948–51* (London: Frank Cass, 1998), p.141.
22. Ibid., p.145.
23. See Fischbach, *Jewish Property Claims*, p.76.

24. Ibid.
25. See Goldstein, 'How Arabs stole Jewish property', *Ynet News*.
26. Pierre-Olivier Aribaud, 'Bien juifs en Tunisie: petit florilège des acrobaties courantes', *Times of Israel*, 10 May 2016, http://frblogs.timesofisrael.com/biens-juifs-en-tunisie-petit-florilege-des-acrobaties-courantes. (Last accessed 26 April 2017).
27. Ibid.
28. Abdessamad Naimi, 'Spoliation immobilière: pourquoi les juifs sont une proie facile', *La Vie Eco*, 1 September 2016, http://lavieeco.com/news/immobilier/spoliation-immobiliere-pourquoi-les-juifs-sont-une-proie-facile.html. (Last accessed 26 April 2017).
29. Richard Smouha, Cristina Pallini, Marie-Cécile Bruwier, *The Smouha City Venture, Alexandria 1923–1958* (CreateSpace, 2014), p.166.
30. Author's conversation with Brian Smouha, London, 13 April 2016.
31. See Smouha et al., *The Smouha City Venture*, p.176.
32. Author's conversation with Brian Smouha, 13 April 2016.
33. See Smouha et al., *The Smouha City Venture*, p.185.
34. See Levin, *Locked Doors*, p.146.
35. Ibid.
36. See Fischbach, *Jewish Property Claims*, p.232.
37. 'Jewish Refugees from Arab and Muslim Countries: Special Report', Israel Ministry of Foreign Affairs, 3 April 2012, http://mfa.gov.il/MFA/ForeignPolicy/Peace/Guide/Pages/Jewish_refugees_from_Arab_and_Muslim_countries-Apr_2012.aspx. (Last accessed 26 April 2017).
38. 'Shemesh draws up Iraqi-Jewish claims petition', *Point of No Return*, 30 December 2009, http://jewishrefugees.blogspot.co.uk/2009/12/shemesh-draws-up-iraqi-compensation.html. (Last accessed 26 April 2017).
39. Adi Schwartz, *Haaretz*, republished as 'All I wanted was justice' on adi-schwartz.com, 4 January 2008, http://www.adi-schwartz.com/israeli-arab-conflict/all-i-wanted-was-justice/. (Last accessed 26 April 2017).
40. Correspondence with Raphael Bigio, 15 December 2016. For background to the case see Bigio Family website, http://www.bigiofamily.com/11801.html. (Last accessed 26 April 2017).
41. Nathan Guttman, 'Rapprochement with Libya falters as new sanctions contemplated', *The Forward*, 3 July 2007, http://forward.com/news/11097/rapprochement-with-libya-falters-as-new-sanctions-00103/. (Last accessed 26 April 2017).
42. Sandy Rashty, 'Iraqi Jews did wonders for us', *Jewish Chronicle*, 3 January 2013, http://www.thejc.com/news/uk-news/96347/iraqi-jews-did-wonders-us%E2%80%99. (Last accessed 26 April 2017).
43. 'Cancellation of Egyptian roots trip – update', *Point of No Return*, 29 May 2008, http://jewishrefugees.blogspot.co.uk/2008/05/cancellation-of-egyptian-roots-trip.html (Last accessed 26 April 2017).
44. 'Egypt seizes Jewish documents (update)', *Point of No Return*, 30 October 2012, http://jewishrefugees.blogspot.co.uk/2012/10/egyptians-seize-jewish-documents-update.html. (Last accessed 26 April 2017).
45. 'Arabs fear the Jews want their property back', *Point of No Return*, 15 August 2012, https://jewishrefugees.blogspot.co.uk/2012/08/arabs-fear-jews-are-coming-to-claim.html, (Last accessed 26 April 2017).
46. Sarah Mishkin reported that two members of Egypt's parliament had been embroiled in a scandal to forge documents that they then used to improperly and illegally sell Jewish property they did not own, 'Undersold', *The Tablet*, 21 September 2010, http://www.tabletmag.com/jewish-news-and-politics/45162/undersold. (Last accessed 26 April 2017).

47. Jonathan Beck, 'Egyptian bank claims it part-owns Israel's King David's Hotel', *Times of Israel*, 7 July 2015, http://www.timesofisrael.com/egyptian-bank-sues-to-reclaim-king-david-hotel-stocks/. (Last accessed 26 April 2017).

48. Roi Kais, 'Iraq to sue Israel for destroying Iraq's nuclear reactor in 1981', *YNet News*, 15 June 2016, http://www.ynetnews.com/articles/0,7340,L-4816100,00.html. (Last accessed 26 April 2017).

49. Edy Cohen, 'Iraq's absurd lawsuit against Israel', *Israel Hayom*, 16 June 2016, http://www.israelhayom.com/site/newsletter_opinion.php?id=16415. (Last accessed 26 April 2017).

50. 'Conspiracy theory of the day: Jews to colonize Iraq!', *Elder of Ziyon*, 19 February 2009, http://elderofziyon.blogspot.com/2009/02/conspiracy-theory-of-day-jews-to.html. (Last accessed 26 April 2017).

51. Miriam Kresh, 'The soldier in the Mukhabarat: Saddam Hussein's trove of Jewish artifacts', *Jerusalem Post*, 21 February 2016, http://www.jpost.com/Metro/The-soldier-in-the-Mukhabarat-443108. (Last accessed 26 April 2017).

52. Ari Werth, 'The struggle for the scrolls', *Aish.com*, 25 August 2012, http://www.aish.com/jw/s/Struggle-for-the-Scrolls.html. (Last accessed 26 April 2017).

53. For a comprehensive discussion, see Bruce M. Montgomery, 'Rescue or return: the fate of the Iraqi-Jewish archive', *International Journal of Cultural Property*, 19 June 2013, https://www.cambridge.org/core/journals/international-journal-of-cultural-property/article/rescue-or-return-the-fate-of-the-iraqi-jewish-archive/D3EB2F8E907F004E63E828F815D7F721. (Last accessed 26 April 2017).

54. See the websites of the Nebi Daniel Association at www.nebidaniel.org and the Historical Society of Jews from Egypt, http://www.hsje.org/.(Last accessed 26 April 2017).

55. 'People of the book lose books to Egypt', *Point of No Return*, 18 April 2016, http://jewishrefugees.blogspot.co.uk/2016/04/people-of-book-lose-books-to-egypt.html. (Last accessed 26 April 2017).

56. Jenni Frazer, 'Vital papers proving Jewish identity held back by Egypt', *Jewish Chronicle*, 12 April 2017.

57. Dr Adam Reuter, 'Can Jewish refugees claim billions from Arab states?' *YNet News*, 3 August 2015, http://www.ynetnews.com/articles/0,7340,L-4686648,00.html. (Last accessed 26 April 2017).

58. 'Lobby drafts historic' compensation' bill, *Point of No Return*, 17 December 2015, http://jewishrefugees.blogspot.co.uk/2015/12/lobby-drafts-historic-compensation-bill.html. (Last accessed 26 April 2017).

59. Yaakov Ahimeir, 'Price of peace', *Israel Hayom*, 4 February 2014, http://www.israelhayom.com/site/newsletter_opinion.php?id=7249. (Last accessed 26 April 2017).

60. Larry Collins & Dominique LaPierre, *O Jerusalem!* (Simon & Schuster, 1988).

61. 'Land sale to non-Palestinians', *Palestine (West Bank and Gaza) Business Law Handbook*, Volume I, p.48.

62. Hezi Baruch and Avi Yashar, 'The struggle to keep Eastern Jerusalem property in Jewish hands', *Arutz Sheva*, 15 October 2014.

63. Elliot Green, 'Simon's tomb and Jewish refugees', *Jerusalem Post*, 15 December 2010, http://www.jpost.com/Opinion/Op-Ed-Contributors/Simons-Tomb-and-Jewish-refugees. (Last accessed 26 April 2017).

64. 'Jews expelled from E. Jerusalem in 1929', *Point of No Return*, 22 October 2014.

65. Yemenite Jews were first in Silwan, *Point of No Return*, 8 October 2014.

66. Lyn Julius, 'Breaking the silence on Jewish Property Rights', *Times of Israel* , 4 May 2012. Jews have also demanded restitution of property in Hebron (Ezra Halevi, 'Pre-state Hebron Resident joins defence against Peace Now', *Arutz Sheva*, 17 October 2007,

http://www.israelnationalnews.com/News/News.aspx/123952 (Last accessed 26 April 2017)).

67. Yair Altman, 'Jews seek to reclaim houses in Sheikh Jarrah', *Ynet News*, 14 October 2010, http://www.ynetnews.com/articles/0,7340,L-3969735,00.html. (Last accessed 26 April 2017).

68. Rafael Broch, 'Erasing facts from the Israel eviction story', *The Guardian*, 6 August 2009, https://www.theguardian.com/commentisfree/2009/aug/06/israel-eviction-palestinian-east-jerusalem. (Last accessed 26 April 2017).

69. Aaron Klein, 'Palestinians, UN, build on Jewish-owned land', *WND*, 4 November 200, http://www.wnd.com/2007/04/41035. (Last accessed 26 April 2017).

70. Gil Zohar, 'Squatters rights and wrongs', *Jerusalem Post*, 27 July 2007, http://www.gilzohar.ca/articles/israel/i2007-15.html. (Last accessed 26 April 2017).

71. One *dunum* is a unit of land area enclosing 1,000 square metres.

72. See Fischbach, *Jewish Property Claims*, p.85.

73. 'Jews legally own land in the territories', *Elder of Ziyon*, 9 February 2011, http://elderofziyon.blogspot.co.uk/2011/02/palestine-papers-jews-legally-own-land.html#.Vtv5pBiU1JM. (Last accessed 26 April 2017).

74. See Fischbach, *Jewish Property Claims*, p.36.

75. CAMERA, 'Diaa Hadid, Recycling old stories about the Old City', 15 January 2016, http://www.camera.org/index.asp?x_context=2&x_outlet=35&x_article=3222. (Last accessed 26 April 2017).

76. Official moves to evict 'illegal Jewish settlers' from the West Bank should be applied consistently to the thousands of Arab squatters occupying Jewish property in Jerusalem, Mayor Nir Barkat has argued. Conversely, if Israel legalises 'illegal' settlements, this has implications for Arabs occupying property 'illegally'. See *Arutz sheva*, 6 November 2016, http://www.israelnationalnews.com/News/News.aspx/219880. (Last accessed 26 April 2017).

77. Daniel Halper, 'Palestinian sentenced to death for selling a home to Jews', *Weekly Standard*, 23 April 2012.

78. Oren Liebermann, Israel suspends ties with UNESCO in spat over Jerusalem holy site', *CNN*, http://edition.cnn.com/2016/10/14/middleeast/israel-unesco-jerusalem-holy-site/. (Last accessed 26 April 2017).

79. Lyn Julius, 'UN attempts to save Jewish sites from ISIS – too little, too late?'*Arutz Sheva*, 7 December 2014, http://www.israelnationalnews.com/News/News.aspx/188324#. VIW19oeprQS. (Last accessed 26 April 2017).

80. Shimon Cohen, Ari Yashar, 'UNESCO debates ISIS erasing of Jewish history', *Arutz Sheva*, 1 December 2014, http://www.israelnationalnews.com/News/News.aspx/188081. (Last accessed 26 April 2017).

81. Moshe Kantor, 'UNESCO has been used as a weapon to wage a cultural war', *Newsweek*, 16 November 2016, http://www.newsweek.com/unesco-has-been-used-weapon-wage-cultural-war-521788. (Last accessed 26 April 2017).

9

Mizrahi Wars of Politics and Culture

One word encapsulates the Mizrahi refugee experience in the Israel of the 1950s and 1960s: *ma'abara. Ma'abarot* were transit camps of fabric tents, wooden or tin huts. They were conceived by Levi Eshkol of the Jewish Agency to provide temporary housing and jobs. The first *ma'abara* was established in May 1950 in Kesalon in Judea.[1]

The EU as a whole, with a population of over 300 million, has been taking in as many immigrants as Israel, a country of half a million, absorbed in the early 1950s. As well as 100, 000 Holocaust survivors, the tiny struggling country took in 585,000 Jewish refugees from Arab countries, most of them destitute. By the 1960s, the refugees had tripled the country 's population.[2] The size of Israel's endeavour was Herculean. A nation of 650,000 absorbed 685,000 newcomers, some arriving with dysentery, malnutrition, ringworm, trachoma[3] and TB.[4] During the first years of statehood, roughly two-thirds of Jews from Muslim countries availed themselves of the Law of Return, passed by the Israeli Knesset in 1951. The newcomers came to Israel on some of the largest airlifts in history. It was a miracle that there were no accidents. The chartered aircraft were overloaded and fuel was short. Desert sand damaged the engines. It took sixteen hours for Yemenite Jews to reach Israel, and planes from Iraq were, at first, not permitted to fly direct.

Beit Lid *Ma'abara*, 1949. There were 113 *ma'abarot* in Israel. Some residents lived in these transit camps for up to thirteen years (ZoltanKluger/Israel Government Press Office)

The *ma'abarot* had no running water or electricity and only rudimentary sanitary facilities.
Yemenite Jews at Camp near Ein Shemer, 1950 (Hans Pinn/Israel Government Press Office)

Conditions in the *ma'abarot* were deplorable – too hot in summer, too cold in winter, exposed to the wind and the rain. Everything from food to detergent was rationed.

Refugees had to line up to collect water from standpipes. The water had to be boiled before it could be drunk. The public showers and toilets were rudimentary. The 113 *ma'abarot* housed a quarter of a million people in 1950. Slowly the *ma'abarot* turned into permanent towns. Some residents stayed in the camps for up to thirteen years.[5] 'Bring a million Jews', declared Ben-Gurion. But news of what awaited them deterred those Jews still in Arab countries from joining their relatives in Israel. Bitter and disappointed Iraqi Jews spread rumours that the Mossad had planted bombs in order to make them leave the 'paradise' that was Iraq. Later, there arrived in Israel Moroccan Jews, disparaged as '*Morocco sakin*'[6] (cut-throats),

Sallah Shabati was a 1960s satirical film on the absorption of immigrants from Arab countries starring Topol and written by Ephraim Kishon.

Wedding photograph and invitation to the wedding ceremony of Shafiqa and Sa'adya Nuri in a wooden hut

Sakiya (Or Yehuda), 1957
Courtesy of Yafa Masasa

תצלום חתונה והזמנה לטקס הכלולות
בצרוף של שפיקה וסעדיה נורי

סקייה (אור יהודה), 1957
באדיבות יפה מססה

1957 Photo and invitation to the wedding of Iraqi immigrants Shafiqa and Saadiya Nuri in a wooden hut (Or Yehuda, Courtesy of Yaffa Masasa)

who, faced with multiple hardships, idealised the sultan of Morocco as their protector and saviour.

The male heads of household in particular never got over the degradation of becoming refugees. Raphael Luzon writes of his father, who once owned several pharmacy and cosmetics stores in Benghazi, Libya, until the family were forced to leave in 1967:

> After his soul surrendered, his body followed and soon he became ill with kidney failure. Apart from a brief stint in employment, he refused to work. Once a man of wealth, he never would have thought about standing in line at the soup kitchen with charity coupons to get meals for himself and his family. My mother urged him to fight back, but her words fell on deaf ears. He had long ago lost the will to live.[7]

Other newcomers remained quietly philosophical: Egyptian Jews incongru-
ously maintained their bourgeois cultural habits in the camps – playing cards
and ballroom dancing on a Friday evening.[8]

The Jewish state wished to build a new national identity and fashion
those Jews who did reach its shores in its own Western image. Many refugees
launched themselves with gusto into the task of nation-building, making an
effort to speak only Hebrew (Arabic was often associated with unhappy
memories) and even Hebraising their family names. The young people were
carted off to kibbutzim to learn Hebrew and controversially secular Western
values, wear shorts and mix socially with the opposite sex for the first time,
as Eli Amir describes in *Scapegoat*.[9]

But these values were actually 'only slightly Western', as Yitzhak Bar
Moshe discovered when he arrived from Iraq. Israel was the state of Eastern
European Jewry. With the exception of rare figures like President Yitzhak
Ben Zvi, it did not know about Mizrahi Jewry – worse still, it did not want
to know about them, their sages, their rabbis, authors, *paytanim* (poets) or
judges: 'We understood that we were one of many communities. We left Iraq
as Jews and we entered Israel as Iraqis.'[10]

Still, cultural adjustments were necessary in all facets of life. Shmuel
Moreh's father could not comprehend the lack of corruption in Israel:

> He used to say, gritting his teeth: 'By God, I don't understand this up-
> side-down country. May the Lord have mercy on Iraq. There we knew
> how to calculate our steps. Open your hand a bit, slip a few dinars into
> the official's hand in order to grease the process of your request a bit and
> everything will fall right into place. Here there is no bribery, there is no
> cronyism and there isn't the magical religious saying: 'Do it for the sake
> of God! Do it for the sake of the Prophet Muhammad!' Here everything
> is according to the dark law of the inhabitants, a law I don't understand.'[11]

For the family of Chochana Boukhobsa, who came to Paris from the small
Tunisian town of Sfax, cultural differences had some hilarious side-effects.
Her grandfather, a ritual slaughterer, had brought with him his sharp knives
and the habits of a lifetime. Her mother paid top price for a cockerel she
found on the Seine quayside.

> The cockerel stayed under the kitchen sink of our tiny apartment on
> the rue de la Roquette. He crowed at the crack of dawn. Puzzled
> neighbours searched the whole block looking for him. 'Did you hear
> a cockerel crow?' They asked my mother. 'No', she answered, morti-
> fied. As soon as the door shut, she told my grandfather. 'Quick, kill
> that cockerel and be done with. In this city, the police come after
> those who keep live birds in their apartments.'[12]

Suppression of Mizrahi Culture

Rachel Shabi's book *Not the Enemy: Israel's Jews from Arab Lands*[13] catalogues the 'European' prejudices which Mizrahi Jewish refugees encountered when they arrived in Israel in the 1950s and 1960s. 'Israel's leadership was perennially paranoid about the possibility of the Jewish state sinking to a Levantine cultural level', she writes.[14] She sees every injustice through the prism of identity politics; blue-eyed, privileged Ashkenazim forced dark-skinned, deprived Mizrahim to speak Arabic only in private lest they be taken for Arabs, gave them the worst education and housing, and consigned them in the dead of night to frontier development towns, and to the ranks of Israel's poor and criminal classes. Cherry-picking examples of cultural repression, Shabi meets actors rejected for their guttural accents, and claims that Arabic music, available only on pirated cassettes at the Tel Aviv bus station, was 'scorned and hushed up, decreed as belonging to the enemy camp and considered low-quality – like all things Oriental'.[15]

The Moroccan-born poet Sami Shalom Chetrit and the sociologist of Iraqi-Jewish descent Yehouda Shenhav founded the Mizrahi Democratic Rainbow Coalition[16] in 1996 to challenge Ashkenazi hegemony in Israeli society and the idea that Ashkenazim were more 'civilised' than Mizrahim. Sami Michael, a popular author now in his nineties, is among a number of Jewish communists from Arab countries who continue to inveigh against Israeli 'racism'.[17] Other activists include Reuven Abergil and Tom Pessah. Almog Behar heads the Ramat Gan Committee,[18] which purports to speak for Iraqi Jews, but in fact consists of a tiny coterie of Arabic literature ex-students from Tel Aviv University.

Although Ashkenazi contempt for Mizrahi culture was undeniable in Israel's early years, the 'discrimination' narrative has become an instrument by which 'progressives' and the far left denigrate Zionism.

A handful of Mizrahi radical leftists has been pushing the line that Mizrahim have been torn away from their Arab brethren by Zionism, which has prevented them from making common cause with the Palestinians. The Mizrahim allegedly suffer from a 'false consciousness',[19] alienated from their true 'Arab' selves. The radicals align themselves with anti-Zionists who argue on behalf of an 'Arab-Jewish' identity as a way of repudiating Jewish nationalism. They presuppose that Jews were just another faith group in the Arab world, that Arabs and Mizrahi Jews are natural allies,[20] and that both are postcolonial victims of the Ashkenazim, who lured Mizrahim to Israel under false pretences as a reservoir of cheap labour.[21]

Zionism is presented as a purely a European colonial movement. Jews in Arab lands were not Zionists, we are told; only European Jews were Zionists.[22] Accounting for just 10 per cent of the total Jewish population, Mizrahim, it is said, did not attract much attention from the Zionist movement.

The Moroccan-Jewish scout movement still had a Zionist orientation in the 1950s (Montreal Jewish Museum)

Although Middle Eastern and North African Zionists were represented from the very beginning at the First Zionist Congress in Basle – there were two delegates from Constantine, Algeria, and embryonic groups in Tunisia, Morocco, Afghanistan and Egypt sent their greetings to subsequent meetings[23] – it is true that the modern Zionist movement had little support among Jews in the Arab world. Its secular socialism did not appeal to the more traditionally-minded Mizrahim. This was partly because the Zionist movement was not especially interested in the oriental Jewish minority before the Second World War, partly because Zionist activities in Arab countries were curtailed or forced underground, and partly because the British restricted immigration of Jews into Palestine.

During the British mandate in Palestine, the Ashkenazi-dominated Zionist leadership imposed strict entry selection criteria, allocating to what it considered the more deserving (and desperate) Jews from Europe, in preference to Jews from the Middle East and North Africa, the precious few legal permits into Palestine that the mandate was willing to give Jewish immigrants. In 1944, as the terrible toll of the Holocaust was becoming apparent, the Jewish Agency in Palestine approved the One Million Plan: for the first time this incorporated 800,000 potential immigrants from Arab lands.[24]

The Mizrahim who flocked to Israel after 1948 were non-Zionist in the sense that, by and large, they were not members of the modern Zionist movement. All communities were fired up with a passive interest in, and sympathy for, a Jewish home in Palestine just after the First World War.[25] But the fledgling Zionist movements in Arab lands were suppressed and the leadership of Jewish communities in Arab countries changed course: for reasons of survival they bent over backwards to express reservations about Zionism. In

Iraq, Jewish communists led the League against Zionism. Jewish members of the main Egyptian communist party founded a league for the struggle against Zionism.[26] Syrian-Jewish leaders improbably announced their intention to hold a banquet for Fawzi al-Qawuqji, a former Syrian officer who had served with the Mufti's forces in Palestine.[27]

Biblical Prophecy Fulfilled

Pushed out by Arab and Muslim anti-Semitism, many refugees, especially the devout Yemenite and Maghrebi Jews, were Zionists in the sense that they were motivated by the spiritual 'pull' of *Eretz Yisrael*. The return to Zion in the twentieth century was not quite what Ben Gurion and the European Zionists had envisaged following the annihilation of one third of Jewry in the Holocaust, but for the Mizrahim, it was the fulfilment of biblical prophecy, and the realisation of centuries of dreams and prayers.

Because the lands where they lived had never undergone a secular enlightenment, there was little tension between Judaism and the Mizrahi brand of Zionism. Eastern diaspora communities – often known as little Jerusalems – were naturally pious. They had always had an atavistic sense of their origin in Judea. With the advent of Western education, the Jewish elites tended to be more secular, but still had a strong sense of tradition and belonging.

For 2,000 years Jews outside Palestine felt as if they had personally been exiled from the Land of Israel, with which they harboured strong spiritual ties. The ingathering of the exiles in *Eretz Yisrael* is considered the necessary prelude to the coming of the Messiah. Twenty-one of the 613 commandments in the Torah can only be observed in Israel. All pious Jews, wherever they are in the world, pray three times a day for the return to Zion and 'Next year in Jerusalem' at Passover. Jerusalem is invoked at a baby's circumcision. A bridegroom crushes a glass under his wedding canopy to recall the destruction of the Temple in Jerusalem. Soil from the Holyland is sprinkled on the corpse at Jewish funerals. Religious Jews (and until the eighteenth century Enlightenment, there was no other kind) had, through the ages, aspired to end their days in *Eretz Yisrael*, or at least be buried there. What could have been more natural than for traditionalist twentieth century Jewish communities to see Zionism as the fulfilment of the exiles' centuries-old longing to return to their ancestral homeland?

Every year, all observant Jews mourn the destruction of the Temple in Jerusalem on the festival of Tisha B'Ab. Six days a week during the rest of the year, the pious Jews of Djerba in Tunisia would wear a black band, the *sawal*, on their legs, exchanging it for a white band on the Sabbath,[28] to recall this disaster, 2,000 years previously, and the Jews of Yemen would rationalise the rags they were made to wear as humiliated *dhimmis* as the garb of mourning for the destroyed Temple. The story is told of a Moroccan rabbi who would collect in a vial the tears he shed – for Jerusalem.

'Every year on Tisha b'Ab Iraqi Jews weep for the Temple as if it happened yesterday', Professor Shmuel Moreh told the *Manchester Jewish Telegraph*. 'They weep when they sing the psalm *On the Rivers of Babylon*. Every Jewish house had a strip of black paint around its walls to remember the destruction of the Temple.'[29]

Jewish religious festivals recalled the seasons and conditions in *Eretz Yisrael*, and the use of both Hebrew and Aramaic in the liturgy testifies to the tribal Middle Eastern origins of the Jewish people.

Palestine had never been devoid of Jews, although 'lawlessness and misrule' kept their numbers low[30] until the twentieth century. Sephardi Jews settled in the Holyland after the fifteenth century Spanish Inquisition. The medieval poet Yehuda Halevi penned these 'Zionist' words in Spain: 'I am in the West but my heart is in the East'. Rabbi Yehuda Bibas, who was appointed, in 1831, as the chief rabbi of Corfu and witnessed the Greek war of independence against the Ottoman Empire, was a forerunner of modern Zionism. He travelled to many communities in Europe spreading the message: 'We are Jews, we must come back to Zion'. He ended his days in *Eretz Yisrael* and is buried in Hebron.

In the nineteenth century, Jerusalem had a majority of Jewish inhabitants. Even before the first *Aliyah* of Ashkenazi pioneers from Russia, Yemenite, Bukharan and Persian Jews had arrived in the Land of Israel. Syrian Jews came fleeing nineteenth century blood libels, before the modern Zionist

Adès synagogue, Nahlaot, Jerusalem was founded by Syrian Jews in the nineteenth century (Ruth Corman)

movement was founded. Desperate to escape terrible conditions, Jews from Yemen arrived in the 1880s in Palestine, some of them on foot. Between the two World Wars, 15,000 Yemenite Jews arrived in *Eretz Yisrael*, even as the modern Zionist movement in Yemen was in its infancy. At the start of the mandate era, Sephardi and Mizrahi Jews made up 40 per cent of the Jewish population of Palestine.[31]

Another precursor of modern Zionism was the Sephardi rabbi Yehuda Alcalay. Theodor Herzl's grandfather was reputed to have listened to his sermons in his Balkan synagogue. Rabbi Moshe Kalfon of Tunisia wrote a book [*The Redemption of Moses*] that paralleled (Theodor Herzl's) *Altneuland*, describing the (ideal future) Jewish state and its character.[32]

This is not to say that 'pull' factors were enough to cause mass migration of Jews into the new state of Israel. They were not. As has been discussed already, Jews went to Israel because they were single-mindedly desperate to leave Arab lands. In most cases Israel was the only country that would accept them.

Arabs of the Jewish Faith?

Widespread is the notion among Arabs and on the radical left, that Jews from Arab countries are not distinct people, but Arabs of the Jewish faith. In other words, the Jews cannot be defined as a people with a right to self-determination. Anti-Zionists claim that a Machiavellian Zionist conspiracy forced these Jews out of their countries of birth. They buy into the myth that Jews are interlopers from Europe and the US – white Westerners who came to 'colonise' and 'steal land' from the 'native' Palestinian people to whom it rightfully belongs. This myth, drawing on Marxist terminology, gained increasing legitimacy after 1967 when Israel annexed East Jerusalem and 'conquered' the West Bank. The notion of 'occupation' and the use of the word 'settlers' reinforce the concept of Israeli 'colonisation' of 'Arab' land.

The colonialism myth supports the idea that Jews are merely adherents of a religion. At the time of the French Revolution, Clermont-Tonnerre said of the emancipation of Jews:[33] 'We must refuse everything to the Jews as a nation and accord everything to Jews as individuals.' This would lead to the Jewish community somehow disappearing, leaving only French citizens of Jewish religion or ancestry.[34]

With the rise of nationalism this concept of the Jew was replaced by a racial stereotype. However, the pendulum has swung back to viewing Jews as a faith community: thus anti-Zionists habitually talk about US citizens of the Jewish faith, Germans of the Jewish faith and now Arabs of the Jewish faith. Mizrahi leftist academics, like Ella Shohat in New York,[35] borrow heavily from Edward Said's post-colonialist bible *Orientalism*,[36] which divides the world crudely into 'the West versus the Rest', viewing both Mizrahim ('Arabs of the Jewish faith') and non-Jewish Arabs (the Rest) as victims of Zionism (the West). Ella Shohat features prominently in a film made in 2002, called *Forget Baghdad*, by the son of an Iraqi non-Jewish communist. The film-maker interviews four protagonists, Jewish members or ex-members of the Iraqi Communist Party including Shimon Ballas, who wrote *Ma'abara*, the first book to describe the experience of refugees in the tent camps. All were forced to flee to Israel, where they suffered varying degrees of cultural alien-ation. In a study, Professor Shohat finds that Israeli cinema depicts orientalist cultural stereotypes, casting Mizrahi Jews as 'boors or buffoons'.[37]

Anti-Zionist Mizrahim like Ella Shohat and Rachel Shabi see their people as conflicted between their binary 'Jewish and Arab' identities and despised by Israel's Ashkenazi establishment. Rachel Shabi writes: 'If Israel could find a way to reconnect with its own Middle-Eastern self, the chances are that this would result in the country having entirely different relations with the region. Because long before they were apparent arch-enemies', she claims, 'Arabs and Jews were culture collaborators, good neighbours – and friends.'[38] Shabi interviews Naima, who was seventeen when she left Iraq. Naima de-clared of her family's relations with their Arab neighbours: 'We got along, and how. Believe me, it was a pleasure.'[39]

Nevertheless, the concept of 'Arab-Jewish' identity remains controver-sial. As one wag put it, 'Mizrahim are not interested in being Arabs – except for the music and the food; a lot of Ashkenazim are not interested in being Jews, period.'[40] Furthermore, many Jews living in Arab countries in the twen-tieth century were influenced by Western – specifically French – culture, bore European first names, and many had a marked preference for the *chan-sons* of Edith Piaf over the ballads of Um Kalthum. No-one stole pure Mizrahi-Arab culture from the Jews of the Maghreb, 'because most of them had lost it long before they came to Israel'.[41] North African Jews arriving in Israel were nicknamed *Frenkim*. 'France was my soul home', writes André Aciman.[42] There are Arab-born refugees in the West who still say they are French so as to avoid having to explain their accents and convoluted life-story.

The writer Jacqueline Kahanoff coined the term Levantinism to describe the multiplicity of identities she enjoyed, growing up in cosmopolitan Egypt. Based on her personal experiences, she advocated a 'Mediterranean' model of coexistence between Jews and Arabs. Egyptian Jews were famously mul-tilingual, speaking an average of 4.5 languages, but often only rudimentary Arabic.[43] It was not unusual for them to have a foreign nationality, go to French schools, be cared for by a Balkan nanny, and a minority were the products of mixed Ashkenazi-Sephardi marriages.

Ellis Douek, an Egyptian-Jewish doctor uprooted to the UK (whose fam-ily had been British subjects since the eighteenth century) said that he had never pretended to be British, but that nowadays he felt more at home in

Britain – not because he became more British, but because Britain had become more foreign. To tell his patients that he was Egyptian confused them: the Arabs among them did not believe that Jews had ever lived in Egypt. Ellis Douek avoided describing himself as Jewish to British people, since they were embarrassed by religion.[44]

One Algerian-born Jewess who had lived in France before coming to England described her identity as Jewish. All through her perambulations, it was the one consistent thread of her identity. 'I've been Jewish all the time, the rest has changed', she said.[45]

A 2008 conference of Iraqi Jews[46] – the most 'arabised' of Middle Eastern Jewries, resoundingly rejected the expression 'Arab Jew' as a badge of identity. Purists define an 'Arab Jew' as one who is steeped in, or familiar with, literary Arabic. University of Haifa professor Reuven Snir, however, emphasised that the Jews who wrote literary works in Arabic in the early twentieth century felt no need to declare themselves Arabs. It might be more appropriate to describe as 'Arabic Jews' those who speak Arabic and have assimilated Arabic culture. Even if Jews from Arab countries were willing to identify as such, where does the expression 'Arab Jew' leave Babylonian, Must'arab, Karaite, Kurdish, Persian or Berber Jews? It is clearly an inadequate description of Haketia-, Ladino- and Aramaic-speaking Jews, not to mention Persian, Afghan, Bukharan and other Jews from the ex-Soviet Muslim republics, who speak Judeo-Farsi dialects and also form part of the 'greater Babylonian diaspora' dating back to the First Exile.

'Who am I?' the Iraq-born author Eli Amir asked rhetorically. 'I'm a bird wandering between two worlds, sometimes I'm in the West, and sometimes in the East. I'm a man whose dual roots allow me to stand strong. My legs still get confused between two worlds, but I'm a Jewish Zionist Israeli.'[47]

The vast majority of Jews have not historically identified as Arabs – in fact most would be offended to be so labelled. Moreover, to talk of 'Arab Jews', when Jews predated the Arab conquest by 1,000 years and lived for the most part under non-Arab Muslim rule, is ahistorical – strictly speaking, it ought only to describe Jews from the Arabian peninsula. Elsewhere the word 'Arab' meant, to many city dwellers, Bedouin – someone who roamed the desert and wore traditional robes.

As well as being an ethnic signifier of comparatively recent vintage, 'Arab Jew' gives equal weight to both elements, an equivalence that neither existed under *sharia* law nor Arab nationalist rule. The 'Arab world' is a community of language and culture, but Arabs have never achieved political union, despite efforts to unite various states into Arab federations. It is legitimate to talk of Egyptian and Iraqi Jews, citizens of nation states. But in the same way we could talk of Spanish Jews – citizens of Spain – we cannot do so of Hispanic Jews of Spanish language and culture, an imaginary construct.

Jews and Christians Compared

To shed more light on these questions of identity, a comparison between Jews and other Middle Eastern non-Muslim communities may be useful. Those Christians who were the most staunch proponents of 'secular' nineteenth century Arab nationalism, describing themselves as 'Arab Christians', have been either Antiochian Greek Orthodox or Melkite Greek Catholics, two sects found mainly in Syria, Lebanon and the Palestinian territories. In 2005, the Melkite Greek Catholic patriarch Gregory III Laham went on the record to say, 'we are the Church of Islam.'[48]

Among Assyrians, Maronites and Copts, however, matters are less clear-cut. Some Maronites subscribe to 'Phoenicianism', which traces a link between the ancient Phoenicians and the Lebanese of today. Among Copts, the notion of 'Pharaonism' emphasises Egyptian identity as a combination of descent from the Ancient Egyptians, Egypt's historically close links with the Mediterranean world, and individual nation-state patriotism. Finally, the Christians of Iraq virtually all reject the term 'Arab Christian'. Instead, they identify as ethnic Assyrians. Some Chaldean Catholics prefer a distinct Chaldean identity. There exist Assyrian and Chaldean nationalists.

Mizrahim? They were Heroes

The poverty and slum deprivation among Jewish immigrants from North Africa who arrived in Israel in the 1950s and 60s was real enough; it spawned Israel's own Black Panther movement in the 1970s. Menahem Begin's Likud

MK Shalom Cohen at Black Panther May Day rally, 1973 (Moshe Milner/Israel Government Press Office)

government was swept to power in 1977 on a wave of Mizrahi support, breaking the Labour Party's monopoly over Israeli politics.

A major watershed in this development was the *Tchaktchakhim* ('riffraff') speech delivered by media personality and comedian Dudu Topaz at a Labour election rally in 1981.[49] By then Mizrahim had earned their spurs in Israel's 1967 and 1973 wars. Topaz memorably said: 'The (Mizrahi) riffraff are in Metzudat Ze'ev (Likud Party headquarters in Tel Aviv). They are barely good enough to serve as guards on a base, if they even enlist. The soldiers and commanders of the combat units are right here.' Topaz's remarks echoed what the then chief of staff Mordechai (Motta) Gur had said in a 1978 newspaper interview about the 'Arab mentality': 'The Mizrahim will not be able to close the gap for another twenty or thirty years. All the money Israel has invested in the Mizrahim has yielded only partial results.'[50] In response Menachem Begin, the leader of Likud, made his 'Riffraff' speech, one of the best of his life. 'Mizrahim? They were heroes', he said. In his days fighting with the Etzel, they didn't know *tchakhtchakhim*. With both fists raised in the air he declared, 'Back then, we all fought together in the underground – Ashkenazim, Sephardim, Jews together!' Begin's speech is credited with winning the 1981 elections for Likud. Topaz spent the rest of his career in the wilderness, and ended up by committing suicide in jail.[51]

The Israeli left mimics the post-modern Western left and overlooks Mizrahi concerns in its enthusiasm to show empathy with the Palestinians: 'The Ashkenazi left doesn't want to hear or listen or know anything about Mizrahi Jews', says film-maker of Egyptian-Jewish background Eyal Sagui Bisawe: 'There is something very annoying for a lot of Mizrahi Jews that the Ashkenazi left go hand in hand with Palestinians but at the same time are ignoring them.'[52] Indeed, such attitudes go back a long way, as author Sami Michael, who joined the Communist Party in Israel in the 1950s, discovered: 'The Jewish Communist in Iraq was a Communist because he was a Jew, because the ideology was one of equality irrespective of religion ... Meanwhile, the party in Israel emphasized equality only for the Arabs.'[53]

The intelligentsia and media, by and large, treat the Palestinians as victims *par excellence* – the underdog in the Arab-Israeli conflict. The 'colonisation' of the narrative as a consequence of the Palestinian issue is, as we shall see, rampant in coexistence or interfaith initiatives. This has led to complaints that the concept of 'intersectionality' – the idea popular in American universities since the 1980s that oppressed groups should stand up for each other – fails to include oppressed Jews. The Black Lives Matter movement, in its adherence to 'intersectionality', endorses the boycott of Israel but completely disregards the affinity between the parallel civil rights struggles of indigenous Jews and Africans – both groups having suffered a history of oppression and enslavement by Arabs.[54]

Absent from Peace Projects

The 'Mizrahi story' is routinely omitted from coexistence and peace initiatives. When Janet Dallal, an Iraqi-born peacenik, attended a conference at the Neve Shalom/Wahat al-Salam Jewish-Arab village near Jerusalem, she was shocked that one session examining the 'healing of communal wounds to achieve reconciliation' did not recognise the trauma of Iraqi Jews – nor indeed the trauma suffered by any Jews from Arab countries. 'All they wanted to talk about was the Holocaust and the Arab *Nakba* [catastrophe]', she complains.[55]

As a teenager in Iraq, Janet lived through the trauma of Saddam Hussein's persecution of Jews in Iraq in the late 1960s and early 1970s. In 1972, her schoolmate Joyce Kashkoush and family were murdered in their own home and their bodies dismembered and put into the suitcases with which they intended to leave Iraq just a few days later. After introducing the subject, the Neve Shalom session moderator said: 'the most important step for healing is acknowledgement'. Our peacenik Janet could contain herself no longer and improvised a passionate speech. 'This is a crazy attitude. People lost their lives, others were hanged or slaughtered like sheep!' she exclaimed. The moderator promised that the issue would be included in future sessions, but a sea change is needed. The peace agenda is seriously skewed when a trauma afflicting more than half the Israeli population – those who descend from refugees from Arab and Muslim countries – has been airbrushed out of dialogue and coexistence projects.

These peace initiatives involve a disproportionate number of Ashkenazim, mostly on the political left.[56] Peaceniks generally see Israel as the guilty party and the Palestinians as innocent victims. Many may be genuinely ignorant of the plight of Jews who fled Arab countries with their lives and a suitcase, or they may be moral narcissists, or both. Their instinct is to reach out to victimised Palestinians, disadvantaged Arabs and even non-Jewish Africans in Israel, leapfrogging over the Mizrahim.

Why is it that Jews on the left hurry to support the Palestinian cause, yet show contempt for the rights of Mizrahi Jews? One could say it is ignorance, or the Eurocentricism of 'white', European Jews, some of whom have bought into the 'Israel-as-colonial-implant' myth. In truth, post-colonialism cannot admit that the relationship between Muslim rulers and their subservient Jews and Christians resembled that between colonisers and colonised. As one commentator puts it: 'The Western left can't talk about Muslim anti-Semitism because it would also have to talk about Muslim colonialism. And then the entire basis of its approach to the Arab and Muslim world would collapse.'[57] Because a 'right-wing' government under Benjamin Netanyahu gave its official blessing to the campaign for Justice for Jewish refugees, some members of the elite and media treat it as a cynical political ploy. They mutter disapprovingly about the politicisation of the Jewish refugee issue, without questioning the Palestinian politicisation of their 'refugee' issue. Thus genuine ex-refugees who are deterred by violence and hatred from returning to their countries of birth are ignored, while the radical left promotes the 'Palestinian narrative' of third- and fourth-generation 'refugees' who have never seen Palestine but insist on 'returning' there.

Mizrahim and the Arabs are depicted as blood brothers in leftist circles, yet Loolwa Khazzoom, the feminist and activist daughter of an Iraqi Jew,[58] discovered little sympathy for the Mizrahi cause among Arabs – unless Jews from Arab countries are prepared to ally themselves with Arabs against Ashkenazi Jews and compromise their Jewish identity. To be pro-Palestinian and pro-Jewish rights ought not to be mutually exclusive, yet all but a few feminists toe the anti-Zionist line. Khazzoom, in contrast, asks:

> What about Arabs speaking out about the injustices Mizrahi Jews suffered at the hands of Arabs? There are numerous Jewish organizations – in Israel and abroad – dedicated to giving land to or securing financial compensation for Palestinian Arabs; yet I do not know of one single Arab organization – Palestinian or otherwise – fighting to demand the same for Mizrahim.
>
> I am willing to stand up, speak out about, and fight against current Israeli oppression of Palestinian Arabs – whether at the hands of Ashkenazim, Mizrahim, or anyone else. I challenge my Arab sisters and brothers to be as willing to stand up and speak out about Arab oppression of Mizrahi Jews.

Khazzoom has been to several panels of Arab and Jewish women, where the Arabs were Muslim or Christian and the Jews were white Europeans. 'Every time, I have raised my hand and spoken about the invisibility of Mizrahi women on the panels. And every time, Arab women from the panel warmly have approached me after the program, taking me aside and telling me something like, "You and I are sisters. We are the same people. It's those Zionists that are the problem." Or, as one Arab woman added after a panel, "Those Ashkenazim are pigs."' 'Statements like these have made shivers go up my spine', says Loolwa Khazoom. 'They essentially have asked me to split myself in half, to connect on the basis of one half and forget about the other. They inherently have demanded that I structure my Middle Eastern reality around an Arab construct.'[59]

The Iran-born author Roya Hakkakian[60] has similar thoughts about how Iranians in the West ignore Jews as victims: 10,000 Jews or fewer remain in Iran – 10 per cent of the 1948 Jewish population.

> Such drastic diminishment of any population in the West would surely place that community on the endangered list, warranting the issuing

of buttons and stickers, pasted on car bumpers and the binders of idealistic freshmen in colleges. But somehow Bolivia was closer to the hearts of my compatriots than Ju-bareh, the Jewish district of their own Isfahan, where, as it happens, Jews had, indeed, built underground tunnels to alert each other when pogroms broke out: The extinction of a community to which Iran owes so much of its distinction as a non-Arab nation, a distinction so important to the Iranian sense of self, has never been recognized by Iran's elite, nor eulogised, for with the loss of the Jewish community Iran's claim to tolerance and Persian-ness will be harder to sustain. And so a nearly 3,000-year history is ending in silence.

The Discrimination Narrative

The 'Arab Jew' school of thought pioneered by Ella Habiba Shohat[61] and like-minded academics is a recent development. They attempt to impose an 'Arab-Jewish' identity on Jews which most Jews from Arab countries reject.[62] In a society where communities did not intermarry, Arabs did not consider Jews to be Arabs either. Interestingly, few intellectuals who glory in the label 'Arab Jew', were born in Arab countries, speak Arabic as their mother tongue, or lived in Arab countries for any length of time.

Secondly, discrimination in Israel became more a function of class than ethnicity. One needs to distinguish between the readily employable immigrants of Iraq and Egypt or even the Maghrebi urban mercantile class – multilingual and highly educated, courtesy of the Alliance Israëlite Universelle schools network – and, on the other hand, illiterate Jews, perhaps from the Kurdish and Atlas mountains, who had never seen a flushing toilet. (It is seldom remarked upon that discrimination could cut both ways, with Sephardim and Mizrahim equally suspicious and contemptuous, not just of Ashkenazim, but of each other's communities.)[63]

Thirdly, in its zeal to take the *galut* (diaspora) out of the Jew, Israel was equally hostile to the Yiddish culture of Eastern European Jews. Yiddish theatre was proscribed and Israelis discouraged from speaking their *mammaloshen* (mother tongue). 'That language grates on my ears', said David Ben-Gurion.[64]

Fourthly, many charges of early cultural discrimination no longer hold true in twenty-first century Israel. A survey by the Israel Democracy Institute[65] found that only 4.4 per cent of respondents thought that Ashkenazi discrimination towards Mizrahim was a point of conflict – ranking below the tension between religious and secular, right and left, rich and poor, and Jews and Arabs.

Mizrahi food culture has eclipsed *kreplach*, *kugel* or *lochshen* pudding on Israeli restaurant menus, while 'Mizrahi' music is the staple popular culture, a fact now acknowledged by *The Guardian*.[66] The ancient, religious *piyyutim* (psalms) sung by Mizrahi communities are experiencing a revival, inspiring even secular Israeli musicians. The Sephardi custom of eating *kitniyot* – rice and legumes – at Passover is now so widespread that even the US Conservative movement has ruled that they are permitted.[67] The younger generation of Sephardi Israelis are less pious than their parents, but many follow their traditions faithfully, to the point where tradition defines their identity.

In the first decades of the state, Israel's leadership strove to create a new Israeli citizen out of refugees from 120 countries. It decided what was good for the people, from television to the Beatles. With values infinitely preferable to Levantine corruption, extortion and lack of freedom, Israel boasted it was an outpost of Europe: an argument that has been turned against it by its enemies to considerable effect.[68]

Israel's first prime minister, David Ben-Gurion, reputedly said that the half-a-million Mizrahim flooding into the state in the 1950s and 1960s 'had the worst Jewish and human education'.[69] Jews from the Atlas or Kurdish Mountains may have been 'primitive' by western standards – but they knew their *Gemara* and *Mishna* inside out. But Ben-Gurion also told the Knesset in 1949 that, 'There is no reason to think that Jews from North Africa, Turkey, Egypt, Iran or Aden are fundamentally different from those of Lithuania, Galicia and America. They also have, deep inside, that pioneer spirit, an instinct for hard work and creativity.'[70]

Any Jews with a Western passport, education and connections could choose to go to the Americas or western Europe rather than languish in a leaky *ma'abara* in Israel. (Sometimes the conditions were only marginally better, with the refugees at first consigned to transit camps in France, Brazil or Britain.) Arriving in England after the Suez crisis, the parents of Clemy Lazarus started from rock bottom, determined to integrate into British society:[71]

> From the moment my parents arrived in England, they showed their gratitude to their British hosts by naming their newborn baby Elizabeth after the Queen of England. My father enrolled in night school to learn to speak English and soon spoke English better than any Englishman. My father became a dapper English gentleman, albeit with an Egyptian accent. When he could afford it he bought my mother the finest clothes and had bespoke suits made for himself along with matching bowler hats which he wore jauntily.[72]

The middle classes generally went to France, Britain, Australia, Canada and Latin America. Some have done spectacularly well and acquired international reputations: to name but a few – the public intellectual of Algerian origin Bernard-Henri Levy, the philosopher Jacques Derrida, the singer Enrico Macias, Egyptian-born businessman Sir Ronald Cohen, the Iranian-born textile tycoon Lord David Alliance, the Cairo-born cookery writer Claudia Roden, the Iranian art collector and entrepreneur Nasser David Khalili, the entertainers of Syrian descent Paula Abdul and Jerry Seinfeld, the Egyptian-Jewish movie mogul Haim Saban, the art and advertising tsars of Iraqi origin the Saatchi brothers, and the BBC creative director Alan Yentob. A startling number of Jews of Moroccan origin are Nobel prize-winners: Baruj Benacerraf (Medicine, 1980); Claude Cohen-Tannoudji (Physics, 1997) and Serge Haroche (Physics, 2012).[73]

Although it was then a struggling developing country, Israel took in the stateless, the destitute, the sick and the elderly – because they were Jews. The poorer classes went to Israel. A stubborn focus on discrimination obscures just how far Israel has come. Israel has its Mizrahi superstars: the internationally-renowned popular science professor of Lebanese origin Yuval Noah Harari and the architect Moshe Safdie, for example. Today Mizrahim are generals, accountants, doctors, property developers, bank managers and have held every government post except prime minister.

Most importantly, intermarriage is running at 25 per cent and the mixed Israeli family is fast becoming the norm. Soon there will be no such thing as Mizrahi or Ashkenazi in the Israeli melting pot. Professor Momi Dahan states[74] that the economic gap has narrowed so much that one can pronounce the integration of Mizrahim and Sephardim a palpable success.

Under-represented in Israel's Elite

None of this means the fight for equality has been won. Meyrav Wurmser penned a thoughtful essay[75] in 2005, arguing that discrimination was still very real – Sephardim and Mizrahim remain under-represented in academia and the media, and without doubt, still comprise the poorest and most disadvantaged of Jewish Israelis, especially among the ultra-orthodox. But anti-Zionism, Wurmser insisted, was the wrong cure for the disease. Rather, Mizrahi Jews need to seek solutions *within* the framework of an independent Jewish state.

Despite the existence of a Sephardi chief rabbi – and influential, if controversial, office-holders, like Rabbi Ovadia Yosef – you do not need to be anti-Zionist to lament the modern Ashkenazi dominance of thought and custom in the practice of religion, and the transformation of orthodox Sephardim, represented politically by the Shas party, at one time the third largest in the Knesset, into Yiddish-speaking 'Lithuanian' black-hats. The Ashkenazification of the Sephardi religious establishment has promoted the *shtetl*'s inward-looking view, rather than the easy-going Sephardi tradition, more integrated with the world outside the synagogue. One explanation for this phenomenon is that the mass of orthodox Jewry arriving in Israel from

Arab lands did not go through the Enlightenment, and lacked the confidence to engage with the West. The oriental religious leadership, therefore, felt it ought to tag along to the Ashkenazi religious establishment.

As a consequence of this, Sephardim and Mizrahim might find themselves drawing the short straw when applying to enter some of the most prestigious of Ashkenazi religious academies or Yeshivot. One notorious test case was the Bet Yacob girls' scandal, where parents were accused of pressuring an Ashkenazi seminary into segregating Sephardi girls.[76]

In spite of the inexorable march of assimilation in Israel, lingering resentments simmer below the surface. Every so often, and especially at election time, the 'ethnic demon' erupts into public debate. Benjamin Netanyahu's 2015 electoral victory thrust to the fore the sharp political cleavage in Israeli society between his predominantly Mizrahi support and 'Ashkenazi' backing for the centre-left. 'Drink cyanide, bloody Neanderthals. You won. Only death will save you from yourselves', wrote actress Alona Kimhi on her Facebook page after Netanyahu's win. (She later deleted her post.)[77]

Cultural Wars

An Ashkenazi-Mizrahi cultural war simmers beneath the surface. Addressing a Labour election rally in 2015, Yair Garbuz, head of the Cinematèque, cultural redoubt of the Ashkenazi-dominated elite, could barely disguise his contempt for the predominantly Mizrahi voters who were to secure the victory of the centre-right parties in the 2015 elections. He made disparaging comments about uneducated 'talisman-kissers' and 'tomb worshippers', code for Jews from Arab countries.[78]

Following the release of the Biton report recommending greater emphasis on Mizrahi heritage in the school curriculum, Gidi Orsher, a film critic, unleashed an anti-Mizrahi tirade. 'Next time you want protection from missiles, forget Iron Dome and put a chicken leg on your head', Orsher wrote, referring to a North African old wives' superstition.[79] After intervention by Israel's culture minister in the Netanyahu government, Miri Regev, Orsher was

Artwork by Meir Gal demonstrating how few pages in an Israel schoolbook were devoted to Mizrahi history.

suspended. Regev, of Moroccan origin (who proudly proclaims she has never read Chekhov) has declared war on Israel's snobbish elitists, the self-appointed arbiters of culture and thought. But even voices critical of the anti-Mizrahi outbursts[80] have failed to put their finger on a possible reason for the massive Mizrahi backing for Netanyahu's hawkish policies: cynicism about the prospects for peace based on bitter experience.

The voters were responding to immediate security threats from suicide bombings and rocket attacks. Few of those who demanded that the left do some soul-searching about their attitudes to the Mizrahim, however, pointed to the elephant in the room driving support for the 'right-wing': the subliminal memory of Arab or Muslim persecution experienced by parents and grandparents. They view the Palestinian *jihad* against the Jews of Israel as just the latest chapter in a long story of Arab and Muslim anti-Semitism. It's an anti-Semitism that Israel's Ashkenazi elite, plus a few *wannabe* Mizrahim, are all too ready to ignore or excuse.

Resigned Realism

For Israel's left, it is a bitter pill to swallow that an alliance between Mizrahi voters and hawkish Soviet immigrants has ensured, now and in the future, that the old Labour and leftist parties should remain in the political wilderness.

Israel's once-ruling Labour Party had its Zionist orientalists, romanticising the local Arab as 'a noble savage'. At the same time as Israel's leaders boasted how the country was living by Western norms – like democracy and the spirit of independent inquiry – alien to the rest of the chaotic and cruel Middle East, these orientalists believed that reconciliation with the Arab neighbours lay in convincing them that Israel was a Middle Eastern state like other Middle Eastern states. It would have to 'go native', becoming a genuine Middle Eastern state with the geopolitical priorities and instincts of its neighbours, as described by the historian Paul Johnson.[81]

The former Mossad chief Tamir Pardo recalled a conversation he had with an Arab official early on in his career. The official said:[82]

> How many Jews born in Israel know Arabic? How many are familiar with Arab culture? How many even want to know about it? How can you want to understand me when you live in the Middle East and don't know the language spoken by hundreds of millions around you? How many of your people have ever opened the Qur'an? Not to pray, but to try to understand what is written there – to understand the culture, understand that we are not all the same, and there is a difference between the Egyptian and the Jordanian, Palestinian, Saudi or Lebanese. You are not familiar with anything. You don't know anything. It's easier

for you to move to Canada. You will feel culturally more at home there than you do here; what the hell are you doing here? You still haven't chosen to be part of the Middle East.

We do not know what Pardo said in reply to the Arab official, but it would be a pity if he had nodded in sage agreement, failing to point out that Jews *were* indigenous to the Middle East and that they had helped found the region's culture. Never had the numbers of Jews who spoke and read Arabic and worked alongside their Muslim brethren been greater than at the end of the 1940s.[83] Jews have even been among the top Arabic grammarians.[84] As the author Naim Kattan discovered, a Jew's love of Arabic language and culture did not prevent the Muslim majority from treating him as an outsider.

If some Israeli Jews suffer from a 'colonial guilt complex' and hanker for Israel to 'go native', it was precisely the Jews coming from Arab countries who did not want Israel to be a Middle Eastern state like any other. In an essay on the sixtieth anniversary of the state of Israel, Paul Johnson wrote of the Sephardim/Mizrahim:

> Having suffered at Arab hands, they had none of the dreamy good will of some Ashkenazi founders and their successors. To the contrary, the Sephardim saw Arab and Israeli interests as clearly distinct, and clearly incompatible. Having come to Israel precisely because it was *not* a Middle Eastern state like the rest, they sought to keep it that way.
>
> In due course, these Jewish Middle Easterners played a crucial role in Israeli politics, decisively helping to bring about the fall of Labour and the end of the first phase of Israel's existence: the phase of socialist ideals and illusions, of high hopes deferred and grand visions unrealised. Now, starting in 1977, came the second phase – the phase of resigned realism – which, two decades later, is still with us.[85]

One result of Israel's departure from socialism is that the country has spawned its own 'adversary culture'[86] of alienated academics and politicians, some of whom have become militant anti-Zionists. For more than forty years, the right has won every Israeli election and much to the left's frustration, seems impossible to dislodge. The Mizrahi voter appears 'underneath the lot'.[87]

Meron Benvenisti, the former deputy mayor of Jerusalem, makes no secret of his scorn for Israelis who came from Arab lands. 'If we had not been here to take them in ... what would they be worth? We made a heroic decision to take them all in, and by that decision we effectively committed suicide.'[88] Now an advocate of a bi-national state, Benvenisti echoes the romantic orientalist view of the Arab shared by Israel's founders, David Ben-Gurion and Yitzhak Ben Zvi. 'I am drawn to the Arabs', he explained in an interview. 'I love their culture, their language, their approach to the land.'

The author and academic Joshua Muravchik points out the obvious contradiction between admiration for Arabs and contempt for Mizrahim: 'Of course [the Mizrahim] were culturally similar to the Arabs among whom they had lived for centuries, but apparently the same characteristics he found appealing in an Arab were repulsive in a Jew.'[89]

A Middle Eastern State

In terms of sheer weight of numbers, Mizrahim and Sephardim are destined to play an ever-increasing role in Israeli politics. Before the great Soviet immigration of the 1990s, Jewish refugees from Muslim lands and their descendants formed 70 per cent of the Jewish population in Israel. Today the largest community is the Russian, but with a substantial Mizrahi sub-group of Bukharan, Mountain and Georgian Jews. The second largest is the Moroccan, and the third, the Iraqi community.

Whether the elite like it or not, Israel is also, increasingly, a Middle Eastern state in terms of culture. The hit song *Habib Galbi*, performed in an almost extinct dialect of Judeo-Arabic by the Israeli girl band of Yemenite descent A-wa topped the Israeli charts in January 2016. (It aroused keen interest in the Arab world too – a Youtube video drew over 2 million hits.)[90] Mizrahi pop – or a synthesis of Eastern and Western music – has never been

The Israeli band A-Wa is inspired by Yemenite-Jewish songs (Tal Givony)

more popular. Israeli musicians are experimenting with a whole range of different musical styles and influences. Young Mizrahim are flocking to rediscover their inner Eastern selves at the poetry-reciting sessions by the Mizrahi writers of Ars Poetica. Founded by a Yemenite poet called Adi Keissar, the high-brow name is a pun on the derogatory Hebrew word for 'pimp' or 'chav' – *ars* – commonly applied to Mizrahim.

As the author and journalist Matti Friedman points out:,[91] a cultural and religious *fusion* is taking place:

> If they [the Mizrahim] joined the world of European Jews, the European Jews of Israel simultaneously, and unwittingly, joined theirs. The new identity known as 'Israeli' is a product of that meeting. This is what is not noticed by many observers, even the knowledgeable among them – and even the Israelis among them – who, it sometimes appears, see one country out their window and then sit down and write about another country entirely. As a result, they are left with stale ideas and an out-of-date story that is increasingly useless in explaining the country as it exists right now. They miss the lively and potent fuel that drives the place, and they underestimate its resilience.

Notes

1. Jonathan Kaplan, 'Absorbing the Exiles', *My Jewish Learning* (no date), http://www.myjewishlearning.com/article/absorbing-the-exiles/. (Last accessed 26 April 2017).
2. Joint Distribution Committee archives, 'The 1950s', http://archives.jdc.org/search-the-archives/. (Last accessed 26 April 2017).
3. Eli E. Hertz, 'Arab and Jewish Refugees: the Contrast', 2007, http://www.mythsandfacts.org/conflict/8/refugees.pdf. (Last accessed 26 April 2017).
4. Joint Distribution Committee archives http://search.archives.jdc.org/multimedia/Documents/NY_AR_45-54/NY_AR45-54_Count/NY_AR45-54_00004/NY_AR45-54_00004_01102.pdf. (Last accessed 26 April 2017).
5. Gabriel Lipschitz, *Country on the Move: Migration to and within Israel, 1948–1955* (Kluwer Academic Publishers 1998), Chapter 2.
6. Rebecca L. Torstrick, *The Limits of Coexistence: Identity Politics in Israel* (University of Michigan, 2000), p.235.
7. Raphael Luzon, *Libyan Twilight* (Darf, 2016), p.27.
8. Neta Alexander, 'Alexandria of the 1940s was like Tel Aviv of the 1990s', *Haaretz*, 19 September 2015, http://www.haaretz.com/israel-news/.premium-1.676412. (Last accessed 26 April 2017).
9. Eli Amir, *Scapegoat*, (Am Oved, 2012).
10. Yitzhak Bar-Moshe, *Exodus from Iraq*, in Ora Melamed (ed.) *Annals Of Iraqi Jewry: A collection of Articles and Reviews* Translated by Edward Levin, (Jerusalem: Eliner Library, 1995), pp.35765.
11. Yossi Sadan, 'In exile from paradise', *Haaretz*, 20 August 2010.
12. Chochana Boukhobsa,'Rien sur l'enfance' in Leila Sebbar (ed.) *Une Enfance en Méditeranée musulmane*(Bleu autour, 2012), p.186.

13. Rachel Shabi, *Not the Enemy: Israel's Jews from Arab Lands* (London: Yale University Press, 2009).

14. Lyn Julius: 'Rachel Shabi's Post-Zionism: a critique', *Fathom*, Autumn 2015, http://fathomjournal.org/rachel-shabis-mizrahi-post-zionism-a-critique/. (Last accessed 26 April 2017).

15. Ibid.

16. 'HaKeshet HaDemocratit HaMizrahit', *Wikipedia*, https://en.wikipedia.org/wiki/Mizrahi_Democratic_Rainbow_Coalition. (Last accessed 26 April 2017).

17. Sami Michael, 'Israel, the most racist state in the industrialised world' *+972 Magazine*, 9 August 2012, http://972mag.com/author-sami-michael-israel-is-the-most-racist-state-in-the-industrialized-world/52602/. (Last accessed 26 April 2017). Inter-ethnic tensions could be said to have boiled over in the Wadi Salib riots, Haifa, in 1959.

18. The Ramat Gan Committee of Baghdadi Jews, https://baghdadijews.wordpress.com/english/. See 'Ramat Gan Committee challenges Campaign', *Point of No Return*, 17 September 2012, http://jewishrefugees.blogspot.co.uk/2012/09/ramat-gan-committee-challenges-refugee.html. (Last accessed 26 April 2017).

19. See Shabi, *Not the Enemy*, p.229.

20. See, for example, Ella Shohat 'The Invention of the Mizrahim', *Journal of Palestine Studies*, Vol. 29, No. 1 (Autumn, 1999), pp.5–20, http://www.jstor.org/stable/2676427. (Last accessed 26 April 2017).

21. See Meyrav Wurmser, 'Post–Zionism and the Sephardi Question', *Middle East Quarterly*, Spring 2005, pp.21–30, http://www.meforum.org/707/post-zionism-and-the-sephardi-question. (Last accessed 26 April 2017).

22. Abbas Shiblak, *Iraqi Jews: A History* (Saqi, 2005), p.58.

23. Norman Stillman, *The Jews of Arab Lands: A History and Source Book*, Vol. II (Philadelphia, PA: Jewish Publication Society of America, 1979), p.23.

24. Esther Meir-Glitzenstein, *Zionism in an Arab Country: Jews in Iraq in the 1940s* (Routledge, 2004), pp.35–47.

25. G. Bensoussan, *Juifs en pays arabes: le grand déracinement* (Tallandier, 2012), p.436.

26. Achcar, *The Arabs and the Holocaust: The Arab-Israeli War of Narratives* (New York: Metropolitan, 2009), p.64.

27. Lewis, *Semites and anti-Semites* (New York: Norton, 1986), p.205.

28. Conversation with Rabbi I. Elia, 2015.

29. Doreen Wachmann, 'Shmuel Moreh goes from horrors of Iraq to prizewinning professor', *Jewish Telegraph*, July 2009.

30. Revd J. Parkes, *Arabs and Jews in the Middle East: A tragedy of errors* (London: Gollanz, 1967).

31. Ofer Aderet, 'When Arabs and Mizrahi Jews dreamed of a joint homeland', *Haaretz*, 19 March 2017, http://www.haaretz.com/life/books/.premium-1.777951. (Last accessed 26 April 2017).

32. Yuval Avivi, 'Why is Middle Eastern culture missing from Israeli schoolbooks?' *Al-Monitor*, 8 March 2016, http://www.al-monitor.com/pulse/originals/2016/03/mizrahi-identity-school-litterature-poets-arab-countries.html#ixzz42UM5szPg. (Last accessed 26 April 2017).

33. 'Deux acteurs de la Revolution Française', *Akadem*, http://www.akadem.org/medias/documents/Doc1_deux_acteurs_Revolution_Fr.pdf. (Last accessed 26 April 2017).

34. A group of French- Jewish intellectuals belonging to the Cercle Gaston Crémieux have taken this idea further, relinquishing both synagogue and Zionism to pursue the ideals of the French republic. See J. Friedman, 'Les juifs et le droit à la difference: entre l'idéal de l'état nation et le nationalisme des minorités', https://ccrh.revues.org/2811. (Last accessed 26 April 2017).

35. E.H. Shohat, 'Reflections by an Arab Jew', *Bint Jbeil*, http://www.bintjbeil.com/E/occupation/arab_jew.html. (Last accessed 26 April 2017).

36. Edward Said, *Orientalism*, (Penguin, 2003).

37. Stephen Holden, 'Film review: born in Iraq, living in Israel, pondering issues of identity', *New York Times*, 5 December 2003, http://www.nytimes.com/movie/review?res=9E01E0D8173DF936A35751C1A9659C8B63. (Last accessed 26 April 2017).

38. See Julius, 'Rachel Shabi's Post-Zionism: a critique', *Fathom*, Autumn 2015.

39. See Shabi, *Not the Enemy*, p.102.

40. Remark attributed to the apostate Jew Abdullah Schaffer in *Al-Arabiya*. Quoted by Rodin New York *Point of No Return* blog, 14 August 2016, http://jewishrefugees.blogspot.co.uk/2016/08/mizrahi-studies-to-be-mandatory-in.html?showComment=1471203358068#c9212166224335098127. (Last accessed 26 April 2017).

41. Oded Lifshitz, 'The flawed narrative of Israel's deprivation activists', *Haaretz*, 20 July 2016, http://www.haaretz.com/opinion/.premium-1.732108. (Last accessed 26 April 2017).

42. André Aciman, 'An Alexandrian in search of lost time', *Newsweek*, 2 June 2011.

43. Racheline Barda, 'The Second exodus of the Jews of Egypt 1948–67', unpublished PhD thesis submitted to Sydney University.

44. Ellis Douek interviewed by Bea Lewkowicz, *Sephardi Voices UK*, 2016.

45. Jocelyne Shrago interviewed by Bea Lewkowicz, *Sephardi Voices UK*, 2015.

46. Vered Lee, 'Conference asks: Iraqi-Israeli, Arab Jew or Mizrahi Jew?' *Haaretz*, 18 May 2008, http://www.haaretz.com/print-edition/features/conference-asks-iraqi-israeli-arab-jew-or-mizrahi-jew-1.246035. (Last accessed 26 April 2017).

47. Eli Amir in conversation with Tsionit Fattal Kuperwasser at the Babylonian Heritage Center, Israel, April 2017.

48. Interview in *30 Days in the Church and the World*, no.10, 2005, published by the Synod of Bishops.

49. 'Dudu Topaz arrested for ordering attack on TV executives', *The Jerusalem Post*, 31 May 2009.

50. Lily Galili,'Up the down escalator' *Haaretz* ,25 January 2007.

51. Ibid.

52. Alex Shams interviewing Eyal Sagui Bisawe in *Jadaliyya*, 7 July 2015, http://www.jadaliyya.com/pages/index/22090/arab-film-on-israeli-television_an-interview-with-n. (Last accessed 26 April 2016).

53. T. Morad, D .Shasha and R. Shasha (eds), *Iraq's last Jews*, (Palgrave Macmillan, 2008), p.70.

54. Micha Danzig, 'The real intersectionality of European and Arab oppression and persecution of Jews and Africans', *Times of Israel*, 22 August 20126, http://blogs.timesofisrael.com/the-real-intersectionality-european-and-arab-oppression-and-persecution-of-jews-and-africans/. (Last accessed 26 April 2016).

55. Lyn Julius, 'How coexistence projects can hinder peace', *Jerusalem Post*, 23 November 2011, also at *Point of No Return* http://jewishrefugees.blogspot.co.uk/2011/11/how-co-existence-projects-can-hinder.html. (Last accessed 26 April 2017).

56. Tom Mehager, 'Why Mizrahim don't vote for the Left', + *972 Magazine*, 24 January 2015.

57. Daniel Greenfield, 'Don't excuse Muslim antisemitism', quoted in *Point of No Return*, 24 January 2015, http://jewishrefugees.blogspot.co.uk/2015/01/dont-excuse-muslim-anti-semitism.html. (Last accessed 26 April 2017).

58. Loolwa Khazoom blog, 'A piece is missing from this peace', http://www.loolwa.com/archive/articles/pgs/piece.html. (Last accessed 26 April 2017).

59. Ibid.

60. Roya Hakkakian, 'Smelly little orthodoxies', *Tablet*, 4 September 2014, http://www.tablet-mag.com/jewish-news-and-politics/182845/iran-intellectual-left. (Last accessed 26 April 2017).

61. Shohat, 'Sephardim in Israel: Zionism from the Standpoint of its Jewish victims', *Social Text*, Autumn 1988, https://palestinecollective.files.wordpress.com/2013/10/sephardim-in-israel_-zionism-from-the-standpoint-of-its-jewish-victims.pdf. (Last accessed 26 April 2017).

62. See Lee, 'Conference asks'.

63. The snobbery of those who claimed to be *Sephardi tahor* (pure Sephardi) is legendary. Until the twentieth century it was unthinkable for a Sephardi to marry an Ashkenazi *todesco* (German). ['A Spanish attitude': Elias Canetti's childhood reminiscences of Bulgaria 1905–1911' in Julia Phillips Cohen and Sarah Abrevaya Stein (ed.) *Sephardi Lives* (Stanford University Press, 2014), p. 80]. Those Ashkenazim who had moved to Egypt were known by the majority Sephardi community as *schlechtes* (dirty). [1925 report by Julius Berger quoted in Gudrun Krämer, *The Jews in Modern Egypt* 1914 –52 (IB Tauris, 1989), p.87].

64. Eli Kavon, 'When Zionism feared Yiddish', *Jerusalem Post*, 5 November 2014, http://www.jpost.com/Opinion/Op-Ed-Contributors/When-Zionism-feared-Yiddish-351939. (Last accessed 26 April 2017).

65. 'The social realm', *Israeli Democracy Index 2015*, p.69, http://en.idi.org.il/media/4256544/democracy_index_2015_eng.pdf. (Last accessed 26 April 2017).

66. Peter Beaumont ,'Israel's sidelined Mizrahi Musicians and artists reclaim centre stage', *The Guardian*, 17 January 2017, https://www.theguardian.com/world/2017/jan/17/israels-sidelined-mizrahi-musicians-and-artists-reclaim-centre-stage. (Last accessed 26 April 2017).

67. Lisa Schoenfein, 'Conservative movement overturns 800-year old Passover ban on rice and legumes', *Forward*, April 2016, http://forward.com/culture/food/338525/conservative-movement-overturns-800-year-old-passover-ban-on-rice-and-legum/. (Last accessed 26 April 2017).

68. See, for example, Chandra Kumar, 'Herzl's Vision Realized: Israel as Outpost of Western Civilisation in Asia', *The Palestine Chronicle*, 12 December 2014.

69. Sylvia Schwartz, 'How Long can Israel depend on Mizrahi docile loyalty? Smadar Lavie asks in her new book', Mondoweiss blog, 7 July 2014.

70. D. Ben-Gurion, *Israel – A Personal History*, p.371, quoted in Martin Gilbert, *In Ishmael's House*, p.313.

71. 'Suez 1956: how we survived exile from Egypt', *Point of No Return*, http://jewishrefugees.blogspot.co.uk/2017/02/suez-1956-how-we-survived-exile-from.html. (Last accessed 26 April 2017).

72. Ibid.

73. Oded Lifshitz, 'The flawed narrative of Israel's Mizrahi deprivation activists', *Haaretz*, 20 July 2016, http://www.haaretz.com/opinion/.premium-1.732108. (Last accessed 26 April 2017).

74. Anat Georgi, 'Melting-pot Culture Has Proved Recipe for Success in Israel, Claims Mizrahi Professor' *Haaretz*, 19 July 2016, http://www.haaretz.com/israel-news/business/.premium-1.666435. (Last accessed 26 April 2017).

75. Wurmser, 'Post-Zionism and the Sephardi question', *Middle East Quarterly*, Spring 2005, pp. 21–30, http://www.meforum.org/707/post-zionism-and-the-sephardi-question. (Last accessed 26 April 2017).

76. Yair Ettinger, 'Court to weigh sanctioning parents for school segregation', *Haaretz*, 29 April 2010, http://www.haaretz.com/court-to-weigh-sanctioning-parents-for-school-s-segregation-1.287363. (Last accessed 26 April 2017).

77. Lyn Julius, 'A dose of Neanderthal realism', *Times of Israel*, 25 March 2015, http://blogs.timesofisrael.com/a-dose-of-neanderthal-realism/. (Last accessed 26 April 2017).

78. Dimi Reider, 'Underneath electoral hype, Israel's ethnic divide', *Middle East Eye*, 15 March 2015, http://www.middleeasteye.net/columns/underneath-electoral-hype-israel-s-ethnic-divide-604876824. (Last accessed 26 April 2017).

79. Seth Frantzman, 'An Israeli film critic's rant and the legacy of 1950s racism', blog, 10 July 2016, https://sethfrantzman.com/2016/07/10/an-israeli-film-critics-rant-and-the-legacy-of-1950s-israeli-racism. (Last accessed 26 April 2017).

80. Ari Shavit, 'Israel's Center-left is sick, sterile and detached', *Haaretz*, 18 June 2015, http://www.haaretz.com/opinion/.premium-1.661791. (Last accessed 26 April 2017).

81. Paul Johnson, 'Israel: the miracle', *Commentary*, reproduced in *Jewish Ideas Daily*, 10 May 2011, http://www.jewishideasdaily.com/878/features/israel-the-miracle/. (Last accessed 26 April 2017).

82. 'Israel faces no existential threats, says departing Mossad chief, *Times of Israel*, 16 January 2016, http://www.timesofisrael.com/israel-has-no-existential-threats-says-departing-mossad-chief/?utm_source=dlvr.it&utm_medium=twitter. (Last accessed 26 April 2017).

83. Abitbol, *Le Passé d'une Discorde: Juifs et Arabes depuis le VIIe siècle* (Paris: Perrin, 2003), p.427.

84. Kattan, *Adieu Babylone* (Montreal: La Presse, 1975), p.26.

85. See Johnson, 'Israel: the miracle', *Commentary*.

86. Joshua Muravchik, *Making David into Goliath* (New York: Encounter Books, 2014), p.137.

87. The expression derives from T.S. Eliot's famous poem, *Burbank with a Baedeker, Bleistein with a Cigar*.

88. Joshua Muravchik, *Making David into Goliath* (New York: Encounter Books, 2014) , p.143.

89. Ibid.

90. 'Jewish-Israeli band making waves with Arabic song', *Al-Jazeera*, 12 Jan 2016, http://www.aljazeera.com/news/2016/01/jewish-israeli-band-arabic-song-160112132639331.html. (Last accessed 26 April 2017).

91. Matti Friedman, 'Mizrahi Nation', *Mosaic*, 1 June 2014, http://mosaicmagazine.com/essay/2014/06/mizrahi-nation. (Last accessed 26 April 2017).

Myths, Lies and Omissions

On the Jewish festival of Shavu'oth, on 1 and 2 June 1941, a pogrom broke out in Iraq which claimed the lives of hundreds of Jews. It is not known how many exactly were murdered – figures vary from 145 to 600. Thousands of Jews were injured, women raped, babies mutilated, property wrecked and looted. Some brave Arabs saved their Jewish neighbours. Others turned against them. The mayhem went on for two days until the British army, camped out on the outskirts of Baghdad, belatedly intervened against the rioters. The *Farhud*, as it was known, became seared in the memory of those who survived, and sounded the death knell for the ancient Jewish community of Iraq. Ten years later almost all the Jews had left.

These had been the facts about the *Farhud*. Until an Israeli professor tried to change them.[1] The story begins in January 2007, when I stumbled upon a lecture which Professor Sasson Somekh, an emeritus professor of Modern Arabic Literature at Tel Aviv University, had given at Vanderbilt University, USA, the previous November. One paragraph, though, sounded particularly controversial. Professor Somekh stated: 'We forget that although 150 Jews were killed, at least 200 Muslims were killed at the same disturbances and those 200 Muslims because they wanted to defend their Jewish neighbours. And this must be written in letters of fire.'[2]

Sensing that something did not ring true, I alerted Salim Fattal, a Baghdad-born broadcaster and author who had interviewed survivors of the *Farhud* for a series of TV programmes. Fattal challenged Somekh, who blamed a reporter on the Vanderbilt newsletter for misquoting him. But Somekh's words had been recorded for all to hear.[3]

Salim Fattal then rubbished Somekh's claim:

> The new theory that 250 Iraqi Muslims sacrificed their own lives only to save or defend their Jewish neighbors is absolute nonsense. This is a new, pathetic attempt to add to the bloody massacre some rosy color and to twist the very simple truth that Arab society was hostile or, in the best case, indifferent to the Jewish tragedy.
>
> At the time, Arab public opinion in Iraq, as well as in other Arab countries, including North Africa, was openly admiring of Nazi Germany and was fanatically against the British and the Jews as well. My uncle Meir Kalif and his partner Nahom Qazzaz were assassinated

in the pogrom. Their bodies were never found. Our two families were very much involved in searching and tracing their disappearance but in our entire search we never heard such a legendary story.

Researching his TV documentary series, Fattal interviewed over 100 Jews; not one of them claimed that Muslims were killed defending their Jewish neighbours, or simply killed. On the contrary, he heard that some Muslims had joined the rioters in killing or looting from their Jewish neighbours. The revisionist version of the facts was an insult to those many Muslim rescuers of Jews who were living heroes:

> If 250 Muslims were killed while defending Jews and only 150 Jews were killed, if, out of a total of 400 victims, nearly 65 per cent were Muslims and nearly 35 per cent were Jews, then we can definitely say that the pogrom initiated and carried out by Muslims was not directed against Jews but against Muslims. Can anybody conceive such absurdity?
>
> Yes! There were some Muslims who gave shelter to their Jewish neighbors. Some Muslims challenged the rioters by telling them that 'if you want to kill my neighboring Jews you have first to kill me'. They were noble citizens but none of them was killed. Rioters didn't kill Muslims. And yes, hundreds of Muslims were killed in the second day of the pogrom. But they were killed as rioters by the forces of law and order.

The Israeli 'new historians' have done much to smash up the sacred cows of Israel's 'Zionist' narrative, especially the events of the 1948 war of independence. Now the sacred facts of Iraqi-Jewish history were being rewritten and an anti-Jewish pogrom stripped of its Jewish significance. Realising that something must be rotten in the Israeli academy if Somekh's fabrications could be freely disseminated, Salim Fattal decided to write a book. *An idol in the Temple of the Israeli Academy* not only sets the record straight on the *Farhud*, but inveighs against revisionist academics with a post- or anti-Zionist political agenda.

The facts have been distorted and, as in the above example, Jews from Arab countries are often themselves to blame for distorting their own history 'to flatter' their enemies. Such a tendency can be viewed as a symptom of the *dhimmi* syndrome – centuries of ingrained Jewish insecurity and dehumanisation.[4]

Living in freedom in Israel or the West after fourteen centuries of humiliation and alienation may not be enough to bolster a Mizrahi Jew's confidence, self-esteem or sense of empowerment. For instance, one Moroccan Israeli named Mordechai never shared his story with his own grandchildren. The owner of a large and prosperous factory in Marrakesh, Mordechai abandoned his business, house, and motherland to come to Israel with nothing: his daughter Rachel, diagnosed with a rare disease, was refused treatment in Morocco because she was Jewish. She eventually became blind because she was not treated in time. Yet Mordechai told his Israeli-born children and grandchildren that his motive was 'Zionist'.[5]

A second category of Jews are those who like to act as ambassadors for Arab countries (specifically Morocco and Tunisia). The well-to-do, who could bribe their way out of trouble, ignored or denied the persecutions afflicting the poorer classes. Business interests often dictate that they downplay the suffering endured by their less fortunate brethren, emphasising the points of connection between Jews and Arabs.[6]

Another variant of 'Jewish denial' has been identified by Robert Satloff, author of *Among the Righteous*. He found some Jews were so anxious to put a positive spin on the way they were treated, they even claimed that the 'Nazis were not so bad':

> As the last remnant of a people who had mastered the art of living as a tolerated community – sometimes protected, often abused, always second class – over 1,400 years of Muslim rule, these Jews long ago made peace with their lot. Their silence about the persecution they suffered at the hands of the Nazis and their Vichy and Fascist allies is just the latest in a string of silences.[7]

There is no simple explanation for 'Jewish denial'. Levantine peoples are known often to be reluctant to share their private thoughts. There are also cultural factors – a sort of shame/honour reticence to talk about painful or unpleasant memories. It is beneath their dignity to revisit hurt and humiliation. But there is also the silence of the 'internally colonised': communities remaining in Arab and Muslim lands could be said to suffer from this *dhimmi* syndrome. They are desperate to show their appreciation of Muslim 'tolerance'. Their survival has depended on their keeping on the right side of those in power in Arab and Muslim autocracies. It was to ingratiate itself with the powers-that-be that, in 2014, the microscopic Jewish community in Egypt hosted an *iftar* dinner (the meal that concludes the Ramadan fast).[8] The dwindling Jewish community of Turkey did the same in 2015.[9]

Tunisian-Jewish leader Roger Bismuth reserved his highest praise for the country's autocratic president, Zine el-Abidine Ben Ali, who had been in office since seizing power in a bloodless coup in 1987. 'The president is good to us', Bismuth told the reporter, Larry Luxner of the *Jewish Telegraphic Agency*,[10] praising Ben Ali for restoring synagogues and assuring Jewish community security. But after Ben Ali was ousted in 2011and denounced by his countrymen as a corrupt and nepotistic dictator, Bismuth abruptly changed his tune in accordance with the *zeitgeist*. 'He was behaving like a crook', Bismuth announced. 'He and his family stole property from people and the state, and they destroyed everything they could put their hands on.'[11]

Silence and Distortion

In the decades while nothing was said about Jews from Arab countries, myths and lies filled the vacuum. 'Because we never wrote the history of the Jews from Arab lands, the Arab states and Palestinians have written it for them', said Jean-Claude Niddam, ex-head of the legal department in Israel's Ministry of Justice.[12] Efforts in Israel and the West to raise awareness of the mass displacement of Jews from Arab lands – feeble, underfunded and piecemeal though they have been – crash into numerous brick walls, both inadvertent and ideological. These perpetuate a 'colonisation of the facts'.

A key reason for the invisibility of the Jewish *Nakba* is that the diaspora Jewish leadership and international Jewish groups fighting anti-Semitism and Israel's cause are overwhelmingly of European background, and tend to project a Eurocentric world view. Their frame of reference is Europe and the Holocaust, not the destruction of the Jewish communities of the Muslim world. The Ashkenazi-dominated diaspora in general sees the 'Mizrahi' issue as a niche concern of interest only to Sephardim and Mizrahim. The situation is not helped by the folklore that passes for Mizrahi history in the Jewish press and media – the nostalgic celebration of tradition, costume, music and food.

US Jewish liberals see Israel through the lens of conflict and universalise their concern for civil and social issues. One journalist found it impossible to interest the US Jewish press in an article on Mizrahi poverty in Israel: 'While poverty may be a Jewish concern abroad, wrapped up in such concepts as *tikkun olam* [repairing the world], it isn't a sexy issue. African refugees in Israel are interesting, Jews from Africa less interesting.'[13] Arab and Muslim anti-Jewish prejudice, like anti-Semitism generally, is often ignored, derided or downplayed.[14] 'Islamophobia', however, seems to demand equivalent attention.

Even where there is awareness of the mass expulsion of Jews from Arab lands, they are not generally seen as victims: their plight was apparently successfully resolved. In the fashionable 'hierarchy of oppression' of marginalised groups, Jews rank well down the list. They are seen to enjoy power, despite their history as a vulnerable minority, and 'white privilege', despite their ethnic origins in the Middle East.

When the US government introduced a 'Middle East' category in its census,[15] a number of US Jews hesitated to describe themselves as 'people of colour', perhaps in order to de-emphasise their Jewish identity so that they might more easily assimilate in US society. Even Mizrahi Jews living in the US could not bring themselves to tick the 'Middle East box', thinking they had not experienced the requisite marginalisation associated with 'people of colour'. [16]

In Israel, where Jews of Middle Eastern and North African descent form a majority, the Ashkenazi elite remains resistant to telling their story. Schools have done little to educate about Jewish history and heritage in Arab countries. Every schoolchild knows about the Kishinev riots of 1903, which claimed 49 Jewish lives, but not many have heard of the *Farhud* in Iraq, which took 179 identified Jewish lives. They learn about the *Bilu'im* – the waves of Ashkenazi pioneers who settled the land and founded the *Yishuv*'s institutions – and nothing about the Yemenite Jews who preceded them. In 1997, the artist Meir Gal ridiculed this state of affairs in a tableau called 'Nine out of 400', with himself holding the 9 pages out of 400[17] which covered the history of Jews in Muslim lands in an Israeli school textbook.

This resistance to acknowledging a balanced view of history is reflected in the public space and media and extends to amnesia about recent history. Israel's official spokesmen hardly ever mention the 850,000 Jewish refugees expelled from Arab lands. In spite of recent moves to introduce more Mizrahi content into the Israeli school curriculum, as recommended by the Biton Report, the lingering cultural dominance of the Labour-supporting Ashkenazi elite in education and public diplomacy has ensured that the Jewish *Nakba* is invisible – absent from the history books.

The Israeli film-maker of Iraqi origin Duki Dror accused the Arts Commission in charge of recommending the *Sal Tarbut* – works approved for teaching or showing in schools – of 'deleting 2,000 years of Jewish history in the Middle East and North Africa' when it rejected *Shadow in Baghdad*, Dror's documentary about Linda Menuhin's desperate search for traces of her father, abducted in 1972. Although it acknowledged that *Shadow in Baghdad*, which has been internationally acclaimed and shown at film festivals worldwide, was one of the few films that depicted Jewish history in Arab countries, the Commission's rejection letter cited 'the violent images of executions in the film as being inappropriate for young children'. The film shows actual footage of nine Jews hanged in Baghdad's Liberation Square in 1969 as alleged spies. Yet, Dror pointed out, Israeli schoolchildren are regularly exposed to horrific images of the Holocaust.

Israel has also suffered from a string of left-leaning ministers of education[18] who have been more enthusiastic about teaching the Palestinian *Nakba* than informing the more than 50 per cent of Israeli schoolchildren with Mizrahi and Sephardi backgrounds of their own history and heritage.

Misguided attempts to arabise the school curriculum may end up condemning the distinctive Judeo-Arabic culture to death. For instance, dialects preserved over millennia will die with the generation born in Arab

A memorial in Ramat Gan, Israel, to Iraqi Jews executed in January 1969.

lands. Well-meaning attempts to teach Arabic in schools[19] may kill off any attempt to pass on Judeo-Arabic to Israeli schoolchildren by insisting that the teachers instruct only Palestinian Arabic.

So if Jews themselves repress the facts, are apt to idealise their history, are ignorant of it, or Israel barely teaches it, what hope is there of 'de-colonising' the narrative – persuading the outside world of the importance of the issue and the justness of the Jewish refugee cause?

In the reams written about the Arab-Israeli conflict, it is rare to find any mention in the mainstream media of Jewish refugees from Arab countries. The Palestinian Arab refugee narrative hogs the limelight. The behaviour of Jews in Israel, many believe, is driven by paranoia resulting from the European Holocaust. The Israel-Palestine conflict plays a primary role in 'virtue-signalling', and suits those who wish to promote the idea that Palestinian refugees were the sole victims of an Israeli injustice. In order to gain credibility, the 'colonisation of the facts' must promote a 'narrative' of Palestinian exceptionalism. The injustice of the Arab *Nakba* is set alongside the European Holocaust – resulting in an Israel 'born in sin' – as two sides of the same coin, instead of being positioned alongside the injustice of the Jewish *Nakba*.

Although it is one of the largest of refugee movements from the Arab world until the Islamic State Iraqi insurgency and the Syrian civil war, the story of the forgotten Jewish refugees is invariably omitted from Western coverage of the Israeli-Arab (or more commonly, Israel-Palestinian) conflict. In December 2015, *The Washington Post* refused to correct an infographic on refugees worldwide since the Second World War[20] omitting altogether any mention of the 856,000 Jewish refugees.[21]

The 'colonisation' of the facts' afflicts higher education. The post-modern academic study of the Middle East has become politicised – and the inflow of massive sums of Arab petrodollars has corrupted Middle Eastern studies departments in Western colleges and universities: the displacement of Jews from Arab countries has been brushed under the 'Persian' carpet. When Muslim-Jewish relations are examined, universities often present a politically-correct version of history which sanitises the points of division or erases them altogether. You could term it '*dhimmi* denial', the eastern counterpart to Holocaust denial. Anyone brazen enough to call out 'Muslim anti-Semitism' is accused of 'islamophobia'.[22]

Political correctness blocks research. In the words of Professor Jeffrey Herf:

> Avoidance of facts about the affinities between Islamism and Nazism – with the European extreme right – has become a leftist academic signal of anti-colonial militancy. Rarely if ever has avoidance of research on the history of anti-Semitism found a more effective banner than that of the slogans of leftist anti-racism and anti-Zionism.[23]

The deck is stacked against a balanced study of historical events. The archives of the Arab states remain closed. Although the 'Arab Spring' has brought forth more interest in the past, much nostalgia for it and more freedom for Arabs to express themselves about it, Arab scholars have traditionally acted more like official servants of their regimes than *bona fide* historians. Arab states do not want to acknowledge their responsibility for expelling the Jews from Arab countries. Those that do, like the Moroccan specialist in Jewish history, Mohamed Kenbib, blame the Jews for their own misfortune.[24]

Only a handful of Western historians specialise in Jews from the Middle East and North Africa, and their work rarely penetrates the mainstream, with the possible exception of Sir Martin Gilbert's *In Ishmael's House*, published in 2010. Modern histories of the Middle East ignore, downplay or excuse persecution of Jews. This has led to what the Israeli columnist Ben-Dror Yemini, turning Michel Foucault's famous phrase on its head, has called, 'the power of ignorance'.[25] Propagandists eagerly exploit this ignorance to perpetuate the lie that Israeli Jews are all from Europe and America.

In the West, 'progressive' academics and activists make pernicious comparisons between the Nazi Holocaust and Palestinian *Nakba*, as if the two events were on a par. What's more, Palestinians 'paid the price' for the catastrophe that befell European Jewry. The Middle East debate is commonly framed to show Israel as the aggressor. Charges of 'apartheid' and racism against the Jewish state, an obscene inversion of the facts, remain unchallenged: few ask themselves, what individual can simply practise Judaism without fear in *judenrein* Arab states, let alone proudly declare himself a Jew?

A substantial number of opinion-formers, unions and some churches [26] view the Arab-Israeli conflict through the prism of the 'occupation'. Violence against Israel and Jews is explained away by Palestinian or Muslim grievances, while scant attention is paid to minority rights and Palestinian eliminationist anti-Semitism predating the creation of Israel. It is not 'politically-correct' to refer to the hatred Grand Mufti Haj Amin al-Husseini incited against the Jews of Palestine and the Arab world, and his role in laying the groundwork for the Jewish *Nakba*. Current public discourse has little inkling that the genocidal anti-Jewish hatred of the 1930s, and the Mufti's pivotal role in disseminating it, still informs the huge wave of anti-Semitism sweeping the Arab and Muslim world today.

Without an accurate picture of the root causes of religiously-inspired bigotry in the Middle East, scholarship is being ill-served and commentators are making their observations on the basis of falsified and incomplete information. Fearful that they may lay themselves open to Islamist aggression or become terrorism targets, Holocaust museums are intimidated into leaving out the Arab-Nazi wartime alliance altogether.

On the rare occasions when the Western media mention Jews from Arab countries, they are depicted as wracked by nostalgia or 'fish out of water' in their new lands. For example, in one *Al-Jazeera* (English) report, Ezra Levy is one of six Baghdad Jews who resettled in Israel after the 2003 US invasion but, we are told, he only left Iraq for Israel to find his first love Daisy. In Israel he appears only really comfortable with his Arab cleaner, and only really happy at her family celebration.[27]

The left has an ignoble tradition of anti-Semitism, often described as the 'socialism of fools', morphing into 'anti-semitic anti-Zionism'. Grafted on to this is the post-Zionist theory that so-called 'Arab Jews' 'alienated from their true selves' by white Ashkenazim should make common cause with Arabs.

The litmus test of contemporary liberalism is devotion to the Palestinian David's struggle against the Israeli Goliath. The theories of Jean-François Revel, Michel Foucault and Edward Said hover in the background of many a 'progressive' Westerner's' views of the Middle East. Class conflict has been replaced with conflict between nations and ethnicities. In the 1970s, Israel became the main focus for the 'anti-imperialism of idiots' when vicious, well-funded and long-running anti-Zionist campaigns were conducted by the Soviet Union.[28] Even culturally, Israelis are accused of appropriating Arab foods, such as falafel and hummus, although Middle Eastern Jews have been eating them for centuries, if not millennia.

Despising narrow national solutions gives New Leftists with an agenda to 'bash' Israel a free pass. While the 'bash-Israel' brigade[29] pour over every flaw and imperfection of the Jewish state, 'Third Worldism' makes people in the West inclined to overlook the misdeeds of Arab and Muslim states or to indulge in apologetics for them. To give a flagrant example, the Taubira law memorialising slavery (adopted in France in 2001) mentioned the 11 million victims of the transatlantic slave trade, while ignoring the 17 million slaves trafficked by Arabs and Muslims.

Western journalists, says one commentator, 'have a kind of guilt about being white and Western, and the history of their own colonisation. Israel is perceived as a white country and the Palestinians are perceived as non-white, even though, in fact, many Palestinians have lighter skin than some Israelis.[30] But the theory that Israel is a colonialist and imperialist interloper only works if vital information is suppressed – that Israel is a *de facto* Middle Eastern nation; that indigenous Jews were colonised and ultimately victimised by Arab and Muslim racism, and more were driven out by their neighbours' genocidal intentions than Palestinian Arabs who fled Israel. To introduce into the discourse the Jewish refugees to receptive audiences is to deliver a 'knock-out punch', according to one Norwegian pro-Israel group.[31]

To focus on Arab and Muslim anti-Semitism and the expulsion of their Jews shatters the lens of moral equivalence with which many post-colonials have come to view the conflict, or the moral narcissists who infantilise the Arabs as lacking agency. For them, the onus is always on Israel to show initiative and make concessions. Post-colonialism turns the truth on its head: it refuses to see that Arab and Muslim rule is a colonialism that predates Western European colonialism.

The Suppression of the Jewish Nakba

The 'colonisation of the facts' is so egregious that even when Jewish leaders and activists are aware of the Jewish *Nakba*, they may come under pressure not to mention it. In 2014 the Simon Wiesenthal Center held an exhibition at UNESCO headquarters: *People, Book, Land: 2,500 years of Jewish relations with the Holy Land*. While it was a considerable achievement to hold an exhibition within the precincts of the UN legitimising the Jewish presence in the land of Israel, the exhibit had one gaping hole: the story of the movement of Jews from Arab countries to Israel. There is one sentence in the panel entitled 'Israel among the nations' which says, 'By 1968, Middle Eastern Jews already represented 48 per cent of the entire Jewish migration to Israel.' And that was it.[32] This was the only statistic in the entire exhibit which disbelieving UNESCO officials had demanded be backed up with a reference to its source – Israel's Central Bureau of Statistics.

The academic who wrote the panels, Robert Wistrich, had prepared a whole panel on Jews from Arab countries for the exhibit, but nervous UNESCO officials vetoed it. It was made clear to Wistrich and the Simon Wiesenthal Center that, if they insisted on this particular panel, the exhibit would not take place.[33]

Underpinning denial, or omission, of Arab anti-Semitism, we encounter our old friend – the myth of peaceful Jewish-Arab coexistence. Even Chaim Weizmann, Israel's first president, believed the myth. Addressing the 1946 Anglo-American Committee of Enquiry, he said: 'I would not like to do any injustice. The Muslim world has treated the Jews with considerable tolerance. The Ottoman Empire (of which the Arabs were a major part) received the Jews with open arms when they were driven out of Spain and Europe, and the Jews should never forget that.'

The myth of the absence of anti-Semitism in the Arab and Muslim world before the establishment of Israel persists among the staunchest defenders of the Jewish people. Anti-Semitism is perceived, first and foremost, as a European problem. Moreover, there is a widespread inversion of cause and effect. As a schoolboy in the 1950s, Aldo Naouri endured successive put-downs from his Algerian Muslim teacher because he, a Jew, had the temerity to excel in Arabic. He reflects: 'It is not without some despair that I am witnessing the growth of a myth relativising Muslim anti-Semitism so as to make it the result solely of the Israel-Palestinian conflict.'[34]

The Mirage of Coexistence

Myriad coexistence projects ensure Jews and Arabs are humanised to each other in the belief that peace is made from the grassroots upwards. With the almost total absence of Jews in Arab and Muslim countries, there is scant chance a Muslim would ever meet a Jew in his life.[35] There is no doubt that 'coexistence' projects are important, given that polls show 74 per cent of MENA respondents harboured a deep hatred of Jews,[36] but a racism of low expectations operates: even when a place has hardly any Jews left or they are six feet under, examples of Muslims caring for Jewish graves or synagogues are hailed by the media as 'coexistence'.

In July 2015, *Morocco World News* published a report boasting the headline: 'Over 2,000 Jews live in Morocco'.[37] In other settings, this news would be taken as a disaster – there were almost 300,000 Jews in 1948. The Jewish population has thus dwindled to less than 1 per cent of what it once was. International travel writers enthuse about Morocco's shared Jewish-Arab heritage. One *New York Times* article gushed that Muslims even joined Jews in veneration of Solika Hachuel, the beautiful Jewess who had chosen death rather than submitting to forced conversion to Islam![38]

Nineteenth century execution of a Moroccan Jewess painted by Alfred Dehodencq. Solika Hachuel paid with her life for refusing to convert to Islam.

When discussing the 10,000 or fewer Jews still living in Iran, the Western press is fond of saying that Iran has 'the largest Jewish community' of the Middle East [39]– but rapidly glosses over the fact that Iran has forced four-fifths of its Jews into exile.

Other countries with just a handful of Jews have clambered on to the 'coexistence' bandwagon. *Judenrein* states are not deterred from creating phantom communities complete with representative organisations for invisible Jews.[40] Restoring synagogues seems to win favour with the Americans, perfecting the art of getting good PR for restoring Jewish buildings without the inconvenience of live Jews. The Maimonides synagogue was restored but promptly closed 'for security reasons', soon after it was inaugurated in Cairo. The Maghen Avraham synagogue in Beirut was recently renovated, but has yet to open at the time of writing. For decades, the Moroccan government has been restoring Jewish sites and instrumentalising Jews through films, exhibitions and festivals to project an image of cultural harmony and social diversity in order to impress the West. Rarely, however, do the points of division get aired. Mention of the Jewish *Nakba* is either dismissed without comment or causes an earthquake of outrage. Coupled with a celebration of the points of connection between Jews and Arabs – the music, folklore and food – is a desperate desire for peace through practical demonstrations of Arab-Jewish coexistence. Thus a workshop held at the School of Oriental and African Studies (SOAS) in London in June 2015 highlighting minority contributions to the Arab world[41] glossed over their mass displacement. An earlier conference, sponsored by the Woolf Institute in June 2009, placed Mizrahi Jews and Arabs from Palestine in the same basket, in keeping with the post-colonial view that Mizrahi Jews are Arabs of the Jewish faith who have more in common with each other.

The Moroccan government is systematically restoring Jewish cemeteries and synagogues, such as the Reuven Bensa'adoun Synagogue in Fez (P. F. Marsol, Dafina.net)

The bombing of the Alliance Israëlite school in Beirut, January 1950 (Alliance Israëlite Universelle Photolibrary, Paris)

A (Bahrain-sponsored) conference at London's SOAS in November 2010[42] celebrated Jewish achievements in literature, music and architecture in the Arab world. However, it sidestepped the elephant in the room: the Arab and Muslim anti-Semitism which drove the Jews out. The conference presented Jews as torn between Arab nationalism and communism, and all but ignored the third position, Zionism, which gained mass popular support as a practical response to Arab anti-Semitism.

'We would have liked to be Arab Jews,' muses Albert Memmi in his essay *Who is an Arab Jew?* He adds, 'If we abandoned the idea, it is because over the centuries the Muslim Arabs systematically prevented its realisation by their contempt and cruelty.'[43]

The 'Shared Culture' Delusion

The prominence given by post-modern academics to cultural and socioeconomic factors over people, historical events and politics has also served to falsify the history of Jews from Arab countries. Take for example the work of Orit Bashkin, whose *New Babylonians* was reviewed by Norman A. Stillman:

> Bashkin's chronicling of the watershed events of the 1940s leading up to the mass exodus of 1951 lacks the same degree of analytical insight.

This is due, I suggest, to her basic approach as a cultural studies scholar who interprets texts, but does not fully take into account the actual events, people, and politics. It is also due to *a priori* ideological assumptions. Bashkin from the very outset acknowledges her intellectual debt to contrarians such Sami Zubaida, Ella Shohat, and Gilbert Achcar, and the ghost of Edward Said often lurks in the background unnamed. Previous historical work on the Jews of the Islamic world is reduced to an oversimplified caricature: 'a model of harmonious coexistence' or 'a tale of perpetual persecution,' and 'alongside these ideas, an orientalist [sic] interpretation'. More seriously, there is an element of naïve wishful thinking which constantly views positive examples of Jewish acculturation and patriotism, on the one hand, and the openness of some Arab liberal intellectuals and politicians, on the other, as proving that the dark forces of radical Arab nationalism were not really as powerful as they appeared in retrospect.[44]

A shared culture and language with Arabs did not save the Jews of Iraq, any more than the Jewish contribution to German culture saved German Jews from Nazism. The most arabised of Jews were forced to take the road to exile. Instead of causing displaced Mizrahim to empathise with displaced Palestinians, the Jewish refugee experience created a legacy of hurt, bitterness and mistrust. Mizrahim are commonly more hostile to Arabs than Ashkenazim: this painful history, and not 'discrimination' by Israel's Labour-left establishment – although resentment of its patronising attitudes plays a part – explains why they are known to vote for 'rightwing' parties.

Coexistence initiatives like the Aladdin Project, which aims to combat Holocaust denial in the Arab world, end up deepening the Palestinians' sense of victimhood by projecting the Holocaust as a purely European phenomenon. Palestinian complicity with the Nazis is passed over in silence. Worse still, the Nazi legacy of anti-Semitism/anti-Zionism, a central theme in the philosophy of reactionary streams of Islamism, is ignored. One conference sponsored by the Aladdin Project[45] concealed the Sephardi/Mizrahi 'forgotten exodus' from Arab countries. In other words, Ashkenazi and Sephardi narratives of suffering were made to compete: the Ashkenazi 'won'. The Arab/Muslim world condemned Holocaust denial, but at the expense of historical truth, and with dubious dividends to Jews and Israel. The journalist Véronique Chemla stated:

> We need to go beyond the perennial 'We are brothers, cousins, *shalom, salam!*' and engage in a real dialogue with the Muslim world in which we recognise what unites us but also what divides us. We

need to air our disagreements in order to build enduring and deep relationships.[46]

Under the auspices of the Aladdin Project, sponsored by UNESCO, the French veteran Nazi hunter Serge Klarsfeld, whose father was deported to a death camp, went on a tour of Arab countries.[47] Klarsfeld set up a false moral equivalence between Jewish suffering under the Nazis and Muslim suffering at the hands of the Israelis. At a lecture in Baghdad he urged Muslims and Jews 'to learn about their mutual suffering as a way to bring them closer': 'We must spread knowledge about works showing the common ties between Jews and Muslims, because Muslims also suffered from colonialism and humiliation ... I understand that those who have lived under English and French colonialism would also want to speak of their suffering and of those who suffer Israel's presence on what they consider their land.'[48] By making the link, Klarsfeld not only trivialised Jewish suffering, but played into the hands of those who spread offensive and malicious propaganda that Israelis are the new Nazis.

Was Serge Klarsfeld aware that Baghdad was the scene of a pro-Nazi coup in May 1941, leading directly to the deaths of more Jews than perished in *Kristallnacht*? Did he know that the pro-Nazi government had planned to deport Iraq's Jews to detention camps and liquidate them in the desert? Did he know that, after the Second World War, Arab countries welcomed fleeing Nazi war criminals with open arms, giving them cover and employment?

It is an irony which seems to have been lost on Serge Klarsfeld that his final lecture was delivered at the French embassy in Baghdad – a building which was abandoned by the Jewish Lawee family following the pro-Nazi *Farhud*.

Exaggerating Arab Heroics

There is an overall post-modern trend to exaggerate the heroics of Arabs who saved Jews, to promote the concept of the 'Golden Age of peaceful coexistence', ignore instances of Jewish oppression by Arabs, minimise diaspora links with the land of Israel and let Islam take credit for the achievements of non-Muslims.

Examples include a touring exhibition featuring the Albanians who practised their Besa code of honour to save Jews during the Second World War (this code was not limited to Muslim Albanians); the film Les *Hommes Libres* claiming that the rector of the Great Mosque in Paris under the Nazi occupation, Si Kaddour Ben Ghabrit, issued false Muslim certificates to Jews (there is scant evidence of this: on the contrary, he may have denounced Jews)[49]. Proposals to Yad Vashem to name the Tunisian Khaled Abdul Wahab a Righteous Gentile were rejected because he did not risk his life to save the Jewish Boukris and Ouzzan families.[50]

A big-budget glossy coffee table book, *Encyclopaedia of Jewish-Muslim Relations*,[51] published in its English language version by Princeton, represents, according to the French sociologist Shmuel Trigano: 'An incredible publicity and ideological campaign ... Its target is world public opinion by way of the Jews, and more specifically Sephardi Jews – sorry, "Arab Jews"'.[52] Among the Encyclopaedia's sponsors are 'The Alliance of Civilisations', a front for the Organisation of Islamic Cooperation, whose task is to 'change the narrative'[53] by promoting the Spain of the Three Religions and the Andalusian Golden Age. The project received grants from the French regions -- as well as various liberal media, such as the *Nouvel Observateur*[54] – presumably because sectarian conflict between Jews and Muslims puts at risk the social fabric in France, and these initiatives work to put aside intractable differences of religious belief in favour of a shared civic identity.

The Encyclopaedia of Jewish-Muslim Relations fails to mention the 1033 pogrom of Fez in its description of the medieval golden age of Arab-Jewish relations. In addition to sloppy editing and errors of omission and commission, it may be criticised, to give just a few examples, for downplaying, or erasing, the Jewish contribution to mathematics. Muslim influences on the great medieval Jewish rabbi Maimonides are exaggerated, his Jewish background as the son of a Talmud scholar is ignored, and his burial place is cited not as Tiberias, but as old Cairo (Fostat), in order to downplay his links with the Holyland. In the same vein, the role of the pro-Nazi Mufti of Jerusalem is minimised.

Compared to the lines devoted to the aid or rescue of Jews in Morocco (102), Jews in Algeria (52) or Jews in Tunisia (89), a chapter by Professor Henry Laurens devotes just 48 printed lines to the pro-Nazi Mufti of Jerusalem, about whom the Palestine Liberation Organization (PLO) leader Yasser Arafat boasted: 'I was one of his troops.'[55]

In summary, Israel may have been victorious in its military campaigns against the Arab world, but truth has been the first casualty. Much public opinion has been 'colonised' by the Arab 'narrative' of the Arab-Israeli conflict. This threat is at least as important as the military threat, and some think the greatest threat to the Jewish people today is the falsification of history.

Notes

1. 'Fighting revisionism and this blog's part in it', *Point of No Return*, 19 May 2010, http:/jewishrefugees.blogspot.co.uk/2010/05/fighting-revisionism-and-this-blogs.html. (Last accessed 26 April 2017).

2. Ibid.

3. Recording of lecture by Sasson Somekh at Vanderbilt University, January 2007, http://www.vanderbilt.edu/News/newsSound/SassonSomik.mp3. (Last accessed 26 April 2017).

4. Bat Ye'or, *The Dhimmi* (Associated University Presses, 2003), p.143.

5. Adi Schwartz, 'Reasons for the Moroccan exodus erased', *Point of No Return*, 2 June 2013, http://jewishrefugees.blogspot.co.uk/2013/06/reasons-for-moroccan-exodus-erased.html. (Last accessed 26 April 2017).

6. Penina Elbaz, 'The truth about Morocco: fear made Jews leave', *Point of No Return*, 11 September 2016, http://jewishrefugees.blogspot.co.uk/2016/09/the-truth-about-morocco-fear-made-jews.html. (Last accessed 26 April 2017).

7. Robert Satloff, *Among the Righteous* (Public Affairs New York, 2006), p.178.

8. 'Jewish synagogue hosts Ramadan iftar in Cairo', *Egyptian Streets*, 10 July 2014, http://egyptianstreets.com/2014/07/10/jewish-synagogue-hosts-ramadan-iftar-in-cairo/. (Last accessed 26 April 2017).

9. Fatih Semsettin Isik, 'Turkish Jews host Iftar in landmark synagogue', *Daily Sabah*, 22 June 2015, http://www.dailysabah.com/politics/2015/06/22/turkeys-jews-host-iftar-in-landmark-synagogue. (Last accessed 26 April 2017).

10. Uriel Heilman, 'Reluctant exiles: Jews from North Africa and the Middle East', *B'nai B'rith magazine*, Spring 2011, http://www.urielheilman.com/0411-jews-in-arab-lands.html. (Last accessed 26 April 2017).

11. Ibid.

12. Eetta Prince-Gibson, 'Right of Return', *Jerusalem Post*, 8 August 2003.

13. Seth J. Frantzman, 'A blindspot of Diaspora Jews on Israel', *Jerusalem Post*, 24 July 2016, http://www.jpost.com/Opinion/A-blind-spot-of-Diaspora-Jews-on-Israel-462249. (Last accessed 26 April 2017).

14. Michelle Huberman, 'Who are the Ashkenazim?' *Clash of Cultures* blog, *Jerusalem Post*, 3 March 2012.

15. Binyamin Arazi 'Reclaiming Jewish identity: An aboriginal people of the Middle East', *Huffington Post*, 2 July 2016, http://www.huffingtonpost.com/binyamin-arazi/reclaiming-jewish-identit_b_7715528.html. (Last accessed 26 April 2017).

16. Taly Krupkin, 'Mizrahi is the new Black for American Jews', *Haaretz*, 18 October 2015.

17. See artwork by Meir Gal, 'Nine Out of Four Hundred (The West and the Rest)', 1997, http://meirgal.squarespace.com/exhibitions/nine-out-of-four-hundred-the-west-and-the-rest-1997/5060044. (Last accessed 26 April 2017).

18. Education ministers have included Shulamit Aloni, Amnon Rubinstein and Yossi Sarid of the Meretz Party and Yuli Tamir of the Labour Party (source: *Wikipedia*).

19. Lahav Hartov, 'Ministers approve mandatory Arabic studies from first grade', *Jerusalem Post*, 25 October 2015, http://www.jpost.com/Israel-News/Politics-And-Diplomacy/Ministers-approve-mandatory-Arabic-studies-from-first-grade-430017. (Last accessed 26 April 2017).

20. 'A visual guide to seventy-five years of major refugee crises around the world', *Washington Post*, 21 December 2015, https://www.washingtonpost.com/graphics/world/historical-migrant-crisis/. (Last accessed 26 April 2017).

21. Maurice Roumani, 'The Case of the Jews from Arab Countries: A Neglected Issue', (WOJAC, 1987), http://www.asfonline.org/portal/ArabLandsDisplay.asp?article_id=8&. (Last accessed 26 April 2017).

22. In January 2017, the French historian Georges Bensoussan was tried in a criminal court for 'hate speech': he was paraphrasing an Arab sociologist's words to the effect that Arabs imbibe anti-Semitism 'with their mother's milk'. He was acquitted.

23. Jeffrey Herf, 'Middle East Studies blind spot', *History News Network*, 27 September 2015, http://historynewsnetwork.org/article/160546#sthash.2K6xP1nn.dpuf. (Last accessed 26 April 2017).

24. G. Bensoussan, 'L'histoire enchantée des juifs du Maroc' *CRIF*, 13 June 2012, http://www.crif.org/tribune/l%E2%80%99histoire-enchant%C3%A9e-des-juifs-du-maroc/31573. (Last accessed 26 April 2017).

25. Ben-Dror Yemini, speech at the UN, 2 December 2015, http://webtv.un.org/watch/the-untold-story-of-850000-refugees-%E2%80%93-the-tale-of-ancient-jewish-cultures-in-ar ab-lands/4641983532001. (Last accessed 26 April 2017).

26. Supporters of the Arab position include prominent figures such as Archbishop Desmond Tutu, ex-US President Jimmy Carter, the UK National Union of Teachers, the African National Congress and the Presbyterian, Methodist and Episcopal churches. See also Robin Shepherd: *A State beyond the Pale: Europe's Problem with Israel* (W&N, 2009).

27 'The last Jew of Babylon' Pt 1, *Witness*, 15 July 2007, interview by Inigo Gilmore, https://www.youtube.com/watch?v=X7kJIkW1r3A. (Last accessed 26 April 2017).
The BBC talks of 'Arab Jews', forcibly torn from their natural habitat, the Arab world. 'BBC asks: will Arab Jews return?', *Point of No Return*, 27 April 2013, http://jewishrefugees.blogspot.co.uk/2013/04/bbc-asks-will-arab-jews-return.html. (Last accessed 26 April 2017).

28. Stan Crooke, 'Stalinist roots of left antisemitism', *Workers' Liberty* site, http://www.workersliberty.org/story/2004/02/24/stalinist-roots-left-anti-zionism-1/ in alliance with the authoritarian Arab states and parts of the Western New Left. Quoted by Alan Johnson, 'The left and the Jews: time for a rethink', *Fathom*, Autumn 2015, http://fathomjournal.org/the-left-and-the-jews-time-for-a-rethink/. (Last accessed 26 April 2017).

29. See Giulio Meotti, 'The Israel-bashing industry's "intellectuals"', *The Gatestone Institute*, 16 March 2016, https://www.gatestoneinstitute.org/7610/israel-bashing-intellectuals. (Last accessed 26 April 2017).

30. Dafna Maor, 'Why journalists say Israeli-Arab reporting is rigged', *Haaretz*, 14 September 2014. Dispatch by Tom Gross, 'Why journalists say Israeli-Arab reporting is "rigged"' 14 September 2014, http://www.tomgrossmedia.com/mideastdispatches/archives/001485.html. (Last accessed 26 April 2017).

31. David M. Weinberg, 'The winning issues', *Jerusalem Post*, 6 June 2013, http://www.jpost.com/Opinion/Op-Ed-Contributors/The-winning-issues-315754. (Last accessed 26 April 2017).

32. David Matas, 'UNESCO silence on Jews from Arab Countries', *Jerusalem Post*, 21 June 2014, http://www.jpost.com/Opinion/Columnists/UNESCO-silence-on-Jews-from-Arab-countriesdav-360130. (Last accessed 26 April 2017).

33. Conversation with R. Wistrich at the exhibition opening, UNESCO, Paris, June 2014.

34. Aldo Naouri, 'Sauf votre respect' in Leila Sabbar (ed.), *Une Enfance juive en Méditerranée musulmane* (Bleu autour, 2012), p.259.

35. According to a 2015 ADL poll – *ADL Global 100: an index of antisemitism*, http://global100.adl.org/ – 74 per cent harbour negative attitudes towards Jews.

36. The figure is 93 per cent in the West Bank or Gaza.

37. 'Over 2,000 Jews live in Morocco', *Morocco World News*, 5 July 2015, https://www.moroccoworldnews.com/2015/07/162537/over-2000-jews-live-in-morocco-report/. (Last accessed 26 April 2017).

38. Michael Frank, 'In Morocco, exploring remnants of Jewish history', *New York Times*, 30 May 2015, http://www.nytimes.com/2015/05/31/travel/in-morocco-exploring-remnants-of-jewish-history.html?_r=0. (Last accessed 26 April 2017).

39. See for example Kim Sengupta, 'Iran's Jews on life inside Israel's enemy state: "We feel secure and happy"', *The Independent*, 16 March 2016, http://www.independent.co.uk/news/world/middle-east/irans-jews-on-life-inside-israels-enemy-state-we-feel-secure-and-happy-a6934931.html. (Last accessed 26 April 2017).

40. 'Algeria creates Jewish Association for phantom Jews', *Point of No Return*, 30 July 2009, http://jewishrefugees.blogspot.co.uk/2009/07/algeria-creates-jewish-association-for.html. (Last accessed 26 April 2017). There was also created a Directorate for Jewish Affairs in Kurdistan, even though no Jewish community has existed there since the mass airlift of 18,000 Kurdish Jews to Israel in 1950–1.

41. Woolf Institute, June 2015 workshop programme, http://www.woolf.cam.ac.uk/uploads/General%20Programme.pdf. (Last accessed 26 April 2017).

42. 'Bahrain sponsors conference on Jews from Arab lands', *Point of No Return*, 10 November 2010, http://jewishrefugees.blogspot.co.uk/2010/11/bahrain-sponsors-conference-on-jews-of.html. (Last accessed 26 April 2017).

43. A. Memmi, 'Who is an Arab Jew?' February 1975, http://www.sullivan-county.com/x/aj1.htm. (Last accessed 26 April 2017).

44. Norman A. Stillman, 'Review' in Orit Bashkin, *Research Gate of New Babylonians: A History of Jews in Modern Iraq*, http://www.researchgate.net/publication/265697032_New_Babylonians_A_History_of_Jews_in_Modern_Iraq_by_Orit_Bashkin_. (Last accessed 26 April 2017).

45. Véronique Chemla, 'La conférence islamiquement correcte de lancement du Projet Aladin', *Véronique Chemla* blog, 25 February 2015, http://www.veroniquechemla.info/2009/10/la-conference-islamiquement-correcte-de.html. (Last accessed 26 April 2017).

46. Véronique Chemla interviewed on *Radio Chalom Nitsan*, 25 March 2010, http://www.veroniquechemla.info/2010/04/interview-par-radio-chalom-nisan.html. (Last accessed 26 April 2017).

47. 'Holocaust: a call to conscience', *Aladdin* website, http://www.projetaladin.org/holocaust/en/newsletters-3/reading-primo-levi-in-the-muslim-world.html. (Last accessed 26 April 2017).

48. Ibid.

49. See G Bensoussan, *Les juifs du monde Arabe: la question interdite*, p.100.

50. Irena Steinfeldt, 'Why Khaled Abdul Wahab does not deserve to be called righteous', *Jerusalem Post*, 8 April 2009, http://www.pbs.org/newshour/among-the-righteous/2010/03/op-ed-2.html. (Last accessed 26 April 2017).

51. Abdelwahab Meddeb and Benjamin Stora (eds), *Histoire des relations entre Juifs et Musulmans des origines à nos jours* (Albin Michel, 2013).

52. Lyn Julius, 'A perplexing rewriting of history', *Times of Israel*, 16 April 2014, Also at *Point of No Return*, http://jewishrefugees.blogspot.co.uk/2014/04/a-perplexing-rewriting-of-history.html. (Last accessed 26 April 2017).

53. Rudi Roth, 'Réécriture de l'histoire des juifs et des arabes', *Philosemitisme* blog, in 'Qu'est-ce qu'un acte antisemite?' *Pardès* 55, pp.273–303.

54. Shmuel Trigano, 'Les Juifs sont des arabes "comme les autres", une opération de grande ampleur', *DesInfos* website, 11 November 2013, http://www.desinfos.com/spip.php?article38444. (Last accessed 26 April 2017).

55. Rudi Roth, 'Réécriture de l'histoire des juifs et des arabes', *Philosemitisme* blog,-in 'Qu'est-ce qu'un acte antisemite?' *Pardès* 55, pp.273–303.

11

The Quest for Justice for Indigenous Peoples

> Where there is no remembrance, there will be no truth,
> where there is no truth, there will be no justice, where there
> is no justice, there will be no reconciliation, where there is
> no authentic reconciliation – between the parties and not just
> between the states – there will be no genuine peace.
>
> **Irwin Cotler,**
> Human Rights lawyer
> and former Minister of Justice, Canada

The Jews from Arab countries are the victims of an injustice. Until they are offered recognition and redress, a Middle East Peace settlement fair to all parties will not be possible.

The Israeli government has come late to this realisation. While matters have improved in the last few years, Israel has been obliged to 'play catch-up' with the Palestinian cause. And when Jews from Arab countries do appear in the discourse, it is often only to reinforce the myth of peaceful coexistence between Arabs and Jews before Zionism. Israel has become the bogeyman, instead of being the necessary response to Arab/Muslim anti-Semitism. These Jews have been doubly betrayed, firstly by Arab nationalism and secondly, by Europe which, having offered them an escape route from *dhimmitude*, committed Jewish genocide – the greatest betrayal of the twentieth century.[1] The issue of recognition and redress for the refugees is overshadowed by pseudo-colonial allegations of 'discrimination' that Mizrahi Jews suffered on arrival in Israel.

With no outside help, Israel successfully resolved the Jewish refugee problem: no Jew today considers himself a refugee. It failed in two major respects, however. The Palestinian refugee problem was left unsolved, a festering sore. The Palestinians became a *cause celèbre*, while Israel failed to raise the moral imperative of Justice for Jewish refugees from Arab lands in a clear and forthright manner. Israel failed to put forward the case for these Jews in the court of public opinion, let alone brand them as a model for the resettlement of Palestinian refugees by Arab states.

The Jewish refugee issue remains a crucial human rights issue. Hundreds of thousands of people were wronged, and they deserve recognition and redress – the law says there is no statute of limitations – whether they now live in Israel or the West.

In spite of Arab denial, the Nazi project to commit genocide against the Jews is not just a European story; it is an Arab story, with a direct link to the mass exodus of Jews from Arab countries. Arab regimes have deliberately encouraged the flight of their Jews; they have shown not a shred of remorse for the wholesale destruction of their millennial Jewish communities over a single generation. The Jews have been airbrushed from Middle Eastern history, as if they had never existed. Such is anti-Jewish hatred that the word 'Jew' is used only to insult or discredit a leader or a politician.[2] Holocaust denial and conspiracy theories about Jewish power permeate the Arab and Muslim world.

Arabs states have never recognised, much less apologised for the mass displacement of loyal citizens and the violation of their human rights. The Jewish refugees have never been compensated for stolen property: the Arab and Muslim quarrel with Israeli 'imperialism' becomes absurd when viewed against the claim that Jews lost privately-owned land in Arab states amounting to four or five times the size of Israel, itself just 0.01 per cent of the land area occupied by Arab states.

Israel missed a unique opportunity to settle the question of seized Egyptian-Jewish property when it signed the 1979 peace agreement with Egypt. There has been no closure for either side. Egypt may seem too poor to offer compensation, but it still trembles at the thought that the Jews will return to claim back their property. Post-Saddam Iraq also failed to settle accounts with its Jewish former citizens. The tug-of-war between Iraq and its displaced Jewish community over the water-stained mementos, religious books, school reports and humdrum communal correspondence which comprise the Iraqi-Jewish archive demonstrates that Iraq is not prepared to make the slightest concession to the Jewish refugees it robbed and drove out.

As long as Palestinians call for a mass return to Israel for its refugees and their descendants, they must be reminded that an irrevocable exchange of roughly equal populations took place.[3] No different from other exchanges – for example, the Greek/Turkish and the Indian/Pakistani exchanges of population – resulting from other post-colonial conflicts, this exchange cannot be reversed. Of all twentieth century conflicts, the Arab-Israeli conflict is the only one in which the population transfer failed as a result of the Arab refusal, except in Jordan, to absorb their refugees.

Refugees and Peace

As I write, the Middle East peace process is dormant. The Israel-Arab conflict has slipped right down the priority list as intra-Arab conflicts rage. If and when the parties do sit down to a political agreement, the refugee issue should be central, if not the key to reconciliation. As long as the Palestinian Arabs see themselves as the sole victims of an egregious injustice, they will never be able to reconcile with the Jews. As long as they ignore the 'colonised' history of indigenous Jews under Muslim rule and their eventual 'ethnic cleansing', they will never comprehend why Jews need to have their own sovereign state in the Middle East. And as long as Arabs and Muslims, bolstered by Western intellectual opinion, portray the Jews as foreign interlopers in the region, then peace has little chance.

Since February 2010, Israeli governments of all political stripes have been bound by a Knesset law committing them to secure compensation for Jewish refugees in any peace deal. The 50.2 per cent of Israel's Jews who descend from refugees forced out by Arab and Muslim persecution have a right to expect that a peace deal will be signed that does not ignore their painful history. They cannot reasonably be asked to approve a peace plan that only provides rights and redress for Palestinian refugees, without providing rights of remembrance, truth, justice and redress for Jews displaced from Arab countries, as mandated under humanitarian law.

The Palestinians, it is widely believed, cannot be held responsible for what happened to the Jewish refugees. Even Israeli government negotiators, such as Tzipi Livni, who served as Israel's Minister of Justice, declared in 2013 that 'there was no connection between Jewish and Palestinian refugees'.[4] She asserted that, while Israel could legitimately discuss Palestinian refugees in peace talks, Jewish refugees would have to address their grievances to Arab states.

It is a fact, however, that both refugee populations were created by the Arab countries' belligerent refusal to accept the 1947 UN Partition Plan; both groups became refugees during the same period in history; and both were declared to be *bona fide* refugees, under international law, by the appropriate UN Agencies – the United Nations High Commission for Refugees (UNHCR) and the UN Works and Relief Agency (UNRWA).

The common objection to the Jewish refugee issue – that the Palestinians had nothing to do with it – is an easily-demonstrable fallacy. Seven Arab states declared the 1948 war against Israel. However, an extremist Palestinian leadership, which collaborated with the Nazis and incited anti-Jewish hatred all over the Arab world in the decades preceding the creation of Israel, played an active part in all Arab League decision-making and dragged Arab states into conflict with the new Jewish state – a conflict they lost and whose consequences they must suffer. It cannot escape some measure of responsibility for both the Arab and the Jewish *Nakbas*.

Indeed, the idea of expelling the Jews of Arab countries was adopted by the Palestinians as a policy. According to the well-connected Egyptian-Jewish journalist Victor Nahmias, the Palestinians were a major factor in the Jewish migration to Israel in 1950–1.[5] Still today, most Palestinians[6] appear both uncompromising and unrepentant. As a consequence, any proposed solution that calls for return of Palestinian refugees, even in paltry numbers, without taking into account the Jewish refugees, perpetuates the injustice to Jewish refugees by letting both the Palestinian leadership and the Arab states off the hook.

When all's said and done, if Israel were to concede an independent Palestinian state, and if agreement were reached on borders, settlements and even Jerusalem, peace negotiations would still founder on the immovable rock of the Palestinian 'Right of Return'. The Right of Return cannot be dismissed as meaningless rhetoric. This form of 'demographic subversion'[7] remains the single biggest stumbling block to peace, if not a recipe for continuing bloodshed. Even Fatah 'moderates' will not give up their 'right' to arabise Israel by flooding it with the millions of descendants of Palestinians, who, under the aegis of the UNWRA, are uniquely permitted to pass on their refugee status from generation to generation.

In 2009, Omar Barghouti (the founder of the Boycott, Divestment and Sanctions movement), told *The Electronic Intifada*, that 'people fighting for refugee rights like I am, know that you cannot reconcile the Right of Return for refugees with a two-state solution. That is the big white elephant in the room and people are ignoring it.'[8] As long as the Right of Return is the cornerstone of the Palestinians' strategy, the Jewish refugees from Arab lands remain its antidote.

Linkage between the two sets of refugees opens up a window of opportunity for a political accommodation. A Right of Return for Palestinian Arab refugees to Israel – a state where they were not citizens – is a concept non-existent in international law.[9] It is, in any case, a non-starter, for it promises nothing but upheaval and strife between Arabs returning to 1948 Israel, and resident Israeli Jews. A Right of Return for one set of refugees is morally untenable – it is not equitable to give one set such a right without giving the same right to the other. Apart from the chaos and turmoil it would generate, however, giving Jews from the Arab world a Right of Return to countries which spat out them out is like asking a prisoner who has tasted freedom to go back to jail. 'The masts of our ships are broken, our sails are torn', says Baghdad-born Professor Shmuel Moreh, poetically. 'Iraq is no place for us. If the Muslims are slaughtering their brothers, how can we return?'[10]

Three generations of Jews have now been resettled in Israel and the West after their painful uprooting. No Jew would wish to return to an Arab country in present circumstances, except perhaps as a tourist, unless they are Jews who, in 1948, lost their homes in Jerusalem and areas which have fallen under Israeli control, and are seeking restitution.

One might argue that no comparison between the two groups of refugees is possible – one problem has ostensibly been resolved, the other has not. It is hard to justify a position which defends the non-resettlement of Palestinian refugees – an abuse of their human rights. The biggest obstacle to their absorption is the existence of the UNWRA, the UN agency dedicated to perpetuating refugee status through the generations. It is extraordinary and concerning that UNWRA should attract one third of the budget for the UNHCR, the agency that deals with all refugees globally – excluding Palestinians – and that it should have four times the number of staff.[11]

Israel should not be penalised for 'doing the right thing' by absorbing its Jewish refugees. Palestinian Arab refugees need to follow the model of successful Jewish refugee resettlement by being allowed to acquire full citizenship in a future Palestinian state – a right which the Palestinian leadership has, to-date, declared no intention of granting them[12] – or in their host Arab countries, instead of being fed the vain hope of a Right of Return to Israel, a country that most 'refugees' have never seen.

An international fund, as proposed by President Bill Clinton, would compensate refugees on both sides, and also be used to finance the rehabilitation of refugees in host countries. 'Peace will not bring about the international fund, the international fund will bring about peace', declares Levana Zamir, head of the Israeli organisations representing Jews from Arab lands, for whom establishing the fund is a matter of urgency.[13] The West and Israel would pay into the fund, but it is imperative for reconciliation that Arab countries should also contribute, even if it is only a nominal amount. Compensation should also go to the 200,000 Jews who did not go to Israel but settled in the West. They are also entitled to justice.

Anti-Semitism: A Root Cause of Conflict

The language we use to describe the struggle between Israel and its opponents is distorted by talk of the Israel-Palestine conflict instead of the Arab-Israeli, or increasingly, the Islamist-infidel, conflict. If they do not kill or convert them, Islamists seek to return the Jews and other non-Muslims to their submissive, 'colonised' status under *sharia* law.[14]

We need to recognise that anti-Semitism is a root cause of the Arab-Israeli conflict, not merely a reaction to it. If it is ever acknowledged, Arab collaboration with the Nazis is widely seen as a pragmatic alliance of 'frenemies' against Western colonialism. Had the Arabs' German allies won the War, however, the Jews of the Middle East and North Africa would have been doomed. The Mufti and his followers invented a new ideology of anti-Semitism, cloaked in the language of Islam, which continues to contaminate many minds today. The inability to tolerate difference poisons the relationship between Arab and Jew, between Muslim and Christian, between Muslim and the wrong type of Muslim.

Jews once thronged the cafés of La Goulette, a resort near Tunis .Tourists today stay away for fear of Islamist terrorist attacks (Courtesy Tunisia Inn)

Although the global *jihad* has killed many more Muslims than Jews, the anti-Semitism generated by the Nazi-inspired religious fundamentalism known as Islamism preceded the creation of Israel and remains a core driver behind the terrorism plaguing the West in the first decades of the twenty-first century. Until we confront Islamo-fascism and call it by its proper name, the West cannot hope to defeat it.

Three Colonisations

This book has explored three colonisations: Jews were amongst the indigenous peoples of the Middle East and North Africa colonised by the seventh century Arab conquest and Islam. Jews were colonised by the European powers in the nineteenth and twentieth centuries, a colonisation which promised 'liberation' from the first colonisation. In Arab nationalist eyes, however, it cast the Jews as traitor-collaborators with the Europeans.

The third colonisation is the colonisation of the facts, in the media, churches, community centres and academia, and in the history books: the story of the Jews from the Middle East and North Africa has been erased and falsified. The UN and the human rights community has passed it by. Denial is the cruellest of injustices.

Compare Jews with Christians: the Jews are one of just two non-Muslim Middle Eastern peoples to have achieved sovereignty in their ancestral homeland. The Maronite Christians of Mount Lebanon are the other. Lebanon was carved out of Syria by the French as a safe haven for Maronite Christians, now a dwindling minority in a state controlled by the Iran-backed militia Hezbollah. In his testimony to UNSCOP in August 1947 the Maronite archbishop Ignace Moubarac endorses a Jewish homeland in Palestine, and spells out the affinity that Maronite Christians of Lebanon once felt with Jews in Palestine: 'Major reasons of a social, humanitarian and religious nature require the creation, in these two countries, of two homelands for minorities: a Christian home in the Lebanon, as there has always been ~ a Jewish home in Palestine.'[15] The Jews of the Middle East have achieved success where the Christians, outside Lebanon (itself a debatable success), have failed.

Arabic-speaking Christians sought a solution in the early twentieth century within the framework of pan-Arabism or universalist doctrines, such as communism. While Jews had Zionism, Christians threw in their lot with the Arab-Muslim majority. They have been among the most zealous of champions of the Palestinian cause. In Syria and Iraq, Christians have been cheerleaders for pan-Arab nationalism: they needed a non-Muslim regional identity upon which to ground their legitimacy.[16] Ultimately, the passionate identification of Christians with pan-Arabism and communism was their escape route from institutionalised *dhimmitude*. The Christian nationalists failed catastrophically to find equality with their Muslim brethren. In the twenty-first century, thousands of their co-religionists have fled savage persecution, and in the areas ruled by Daʾesh, faced the bleak choice between conversion to Islam, enslavement or *sharia* subjugation on payment of the *jizya* tax.

A tsunami of extremism has overwhelmed any currents of liberalism and moderation in the Arab world. In the dying days of the Ottoman Empire, liberal Muslims – like the Iraqi poet Jamil Sidqi al–Zahawi and Maruf al-Rusafi, who advocated equal rights – were given the brush-off. A speech Al-Rusafi made in praise of the Ottoman Constitution, which granted religious and ethnic minorities equality, led to bloody riots.[17]

Rising out of the ashes of pan-Arabism, the revolutionary ideology of political Islam, or Islamism, represented by the nihilist jihadists of Daʾesh and the zealots of the Islamic republic of Iran, has yet to be defeated, despite the routing of Daʾesh on the ground. But even 'secular' Arab identity has proved inextricable from Islam. Islam is inscribed as the official religion of state in every Arab constitution, thus relegating non-Muslims to *de-facto* second class status.

With the exception of Ataturk's secular Turkey, now well on the way to being rolled back, no Muslim state has shown respect – as opposed to tolerance – of other religions. To quote Albert Memmi, the great Tunisian Jewish writer:[18] 'The Arabs in the past merely tolerated the existence of Jewish minorities, no more. They have not yet recovered from the shock of seeing their former underlings raise up their heads, attempting even to gain their national independence! They know of only one rejoinder: off with their heads!'

In spite of their portrayal as a tragic minority, the Palestinians are fellow-members of the majority stake-holders in the Middle East, allied with forces who would battle regional minorities into submission.[19] From the outset, the Palestinian cause has been a pan-Arab nationalist cause. It has also had a powerful Islamist, anti-Semitic dimension. In Islamist eyes, the Jews have no claim to a single inch of Palestine.[20]

As I have shown, the anti-Semitism behind the Arab/Islamist dispute with Israel takes the form of an ancient religious contempt for *dhimmi* Jews. But, in the twentieth century, contempt evolved into lethal hatred, coupled with a totalitarian mindset demonising the Other. The former accounts for a deep religious and cultural resistance to the idea of a Jewish state.[21]

The latter emptied the Arab Muslim world of Jews, as well as other sects and minorities, and still drives the conflict with Israel. There can be no peace or coexistence while the totalitarian legacy of the Nazi era, with its tolerance of genocidal anti-Semitism, still lingers.

All talk of resolving the conflict between Israel and the Arab states is academic as long as Islamists engage in a religious war to win back for Islam every inch of what was once Muslim *Wakf* land. Muslim orthodoxy abhors Jewish rule – let alone sovereignty on any inch of land that was once ruled by Islam. The idea of Muslims under Jewish rule is a travesty of everything jihadists believe in.[22]

The Arab shame-honour culture remains a major obstacle to a peaceful resolution of the conflict, shaping Arab attitudes to Jews and Israel. Most shaming of all is to be defeated, not just by one's own subjects – but the most abject and cowardly of them all – the *dhimmi* Jews.[23] Moreover, a non-Muslim *dhimmi* state is an affront to Muslim pride and supremacy. In the Jewish case, a nation of former slaves has committed the unprecedented but unforgiveable sin of overturning the natural order and winning wars. For the humiliated to correct a historical injustice by humiliating their traditional masters is unbearable. A majority-Jewish state sticks in the craw.

If the conflict is to be resolved, the Arab world must also begin to accept responsibility for its failures. Its inability to replace the question: 'Who did this to us?' with: 'What did we do wrong?' means that it will continue to indulge in victimhood and the most conspicuous non-Muslims of the Middle East will continue to be its preferred scapegoats.

A genuine peace calls for a psychological, sociological and cultural revolution in the Arab and Muslim world, reversing the anti-*dhimmi* prejudice against a sovereign Jewish state. The demons of Nazi-inspired genocidal hatred must also be laid to rest, once and for all, for no peace deal is likely while millions in the Arab and Muslim world view Israel and the Jews as the epitomy of evil. A useful litmus test is for the Arab world and Iran to recognise that the Holocaust happened (without making specious comparisons with the Nazi-like treatment of the Palestinians by Israel), that

In 2011 David Gerbi was thrown out of Libya for opening up the 'archaeological site' of the Dar al-Bishi Synagogue in Tripoli (Suhaib Salem/Reuters)

it had a nefarious influence on the region's inhabitants, and is not part of a Jewish conspiracy to play for sympathy. Holocaust denial, as Matthias Küntzel says, contains an appeal to repeat it.[24]

Yet all is not lost: there is an undeniable tradition of pragmatism in Arab politics. Every so often a glimmer of it shines through. Let us not forget that Egypt and Jordan both signed a peace treaty with Israel; unofficial contacts and trade continue to grow between Israel and several Arab states. The common threat of a nuclear Iran has fostered unprecedented cooperation between erstwhile enemies.

While states come together when their national interests converge, peace between peoples is a harder nut to crack. Little might be achieved while a Jew runs the risk of lynching when he visits a country like Libya[25] or when states sanction anti-Jewish incitement and vilification of the Jewish state. The Palestinians and the Arab regimes need to educate for peace.

The Denial of National Minorities

We need a sea change in the way that the Arab world, and indeed the West, views political rights in the Middle East belonging, as of right, to Arab Muslims. Twenty-two Arab states[26] were created on the European model, but only Zionism is treated – and rejected – as a creature of European nationalism. Following the defeat of the Ottoman Empire after the First World War, Kurds, Assyrians and other non-Arab minorities also sought self-determination, but were betrayed by the colonial powers and left stateless. The colonial powers and 'moderate' Arabs surrendered to the demands of the pan-Arab nationalists.

The Ottoman Empire dissolved in a welter of bloodshed and cruelty, but intolerance of the 'Other' as a result of the intertwining of nationalism and Islam is a problem even in non-Arab states such as Turkey, the modern successor to the Ottomans. In spite of Ataturk's militant secularism, there is a deep conviction that if you are Turkish, you are automatically a Muslim.[27] The 'ethnic cleansing' of Pontine Greeks from Turkey has paralleled that of Jews from Arab countries. Numbers have gone down from 1.8 million to 1,700. As with the Jews, there have been fierce pogroms in Turkey, for instance in 1955.

As things stand at the moment, non-Muslim minorities can only be fully accepted in Arab Muslim society by surrendering their distinctive identity. In other words, they must *cease to be themselves*. The Muslim denial of collective minority rights is rooted in the historical rejection of non-Muslim peoplehood. At best, Islam offers them religious autonomy, not national freedom. Its need to retain control is embedded in its very nature.

Instead of giving minorities the right to be different, the Arab nationalist ethos invested an Arab Sunni Muslim elite with power, and oppressed Berbers, Copts, Assyrians and Kurds. The post-1979 Shi'a Islamist theocracy of Iran is a model for the practice of *sharia* law, with its in-built discrimination against minorities, dissidents, death for gays and apostates from Islam, tight control of Jewish institutions and, with the exception of a token MP acting as a mouthpiece for the regime, exclusion of Jews from politics.

The basic question, writes Bernard Lewis, is: 'Is a resurgent Islam prepared to tolerate a non-Islamic enclave, whether Jewish in Israel or Christian in Lebanon, in the heart of the Islamic world?'

> Islam from its inception is a religion of power, and in the Muslim world view it is right and proper that power should be wielded by Muslims and Muslims alone. Others may receive the tolerance, even the benevolence, of the Muslim state, provided that they clearly recognize Muslim supremacy. That Muslims should rule over non-Muslims is right and normal. That non-Muslims should rule over Muslims is an offense against the laws of God and nature, and this is true whether in Kashmir, Palestine, Lebanon, or Cyprus. Here again, it must be recalled that Islam is not conceived as a religion in the limited Western sense but as a community, a loyalty, and a way of life— and that the Islamic community is still recovering from the traumatic era when Muslim governments and empires were overthrown and Muslim peoples forcibly subjected to alien, infidel rule. Both the Saturday people and the Sunday people are now suffering the consequences.[28]

The Arab-Islamist struggle continues to push for the destruction of the Jewish redoubt concentrated on the eastern shore of the Mediterranean – Israel. In this context, it does not seem unreasonable to conclude that Palestinians are the foot-soldiers in a pan-Arab, and now Islamist, irredentist struggle to abolish the Jewish state and re-establish Arab-Muslim majority control over Palestine. The increasingly fashionable 'one-state solution' aims to replace Israel with a single bi-national state under Muslim rule.[29] With the jihadists of Hamas in control, Jews, provided they are permitted to stay after Israel's demise, would be subjugated to minority status under *sharia* law.

In contravention of Article 18 of the UN Charter, all Middle Eastern minority groups are experiencing an abuse of their rights and a struggle for survival. But the Jews are among the few groups to have been almost totally 'ethnically cleansed' from the Arab world.

The very use of the term 'minority' is an unhappy one. The Copt Christophe Ayad said: 'to be a minority is to admit that you are a guest in your own home – it is to give up the idea that you embody the nation's identity, that you descend from the Pharaohs'.[30] Jewish culture is embedded in the very fabric and identity of the region – but Muslim-majority states have indeed treated Jews as guests in their own home.

It is too late to save the Jewish minorities in Arab lands. If things continue as they are, the communities in Turkey and Iran are at serious risk of oblivion too.

Paradoxically, Arab, and an increasing number of Muslim-majority states – from Pakistan to Malaysia – are states without Jews who blame the Jews for everything that goes wrong. They imagine that the Jews are engaged in a global conspiracy to control the world.[31]

Targeting minorities is a sign of a sick society. What is the cure? A healthy civil society does not exclude minorities from the centres of power, and practise cronyism and nepotism. A healthy civil society guarantees human and civil rights and the protection of minorities. The ethnic cleansing of minorities sets a dangerous precedent for society at large. A society that devours its Jews, or its Christians, or its Shi'a Muslims, ends up devouring itself.

The Rights of Indigenous Peoples and Faiths

It is a safe bet, given the widespread oppression of non-Muslim minorities, that this 'ethnic cleansing' of the Other would have occurred even if Israel had never existed. Jews have played the 'canary in the coal mine' for Zoroastrians, Baha'is, Mandaeans, Copts, Assyrian and Chaldean Christians. All are disappearing rapidly from the Middle East. Yazidis, Mandaeans, Chaldeans and even Copts do not aspire to self-determination, but they do wish to have their rights as indigenous minorities protected by the majority.

This means cast-iron physical security guarantees and full integration into the life and the politics of the majority state. A majority can only enjoy civil and human rights if these are also guaranteed to minorities.

As has been discussed, Morocco is the only Arab state to have attempted to redefine itself as a nation inclusive of several identities. The reality does not currently appear to live up to the promise. One Berber student told researcher Aomar Boum:[32]

> Moroccan Jews are like a valuable mortgage that cannot be afforded. Moroccans talk a lot about their Jewish subculture to outsiders and boast about their history of tolerance; yet they refuse to accept that Jews can be Moroccan citizens with full rights and obligations. Our full support and sympathy for the Palestinian cause have blinded us, hindering our acceptance of Moroccan Jews. If we believe that Moroccan Jewish history can be an economic asset worth mortgaging, then we should accept their full rights. Otherwise we have to put it up for sale and stop using it for our economic advantage.

Israel: Yazidis with an Army

With just 4,500 Jews remaining in the Arab world, the expulsion and imminent extinction of Jewish communities has been an object lesson to persecuted minorities. The only way to ensure your survival is to exercise self-defence in your own sovereign state. As the journalist Matti Friedman[33] writes, 'You had better have your own piece of land, and the power to defend it.'

It is not the European Holocaust, but the Jewish *Nakba* in Arab and Muslim lands, which vindicates the idea that Jews should not be at the mercy of a local autocrat, but be responsible for their own defence in a sovereign Jewish state in the region. Jews escaped the gallows of Iraq, the torture of Egyptian prisons, violence and political and economic strangulation, to seek a haven. The establishment of Israel is validated by centuries of Arab/Muslim colonialist subjugation and exploitation of Jews. When news of the terrible tribulations suffered by the Yazidis of northern Iraq at the hands of Da'esh reached the outside world one pundit observed: 'the Israelis are like the Yazidis, only with an army'.[34]

Israel is, however, more than a haven, it is the ancestral homeland of an indigenous Middle Eastern people. The nation-state is the only reliable vehicle in modern times for preserving a people, even if that nation-state is constantly having to fight wars of survival. 'Without a country', said the 19th century prophet of Italian nationalism Mazzini, addressing the Jews, 'you have neither name, nor voice, nor rights, nor admission as brothers into the fellowship of peoples. You are the bastards of humanity.'[35]

As an aboriginal Middle Eastern people, the Jews have an inalienable right, enshrined in the UN Declaration on the Rights of Indigenous peoples,[36] to self-determination – in their ancestral homeland in the Middle East. In the words of Albert Memmi: 'If one were to base oneself on this legitimacy, and not on force and numbers, then we have the same rights to our share in these lands – neither more nor less – than the Arab Moslems.'[37]

The true forces of imperialism in the Middle East have always been Arab and/or Muslim. Some Baluch, Kurds and Amazighen (Berbers) have put on record their empathy and even admiration for Israel as a model they would like to follow.[38] Theirs is a struggle for human and political rights parallel to the national liberation of the Jews and Israel's triumph against all odds.

The Legitimacy of Difference

Jews from East and West form one Middle Eastern people, whose two halves have become re-united. Overcoming social discrimination in Israel's early years, Middle Eastern and North African Jews are free and full Israeli citizens, able to live their lives in dignity and security, and able to defend themselves in partnership with Ashkenazi Jews. Jews from the West were often treated as swarthy aliens during their 2,000-year-old sojourn in Europe, and have closer genetic links with their Mizrahi and Sephardi brethren than they do with non-Jewish Europeans. Nowadays, it is fashionable in certain 'progressive' circles to smear Ashkenazi Jews as Khazar converts with no roots in the Middle East.[39] 'Replacement theology' declares Jesus to have been a Palestinian and the Palestinian Arabs the new Jews.[40] Jews are identified with 'white privilege', success and power.[41]

It was not always thus. As the Israeli novelist Amos Oz wrote: 'When my father was a little boy in Poland, the streets of Europe were covered with graffiti, "Jews, go back to Palestine", or sometimes worse: "Dirty Yids, piss off to Palestine". When my father revisited Europe fifty years later, the walls were covered with new graffiti, "Jews, get out of Palestine."'[42]

In the wake of the Arab Spring, states like Libya, Syria and Iraq are disintegrating into warring tribes but Israel has maintained its integrity. Out of collapse may come opportunity for other non-Arab groups: the breakdown of the Sykes-Picot agreement, in which Britain and France set up a post-First World War order of artificial colonial-ordained boundaries,[43] offers a glimmer of hope to the 30 million Kurds that they might get their longed-for state (at the time of writing Iraqi Kurdistan is independent in all but name). The same cannot be said for those Assyrian Christians who are hoping to achieve a safe haven, and the Berbers who wish to gain some measure of autonomy. In this context, preserving the precious and fragile state of the Jewish people becomes all the more essential.

In what has been described as the 'magnetic pull of Israel-minority cooperation',[44] Israel supported the Christian-led south Lebanese army and the struggle of the Christian and animist South Sudan for independence. It is a pity that *realpolitik* has forced Israel to neglect its affinities with other minorities and their national struggles. In order to preserve relations with Turkey, the Israeli government has stopped short of an unequivocal condemnation of the Armenian genocide. However, Israel has reached out to the Kurds, and they, in turn, have made no secret of their wish to strengthen their relations with Israel. But ultimately, Israel has little to offer them in terms of political support.

The majority of Israeli Jews have never left the Middle East: they merely moved from one area of the region to another in order to form a majority-state on a small sliver of Levantine coastline. The West should be supporting the struggle for the survival of the tiny democratic Jewish state in a sea of strife and extremism. It is a tragedy that many Western liberals do not see the self-determination of a small, indigenous Middle Eastern people – the Jews – as a progressive cause. They see the creation of Israel as expiation for European guilt for the Holocaust. They have also misunderstood the 2,000-year-old communities of Christians in the Middle East, treating them as agents of nineteenth century colonialism and turning a deaf ear to their cries for help from Islamist persecution. Post-colonialism cannot admit that the relationship between Muslim rulers and their subservient Jews and Christians resembled that between colonisers and colonised. Westerners suffer from 'Fanonism':[45] they assume that third world people of colour cannot possibly be oppressors themselves. To their mind, anti-Semitism is solely a product of post-Enlightenment Europe.

The prevailing intellectual discourse needs to change: misled by Edward Said's *Orientalism*, much of liberal public opinion and the New Left has swallowed the canard that Israel is a colonial interloper. Instead, they support the Palestinian campaign against Israel – deceptively cloaked in the language of human rights. In so doing, they have become unwittingly complicit in the unrelenting campaign to re-establish Arab and Muslim supremacy over a *dhimmi* people.

Mesmerised by the romance of the Palestinian cause, the West routinely ignores or minimises the plight of other small non-Muslim and non-Arab peoples who share the Middle East with their Arab and Muslim neighbours. There are almost twice as many Copts as Palestinians,[46] but where are the protests against violations of their human rights? There are more than three times as many Kurds as Palestinians,[47] but the calls for their cultural and political rights have been barely audible. Western church leaders remain mealy-mouthed in their condemnation of the treatment of Middle Eastern Christians.

No Arab government is willing to see that, in the wake of the Holocaust and after having tormented and expelled their Jewish citizens, the vast majority of Jews are now Zionists, and that Israel is a central component of their identity.

Ali Salem, the late Egyptian playwright, once told the story that an Iraqi-Jewish communist named Abdullah went to an anti-Zionist demonstration in Iraq. When he discovered that the mob had stopped chanting 'Death to the Zionists', but had changed their tune to 'Death to the Jews', he understood that there was no future for him in Iraq. He left for Israel and promptly changed his name from the Arabic Abdullah to the Hebrew Ovadiah.[48]

Some Arabs are prepared to acknowledge that the uprooting of the Jewish minority was a disaster for their own countries, politically, economically and culturally. Since the collapse of the old order following the Arab Spring, increasing numbers look back with nostalgia[49] at the brief era of pluralist prosperity in the first half of the twentieth century, acknowledge the contribution made by Jewish communities to their countries, and even see exiled Jews as repositories for their own destroyed cultural fabric.[50] Some view the departure of the Jews as a divine curse on their countries,[51] but very few are prepared to reach an accommodation with the present – the existence of a non-Arab, non-Muslim state in their midst. Their favoured solution is to turn the clock back, to talk of the revival of Jewish communities in Arab countries – a delusion.

The last word belongs to George Deek, an Arab Christian diplomat with the Israeli ministry of foreign affairs:

Inside Ezekiel's shrine in 2010. Will its unique decoration survive? (Canon Andrew White)

The Great Synagogue in Tunis was restored after the 1967 riots.

Tomb of Rabbi Abraham Abeheseira, Bad Marrakesh cemetery, Casablanca.

Courtyard of the Great Synagogue, Aleppo. The Syrian civil war may have inflicted further damage.

Model of Crater Synagogue at the Aden Jewish Heritage Museum, Tel Aviv.

If there is no place in the Middle East for a Jewish State, than there is no place for anyone who is different. And this is why we see today persecution of Yazidis, Christians, Baha'i, Sunni against Shi'a and vice versa, and even Sunni against other Sunni who do not follow Islam exactly the same way. The key to change is connected deeply to our ability as Arabs to accept the legitimacy of others. Therefore, the Jewish State is our biggest challenge, because it has a different nationality, religion, and culture. Jews pose a challenge because as a minority they insist on their right to be different. The day we accept the Jewish State as it is, all other persecution in the Middle East will cease.[52]

Notes

1. G. Bensoussan, *Juifs en pays arabes: le grand déracinement*, (Tallandier, 2012), p.383.

2. See Khaled Diab,' Al-Sisi the Jew?', *Haaretz*, 8 May2014. 'ISIS leader is a Jewish Mossad agent named Simon Elliot', Harry Hibs, *24 USA*, 7 February 2016.

3. Some estimate that there were no more than 300,000 Palestinian refugees. (Yehoshua Porat, quoted by Richard Mather in his blogpost 'Palestinian refugees from 1948' contends they may have numbered less than 300,000', 13 January 2016, https://richardmatherblog.wordpress.com/2016/01/13/palestinian-refugees-from1948-may-have-numbered-less-than-300000. (Last accessed 26 April 2017)).
    Others claim that many could not be described as refugees at all, but internally displaced (see Benny Morris letter to *Irish Times*, http://www.irishtimes.com/opinion/letters/israel-and-the-palestinians-1.896017. (Last accessed 26 April 2017).

4. 'Tzipi Livni: no linkage of refugees', *Point of No Return*, 23 October 2013, http://jewishrefugees.blogspot.co.uk/2013/10/tsipi-livni-no-linkage-of-refugees.html. (Last accessed 26 April 2017).

5. Moreh, and Yehuda (eds), *Al-Farhud* (Hebrew University Magnes Press, 2010), p.143.

6. Hunter Stuart ('How a pro-Palestinian reporter changed his view of the conflict', *Jerusalem Post*, 15 April 2017) reports: 'First of all, even the kindest, most educated, upper-class Palestinians reject 100 percent of Israel – not just the occupation of East Jerusalem and the West Bank. They simply will not be content with a two-state solution – what they want is to return to their ancestral homes in Ramle and Jaffa and Haifa and other places in 1948 Israel, within the Green Line. And they want the Israelis who live there now to leave. They almost never speak of coexistence; they speak of expulsion, of taking back "their" land.'
    This view is born out by a 2015 poll which found that over 80 per cent of Palestinians denied Jewish rights in Palestine (Daniel Polisar, 'Do Palestinians want a two-state solution?' *Mosaic*, 3 April 2017, https://mosaicmagazine.com/essay/2017/04/do-palestinians-want-a-two-state-solution/). (Last accessed 26 April 2017)).

7. Efraim Karsh, 'Why the Oslo process doomed peace', *Middle East Quarterly*, 29 September 2016, http://eliasbejjaninews.com/2016/09/29/efraim-karshmiddle-east-quarterly-why-the-oslo-process-doomed-peace/. (Last accessed 26 April 2017).

8. Ali Mustafa, 'Boycotts work: an interview with Omar Barghouti', *Electronic Intifada*, 31 May 2009, https://electronicintifada.net/content/boycotts-work-interview-omar-barghouti/8263. (Last accessed 26 April 2017).

9. Critics cast doubt on the Palestinian claim to a 'Right of Return' under Article 13 of The Universal Declaration of Human Rights: they were not citizens of Israel at the time of their flight.

10. Doreen Wachmann, interview with Shmuel Moreh, *Manchester Jewish Telegraph*, July 2009.

11. Refugee comparison chart, *Israel Behind the News* (UN data), http://israelbehindthenews. com/library/pdfs/UNRWAchartcomparison.pdf. (Last accessed 26 April 2017).

12. Interview with Palestinian ambassador Abdullah to Lebanon: 'refugees will not be citizens of a new state', *Daily Star*, 15 September 2015.

13. Conversation with the author, 17 April 2017.

14. Samuel Shahid, 'Rights of non-Muslims in an Islamic state', *Answering Islam*, concludes that his study 'shows us that non-Muslims are not regarded as citizens by any Islamic state, even if they are original natives of the land'. http://www.answering-islam.org/NonMuslims/rights.htm. (Last accessed 26 April 2017).

15. Ignace Moubarac, 'Letter To Mr. Justice Sandström, Chairman, UNSCOP Geneva, Switzerland.'The Two Homelands', Beirut, 5 August 1947, *Ha-historion* blog, February 2007, http://ha-historion.blogspot.co.uk/2007/02/relations-between-first-zionist.html. (Last accessed 26 April 2017).

16. A Christian, Michel Aflaq, was the ideologue behind the nationalist Ba'ath party. Constantine Zureiq was a Christian intellectual moderniser who advocated Arab unity based on reason and science.

17. Moreh and Yehuda (eds), 'Introduction' to *Al-Farhud* (Hebrew University Magnes Press, 2010), p.3.

18. Albert. Memmi's essay, 'Who is an Arab Jew?', February 1975, http://www.sullivan-county.com/x/aj1.htm. (Last accessed 26 April 2017).

19. Mordechai Nisan, 'Minorities in the Middle East' in Shulewitz (ed.) *The Forgotten Millions* (Continuum, 2000), p.10.

20. See Hamas (Islamic Resistance Movement) Covenant, https://www.memri.org/reports/covenant-islamic-resistance-movement-%E2%80%93-hamas. (Last accessed 26 April 2017).

21. In the 1950s, the Grand Mufti of Egypt, Sheikh Hasan Mamoun, issued a *fatwa* – signed by the major representatives of all four Islamic schools of jurisprudence – which stated that because 'Jews have taken a part of Palestine and there established their non-Islamic government' it followed logically that *jihad* against the Jews was 'the duty of all Muslims'. (http://www.discoverthenetworks.org/viewSubCategory.asp?id=762). (Last accessed 26 April 2017).

22. Bernard Lewis, 'The Return of Islam', *Commentary*, 1 January 1976, https://www.commentarymagazine.com/articles/the-return-of-islam/. (Last accessed 26 April 2017).

23. See David Pryce-Jones, *The Closed Circle*: An Interpretation of the Arabs (New York: Edward Burlington, Harper & Row, 1988).

24. Karmel Melamed, Q&A with Matthias Küntzel, 'Roots and development of the Iranian regime's antisemitism', *Jewish Journal of Los Angeles*, 26 August 2015, http://www.matthiaskuentzel.de/contents/q-a-kuentzel-on-roots-and-develoment-of-the-iranian-regimes-antisemitism /. (Last accessed 26 April 2017).

25. The case of David Gerbi, who was thrown out of his native Libya in 2011 for wanting to open a synagogue, springs to mind ('My harrowing Yom Kippur', *Point of No Return*, 19 October 2011, http://jewishrefugees.blogspot.co.uk/2011/10/my-harrowing-yom-kippur-and-escape-from.html. (Last accessed 26 April 2017)).

26. Arab League Profile, *BBC News*, 5 February 2015, http://www.bbc.co.uk/news/world-middle-east-15747941. (Last accessed 26 April 2017) .

27. Harold Rhode, review of 'Turkey, the Jews, and the Holocaust' by Corry Guttstadt, *Sephardic Horizons*, http://www.sephardichorizons.org/Volume4/Issue1/turkey.html. (Last accessed 26 April 2017).

28. Bernard Lewis, 'The Return of Islam', *Commentary*, 1 January 1976, https://www.commentarymagazine.com/articles/the-return-of-islam/. (Last accessed 26 April 2017).

29. Daniel Polisar, 'Do Palestinians want a two-state solution?' *Mosaic*, 3 April 2017, https://mosaicmagazine.com/essay/2017/04/do-palestinians-want-a-two-state-solution/. (Last accessed 26 April 2017).

30. Christine Chaillot, *Les Coptes d'Egypte* (Paris: L'Harmattan, 2013), p.15.

31. For examples see Jon Emont, 'How Malaysia became one of the most anti-Semitic countries on earth', *The Tablet*, 8 February 2016, http://www.tabletmag.com/jewish-news-and-politics/196642/anti-semitism-in-malaysia. (Last accessed 26 April 2017); Bilal Ahmed, 'Antisemitism in Pakistan' *Souciant*, 20 February 2013, http://souciant.com/2013/02/anti-semitism-in-pakistan/. (Last accessed 26 April 2017). See also Mehdi Hasan, 'Why the virus of antisemitism has infected the British Muslim community', *New Statesman*, 21 March 2013, http://www.newstatesman.com/politics/uk/2013/03/sorry-truth-virus-anti-semitism-has-infected-british-muslim-community. (Last accessed 26 April 2017).

32. Aomar Boum, *Memories of Absence*, (Stanford, CA: Stanford University Press, 2013), p.155.

33. Matti Friedman, 'Mizrahi Nation', *Mosaic*, 1 June 2014, http://mosaicmagazine.com/essay/2014/06/mizrahi-nation/. (Last accessed 26 April 2017).

34. Jonathan Spyer quoting a colleague, 'Ottomania', *ISBlog*, 1 October 2014, https://jackscohen.wordpress.com/2014/10/01/ottomania/. (Last accessed 26 April 2017).

35. Quoted by Barbara W. Tuchman, *Bible and Sword* (London: Macmillan, 1982), p.225.

36. http://www.un.org/esa/socdev/unpfii/documents/DRIPS_en.pdf. (Last accessed 26 April 2017).

37. See Memmi essay, 'Who is an Arab Jew?'

38. Dr Mohamed Chatou, ('Moroccan Jews' Departure to Israel regretted by Morocco' *African Exponent*, 10 January 2017) testifies to Amazigh sympathy. See also Sharon Udasin and Jan Koscinski, 'Algeria Craves Friensdhip with Israel', *Jerusalem Post*, 27 May 2012. Seth Frantzman, 'Deep in Kurdish Heartland, Finding an Enduring Bond with Israel', *Forward*, 22 June 2015, writes about the positive attitude he found among Kurds.

39. This claim, by radical professor Shlomo Sand among others, was rebutted in this article by Ofer Aderet, 'Jews are not descended from Khazars, Hebrew University Historian Says', *Haaretz*, 26 June 2014, http://www.haaretz.com/jewish/features/1.601287. (Last accessed 26 April 2017).

40. Melanie Phillips, 'Jesus was a Palestinian: The Return of Christian Anti-Semitism', *Commentary*, 1 June 2014, https://www.commentarymagazine.com/articles/jesus-was-a-palestinian-the-return-of-christian-anti-semitism/. (Last accessed 26 April 2017).

41. Rachel Frommer, 'Anti-Semitic "End Jewish Privilege" fliers distributed at Chicago University Rattle Students: School Issues Condemnation', *The Algemeiner*, 16 March 2017, https://www.algemeiner.com/2017/03/16/end-jewish-privilege-fliers-distributed-at-illinois-university-have-students-up-in-arms/. (Last accessed 26 April 2017).

42. Quoted by Stephen Daisley in 'Jeremy Corbyn is no antisemite: he's much worse than that', STV.TV, 28 August 2016, http://stv.tv/news/politics/1327077-stephen-daisley-on-jeremy-corbyn-the-left-anti-semitism-and-israel/. (Last accessed 26 April 2017).

43. A Century On: why Arabs resent Sykes-Picot, *Al-Jazeera*, 2016, http://interactive.aljazeera.com/aje/2016/sykes-picot-100-years-middle-east-map/. (Last accessed 26 April 2017).

44. See Mordechai Nisan, 'Minorities in the Middle East', p.9.

45. David Aaronovitch, opinion piece, *Jewish Chronicle*, 28 August 2015.

46. CIA World Fact Book 2017

47. BBC News Middle East, 'Who are the Kurds?', 14 March 2016.

48. See Ali Salem, *A Drive to Israel: an Egyptian meets his Neighbors* (Dayan Center Papers 128, 2003).

49. Dr Mohamed Chatou, 'Moroccans bitterly regret Departure of their Jews', *African Exponent*, 10 January 2017, https://www.africanexponent.com/blogs/braveafrica/4528-moroccan-jews-departure-to-israel-regretted-in-morocco. (Last accessed 26 April 2017).

50. Samuel Tadros, 'Once upon a time Jews lived here', *Hudson Institute*, 16 March 2017, https://www.hudson.org/research/13456-once-upon-a-time-jews-lived-here.   (Last accessed 26 April 2017).

51. Edy Cohen, 'The Jewish Expulsion – and its Revenge', *Israel Hayom*, 30 November 2016, http://www.israelhayom.com/site/newsletter_opinion.php?id=17777. (Last accessed 26 April 2017).

52. Adi Schwartz, 'Israel's best diplomat: George Deek', *Tablet*, 28 July 2015, http://www.tabletmag.com/jewish-news-and-politics/190615/israels-best-diplomat-george-deek. (Last accessed 26 April 2017).

Appendices

Jewish pop.	Date established	1948	2016
Algeria	1-2nd century CE	140,000	0
Egypt	2nd century BCE	75,000	Less than 15
Iran	3rd century BCE	100,000	8,000
Iraq	3rd century BCE	150,000	5
Lebanon	1st century BCE	20,000	Less than 20
Libya	3rd century BCE	38,000	0
Morocco	1st century BCE	265,000	2,000
Syria	1st century BCE	30,000	Less than 15
Tunisia	1st century BCE	105,000	1,000
Yemen	3rd century BCE	55,000	50

Chart showing displacement of Jewish communities and when they were founded (Source: JJAC, updated by the author)

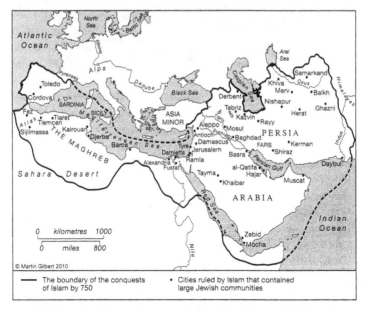

The conquests of Islam by 750, and towns with large Jewish communities (From Martin Gilbert, *In Ishmael's House* [Yale: 2010], p. 356)

Displacement of Jews from Arab Countries 1948-2012

	1948	1958[1]	1968[2]	1976[3]	2001[4]	2005[5]	2012 (est.)
Aden	8,000	800	0	0	0	0	0
Algeria	140,000	130,000	3,000	1,000	0	0	0
Egypt	75,000	40,000	2,500	400	100	100	75
Iraq	135,000	6,000	2,500	350	100	60[6]	50
Lebanon	5,000	6,000	3,000	400	100	~50[7]	40
Libya	38,000	3,750	500	40	0	0	0
Morocco	265,000	200,000	50,000	18,000	5,700	3,500	3,000
Syria	30,000	5,000	4,000	4,500	100	100	~50
Tunisia	105,000	80,000	10,000	7,000	1,500	1,100	1,000
Yemen	55,000	3,500	500	500	200[8]	200	100
TOTAL	856,000[9]	475,050	76,000	32,190	7,800	5,110	4,315

Table showing displacement of Jews from Arab lands between 1948 and 2012. (Source: JJAC)

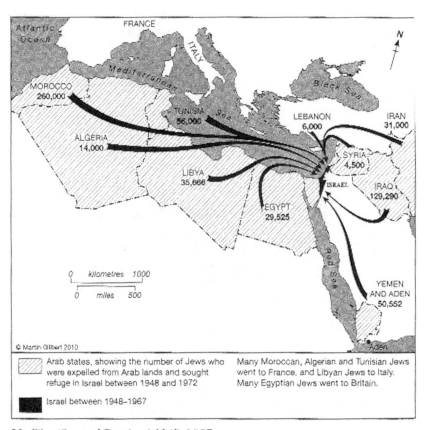

20. The 'Second Exodus,' 1947–1957.

Numbers of Jews who fled to Israel 1947-1957. From Martin Gilbert, *In Ishmael's House* (Yale: 2010) p. 374

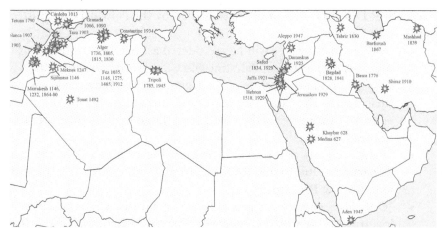

Non-exhaustive map showing anti-Jewish massacres in Muslim countries before 1948 (Torbjörn Karfunkel)

Arab League Draft Law, 1947

A photocopy of this document entitled: "'*Text of Law Drafted by the Political Committee of the Arab League.*'" was discovered affixed to a 19 January 1948 Memorandum submitted by the World Jewish Congress to the UN Economic and Social Council (ECOSOC). It warned that, ' '*all Jews residing in the Near and Middle East face extreme and imminent danger'.

Text of the Law Drafted by the Political Committee of the Arab League
Summary
In 1947, the Political Committee of the Arab League (*League of Arab States*) drafted a law which was to govern the legal status of Jewish residents in all Arab League countries. This law had already been approved by **Egypt, Saudi Arabia and Iraq**, provided that, "beginning with a specified date, all Jews – with the exception of citizens of non-Arab countries – were to be considered members of the Jewish 'minority state of Palestine,' and that their bank account be frozen and used to finance resistance to 'Zionist ambitions in Palestine.' Jews believed to be active Zionists would be interned as political prisoners and their assets confiscated. Only Jews who accept active service in Arab armies or place themselves at the disposal of these armies would be considered 'Arabs.'"[1]

Excerpts of Direct Quotes of the Law drafted by the Political Committee of the Arab League

- "All Jewish citizens…will be considered as members of the Jewish minority of the State of Palestine and will have to register ["within 7 days"] with the authorities of the region wherein they reside, giving their names, the exact number of members in their families, their addresses, the names of their banks and the amounts of their deposits in these banks…"[2]
- "Bank accounts of Jews will be frozen. These funds will be utilized in part or in full to finance the movement of resistance to Zionist ambitions in Palestine."[3]
- "Only Jews who are subjects of foreign countries will be considered 'neutrals.' These will be compelled either to return to their countries, with a minimum of delay, or be considered Arabs and obliged to accept active service in the Arab army."[4]
- "Every Jew whose activities reveal that he is an active Zionist will be considered as a political prisoner and will be interned in places specifically designated for that purpose by police authorities or by the Government. His financial resources, instead of being frozen, will be confiscated."[5]
- "Any Jew who will be able to prove that his activities are anti-Zionist will be free to act as he likes, provided that he declares his readiness to join the Arab armies."[6]
- "The foregoing…does not mean that those Jews will not be submitted to paragraphs 1 and 2 of this law."[7]

Notes

1   *Memorandum Submitted to the U.N. Economic and Social Council by the World Jewish Congress.* (Jan. 19, 1948) Section I. (2) a. June 2, 1948. [ZIIC - This reference is in the document prepared by JJAC and is probably incorrect]
2   Text of the Law drafted by the Political Committee of the Arab League. Paragraph 1.
3   ibid. Paragraph 2.
4   ibid. Paragraph 3.
5   ibid. Paragraph 5.
6   ibid. Paragraph 6.
7   ibid. Paragraph 7. (Paragraph 1 & 2 indicate all Jews must register and disclose personal and banking information and that bank accounts will be frozen and utilized for anti-Zionist resistance.)

US Congress House of Representatives Resolution 185 (2008)

April 1, 2008.

Whereas armed conflicts in the Middle East have created refugee populations numbering in the millions and comprised of peoples from many ethnic, religious, and national backgrounds;

Whereas Jews have lived mostly as a minority in the Middle East, North Africa, and the Persian Gulf region for more than 2,500 years;

Whereas the United States has long voiced its concern about the mistreatment of minorities and the violation of human rights in the Middle East and elsewhere;

seeking an end to the Arab-Israeli conflict in the Middle East and to promoting a peace that will benefit all the peoples of the region;

Whereas United States administrations historically have called for a just solution to the Palestinian refugee problem;

Whereas the Palestinian refugee issue has received considerable attention from countries of the world while the issue of Jewish refugees from the Arab and Muslim worlds has received very little attention;

Whereas a comprehensive peace in the region will require the resolution of all outstanding issues through bilateral and multilateral negotiations involving all concerned parties;

Whereas approximately 850,000 Jews have been displaced from Arab countries since the declaration of the State of Israel in 1948;

Whereas the United States has demonstrated interest and concern about the mistreatment, violation of rights, forced expulsion, and expropriation of assets of minority populations in general, and in particular, former Jewish refugees displaced from Arab countries as evidenced, inter alia, by—

(1) the Memorandum of Understanding signed by President Jimmy Carter and Israeli Foreign Minister Moshe Dayan on October 4, 1977, which states that "[a] solution of the problem of Arab refugees and Jewish refugees will be discussed in accordance with rules which should be agreed";

(2) after negotiating the Camp David Accords, the Framework for Peace in the Middle East, the statement by President Jimmy Carter in a press conference on October 27, 1977, that "Palestinians have rights . . . obviously there are Jewish refugees . . . they have the same rights as others do"; and

(3) in an interview after Camp David II in July 2000, at which the issue of Jewish refugees displaced from Arab lands was discussed, the statement by President Clinton that "There will have to be some sort of international fund set up for the refugees. There is, I think, some interest, interestingly enough, on both sides, in also having a fund which compensates the Israelis

who were made refugees by the war, which occurred after the birth of the State of Israel. Israel is full of people, Jewish people, who lived in predominantly Arab countries who came to Israel because they were made refugees in their own land.";

Whereas the international definition of a refugee clearly applies to Jews who fled the persecution of Arab regimes, where a refugee is a person who "owing to a well-founded fear of being persecuted for reasons of race, religion, nationality, membership of a particular social group, or political opinion, is outside the country of his nationality, and is unable to or, owing to such fear, is unwilling to avail himself of the protection of that country" (the 1951 Convention relating to the Status of Refugees);

Whereas on January 29, 1957, the United Nations High Commissioner for Refugees (UNHCR), determined that Jews fleeing from Arab countries were refugees that fell within the mandate of the UNHCR;

Whereas United Nations Security Council Resolution 242 of November 22, 1967, calls for a "just settlement of the refugee problem" without distinction between Palestinian and Jewish refugees, and this is evidenced by—

(1) the Soviet Union's United Nations delegation attempt to restrict the "just settlement" mentioned in Resolution 242 solely to Palestinian refugees (S/8236, discussed by the Security Council at its 1,382nd meeting of November 22, 1967, notably at paragraph 117, in the words of Ambassador Kouznetsov of the Soviet Union), but this attempt failed, signifying the international community's intention of having the resolution address the rights of all Middle East refugees; and

(2) a statement by Justice Arthur Goldberg, the United States' Chief Delegate to the United Nations at that time, who was instrumental in drafting the unanimously adopted Resolution 242, where he has pointed out that "The resolution addresses the objective of 'achieving a just settlement of the refugee problem'. This language presumably refers both to Arab and Jewish refugees, for about an equal number of each abandoned their homes as a result of the several wars.";

Whereas in his opening remarks before the January 28, 1992, organizational meeting for multilateral negotiations on the Middle East in Moscow, United States Secretary of State James Baker made no distinction between Palestinian refugees and Jewish refugees in articulating the mission of the Refugee Working Group, stating that "[t]he refugee group will consider practical ways of improving the lot of people throughout the region who have been displaced from their homes";

Whereas the Roadmap to a Permanent Two-State Solution to the Israeli-Palestinian Conflict, which refers in Phase III to an "agreed, just, fair, and realistic solution to the refugee issue," uses language that is equally applicable to all persons displaced as a result of the conflict in the Middle East;

Whereas Israel's agreements with Egypt, Jordan, and the Palestinians have affirmed that a comprehensive solution to the Arab-Israeli conflict will require a just solution to the plight of all "refugees";

Whereas the initiative to secure rights and redress for Jews who were forced to flee Arab countries does not conflict with the right of Palestinian refugees to claim redress;

Whereas all countries should be aware of the plight of Jews and other minority groups displaced from countries in the Middle East, North Africa, and the Persian Gulf;

Whereas an international campaign is proceeding in some 40 countries to record the history and legacy of Jewish refugees from Arab countries;

Whereas a just, comprehensive Arab-Israeli peace cannot be reached without addressing the uprooting of centuries-old Jewish communities in the Middle East, North Africa, and the Persian Gulf; and

Whereas it would be inappropriate and unjust for the United States to recognize rights for Palestinian refugees without recognizing equal rights for Jewish refugees from Arab countries: Now, therefore, be it Resolved, That—

(1) for any comprehensive Middle East peace agreement to be credible and enduring, the agreement must address and resolve all outstanding issues relating to the legitimate rights of all refugees, including Jews, Christians, and other populations, displaced from countries in the Middle East; and

(2) the President should instruct the United States Representative to the United Nations and all United States representatives in bilateral and multilateral fora to—

(A) use the voice, vote, and influence of the United States to ensure that any resolutions relating to the issue of Middle East refugees, and which include a reference to the required resolution of the Palestinian refugee issue, must also include a similarly explicit reference to the resolution of the issue of Jewish refugees from Arab countries; and

(B) make clear that the United States Government supports the position that, as an integral part of any comprehensive Arab-Israeli peace, the issue of refugees from the Middle East, North Africa, and the Persian Gulf must be resolved in a manner that includes recognition of the legitimate rights of and losses incurred by all refugees displaced from Arab countries, including Jews, Christians, and other groups.

Attest:

Clerk.

Full text of Knesset Law passed 22 February 2010

The rights to compensation of Jewish refugees from Arab countries and Iran, 22 February 2010

1. Purpose The purpose of this Law is to protect the rights to compensation of Jewish refugees from Arab countries and Iran in the framework of peace negotiations in the Middle East. **2. Definitions** In this Law –— "Refugee Jews from Arab countries and Iran" - who are any of the following: (1) He is a citizen of Israel*, or lived there before the establishment of the state; (2) He was a resident of Arab countries or Iran, and left mostly because he was persecuted on account of his Jewishness and his inability to defend himself against such persecution. (3) He left property** he owned in his country of origin ***"Property" - land, assets, cash, rights, and other property seized by government order.* **3. Negotiations to achieve peace** In negotiations to achieve peace in the Middle East, the government must include the issue of providing compensation for loss of property to Jewish refugees from Arab countries and Iran, including property owned by Jewish communities in these countries. **4. Execution** The Prime Minister is to be in charge of the implementation of this Law. Signed by Benjamin Netanyahu *Prime Minister* Shimon Peres *President* Reuven Rivlin *Speaker of the Knesset*

* Although the Law applies only to Israeli citizens, a mechanism is being sought to cover Jewish refugees living outside Israel, similar to that for Holocaust survivors resident outside Israel.

EGYPT

Jews have had a presence in Egypt since the dawn of civilisation. The modern community was made up of indigenous Jews (Rabbanites and Karaites) and more recent arrivals from elsewhere in the Ottoman empire. Here is a timeline showing how Egypt's Jews were stripped of their rights, beginning with the right to nationality in the twentieth century:

1880: 'Real Egyptian' cabinet formed. In spite of reforms, Jews still considered *dhimmis*. The middle and upper classes sought European consular protection and passports under the regime. **1914:** 10, 000 'foreign' Jews expelled from Palestine arrive in Egypt. **1918:** 80 –- 100, 000 Jews in Egypt. Ethnicisation of Egyptians into separate 'races'.

1922: Egypt becomes nominally independent. **1927**: **First nationality law.** Individual citizens required to apply. **End 1920s/30s**: Muslim Brotherhood (founded 1928) and nationalists launch sporadic attacks on non-Muslims (Syrians/Armenians/Greeks/ Jews.) After 1933, Nazis finance anti-Jewish campaign. **1929**: **Nationality law** establishes *jus sanguinis*. Arabs/Muslims given preference. Only 5,000 Jews receive Egyptian nationality, 40,000 remain stateless. The poor could not afford £5 for a nationality certificate. **1937**: Capitulations abolished. After 1949, Egyptian government responsible for protecting minorities. **1938**: 'Young Egypt' pro-Nazi youth movement leader meets Adolph Hitler and calls for expulsion of Jews. **1942**: Muslim Brotherhood issues anti-Balfour Declaration . **2/3 November 1945:** Anti-Jewish and minority riots. Ashkenazi Great synagogue and other Jewish institutions in Cairo burnt down. Jewish shops looted. Six killed. **1946**: 200 Alexandrian Jews leave for Israel in semi-legal emigration. **1947**: Heykal Pasha, Egyptian delegate to the UN, threatens that a million Jews in Arab countries would be at risk if Palestine Partition goes ahead. **1947**: **Arabisation Company Law** insists that 75% employees must be Arab/Muslim. **1948**: police begin anti-Zionist witch-hunt. Emigration to Israel goes underground.

May 1948: arrest and internment of 1,300, one thousand of them Jews. Sequestration of internees' property. Jewish schools placed under government control and forced to implement Egyptianisation. Some Jews barred from higher education. **June 1948**: martial law imposed. Local Jews considered a Fifth Column. Jewish assets, both communal and private seized during first Arab-Israeli war. Some 20, 000 Jews leave for Israel and Europe. Those with Egyptian nationality stripped of it. **20 June 1948**: Twenty-two Jews killed in bombings of Karaite quarter of Cairo. **July 1948**: 500 Jewish shops including Cicurel and Oreco department stores bombed. A 'Zionist plane' blamed. Some 200 Jews killed during rioting that summer. **September 1948**: 19 Jews killed. Jewish businesses looted. **November 1948** : Jewish shops looted in Cairo. **1950 (revised 1951, 1953 and 1956) nationality law** bans Jews from receiving Egyptian nationality and allows all 'Zionists' to be stripped of their nationality. **Black Saturday, 26 January 1952**: nationalists and fundamentalists attack Greek, Armenian and Jewish property. **1956-57**: Following rise to power of Nasser and the Free Officers, expulsion of 25, 000 Jews in wake of Suez crisis.

1961–62: nationalisation of remaining Jewish property. **1967**: All Jewish males interned after Six Day War. Number of Jews falls to a few thousand. **2016**: Eight Jews remain in Cairo, five in Alexandria.

With acknowledgements to Ruth Toledano Attias's essay 'La denationalisation des Juifs d'Egypte' in *La fin du Judaisme en terres d'Islam* (Ed. S Trigano).

YEMEN and ADEN

The 3,000-year-old Yemenite Jewish community is nearing extinction. At the turn of the twentieth century North Yemen was under the Ottomans/ Zaydi Shi'a Muslims where a strict form of *sharia* law was rigorously enforced. In the south, Aden became a British protectorate.

1881: Jews from Yemen begin leaving for the land of Israel. Jews forcibly converted by Sha'ifis prefer to live under Zaydi rule in north.

1849-72: Ottoman-Zaydi struggle for power.   **1904**: Zaydi ruler Imam Yahya becomes ruler. 7,000 (80 percent) of Jews and 10,000 Muslims die from famine in Sana'a. Many Jews convert to Islam to obtain food. Jews flee to Aden. Many robbed en route.   **1911**: *Sharia* law declared: Jews are inferior *dhimmis*, slightly above blacks in pecking order, equivalent to Untouchables in India. Jews must pay a special tax; amount depends on their profession. Children throw stones at them, murder victims' families get modest blood money but no real justice if the murderer is Muslim. Jews can own property, but interiors must be very simple so as not to arouse Muslim envy.   **1913**: Group of Jews assigned sewage collection from Muslim areas. These form an 'Untouchable' sub-group within the community.

1920: Zaydis declare independence.   **1922**: Orphans' Decree: children who have lost their fathers abducted and converted to Islam.   **1922**: British ban emigration to Palestine.   **1923**: forty-two orphans converted to Islam.   **1928**: twenty-seven orphans converted on pain of torture. **1929**: Fifty children aged 5-13 smuggled out to Aden in the hope that they would reach Palestine. Palestinians in Yemen spread anti-Jewish libels. Jews flee to Aden, but are forced to leave their property. Desperate Yemeni Jews flee wherever they can –- 2,000 move to Egypt; 2,000 to Eritrea, ; 7,000 to India.   **1934**: Mufti of Jerusalem passes through Yemen. Jews banned from leaving for Palestine lest they end up fighting Arabs.   **1935**: Jews oppressed further after rumour that mosques in Jerusalem under threat. After 23,000 Jews pour into Aden, the port is closed to Jews.   **1947**: riots erupt in Aden. Eighty-two Jews killed (87 according to the Aden Jewish Heritage Museum).   **1948**: Imam Yahya is assassinated. Civil war and anarchy follow.   **1949**: Emigration ban lifted.   **1949-50**: 50,000 Jews are ransomed by Israel and airlifted on 'Operation Eagles' Wings'. Those with special skills detained until they could pass them on to Muslims.   **2009**: Over a hundred Jews flee Yemen civil war and radicalisation. In 2016, less than 50 fifty remained.

With acknowledgements to Ruth Toledano Attias's essay, 'Sous la dureté de la *dhimma*: les juifs du Yemen', in *La fin du Judaïsme en terres d'Islam*, (edited by S. Trigano).

SYRIA AND LEBANON

The 2,000 year-old Jewish communities of Syria and Lebanon (30,000 and 20,000 in 1948) have always been intertwined, as has the history of the two countries. Here's a timeline tracing their decline to less than 20 Jews in each country today.

19th century: an era of mass migration for Syrians of all faiths, driven by the 1860 Christian-Druze war and economic crises to move to Egypt and the New World.   **1909**: Young Jews leave to avoid Ottoman conscription law.   **1917**: exiles from *Ertez Yisrael* expose Jews to Zionism.   **1918**: Syria and Lebanon under French mandate.   **1930s**: Anti-Jewish measures introduced, economy in crisis. 2,868 Jews move to Israel. Nazi propaganda and incitement by the Mufti of Jerusalem spreads. 5, 286 Jews leave.   **1945**: 1,000 Jewish children go on *aliya*.   **1945**: Syrian school curriculum becomes compulsory.   **1947**: Partition riots devastate Aleppo. All 18 synagogues, five schools, 150 shops, orphanage and youth club destroyed. Great synagogue of Aleppo badly damaged. Jews cannot buy property. Hundreds arrested. Jews expelled from University of Beirut.

1948: Jews murdered in Beirut. In November, twelve killed in Tripoli, northern Lebanon.   **1949**: Jewish bank accounts seized in Syria, property frozen, no freedom of movement.   **1949**: grenades thrown at al-Menashe synagogue, Damascus: thirteen dead, 32 thirty-two wounded.   **1950**: Jews of Qamishli banned from working in agriculture.   **1950**: Influx   of provincial Jews to Beirut. 10,000 Jews move to Lebanon from Iraq and Syria. Only 5,700 remain in Syria.   **1950**: Syria passes a law seizing Jewish property. Palestinian refugees move into Jewish quarter of Damascus. Attacks on Jews in Damascus, Aleppo and Qamishli. Property and shops looted. **1950**: Bomb explodes at Alliance *Israelite Universelle* school in Beirut. Jewish youth organisations banned. Civil servants sacked. Jews otherwise protected by Phalange militia and free to travel and do business.   **1958-62**: Jews can leave Syria on payment of a ransom. 2,800 Syrian Jews flee to Israel.   **1962**: Travel ban introduced.   **1965**: Arrest of Israeli spy Eli Cohen. Attacks increase.   **1967**: Anti-Jewish riots in Syria. Muslims control two Jewish schools. Travel ban. Jewish chemists and doctors sacked. Jewish jobs given to refugees from Golan Heights. 2,264 Jews go to Israel.   **1967–70**: Of 6,000 Jews in Lebanon, all but a few hundred leave.   **1971**: Wave of kidnappings. Albert Elia, community leader, abducted and murdered in Lebanon.   **1973**: following Yom Kippur War, Jewish homes in Syria have their telephone lines cut off, and are allowed no radios or postal links with outside world.   **1974**: four Syrian Jewish girls raped and murdered.   **1975**: rescue campaign for remaining Syrian Jews, including many single girls, initiated by Canadian Judy Feld Carr.   **1978**: 450 Jews left in Lebanon. Between 1979 and 1980,

30 Jews thought killed in civil war.   **1992**: President Assad allows 2,800 Jews to leave on tourist visas without assets.   **1994**: Jews allowed to leave with their assets. Syrian Chief Rabbi Abraham Hamra leaves for Israel.   **1999**: Sixty Jews remain in Lebanon and between fifty and a hundred in Syria. **2017:** less than 15 Jews remain in either country.

With acknowledgements to 'Comment la Syrie et le Liban se sont totalement vidés de leurs Juifs' by Yaron Harel, in *La fin du judaïsme en terres d'Islam* by (ed. S. Trigano).

MOROCCO

Jews comprised 3 per cent of Morocco's five million inhabitants before 1948. Now there are 2, 500 or fewer, their fate tied to that of the 'protective' royal family; their community is a shadow of its former self. Here is a timeline showing the main stages in a period of dramatic decline.

1912: Fez pogrom: forty-five Jews killed.   **1912**: Establishment of French protectorate signals end of *dhimmi* status of 230, 000 Jews, but they are denied French citizenship, with few exceptions.   **1930s**: Anti-Semitism mounts from the French far-right and Moroccan nationalists.   **1934**: Grand vizir asks French authorities to ban Jews moving in alongside Muslims in New Medina (*Habou* quarter) and new central districts of Casablanca. **1936**: rumour that Jewish girls are having a bad influence on Muslim girls leads to 1937 'pogrom': In Meknes, nationalists ransack 40 Jewish shops. Jews counter with a call for a boycott of German goods.   **3 Oct 1940**: First Vichy statute expels Jews of French nationality from public service, education, law, medicine and media.   **31 Oct 1940**: the sultan signs anti-Jewish *dahir*. Jewish schools and administrative committees remain unaffected; Journals are banned. Converts to Islam exempt.   **Nov 1940**: Muslim girl servants in Jewish homes banned.   **1941**: sultan declares his disapproval of anti-Semitic laws to a Jewish delegation. Sultan delays, but still signs, five more *dahirs* in August 1941 banning Jews from banking, finance, property, law. Jews must declare their assets. *Numerus clausus* in public schools.   **8 August 1941**: Jews sent back from city European districts to *mellahs*.   **1942**: "'There are no Jews, only Moroccans,'" the sultan declares.   **1948**: Riots in Oujda and Jerrada. Forty-four Jews murdered. 10 percent of Morocco's Jews leave for Israel.   **1948-49**: 22, 900 Jews leave for Israel.
1949-57: 110, 000 Jews leave Morocco.   **1953**: Four Jews die in Oujda disturbances.   **1954**: Petit Jean massacre: seven Jews die.
1955: 1,700 Jews escape to the European city of Mazagan after large number of houses in the Jewish Quarter were set on fire and burned to the ground ; 200 Jews left homeless.   **1955**: Wadi Zem: family of five and two other Jews

murdered. **1956**. : Morocco declares independence. Dr Leon Benzaquen named Minister of Postal services. Five Jews named to national consultative council. **Sept 1956**: Independent Morocco imposes emigration ban to Israel. Nevertheless 29, 472 Jews leave secretly with help from the Zionist *Misgueret*. **1958**: Morocco joins Arab League: arabisation. Postal links to Israel cut.

Jan 1961: President Nasser of Egypt visits. Jews roughed up. Jewesses forcibly converted amid nationalist resurgence. **Jan 1961**: Shipwreck of illegal Pisces (Egos) smuggling boat. Forty-two Jewish emigrants and one crewman drown. **1961**: Operation Yakhnin evacuates 87,707 Jews to Israel. Morocco receives 'ransom' of $20 million. **1948-67**: 237, 813 Moroccan Jews arrive in Israel. **After 1967**: 40, 000 Moroccan Jews move to France. **16 August 1972**: attempted coup against King Hassan II fails. **1972**: 30, 000 Jews remain. **2003**: Less less than 5, 000 Jews live in Morocco.

With acknowledgements to *'Mohamed V et ses juifs'* by Guillaume Jobin (*Information juive* Fev/Mars 2015), *Il était une fois le Maroc* by David Bensoussan; Yigal Ben Nun in *'La fin du Judaïsme en terres d'Islam'*, (ed. S. Trigano).

LIBYA

Inhabiting the provinces of Tripolitania and Cyrenaica, Libya's Jewish community traces its origins to the third century BCE. With the Italian occupation in 1911, the Jews made great strides in education and commerce but suffered during grievously during and after the Second World War. By 1941, the Jews accounted for a quarter of the population of Tripoli. Today there are none.

1938: Italian racial laws applied to Libya's 30, 000 Jews.
1942: German occupation of Benghazi Jewish quarter. 2,000 Jews deported across the desert. 600 Jews die in work camp. **1945**: two-day pogrom: 130 Jews killed, five synagogues destroyed. **1948**: fourteen Jews killed in pogrom. 300 homes destroyed.
1948: 3, 000 Jews emigrate illegally.
1949-1952 : 90 percent of Jews flee for Israel. **1951**: Constitution abolished. PM Mahmud Muntassar says Jews can have no future in Libya. **1952**: Independent independent Libya bans emigration, joins the Arab League. **1953**: Libya signs up to anti-Jewish economic boycott. Night-time searches of Jewish homes for 'Zionist' material. **1954**: Maccabi sports club closed. **1958**: Jewish Community Council dissolved by law. **1961**: Law requires a special permit to prove true Libyan citizenship – denied to all but six Jews. **1961**: Assets belonging to Libyan Jews in Israel seized. Only Libyan nationals can buy property (excludes Jews). Jews cannot vote. **1963**: Nasserists press

for closure of US and UK bases.   **1963**: Murder of Jewish leader Halfalla Nahum, aged eighty-four.   **1967**: Six Day War. Jews donate to Palestinian cause. 60 percent of Jewish assets destroyed in Tripoli. Italian and Jewish shops burnt. Ten Jews killed. 300 Benghazi Jews detained for own safety. Two families (fourteen people) massacred. Almost all Libya's remaining 5,000 Jews evacuated out of the country.   **1970**: Gaddafi government sequesters all property of Jews abroad.   **2002**: Esmeralda Meghnagi, Libya's last Jew, dies.

With acknowledgements to 'Le processus de discrimination des juifs de Libye' by Maurice Roumani, in *La fin du judaïsme en terres d'Islam* (ed. Shmuel S. Trigano).

IRAQ

Conditions for Jews in the world's oldest diaspora began to deteriorate in the Thirties with the rise of pro-Nazi sentiment. After the mass exodus of 1950 -1, the remaining few thousand suffered badly under the rule of Saddam Hussein and most tried to escape. In 2016, all that was left of this ancient and illustrious community were five Jews.

1918, 1919 and 1920: Fearful of local Muslim rule, Jews petition the Civil Commissioner for Baghdad for British citizenship, but are refused it.   **1932**: Iraq declares minority rights would be protected, but declines to appoint observer to supervise minority guarantees. Some 600 Assyrians massacred in 1933.   **1932**: German Chargé d'affaires, Fritz Grobba, publishes instalments of *Mein Kampf* in Arabic daily newspaper. Radio Berlin begins Arabic broadcasts.   **1934 - 36:** 600 Jewish clerks dismissed from government, most later re-instated.   **1934**: regulation introduced requiring Jews to deposit £50 to travel abroad.   **1935**: state secondary schools impose quotas on Jewish students. Hebrew and Jewish history instruction forbidden. Only the Bible can be read without translation.   **1936**: government-licensed Jewish businesses must have a Muslim partner.   **1939**: Iraqi public school system begins to follow a Nazi education model.   **1936**: Three Jews murdered in Baghdad, one in Basra. Bomb thrown into synagogue on Yom Kippur.   **1936 - 39:** despite the Chief Rabbi officially dissociating himself from Zionism and a condemnation of Zionism signed by thirty-three Iraqi Jewish leaders, seven murders of Jews and six bombings take place.   **1941**: In the interregnum following a pro-Nazi coup, 179 Jews are killed and 911 houses looted in the *Farhud* pogrom.   **1947**: Iraqi Foreign minister threatens expulsion of Jews as part of coordinated Arab League plan if Partition of Palestine goes ahead.   **1948**: state of emergency declared; 310 Jews court-martialed.   **1948**: Jews receiving letters from Palestine accused of Zionism.   **September 1948**: Shafiq Ades, Iraq's richest Jew, hanged. **May 1948-Dec 1949**: 800 – 1,500 Jews dismissed from public service. Jewish banks lose their foreign exchange trading licences. Restrictions on high school and university students. Jewish community 'donates' 113,000 dinars to war effort against Israel. Fines collected from Iraqi Jews: $80 million. Travel ban on Jews and on buying and selling property. Retroactive tax on Jews. Property of all Jews who had emigrated since 1933 confiscated. Government ceases to service Jewish areas. Property of Jewish prisoners impounded. Jewish newspapers shut down.   **Feb and March 1949**: 100 Jews tried for connections to Zionism.   **March 1950**: Iraqi Parliament Ordinance permits Jewish emigration upon forfeiture of citizenship. Some 120,000 Jews register to leave for Israel including 18,000 Kurdish Jews.   **March 1951**: Law no. 5 deprives all stateless Iraqi Jews of their property.

1963: The rise of the Ba'ath factions resulted in additional restrictions being placed on those Jews who remained in Iraq. Jews are forced to carry yellow identity cards and sale of property is forbidden.

1967: (After the Six Day War) many of 3,000 Jews who remained were arrested and dismissed from their jobs. More repressive measures were introduced, including the expropriation of Jewish property, freezing of Jews' bank accounts, shutting of Jewish businesses; trading permits were cancelled, telephones were disconnected. Jews were placed under house arrest for long periods of time or restricted to cities.

1968: Persecution at its worst. Scores of Jews were jailed allegedly for spying and eleven Jews sentenced to death in staged trials.

27 January 1969: Fourteen men – eleven of them the Jews mentioned previously – publicly hanged in Baghdad and dozens of others abducted, tortured and killed.

1970 -71: 1, 900 Jews smuggled out over the line of control through Kurdistan into Iran.

1972: Some Jews leave with passports.

2003: US troops discover thirty-four Jews in Baghdad.

2016: 5 Jews in Baghdad

With acknowledgements to *The Jews of Iraq: A Forgotten Case of Ethnic Cleansing* **by Carole Basri. (Policy Study no. 26, Institute of the World Jewish Congress)**

TUNISIA

According to legend, Jews first settled in the southern island of Djerba around King Solomon's time and a community still thrives there today . From 105, 000 in 1948, however, numbers have dwindled to 1,500 or less.

1881: French Protectorate established in Tunisia.   **1898**: Fighting breaks out between Jews and Muslims. Jewish homes looted, shops wrecked. Sixty-two Muslims, twenty Jews sentenced.   **1910**: Agudat Tsion founded, 1920 Federation of Zionist organisations.   **1917**: Arab soldiers returning from the First World War riot against Jews who are exempt from army service. Looting, rapes and beatings. One dead, eight wounded.   **1923**: Liberalisation of French nationality. By the Second World War, 6,667 Jews had French passports.   **1940**: Vichy discriminatory laws exclude Jews from public service, Jewish Community Council abolished, inventory of Jewish property drawn up.   **May 1941**: Gabes pogrom. Seven Jews die.   **Nov 1942**: Nazi occupation of Tunisia begins. Italian nationals come under Fascist racial laws. Nazis demand that the Jewish community raises 88 million francs . 2,000 Jews sent to forced labour camps. Sixty deaths from aerial bombardment.   **April 1943**: Aerial deportation to European death camps of 40 Jews.   **1948-49**: Of 100, 000 Jews, 6, 200 emigrate to Israel illegally. Jewish Agency takes over legal migration. 25, 000 emigrate between 1948 and 1955.   **1952**: attempted pogrom against Tunis *hara* thwarted by self- defence groups.   **1952–57**: 10, 000 Jews emigrate to France. **1952**: bloody nationalist riots.   **1954**: Yom Kippur declared an official holiday. **20 March 1956**: Tunisia declares its independence. Rise of pro-Nasser movement.   **1956**: Europeans and Jews attacked and robbed during period of lawlessness.   **1957**: Jewish ministers Andre Bessis and Andre Baruch appointed. President Bourguiba visits Tunis *hara*. Jews begin to join ruling Neo-Destour party. A minority are communists.   **1957**: old Tunis cemetery expropriated.   **1957**: Beth Din religious courts abolished.   **1958**: temporary religious commissions replace Jewish Community Councils.   **1960**: postal links with Israel suspended.   **1960**: Old Great Synagogue of Tunis demolished. **1959**: exchange controls introduced.   **1961**: Bizerte affair. French-Tunisian clashes lead to anti-Jewish reaction. 15, 000 Jews leave.   **1962**: 10, 000 Jews leave for France with one dinar and 11.75 francs in their pockets.   **1962 – 63**: European and Jewish firms nationalised.   **1967**: an ageing population of 26,000 Jews remains.   **6 June 1967**: Jewish-owned shops looted and Tunis Great Synagogue sacked. 18,000 Jews flee, 63 percent to France.   **1976**: 6,700 Jews remain in Tunisia: 1,100 in Djerba, 4,600 in Tunis. Emigrants go mainly to Israel. **1982**: Palestine Liberation Organization establishes offices. More Jews leave. **1985**: several Jews murdered.

With acknowledgements to 'L'échec de l'intégration des Juifs de Tunisie' by Jacques Taïeb in *La Fin du Judaïsme en terres d'Islam* (ed. S. Trigano).

ALGERIA

Although Jews had been settled in Algeria for 2,000 years, the dissolution of their 140,000-member community took place in just three months - when the modern state of Algeria declared independence in 1962.

1830: French invasion of Algeria. All natives declared equal under Article 5 of the surrender of Algiers.   **1845**: *Consistoire* becomes religious governing body of Jewish community.   **24 February 1862**: appeal court deems Jews of Algeria have French nationality.   **14 July 1865**: *senatus-consulte* declares both Muslims and Jews to be French. They may serve in the French army. **24 October 1870**: Crémieux Decree declares Jews to be French citizens (with the exception of those in the M'zab south, their personal and civil status to be governed by French law.)   **1890s**: Far-right French backlash demands abrogation of Crémieux Decree.   **May 1897**: looting of Jewish quarter of Mostagnanem and Jewish shops in Oran. Four far-right supporters of anti-Semite (anti-Dreyfus) Edouard Drumont elected to parliament.   **1914**: Algerian Jews drafted into French army.   **1929, 1933**: Jewish - Muslim clashes, some provoked by far-rightists.   **3-6 August 1934**: Shops looted, 25 Jews killed in city and district. Army does not intervene. Economic crisis aggravates relations between Jews and Muslims.   **October 1940**: Vichy regime imposes *statut des juifs*. Crémieux Decree abrogated.   **June 1941**: quotas on jobs and in education.   **November 1942**: Jews lead Algerian resistance.   **October 1943**: Crémieux Decree reinstated. Jews can serve in the French army. Rise of Algerian nationalism led by the Front de Libération Nationale (FLN).   **1956**: FLN demands that the Jewish community affirm its loyalty to the Algerian nation.   **1st November 1956**: seventy attacks take Jewish community by surprise. Between 1954 and 1962, state declares its opposition to violence. Jews die, some join the pro-French militia, the OAS. **12 December 1960**: Algiers Great synagogue ransacked.   **1961**: Jewish cemetery of Oran vandalised. Jew stabbed to death on his way to New Year synagogue service.   **1961**: musician Sheikh Raymond Leyris murdered. **3 July 1962**: Algeria declares independence. France declares it will repatriate all French citizens, even those of non-French descent.   **May-July 1962**: mass Jewish exodus: of 160, 000 Jews, only 4, 000 remain. 135, 000 Jews flee to France, 10, 000 choose Israel.   **March 1963**: Only Muslims may acquire Algerian nationality.   **1971**: less than 1, 000 Jews remain.   **1992**: less than fifty remain.   **2007**: less than twenty remain.   **2011**: last Jew assisted by Joint Distribution Committee dies.

Based on 'De l'émancipation à l'éxode brutale des Juifs d'Algérie' by Richard Ayoun, in *La Fin du Judaïsme en terres d'Islam* (ed. S. Trigano).

The 19ᵗʰ nineteenth century *dhimmi*

From *History of the Hebrew Nation: From its Origins to the Present Time*
(1841, pp.554-58)
By Revd JW Brooks, London, 1841

**Degraded, despised and abused, such as was the condition of Jews in the
Muslim world, according to a nineteenth century observer.**

The public mind has recently been startled by the report of cruelties and
injustice to which the Jews of Damascus and Rhodes have been subjected,
as if such instances of persecution and oppression were a novelty in these
times. But in the East the Jews have all along been exposed to them, though
their wrongs have failed until now in arresting particular attention. In the
year 1823, at the same Damascus, all the Jews suspected of having property
were thrown into prison, and compelled to pay forty thousand purses or lose
their heads. At Safet, in 1834, their houses were stripped, and great personal
cruelties inflicted upon them, for the like purpose of extorting money; and
generally in Syria they were compelled to work for the Turks without
payment, being bastinadoed if they remonstrated. The lowest *fallaah* would
stop them when travelling, and demand money as a right due to the
Musselman; which robbery was liable to be repeated several times a day
upon the same Jew. Throughout the East they are obliged to affect poverty
in order to conceal their wealth ; the rulers in those countries making no
scruple of seizing what they can discover. And though not interdicted from
holding land, yet the enormous taxes demanded of them (equal to one-third
of the produce, whilst the Mahometans pay only one-tenth), effectually
exclude them from agriculture.

The occupation of Syria by the Egyptians did not mitigate the hard
condition of the Jews of Palestine. They were still defrauded and insulted;
the commonest soldier would seize the most respectable Israelite, and compel
him by blows to sweep the streets, and to perform the most degrading offices.
The contempt indeed in which they are held by Mahometans, however
difficult to be accounted for, exceeds that which they have experienced in
Christian lands. In the East they are truly become a proverb, the term Jew
being applied despitefully, as the most reproachful and degrading known.

Even the Christians of Syria manifest a degree of malignity and contempt
for the Jews, not witnessed in other places: the Nestorians in particular
entertain a bitter hatred toward them; and were a Jew to set his foot within
the church of the Holy Sepulchre at Jerusalem, he would be stoned by the
Christians of all denominations. ...

In Persia the condition of the Jews is worse even than in Syria. Often
whilst they are assembled in their synagogues, a soldier enters with an order

from the Shah for money; they are compelled to work without payment; and their women are unceremoniously taken from them, without their daring to murmur. Their poverty and wretchedness may be best understood by the following graphic description given to Dr. Wolff, before he visited Shiraz, by a Mahometan: "'Every house in Shiraz with a low, narrow entrance is a Jew's. Every coat much torn and mended is a Jew's. Every man with a dirty camelhair turban is a Jew. Every one picking up broken glass and asking for old shoes and sandals is a Jew.'" This description was afterwards confirmed by the doctor's own observation, who found old and young in the street of their quarter sitting and crying to every stranger, with outstretched hand and feeble voice, "'Only one *pool* (penny) for poor Israale !'"

In Morocco they are equally ground down by a barbarous despotism. The Moors consider that the object of a Jew's birth is to serve Musselmen, and he is consequently subject to the most wanton insults. The boys for their pastime beat and torment the Jewish children: the men kick and buffet the adults. They walk into their houses at all hours, and take the grossest freedoms with their wives and daughters, the Jews invariably coming off with a sound beating if they venture to resist. In 1804 those of Algiers were subjected to horrible tortures, being suspended from the walls by long ropes with hooked nails at the ends, merely because they had unsuspectingly lent money to persons who were secretly conspiring against the Dey; nor were they released without the payment of a large sum. In 1827 the Dey threw a rich Jew into prison for no other purpose than to extort from him 500,000 Spanish dollars. At Tripoli the bashaw extorted a large sum from them on account of the drought, which he declared them to be the cause of. Mr. Ewald, after describing the beauty, fertility, and prosperity of the island of Gerba in Morocco, "'where, if any where, (he says) every one lives quietly beneath his own vine and fig-tree,'" next speaks of the Jews as the only exception, among whom he nowhere witnessed greater poverty and oppression; insomuch that he could have imagined he was beholding the Israelites of Egypt in Pharaoh's time, under their taskmasters. They were the quarrymen, hewers of wood, and drawers of water; their food consisted entirely of barley flour with salt and water; and they were altogether in an abject state of slavery. Since the occupation of Algiers by the French, the political condition of the Jews in that part of Morocco is improved; but their religious state, from their having imbibed the French infidelity, is more hopeless.

Via Elder of Ziyon http://elderofziyon.blogspot.com/2016/01/persecution-of-jews-in-muslim-countries.html (Last accessed 26 April 2017)

1967: My ordeal in a Moroccan jail

Born to a Jewish family in Safi, Morocco, Penina Elbaz tells of her ordeal as a fourteen-year-old prisoner in a Moroccan jail. Penina now lives in Montreal, Canada.

Dedicated to my brother Edmond Elbaz, who was only 25 years old when he had to struggle with Moroccan bureaucracy, intimidation and threats to get us all freed.

In 1967, one month after the Six Day War, we finally decided to go to the beach after several days in hiding because Muslims threw stones at us on the streets or at our house, incited to fanaticism by the propaganda news on the radio that was predicting victory and calling for Arabs to destroy Israel and the Jews. They were convinced that the Israelis would lose the 1967 war and that the Arab world was preparing to throw Israelis and Jews into the sea. This is what President Nasser was promising them in the loud radio broadcasts in their homes and in the food stores. As his promise was not fulfilled, the anger over Israel's lightning victory in the Six Day War engulfed the Jews like a wave of rage.

On the beach some sailors from Holland were chatting with young Jewish girls. The sailors began to sing *Hava Naguila*. I was not far away, getting ready to climb onto a swing: I stopped. It was very risky to sing in Hebrew in public. What was about to happen, I felt with apprehension tinged with curiosity, was somewhat surreal.

Shortly thereafter we were surrounded by Moroccan policemen pointing machine guns and shouting, "'All Jews to the police van'". Several people tried to intervene and save us from the forthcoming ordeal, but in vain. We obeyed. The police did not listen, they gave orders. As we were wearing bathing suits, we were permitted to get dressed. I went into a cabin and changed slowly, taking an eternity, before being arrested.

There I was, arrested in Safi, at the age of 14, with a group of Jews, accused of having sung *Hava Naguila* in public to celebrate Israel's victory. We were also charged with being Zionist spies. In my group were Raquel, Simone, Daniel Israel, Poupée, Armand, Guy, Suzy, Lison, Dolly, Nicole, Ruby with her twin babies, and Eleonore. Eleonore explained that she was deaf and dumb, but the police inspector told her that she had clapped her hands in celebration and therefore she was a Zionist.

In the police van we sensed that we were being sucked into a dreadful abyss. At the police station the Dutch sailors came out with ashen-white faces after interrogation and were sent back to their country.

We stood in line. Inspector Berrada called out my name. By nature, I hate injustice and am outspoken. He asked me if I spoke Hebrew. I replied no, but added that I went to the Alliance Israëlite school where we had the right to learn Hebrew and sing prayers and Hebrew songs -- so we did not do anything wrong! He was very shocked and asked me where this school was located. A secretary was typing every word at full speed. Very quickly, I lost my composure and become anguished over seemingly having betrayed my own kind.

Daniel Israel, aged 17 or 18, was particularly badly treated because of his surname. How come he retained his dignity and gentleness? The other two boys, Armand and Guy, showed tremendous resilience, honor and dignity in the face of savage and unjust accusations and ill-treatment. Most of us were holding up as best we could but endured extremely painful moments. We supported each other; building a strong bond out of a nightmare. Lison re-invented herself as a comic, as if by magic transporting us to a different place through laughter.

We were questioned one by one until late. These interrogations were awful. The police inspector was seeking to make us admit that we were singing an Israeli song in public, to celebrate Israel's victory, that we were spies and Zionists. However, no Jew would have had the courage to sing in public, in Hebrew. Only the two sailors from Holland had done the singing. Who knows what damage had been done to the psyche of each of us, our parents, brothers and sisters following our arrest?

We were photographed and fingerprinted as though we were criminals. Did we have a case file? There was no court trial. No lawyer had the courage either to represent or to defend us. Outside the prison gates, fanatical Muslims clamored their hatred. They were there at all times, behind the gates, ready to kill. It was scary to see and hear them whenever the jail gates were opened.

As no lawyer would take our case out of fear, my brother Edmond and Mr. Merran went to Rabat to plead the case for our release. All this was undertaken discreetly. Theirs was a very difficult and risky attempt to reach the King and get us freed. Weaving their way through the bureaucracy, they had to plead, give out bribes and submit to harassment, intimidation and direct threats of arrest. One could not denounce the injustice for fear of inflaming the fanatics.

During twelve days we slept on cold cement. We ate what our families brought us each evening. They came regularly despite the fact they had to run the gauntlet of insults and physical threats.

We slept in the same clothing from the beach, shivering in the night cold. We did not have washing facilities. The three Jewish males took it in turns to watch over us at night. They said they were guarding us from the criminals, delinquents and alcoholics brought in nightly by the police and dumped in the next corridor.

As the days passed, we waited for closure with growing anguish. Myself and other minors were threatened with placement in an institution for delinquents.

Ruby, a mother of children, lost control and began to scream with rage at the absurdity of it all. She wanted to go back to her children and to her secretarial school. The police punished her by isolating her in a one-square-meter dark cell with a hole in the middle for a toilet. The police agreed to return her twin baby girls to their father.

At the end of 12 days the police came to tell us that two of us, Poupée and me, would be released, in the dead of night. The idea of being outside, alone, at night, sent us into a panic. Our fellow inmates gave us beach towels to cover up, money for a taxi and egged us on to leave the jail. The prison was far away. I wanted to go to home, but I did not know where to find my family: they had moved for security reasons, under the constant threat of brutality.

Outside, in the night, Poupée was as coquette as ever. She let her blond hair show even as I begged her to cover up. I was overwhelmed by deep fear, convinced that her blond hair would be our undoing. A taxi stopped at last and took us to her parents. Poupée was yelled at by her mother, who told her: "'Mzrouba yak kolltec matzebess'". "'Miserable girl, I had told you not to go out!'"

We all left Morocco as fast as we were able to. We had to pay large bribes to get passports to leave Morocco. It took many months' worth of my dad's salary to get our passports, otherwise we would have been refused them.

We wanted to go to Canada. Many people from my hometown Safi were not able to get passports. But Moroccan Jews did not need passports to go to Israel.

(Translated from French by David Schwartzmann)

From Harif's *Clash of Cultures* blog, Jerusalem Post, 15 December 2014, http://www.jpost.com/Blogs/Clash-of-Cultures/My-ordeal-in-a-Moroccan-jail-384642. (Last accessed 26 April 2017)

A Jew in pre-1948 Jerusalem

Aharon Nehmad, an 86-year-old Jerusalemite now living in Latin America, is a witness to a long-standing policy of poisonous incitement by the Mufti Haj Amin al-Husseini and his heirs.

Nehmad's family has been settled in the Land of Israel for over 18 generations, ever since they left Aleppo for Tiberias and later for Jerusalem.

Nehmad told *Point of No Return* of an incident prior to World War II.

The Arab revolt was then in full swing. The Temple Mount, then as now, was simmering with rumour and intrigue.

Although Professor Pimienta sounds like a character from *Tintin*, he was a flesh-and-blood fluent Arabic speaker who was a professor of Arabic at the Hebrew University of Jerusalem and also worked for the Department of Immigration. His underground job, however, was for the Jewish secret service. Due to constant plotting and attacks against Jews, he would try and gather as much advance intelligence as possible. One of the best information sources was attending, dressed as an Arab gentleman, the speeches of murderous incitement given by the Mufti to the Muslim worshippers at the Dome of the Rock and Al-Aqsa mosque. He would report back on any plots that were being hatched to attack Jews.

By 1936, declaring his opposition to the British, the Mufti's incitement was at its peak. Professor Pimienta ran a greater risk of being recognised despite his perfect Arabic skills. In 1937, aged eight and also fluent in Arabic, Aharon Nehmad would accompany Professor Pimienta on his mission. Dressed as an Arab boy, Nehmad would loiter and play with other Arab children outside the mosque.

Pimienta had a secret code with the boy. If his cover was blown, he would remove his handkerchief and shake it three times. The boy would then start a commotion pretending his shoes were stolen, screaming and throwing about the worshippers' shoes, and the two would make their getaway.

This is indeed what happened one day in 1937. The boy was horrified to see Professor Pimienta shake his handkerchief. He started screaming and shouting, and together they ran down to safety into the Jewish quarter below.

Aharon Nehmad recalls another incident. It was June 1941 -- the Nazis were on the threshold of conquering Egypt. Propaganda pamphlets showered over Jerusalem announced that the city would be next. Arabs began plotting to drive out and kill the Jewish residents and divvy up their looted homes. Jewish residents found grafitti in Arabic scribbled on their walls -- "'this house is for Ahmed'"; "'this house is for Muhammed'". The Arabs were staking out their loot.

Nehmad was then 12. The Jews declared a day of fasting in anticipation of the Nazi conquest of Jerusalem, wailing and sitting on the floor. But one man was convinced that the Nazis would not come. "'Don't cry,'" Sephardi chief rabbi Ben Zion Uziel told his flock, quoting the Biblical verse: "'Not by might, nor by power, but by my Spirit, says the Lord of hosts.'" (Hosea 1:7).

Beginning in 1929, the Mufti's constant incitement had caused a series of riots in Hebron, Safed and at the Hadassah hospital in Jerusalem, due to long-running disputes over access to the Western Wall and fears over Jewish immigration and land sales to Jews. One historian, Avraham Sela, called the riots 'unprecedented in the history of the Arab-Jewish conflict in Palestine, in duration, geographical scope and direct damage to life and property.'

Fearing a riot in Jerusalem, Aharon Nehmad's family, then living in Musrara, next to the old city, decided to take refuge in the Malon Ma'arav hotel, along with the rest of their Jewish neighbours.

However, one Jewish woman would not budge. She was an old midwife who had delivered hundreds, if not thousands, of Jewish and Arab children. She was well known and beloved by all. She was convinced that the Arabs whom she had delivered as newborn babies -- if the families were too poor, she did not charge them for her services -- would not touch her. Other Arabs managed to persuade her to leave her home. They piled her belongings into a cart and took her to the hotel. It was fortuitous for Mrs Nehmad, who was then heavily pregnant and also taking refuge in the hotel. She was able to have the midwife deliver her first son Aharon.

Point of No Return, 1 November 2015
http://jewishrefugees.blogspot.co.uk/2015/10/a-witness-to-80-years-of-incitement.html
(Last accessed 26 April 2017)

One Jewish girl was abandoned by her family in Egypt

While such stories are rare, it is not unknown for Jewish women especially to be left behind after mass migrations from Arab lands. Jewesses whose Muslim husbands have died have asked to be re-united with their Israeli families, and the offspring of mixed families have discovered their Jewish ancestry.

It was in 1979, soon after the signing of the Israel-Egypt peace treaty. W., a Jewish businessman with connections in high places in the Arab world, was busy arranging for a group of elderly Egyptian Jews (several stripped of their nationality since 1956 -- but that's another story) to visit Israel when he was approached by a tall, gangly Egyptian asking to join the tour.

"'Are you Jewish?'", W. asked. "'No,'" came the reply. Imagining that this Egyptian might be a member of the *Mukhabarat* (secret police) sent to spy on the visitors, W. suggested that the Egyptian wait and join a later tour of Israel he was organising for Egyptian intellectuals.

"'No, my wife and I need to visit Israel as soon as possible. My wife is Jewish, although she doesn't know it.'"

The Egyptian then proceeded to tell the puzzled W. the whole story. The wife was a small child when she was separated from her Jewish family. In their chaotic haste to leave Alexandria for Israel some years before, the family had left their daughter behind. The abandoned girl was taken in by the family's Egyptian neighbours, and brought up as their own. She went on to marry an Egyptian Muslim.

W. duly arranged for the couple to visit Israel. At the airport, they were greeted by the famous Israeli journalist Nahum Barnea. The couple were interviewed on TV, and the wife was told her story.

Before long, a fleet of cars arrived. It was the wife's family, brandishing a photo of her as a child. They had recognised her from the TV screen.

The wife was reunited with her long-lost family. But after a week, she demanded to go back to Egypt. Her links with her Jewish family had been severed for all time and the clock could not be turned back. Egypt would always be home.

The Egyptian authorities must have breathed a sigh of relief. Had the wife decided to stay in Israel, it would have been an embarrassment and a public relations disaster.

Such stories of separation do happen. In 2008 a Jewish woman abducted by a Muslim neighbour joined her family in Israel after 55 years' separation.
From *Point of No Return*, 22 July 2009
http://jewishrefugees.blogspot.co.uk/2009/07/jewish-girl-was-abandoned-by-her-family.html (Last accessed 26 April 2017)

Teddy Nahmias: Final Days in Alexandria 1957

Although his family were Greek subjects, Teddy Nahmias was among 25,000 Jews forced to leave Egypt soon after the 1956 Suez Crisis.

You probably won't believe this, but I was one of the first rock 'n' rollers. As teenagers, we had to identify ourselves with James Dean or Elvis Presley. That was more important than watching our wonderful life collapse before us. That we left that to our parents. We knew it would be over soon, so we wanted to prolong and prolong this life of partying, going to the beach and the movies.

A whole population was preparing to leave. Europe was very cold in the winter, they said – be prepared. Soon warm woollens, coats, and scarves were not to be found in stores. All sold out. Suitcases and large travel bags disappeared from the shelves in days. Farewell gatherings were a daily occurrence. Goodbye … Will we ever see each other again? Classmates promising to meet again somewhere abroad, friends in tears at the thought of parting and, worst of all, members of the same family having to emigrate to different countries and being separated from their loved ones, maybe forever. Sons and daughters following their spouses, grandparents left behind, too old to embark on a new life in faraway places such as Australia or Brazil.

Windows and balconies were covered in heavy blue paper so as to create a 'black out' to protect the city from air attacks at night.

Tension was growing and anyone with European features had to be quite careful when going around town. You would never guess, but I had distinctive streaks of blond hair at the time, and some Arabs in the street shouted *inglesi* at me more than once, frightening the living daylights out of me.

Of course Egypt was at war with Britain and France, as well as Israel. British and French nationals were being expelled daily at 72 hours' notice. Other Jews bearing Greek, Italian, Belgian, Spanish passports etc, realized they had no future in Egypt. Businesses and property owned by Jews were seized. Thousands lost their jobs. Jewish institutions were closed down. Restrictions were imposed and people could only leave with limited luggage and most possessions were left behind. *Khalass* (Finished).

It was impossible to fight the rising tide of Arab nationalism. I recall getting on a bus once with a friend, and as usual we were having a conversation *en français* quite recklessly. Some of the passengers objected and said we should stop speaking French. In retrospect I cannot believe I made a gesture with my hand and said: *Maalesh* (never mind). How foolish. At that moment an arrogant young Egyptian in a grey suit and tie intervened and said, 'I shall cut your hand off if you say *Maalesh* again!' The bus had just come to a stop and we got off in a hurry. Lucky break for us.

My father used to read the daily French paper, *Le progrès Egyptien*. However, he would discreetly cover it with another paper he used to read – - *Taxidromos*, the Greek daily. That, of course, was accepted, as Greeks took the Egyptian side during that conflict.

An interesting activity was the setting up by the Egyptian army of free shooting galleries along the Corniche near Silsila. The targets were the figures of British, French and Israeli soldiers with Union Jacks, *Bleu blanc rouge* flags and *Magen Davids* on their chests. Young Egyptians were queuing to have a go at firing at the enemy. Groups of soldiers were constantly marching all over town and one could not help feeling uneasy and fearful. I cannot forget the fright I had when at the gare de Ramleh suddenly a group of soldiers walked towards me and stopped. One of them came out of the ranks and walked over to me.

Khalass. My knees were shaking, I was probably as pale as a sheet. It was Gaber, my *baoab's* (doorman or porter's) son who was trying to show off his new uniform and machine gun. *Ezzayak ya Teddy*. He laughed at my pitiful sight, and so did the other soldiers. He waved goodbye and they went away with this newly acquired sense of power.

This was not like our peaceful, friendly city of Alexandria at all. I think that by then, we had realised. It was *khalass* – and for good.

From *Point of No Return*, 12 June 2007

http://jewishrefugees.blogspot.co.uk/2007/06/khalass-end-of-my-charmed-life-in.html (Last accessed 26 April 2017)

Memories of the *Farhud*: 1941

This eyewitness account by Steve Acre - as told to Effy Fisher - is one of the most graphic you are likely to read.

Farhud – violent dispossession – an Arabized Kurdish word that was seared into Iraqi Jewish consciousness on June 1 and 2, 1941. As the Baghdadi Jewish communities burned, a proud Jewish existence that had spanned 2,600 years was abruptly incinerated.

As a nine-year-old, I, Sabih Ezra Akerib, who witnessed the *Farhud*, certainly had no understanding of the monumental consequences of what I was seeing. Nevertheless, I realized that somehow the incomprehensible made sense. I was born in Iraq, the only home I knew. I was proud to be a Jew, but knew full well that I was different, and this difference was irreconcilable for those around me.

That year, June 1 and 2 fell on Shavuot – the day the Torah was given to our ancestors and the day Bnei Yisrael became a nation. The irony of these two historical events being intertwined is not lost on me.

Shavuot signified a birth while the *Farhud* symbolized a death – a death of illusion and a death of identity. The Jews, who had felt so secure, were displaced once again. We had been warned trouble was brewing.

Days earlier, my 20-year-old brother, Edmund, who worked for British intelligence in Mosul, had come home to warn my mother, Chafika Akerib, to be careful. Rumors abounded that danger was coming. Shortly after that, the red *hamsa* (palm print) appeared on our front door – a bloody designation marking our home. But for what purpose?

Shavuot morning was eerily normal. My father Ezra had died three years earlier, leaving my mother a widow with nine children. I had no father to take me to synagogue; therefore, I stayed home with my mother, who was preparing the Shavuot meal. The rising voices from the outside were at first slow to come through our windows. However, in the blaze of the afternoon sun, they suddenly erupted. Voices – violent and vile. My mother gathered me, my four sisters and youngest brother into the living room, where we huddled together. Her voice was calming.

The minutes passed by excruciatingly slowly. But I was a child, curious and impatient. I took advantage of my mother's brief absence and ran upstairs, onto the roof. At the entrance to the open courtyard at the center of our home stood a 15-foot date palm. I would often climb that tree. When there was not enough food to eat, those dates would sustain us. I expressed gratitude for that tree daily. I now climbed that tree and wrapped myself within its branches, staring down at the scene unfolding below. What I saw defied imagination.

On the narrow dirt road, 400 to 500 Muslims carrying machetes, axes, daggers, and guns had gathered. Their cries – *Iktul al Yahud,* Slaughter the Jews – rang out as bullets were blasted into the air. The shrieks emanating from Jewish homes were chilling. I hung on, glued to the branches. I could hear my mother's frantic cries: "'*Weinak! Weinak!*'" (Where are you?)

But I could not answer, terrified of calling attention to myself. Amidst the turmoil, I saw our landlord sitting by our door, wearing his distinctive green turban. He was a hajji, considered a holy man because he had made the mandatory pilgrimage (hajj) to Mecca, Saudi Arabia. Demanding, raging men were remonstrating with him, and then, inexplicably, they moved on.

For some reason, our home was left undisturbed. Only later were we told that our landlord had explained to the men that a widow with nine children lived inside and had asked for his protection. Kindnesses abound when least expected, and for this I thanked G-d.

The horrors continued to unfold. The killing of men and children and attacks on Jewish women were rampant. Four doors down – at the home of Sabiha, my mother's good friend – a Muslim emerged carrying what appeared to be a bloodied piece of meat. We learned afterwards that Sabiha had been killed and mutilated. My mother's sorrowful refrain would later ring out: " 'Sabiha! They attacked her! They cut her throat! They mutilated her!'"

At the same time, Jews were scampering over the roofs, running for their lives. If not for the looting taking place below, more would have been murdered. No authorities came to help; barbarism ruled.

All the anger and jealousy that had been pent up over the centuries erupted in these horrific moments. Neighbors with whom we had shared a nod, a smile – and even attended their sons' circumcisions – had metamorphosed into sub-humans intent on annihilation.

And then, the fires started. Houses were being torched amidst the cries of their destroyers. Black smoke ascended towards the heavens. The putrid smell of smoke filled my nostrils – together with the smell of burning flesh. I will never forget those smells. How long was I up there – one hour, two hours? I finally jumped down onto the roof, running into my mother's arms. Shaking, she slapped me – a slap of love.

We later learned that after leaving Dahana, these teeming masses of men, joined by others, went on to rampage the other impoverished neighborhoods, later making their way into the wealthier districts. The red hamsa signified their targets. All along Baghdad's main Rashid Street, Jewish shops that were closed for Shavuot were broken into and robbed. What the mob couldn't steal, they destroyed. The multitude of synagogues lining the streets were equally ravaged – sifrei Torah going up in smoke.

The destruction was absolute and relentless. On June 2, the second day of the Farhud, an eerie calm descended. Again, I ran upstairs and climbed the tree. In the distance were airplanes buzzing and bombs dropping. The British, who had camped on the outskirts of town as our communities burned, were finally moving into the city and reclaiming what had so tragically gone awry. But for the Jews of Baghdad this was too little, too late. What had been witnessed and experienced during those 24 hours would ring the death knoll for Iraqi Jewry. Many of us now understood that after 2,600 years, it was time to move on.

'On Fire in Baghdad: An Eye-witness Account of the Destruction of an Ancient Jewish Community', Steve Acre as told to Effy Fisher - *AMI magazine*, **3 August 2011**
http://www.mikecohen.ca/files/steve-acre-farhud-article.pdf (Last accessed 26 April 2017)

A Libyan Holocaust survivor's story

More people would know that the horrors of the Holocaust touched North Africa if the media had shown greater interest in individuals like Shimon Teshuva, a Libyan survivor. Shimon's story, which appeared in the Hebrew evening daily *Maariv* **of April 2013, was translated by the late Orna Moses.**

When we talk about the Holocaust, the first thing that comes to mind is the famous picture of Auschwitz; Birkenau or the fact of six million dead.

Most of the evidence and films deal with the European Jewry, that is why it is important to hear Shimon Teshuva's story (85) from Michmoret.

It started in 1940 in Benghazi, when the Teshuva family was one of the important families in the community. Benghazi had changed hands five times between the Italians, Germans and British. Every time, there were lootings; pogroms; the burning of shops.

"'I remember one night when there was loud knocking on the door and then the door was broken down and people came to our house looking for gold and valuables. We moved to Puerta Barida – a small town near the Egyptian border. I remember Mussolini coming to visit us. There was an increased antisemitic atmosphere, Jews were forced to open their shops on Shabbat, at school children were called "'donkey"' and made to walk on all fours. I never went back to that school.

My father sent me back to Benghazi for my education but he was not aware that the situation had become worse there –- Jewish children were not allowed to study at Italian schools anymore so we studied at home with private tutors.

In April 1942 Mussolini ordered all the Jews to a concentration camp in the desert: they were allowed to take clothes and bedding only. It was a five-day journey; we were loaded like cattle onto the lorries. During the day, we were in the terrible desert sun and at night freezing desert cold. I was 12 years old then. We arrived at a military base in the middle of the desert surrounded by mountains: 2,700 families were at the Giado camp.

'The area was divided and each family was given 1 meter squared marked off by a rope. A long wooden plank with holes was used for latrines. There were no showers; no running water, we were covered in lice.

The majority of the camp inhabitants contracted illnesses, including typhoid. There were no doctors in the camp as Jews were generally employed in the Civil Service or Commerce. It was a miracle that I survived.

People brought with them (smuggled) gold and valuables and they managed to bargain with the Bedouins around them. My mother smuggled a small sewing machine which she used to sew colourful scarves for the Bedouin women.

There was nothing to do on the camp; we could not run away as there was nowhere to go to.

I lost my father, my brother and five more from my extended family to illness.'"

Giado Camp operated from April 1942 to March 1943 when the British managed to take control, after defeating the Germans.

When the family returned to Benghazi they found that it was destroyed. Their father dead and their mother a seamstress – the family fell on hard times.

Shimon was only 13 years old but he realised then that the Jews had no future in Libya; but he had to stay and look after the family.

Shimon tried to get a job at the British Army camp and after a few attempts, with lots of help, he got a job there. "Around this time I started thinking of *Aliya*. I managed to grow a small vegetable plot which made the Israeli soldiers think that I was serious.'"

In 1945 he obtained a uniform and paperwork. He parted from his family;' the night before he left Libya, he received his mother's blessing.

He spent the first year in Israel in Ein Vered then he transferred to Ben Shemen boarding school. At the time the students were surrounded by Arabs who stoned their bus and made life very difficult. He was drafted to the Israeli army in 1948 and fought in many wars.

Asked why not many people know about this aspect of the Holocaust, he replied that if the media took interest, then it would have been better known. People are not aware of this story as the media chose not to emphasise it.

He concludes: 'I am very proud to have survived all hurdles. Israel is my home – there is no other place.'

English translation by Orna Moses of article in *Ma'ariv*, *Point of No Return*, 5 April 2013
http://jewishrefugees.blogspot.co.uk/2013/04/a-libyan-holocaust-survivors-story.html (Last accessed 26 April 2017)

Escape from Saddam, 1970,
Emil Somekh's Story

The Somekh family – like all Jews forbidden from leaving Iraq – blazed the trail in 1970-1 to attempt the smugglers' route into Iran after a truce had come into force between the Iraqi regime and the Kurds. Almost 2,000 Jews were to follow, but the families waiting in Erbil immediately after Emil's escape were all arrested.

It was a long trip of several hours. In the evening we finally reached Sulaymaniyah and the taxi took us to the open air restaurant where we had fixed our *rendez-vous* with the smuggler. I noticed that the place was nearly empty and the smuggler was nowhere to be found. After some time he showed up stealthily and told me that he had spotted some secret government agents in the place and that he could not take us now.

He advised us to sit there, order food and he would come to pick us up later. As we were eating some starter delicacies I was wondering if it could be our last meal. We also ordered main dishes with grilled meat on skewers. But it was delayed. I was thinking that the smuggler might come at any time and I did not want to miss the delicious meal. I went to the place where they prepared the meat on the fire and I was urging them to hurry up. Just as the meat was ready, the smuggler arrived. So I asked them to wrap the grilled skewers for us and we paid and left the restaurant with the smuggler.

Just as we left the restaurant we saw the smuggler's truck. It was a standard truck for transporting goods with a cabin that could seat just two passengers besides the driver. So my father, mother and my young sister Zetta squeezed besides the driver. The funny thing was that Zetta was then 12 years and she was dressed in a mini-skirt and high-heel shoes. No matter how much we entreated her in Baghdad to wear something more suitable, our requests fell on the deaf ears of a typical teenager. So my mother had to cover her legs with a cloth as she squeezed between my father and mother beside the driver!

My brother Terry and I were instructed by the main smuggler to climb on top of the driver's cabin and to sit there in full view with our Baghdadi clothes, which were completely out of place in this area where everybody was dressed in Kurdish clothes. The smuggler told us that if the army stopped him he planned to tell them that our car has broken down and he had found us and picked us up! That is why he did not give us any Kurdish clothes to wear and he left us in our Baghdadi clothes. So it looked to me that maybe he was preparing simply to abandon us to the Iraqi army at the first obstacle – not an easy feeling at the start of the second phase of our perilous journey into the unknown!

In a short while I realized how perilous our escape really was! It turned out that the route the smuggler chose took us right through the Iraqi army camps. It seemed that according to the terms of the armistice agreement signed in March of that year between the Iraqi government and the Kurdish rebels, the Iraqi army was supposed to give free passage to the Kurdish fighters.

It was like a scene from a James Bond movie. My brother and I were sitting openly at the top of the driver's cabin, in full view of the soldiers in the Iraqi army camps. I was incredulously looking down at the Iraqi soldiers going about their business -- just a few hours earlier we had been in Baghdad, scared of our own shadows. We took a few minutes to pass several Iraqi army bases. We saw tanks, trucks, soldiers, and army barracks. Then the smuggler told me and my brother to get down from the top of the driver's cabin and to sit inside the enclosed part of the truck, where goods are usually stored. He said the fact that all the army camps we passed till now have not stopped us is nothing since they could have radioed to the last camp, to which we were arriving and they could stop us there. My father, mother and sister were still sitting beside the driver, in full view of everybody.

As we entered the last army camp, the smuggler started to pray. I knew we were entering the really serious phase of our escape. My brother Terry was looking through a hole in the truck's side and I kept asking him whether we were out of the camp. It was a really big camp; the last Iraqi army camp before the Kurdish autonomous area. It took us about 10 minutes to pass through this camp. Finally we reached a bridge that had Iraqi soldiers at either end. This was the last bridge controlled by the Iraqi army before the Kurdish Autonomous Region. The soldiers at the start of the bridge waved us through. But as we approached the end of the bridge we saw the soldiers giving a sign to stop.

At this moment, instead of stopping, the driver put his foot on the gas pedal and speeded up. A shouting match ensued between the Iraqi soldiers and the armed smuggler and his assistant Kurdish fighter, who were hanging out of either side of the truck. We zoomed past the soldiers stationed at the end of the bridge and I waited for the shooting to start as we rapidly travelled away from them. But the shooting never occurred and we sped away from the soldiers around the bend of the road and into the mountains.

My take of the encounter was that the soldiers had met the smuggler and his team before, when they were moving goods along this road. According to the armistice agreement signed half a year earlier in March between the Iraqi government and the Kurds, the government soldiers were not supposed to stop the Kurdish smuggler. But seeing that he had Baghdadi people with him was something new -- and that is the reason why the soldiers probably wanted him to stop. He decided to take his chance and he dared not stop. He called their bluff and they did not dare start a firefight with him -- this could ruin the armistice agreement.

As we turned the bend in the road into the mountain and away from the Iraqis, I thought the difficult part of our escape was over. It was 2 am in the morning and a moonless night. But suddenly the driver turned off the main headlights of the truck as he drove along the narrow mountain road. I asked the smuggler why: he said we were now in an area with no government. It had become a No Man's Land full of dangerous bandits. We travelled without lights along these dangerous mountain roads to avoid being spotted by the bandits. After about one hour of driving we stopped for a rest by a mountain stream.

We decided to eat the meat that we had picked up at the restaurant in Sulaymaniyah at the start of our journey with the smuggler. It was totally quiet in the mountain; we just heard the sound of the flowing water. I was a bit nervous and I preferred chatting with the smuggler. He was boasting to us about the weapons supplied to the Kurds by the Israelis and how he had smuggled the arms to the Kurdish fighters.

After resting we continued our journey in the truck towards the Iranian border. We were about to reach the part of our journey where we would have to continue by foot. The smuggler was saying to me that my mother had packed too many clothes in the suitcases he had taken from us and they were too heavy to carry in our journey on foot. He asked me to open them and throw away some of the contents, without my mother knowing. I told him I did not want to do this. He gave up on the idea.

Finally we reached a spot in the mountains where the truck stopped and we continued on foot, the smuggler assisting us with the suitcases. My young sister was still wearing her heels and she had difficulty walking on the mountain trail. We walked for about half an hour. As we were walking along a road alongside the mountain, the smuggler said we had to stop there: we were very near the border and he could not continue with us. The Iranians might accept us but for him it was dangerous to get close to the Iranian border post. He said he would leave us there and we should wait till daybreak and then continue along this road until we reached the Iranian border post. He said he would be waiting close by in a Kurdish village called Tuwaila and if the Iranians turn us back he would take us back to Baghdad! It was a crazy idea, I thought – coming all the way here to the Iranian border and then having to return back to Baghdad –- no way, I said to myself! The smuggler wanted to leave, but my mother did not accept and told him to wait with us. So he stayed.

But he was nervous. We were sitting there by a deserted road at the edge of the mountain, all five of us in Baghdadi clothes, our suitcases around us, in this location in the mountains, which the smuggler claimed was very close to the border, hoping that he was telling the truth. As time passed, the smuggler was getting more and more nervous and he kept asking my mother to let him go because he was scared of the Iranians. Finally my father, who was restless and pacing back and forth, got angry at my mother and he told her that she should let him go.

Now we had to give him half the money, as agreed – 1, 000 dinars – and give him a code word that he could relay to my uncle Naim back in Baghdad so that he could claim the other half – another 1,000 dinars! Now a code word had been agreed with my uncle to indicate whether the escape route was a good one –- since we were the first to try it, and other Jews would need to use it. I had agreed with my uncle that if I felt it was a good and safe escape route then the code word would be TV – if it was an average escape route, then the code word would be RADIO. My uncle's wife said jokingly back in Baghdad that if it was a bad road then the code word would be GRAMOPHONE.

At this point I could not faithfully convey a meaningful message to others who might follow about how good and safe the route was. The road itself was quite dangerous passing through the Iraqi army camps. The smuggler had not been frank with us about this at all, knowing that we would never have come with him had he told us. It was clear he was using us as guinea pigs to try this escape route out and, by keeping us in our Baghdadi clothes, he was hedging his bets and planning simply to turn us over to the Iraqi army if he could not pass through. There was also the very tense and dangerous near-armed confrontation with the Iraqi soldiers at the end of the last bridge before the Kurdish area.

To cap it all, we were now in some location in the mountains, without really knowing how near the Iranian border we really were. We had to take the smuggler's word for it. So according to all these factors the code word should actually have been GRAMOPHONE. But on the other hand I thought maybe he was telling the truth, and we were very close to the border.

I thought if I said GRAMOPHONE then all the Jews of Baghdad would think that something really bad had happened to us and their imaginations would run wild with theories of what had befallen us! So I decided to hope for the best and assume the smuggler was telling the truth –- that we were close to the border. In that case, what we went through was nothing if the outcome was successful in leaving the Iraqi hellhole and reaching freedom in Iran!

So I gave the smuggler his 1,000 dinars and told him the code word was TV!

We bade him farewell and he left us. Before leaving, he told us to wait until the first sign of daybreak. We should then continue along the road to the Iranian border post, which he assured us was just around the bend in the road. He said my mother and sister should go about 100 meters ahead so that the Iranian soldiers would see women first. He also warned us that if any local people passed by us then we should continue immediately to the Iranian post.

We sat there in the middle of nowhere, waiting for daybreak. Time passed slowly. We were listening to the sounds of wild animals that roamed the forests of the mountains at the Iraqi-Iranian border. Just as were seeing the first small signs of daybreak, we saw a local Kurdish man coming towards us. He saw us sitting there, completely out of place, but he just greeted us, SALAM ALEIKUM, and continued on his way.

At this point we decided to move on. Just as the smuggler instructed, my mother and sister went first and we followed them, carrying our bags. Just as the smuggler said, as soon as we turned the bend in the road we saw the Iranian border post in the distance. Since my mother and sister were not carrying anything and we were laden with bags, some distance opened between us. I saw far away that the border crossing had gone up and that my mother and sister had gone through. We continued with the suitcases and soon reached the border post and went in. The Iranian soldiers escorted us to their commander's cabin, which was atop a mountain overlooking the whole area. Just as we climbed to his post, the sun came out and we saw the most beautiful view we could have set eyes on – right at our feet, down in the valley, we saw the whole route that we had travelled at night with the smuggler. When he had pointed in the darkness towards some point in the mountain and said that was where the Iranian command post was, he was referring to the place where we were now. The commander told us to look down at awful Iraq: he gave us his binoculars to look through.

My father, who has been in Persia for a short time about thirty years earlier, was so exhilarated that he suddenly started talking Persian! He remembered what he had learnt in that short time, thirty years ago. We learned that the reason for the warm welcome we got from the Iranians was that the border posts were alerted by the government of the Iranian Shah, which had good relations with Israel, that Iraqi Jews were trying to escape. Still, we were the first Jews who escaped through this specific border post. After a short time at the border post, we were taken by military car to the nearest Iranian army camp for interrogation. There were two major offenses for which you could be killed in Iran: if you were smuggling drugs or if you were a communist. My father told the interrogators that we were Jews and we were neither communists nor drug smugglers. We were treated very nicely by the Iranian soldiers in this army camp. The camp commander's wife cooked lunch for us. At night, some of the soldiers gave us their beds to sleep in. The next morning they got us a mini-bus and we were sent, with armed escort, to the nearest big city – Kermanshah – to continue our interrogation.

In Kermanshah we were put under arrest in a hotel. Delicious meals were brought to our rooms – white rice with *chelo kebab* was my favourite. Just before leaving Baghdad, I had bought shoes with thick soles for me, my father and brother. I had opened the soles and put several $100 bills in each shoe and then glued the soles back. With these shoes, full with the $100 bills, we had crossed the Iranian border. Now my father said that his shoes were dusty and needed cleaning and polishing. So he decided to send them out to a local shoe polish boy.

No matter how much I tried to convince him that there was too much money in them to just send them out, he persisted. The shoes came back with the money inside. I assume the kid who polished it would never again have so much money so close to hand!

After three days in this hotel, with no possibility of leaving, we finally got the permit to move on to Tehran. We were finally completely free.

From *Point of No Return*, 5 April 2013
(Last accessed 26 April 2017)
Reprinted from Emilsomekh.com
    http://jewishrefugees.blogspot.co.il/2013/03/escape-from-iraq-emil-somekhs-story.html

Tunisian Jew: My Right of Return – to Reason

Jean-Pierre Chemla reflects on his childhood in Tunis.

It is about time we refuted the delusion that many of us have wished to nurture these last hundred years –- the myth of coexistence between Jews and Arabs in the Maghreb countries.

I was born in 1952 in a business district of central Tunis.

My earliest memories are of lights, smells and sounds : carts, horses' hooves on the asphalt, the cries of peddlars of all sorts.

There were ten of us –- eight children and our parents –- living in a three-room apartment in a business district of central Tunis. Noise was everywhere –- not hushed and discreet conversations, but clatter in the kitchen, whistling cooking pots, breaking glass, heated discussions about news, politics and sport. Every square metre buzzed with life, impulsiveness, humour and love. As the youngest of this fabulous brood, I benefited from the enrichment which each of my siblings brought with him.

Our status was privileged compared to that of our immediate antecedents. To live in a sunny apartment overlooking a wide avenue on one side and a large garden on the other -- built, unfortunately, over a desecrated Jewish cemetery* -- would never have been possible for my grandfather on my father's side who was made to live in the Hara Hafsia, the Jewish ghetto, whose gates were shut at night to prevent Jews from wandering among the Arab population.

My father, who was a teacher at the Alliance Israëlite Universelle, was probably the first white collar worker in his family. Such social promotion allowed his offspring access to higher education and jobs that were a far cry from the only trades open to Jews at the end of the 19th century -- butcher, cobbler, grocer, etc.

Of course this improvement in our living conditions had not happened by accident nor because Arab leaders had willed it. Everything suddenly changed in 1881.

At that time, shut away in their Hara in rather wretched conditions, the Jews lived in hovels without light or ventilation. There was no sanitation, they were prey to epidemics, received only a rabbinic education and were 'dhimmis' subject to a special tax and to all sorts of humiliations and taunts (Read *The Dhimmi* ' by Bat Ye'or).

The Jewish presence in these countries, which predated that of the Arabs, was a historical reality that many would not have known about at the time. In any case, if some did, it would have been carefully hidden in order to maintain intercommunal relations to the Arabs' advantage. The Jews were just 2 percent of the population of Tunisia (100,000 of 5 million).

France had already been in Algeria for 50 years and took advantage of a few incidents at the Algerian-Tunisian frontier in order to intervene and make Tunisia a protectorate. The Bey at the time was forced to sign the Treaty of Bardo to formalise its status.

France was anxious for all its subjects on Tunisian soil to have equal rights and created a new situation which allowed the Jews to emerge, like zombies out of the grave, from their age-old prison.

Very quickly a large number of them tried to draw closer to their saviours, abandoning Judeo-Arabic for French, adopting western dress, changing their first names and even their surnames in order to Frenchify them.

They threw themselves with gusto into a period of economic growth stimulated by the French, under the irritated gaze of their Arab co-citizens, who saw their power being usurped, something they were not used to.

As with any revolutionary change, there were excesses: denial and obliteration of any reference to the hardships of the past. Some flatly refused to express themselves in their mother tongue. Others abandoned religious customs which themselves symbolised centuries of humiliation. These surreal characters became the butt of Tunisian Jewish jokes.

Generally speaking, rather than lose its identity, the Tunisian Jewish community rediscovered and cultivated it during the enchanted interlude between 1881- - 1956, 1956 being the year when the first president, Habib Bourguiba, despite being a friend of the Jews, was not able to prevent them being excluded from Tunisian society.(...)

For myself, the memory of this house, this avenue, this garden is still with me. I can still mentally trace my way to the Lycee Carnot. The apricot stones, the silk worms, the honey pastries and others, the bunches of jasmine, I've told my children about them over and over again in case the colours sink for ever into oblivion, to preserve a small imprint of the person I am. I only spent the first 11 years of my life in Tunisia but they seem like a hundred and I am essentially the product of that child.

Yet there was never any question of an UNWRA for us. We never kept the key nor the title deeds in order to exploit them many years later.

On the 29th June 1964 we caught the plane for Marseille and chose to look straight ahead of us and build a new future. We are not dehumanised for having done so. To have acted otherwise would have been deadly.

To maintain in the heads of young Palestinians who have not even known 'the land that belongs to them' the idea of a right of return is a brazen political swizz. It's about time that the international community ceased conniving in it. Today I proclaim, loud and clear, my Right of Return –- to reason and intellectual honesty.

My brother Gerard has this to add about the Jewish cemetery: This garden was one of the factors behind our departure. It was a Jewish cemetery bought in the 19th century with the community's resources outside the town of Tunis. But the modern town spread from the Porte de France to the Belvedere, gobbling up the cemetery where famous *Sadikkim* were buried such as Rabbi Hai Taieb (Lo met) who 'protected the family when it was passing its school exams thanks to Mother's prayers. She opened the windows of the end room to appeal to him with arms outstretched.'

When independence came the government decided to expropriate the cemetery (without compensation). It had been agreed that the bodies would be exhumed grave by grave and sent to Israel. I spent many hours at the window witnessing the exhumation. When Rabbi Hai Taieb's bones were dug up there was a long prayer procession around the cemetery. But as far as the Tunisian authorities were concerned it was taking too long. Suddenly, one fine day, bulldozers broke through the cemetery boundary and overturned the earth, mixing it for all time with our ancestors' remains.

This was done despite the community's protests, but we no longer had a say. The community leader, Maitre Haddad, then decided to leave Tunisia. I should like to see a similar situation arise in Israel with a Muslim cemetery. The whole world would be up in arms.

The community was represented by a CRIF-style (Board of Deputies) body but at independence Tunisia refused 'a state within a state' and banned any civil organisation representing the Jewish community (the Beth Din was allowed to continue but under state control). The first article of the Tunisian constitution clearly stipulates that the Tunisian Republic is Muslim. That means that all non-Muslims, even those of Tunisian nationality –– 75,000 Jews –– would from then on be considered second-class citizens.

Today Arabs claim that it is scandalous for Israel to see itself as a Jewish state and that the land must be shared between Jews and Arabs. What are they on about? We who lived there for millennia, we of Tunisian nationality, whose intellectuals fought for Tunisian independence, we do not have the right to share the land because we are non-Muslims.   I who have lived through independence I did not consider myself part and parcel of the country. I turned to France (of course my French nationality helped me. What a worry for Jews of Tunisian nationality).

I have to say that the many incidents I lived through (fights, actually) drove me further away every day from that country. We had no more rights and if the police turned up to an incident we were always in the wrong. We had become *dhimmis* again. So goodbye Tunisia and long live France .

From *Harissa* blog (Last accessed 26 April 2017)

***Point of No Return* in English translation, 12 July 2005**

http://jewishrefugees.blogspot.co.uk/2005/07/my-right-of-return-by-tunisian-jew.html

(Last accessed 26 April 2017)

Suez 1956: one Jewish family's flight from Egypt

Clemy (Menir) Lazarus arrived in England in 1957 as a five-year-old refugee from Egypt. Here is the story of her family's flight.

The year 1956 was not the first recorded time that the Menir family was exiled from the land of their birth. The Encyclopaedia Judaica records that we lived in Tudela, Spain in the 13th Century, and by the time of the Spanish Inquisition of 1492, we left Spain and had followed the same route to Egypt as the Rambam (Maimonides).

I was born in Cairo, Egypt in 1951, and by 1956 my family was caught up in the conflict that became known as the Suez Crisis. This was for two reasons. Firstly we were Jewish and secondly my mother was a British Subject. My mother had acquired this status along with a British passport by virtue of the fact that her grandfather had worked for the British in India, generations earlier. My father's classification, however, was 'stateless'. Although he and his antecedents, for many generations, had been born and lived in Egypt, they were, nevertheless, deprived of any rights, recognition, or entitlements of citizenship because we were Jewish. I believe the official status is *dhimmi*. In essence we were subjugated and lived as second class citizens. However, we did enjoy a very good standard of living. My father established a successful cardboard box manufacturing business in Cairo.

My father was one of four siblings. He was the eldest and he eventually joined my mother in England. The second sibling established a life in Paris. The third went to live in the fledgling state of Israel where he lived under very difficult conditions in corrugated tin huts in a *ma'abara* for many years. The fourth, a sister, remained in Egypt with her aged parents until my grandfather passed away after which time she and my grandmother eventually moved to Israel.

As a consequence of the Suez Crisis, my mother, along with all British and French 'citizens' were unceremoniously expelled from Egypt. I have a memory of military personnel marching through our apartment delivering the expulsion order.

This caused my parents and grandparents severe heartache as my parents had five children and my mother was, at the time, six months' pregnant with number six. She was obliged to leave for England on her own, without her husband, but with five children in tow. She was 24 years of age at the time. She spoke French and Arabic but no English and she knew no other culture than the Jewish/Egyptian one in which she grew up.

She was compelled to leave without any money or possessions of any value. She did, however, manage to buy a few gold bangles that she wore as jewellery and sold for the purpose of sustaining us down the line.

Once in England, my mother was housed in a refugee camp, first in Leeds and then in Kidderminster. These were essentially former wooden army barrack huts. When my mother was ready to deliver her baby, my siblings and I were placed in the guardianship of the British Red Cross and she was taken to the local hospital to give birth. This was a particularly harrowing time for her as she had no means of communicating her concerns. During this time our suitcases were ransacked and many fine Cacharel clothes were stolen. Added to this, my mother returned from hospital to find that one of her children was missing. Her youngest, Vivienne, had developed measles and had been placed in isolation.

After six months my mother was at the end of her tether. My mother is the sweetest, most mild-mannered, excruciatingly shy woman. Nevertheless, astonishingly, she found the strength to march into the office of the commander of the refugee camp. She banged on his desk, swiped all the paperwork to the floor and in her best newly-acquired English she declared, "Captain Marsh, bring my husband!" To his credit, Captain Marsh did his utmost to make this happen and shortly afterwards my father joined us in the camps.

My father had been given permission to leave Egypt on condition that he abandoned his business, his home and all his possessions. Everything was confiscated by the Egyptian authorities and to this day we have received not a penny in compensation.

The early years in England were extremely difficult for my parents. They had no money, no home and no livelihood. Added to this, it was against every economic, social and spiritual tide that my parents maintained a strictly orthodox home.

Shortly after this we were welcomed by the Birmingham Jewish community, where we were housed in a Victorian tenement building along with half-a-dozen other refugee Jewish/Egyptian families, and committed to paying a nominal weekly rent.

My parents, who started from rock bottom, worked unbelievably hard, living a life of deprivation and self-sacrifice. They devoted all their time and energy to caring for their family's wellbeing and education, to the exclusion of all else. After many attempts to work for others my father was eventually able to set up a small cardboard box manufacturing business which subsequently grew into a highly successful one. In this way he himself was then able to provide employment for many other needy individuals.

From the moment my parents arrived in England, they showed their gratitude to their British hosts by naming their newborn baby Elizabeth after the Queen of England. My father enrolled in night school to learn to speak English and soon spoke English better than any Englishman. My father became a dapper English gentleman, albeit with an Egyptian accent. When he could afford it he bought my mother the finest clothes and had bespoke suits made for himself along with matching bowler hats which he wore jauntily. The pinnacle of his achievement was when he managed to buy himself a Rolls Royce. As a *mitzvah*, he shared his good fortune by using his car to drive many a bride to the *Chuppah*.

I and my siblings are certainly 'forgotten refugees', but the point is that at no time in our life did my parents define the family as such. At no point was that label used as a yoke that bound us to our unfortunate early life. My parents embraced their new life in exile and worked hard to improve their lot.

Clash of Cultures, **Harif blog at the *Jerusalem Post*, 18 February 2017**
http://www.jpost.com/Blogs/Clash-of-Cultures/Suez-1956-one-Jewish-familys-flight-from-Egypt-481882 (Last accessed 3 April 2017)

A Jew in Syria – Joseph Esses

Michelle Devorah Kahn interviewed her Syrian-born grandfather for a school project – and turned his harrowing story into a documentary.

All it took to get from one end of the room to the other was a slight step forward. Every couple hours, a man would walk by his cell and spit on him. There was no food. There was no water. There was no light. There were no comforting words, only brief moments when hopeful thoughts would fleetingly pop into his head. From 1948 to 1950, my grandfather had one job: He was a prisoner; a convicted Jew.

Joseph Avraham Esses was born on 16 October, 1919, in Aleppo, Syria. His father was a textile merchant and he was the eighth of 14 children. Although he enjoyed a happy childhood –— filled with love, laughter and an abundance of Baklava –— living side-by side with his Muslim Arab neighbours, things would take a turn for the worse. This was the point in his life he never spoke about; the point I was most curious about.

So in 2007, for a class project, I set up two chairs, directed a camera at my grandfather and interviewed him. My grandfather was a very closed and cautious man at the time, and after much debating and negotiating with him, I began to understand why.

He explained to me that as the end of the 1940s approached, everything changed and the attitude towards the Jewish people, who were once the "'brothers and sisters'" of the Muslim Arabs, shifted greatly. At the time of the establishment of the State of Israel, my grandfather, then a young adult, owned and managed his own shop, selling clothing and incidentals (perfume, cologne, accessories, etc.).

One evening, after closing up his shop, he was walking home when three young Muslim men cornered him in the middle of the street and began beating him with their fists and whatever pathetic weapons they had (sticks, rocks, etc.) and shouting, "'You want a country? You want a country?! Here is your country!'"

Along with the entire Jewish community of Aleppo, he witnessed many atrocities. Friends and family members often disappeared, never to be heard from or seen again, or were slaughtered during broad daylight for all to see. One incident involving a Jewish family man who was hiding from the Muslims, lead to his three young daughters being kidnapped from the marketplace and held captive for days, where they were tortured and ultimately killed. A few days later, their cut-up bodies were delivered to the family's home and left on their doorstep in a sack.

Being Jewish became a crime and my grandfather was convicted of it. Men, women and children were often hung for this crime in the town square, as the Arabs cheered. My grandfather was luckier than most.

He had established strong, positive relationships with both the Arabs and Jews over the years (professionally and socially), and boasted about having the son of Syria's chief of police as his best friend. But, at the risk of appearing disloyal, everyone had no choice but to put aside their personal feelings for political ones.

So my grandfather was allowed to live, but he was thrown in jail. Many were left in there for days on end, starved, tortured and belittled, and left to stand in dirt and faeces. Even luckier for him was that his relationship with the Arabs secured him a nightly release, but each morning he was put back into that same jail cell.

Never knowing if things would improve, or if they would continue to worsen, his family had no choice but to leave. Slowly, he began securing the escape of his younger siblings and his dear mother.

One night, being the final family member left, Joseph turned on all the house lights, left the radio at full blast, unlocked the front door and left forever. He escaped across the border into Lebanon with a fake passport, which listed his birthplace as Philadelphia. He left behind all his cherished family heirlooms, belongings, money and memories. When he crossed the border safely into Lebanon, he ran out from the vehicle, kissed the ground and began singing a song of freedom.

This was not an easy interview for me to sit through. It was the first, and maybe the only, time he had ever spoken about this in his life. Most of my family didn't know what I did. I knew he was in pain and I knew he was afraid of people knowing the truth. But I also knew I had a duty to my ancestors and my heritage to learn what really happened. I began interviewing other family members and gathering stories and photos. In the end, I had a full-length documentary on my grandfather's life titled, *Wanted: The Joseph Esses Story*.

Michelle Devorah Kahn: 'Tales of a Convicted Jew's Escape from Syria'
***National Post (Canada)*, 1 December 2014**
http://news.nationalpost.com/full-comment/michelle-devorah-kahn-tales-of-a-convicted-jews-escape-from-syria (Last accessed 26 April 2017)

Forced out from Cairo, 1956

Jenny Stewart's family was among the first to be expelled from Egypt in the aftermath of the Suez Crisis in 1956. Here is her story, as told to *Point of No Return*:

My name is Jenny Stewart (nee Setton). I was born in Cairo in 1935. I went to a convent boarding school. Our family was amongst the first Jews to be forced out of Egypt in 1956. I was then 21, a primary schoolteacher. The Suez

Crisis had just broken out: Britain and France in alliance with Israel were attacking Nasser after he nationalised the Suez Canal. We were among 25,000 Jews expelled from Egypt.

It was November 1956. There was a knock at our door. It was Mrs Kromovski, an Ashkenazi lady from Poland. She begged us to take her in: she had been turned out of her home in Suez which had become a military zone. Two officers came to our door and gave us three days to leave. We do not know if Mrs Kromovski's arrival and our subsequent expulsion were linked.

We packed our suitcases with warm clothes. My mother had a UK passport, but I had none. I had to get a travel permit from the Swiss embassy. My stepfather was stateless.

We were allowed to take out only 20 pounds each. I sewed a £10 note in the hem of my dress. My mother insisted on taking her jewellery with her. It was all confiscated by the immigration officers when we arrived at the airport.

After a long and complicated journey –- we left Cairo on a UN transport plane –- I remember arriving at London airport, which consisted then of just a few corrugated shacks. The cold and damp weather made my stepfather very ill. Having previously contracted TB he only had one kidney and asked to be sent to the Jewish hospital in the East End of London. He spent six months there. My mother became so depressed she had spells in a mental hospital under sedation.

Jews who arrived in England after us were sent to refugee camps in the north of the country. My father, an import-export merchant in Egypt, was taken to prison. An Egyptian army officer had designs on the apartment he lived in, and had him arrested on trumped-up charges. My father spent about eight months in jail with robbers and thieves. When he was released he was put on a ship for Italy, and then another to Israel. Life was a struggle: he started working as a postman; as he was well-educated and multilingual, he managed to rebuild his life in Israel.

Our family business in Egypt involved running two shops selling French designer clothing and children's wear. On our hurried departure we left the shops in the hands of my brother-in-law, but later he too had to flee Egypt, leaving all our property behind. We later found out that we owned a plot of land in Alexandria, the site of an ancient Greek temple. It must have been purchased before King Faroukh ascended the throne: afterwards, Jews were not allowed to inherit property.

After 1979, when Egypt and Israel signed a peace treaty, we visited Egypt. I remember staying in a palace in Zamalek, converted into a hotel, that I used to walk past as a child. The Egyptians welcomed us very warmly. But I felt Egypt had gone backwards. The shops still had their original names. Their owners of the large department stores, such as Gattegno and Cicurel, had fled Egypt with nothing. The street names, however, had all changed.

We were recommended an Egyptian lawyer to try and get us compensation for our losses. We paid him his fee, but nothing came of it.

From *Point of No Return*, 20 November 2012
http://jewishrefugees.blogspot.co.il/2012/11/

Tisha B'Ab in Aden

This is an Ashkenazi traveller's account of his visit to the main synagogue in Aden in the 1950s during the 9th of Ab. This is the saddest festival in the Jewish calendar, mourning the destruction of the two Jewish temples in Jerusalem and other disasters in Jewish history.

At night, a scene right out of the *Arabian Nights* meets me in the synagogue for the Tisha B'Ab services. The men wear red fezzes, are dressed in white, flowing robes, and are followed by their sons and grandsons. Clusters of these families place themselves comfortably in various spots of the synagogue. The grandfather, patriarchally placed in the middle, sits on a carpet, sometimes barefoot, resting against a high cushion or box; next to him his son, also a little on the heavy side, but without the elder's flowing white beard and side curls.

Around the group are children, usually barefoot, of all ages, of whom the youngest will soon fall asleep while the older ones compete with the grownups in chanting the *Kinot*. With the synagogue built for a community of thousands, only a few hundred are left; the enormous spaciousness of the basilica-type synagogue leaves room for approximately fifty adults and an equal number of children to disappear into their respective corners.

For the youngsters, it is like Purim or Simchat Torah. Happy groups of boys in holiday dress, barefoot, with Israeli-made skullcaps on their heads, run back and forth. Then a stern looking young man with a red fez and black beard strikes the air with his rod with a whistling sound, but miraculously misses the children each time he charges into the groups. For a while he gets them to congregate at the foot of the Ark and even gets them to chant a few lines, but soon they are dispersed again in mirth, to the charging of the *melamed*.

Behind the bars along the east wing, women are following the services in a darkened hall. I noticed that their faces are uncovered, although their heads are covered by kerchiefs. Surrounded by Moslems whose married women are literally mummified from head to toe, it must have required enormous strength of character on the part of the Jews not to force their women into adopting similar garb.

As the reading of the Lamentations proceeds, I am struck by the peculiar Yemenite pronunciation applied. Each *komatz* is pronounced as an 'o' and each *cholem* is pronounced—similar to the Lithuanian manner—as an 'ay.' (A typical Oriental differentiation between the *aleph* and *ayin*, between *kof* and *qof*, between the 'hard' and 'soft' sounds, is observed. This mixture of Oriental consonants and 'Lithuanian' vowels creates a rather weird-sounding Hebrew.)

After the services, as a group of worshippers gathers around me for conversation, I query them about this. They reply that their forefathers have lived in Aden for over two thousand years and that they have no other pronunciation. When I asked them why their cemetery as well as their synagogue faces north and not east, they shake their heads in wonderment, since they have never heard of another direction other than north for praying and burying their dead. After all, Aden is practically due south of Israel. I am informed about their institutions, their yeshivot for boys up to the age of fifteen, their *shechitah*. I meet their rabbi, Rav Zecharyahu, a venerable sage with a long white beard and wise, knowing eyes. I hear complaints about the unhappy lot of the approximately one thousand Jews still living in neighboring Yemen, whose king refuses them the right to emigrate.

Reprinted from JJAC website.
From *Point of No Return*, 24 July 2015
http://jewishrefugees.blogspot.co.uk/2015/07/tisha-b-av-with-jews-of-aden.html
(Last accessed 26 April 2017)

The 1947 riots in Aden

Below is a first-hand account of the events, in a letter to the *Jewish Chronicle* (published in the issue of 2 January 1948) by a Jew signing himself 'An Adenite'.

The first day of the three-day Arab strike against partition, on 2 December, passed off quietly, despite a demonstration outside the Jewish quarter [in Crater]. On the evening of that day, a meeting was addressed by Arab leaders, and at 6 p.m. the crowd, followed by thousands of Arabs, attacked the Jewish quarter. Those of us who were in the streets had to take shelter in the nearest house. This lasted up to about 10.30 p.m., when some British sailors surrounded the Jewish quarter and dispersed the mob.

Next morning, since Aden Protectorate Levies (Moslem Troops) were stationed in the Jewish quarter, many [Jews] came out on the streets, trusting that peace and order would be maintained. Suddenly, news reached us that Jewish shops situated in the leading bazaars were being looted.

Eyewitnesses saw Arabs set fire to buildings under the eyes of the Levies. They also saw Indian merchants openly abstracting bales of textiles from godowns [warehouses] in the Jewish quarter.

Following that, many houses were burned, as well as a synagogue. The reason that very few lives were lost in them was due solely to the fact that the inhabitants had fled. At least one-third of the Jewish quarter was destroyed, looted, or devastated.

In many of the houses, mobs broke in, looting and beating the inhabitants, and in some cases threatened them with death if they did not "accept the Mohammedan religion." Some were kidnapped by Arabs, and five are still missing.

Jewish deaths total 74 (*The Aden Jewish Heritage Museum in Tel Aviv puts the toll at 87 – ed)*, including men, women, and children. Many others were wounded. The only ones killed by the Arabs were one man slaughtered by rioters, and probably a few more by looters, in their homes. The Levies were responsible for nearly all the deaths because of their constant shooting at our homes....

An amazing allegation is contained in a cable dispatched by the Governor himself [Sir Reginald Stuart Champion] to the Secretary of State [for the Colonies, Arthur Creech Jones], on 5 December. It reads: "Curfew retained in Crater and situation there generally quieter, but alleged hostile activity of Jews created new dangerous tension, especially after killing of a Levy and an Indian Moslem Government doctor almost certainly by Jewish snipers ....

I can hasten to assure His Excellency and the Governor that this allegation is completely untrue. The doctor in question is well known to the Jews as a kindly man and as a particular friend of a Jew called Mori Dawood. The real facts are that one of the sons, named Yehia, was shot on Wednesday, in his own home by the Levies. His family risked their lives under fire to reach a Jewish house where a telephone was available for the purpose of arranging for an ambulance to take Yehia to hospital and also telephoned the Audit Officer in whose office one of the sons is a clerk. All the replies were 'Busy' and 'Wait.'

It was only the next morning that the doctor came and removed Yehia to the ambulance while he was speaking to his brother Hayeem near the house, the Levies shot them both. The doctor died instantly and Hayeem is still under treatment for wounds. Yehia died later in hospital.

What is needed is an impartial inquiry. I declare bluntly that the attack upon us was organised beforehand. How else can one account for an all-round attack, not only in the Crater, but also in Tawahi, Shaikh Othman, and Maalla? It was in the Crater that the events already described took place. But in Tawahi, a port six miles from the Crater, the total number of Jewish steps is five.

In Shaikh Othman, about eleven miles from the Crater, 14 Jews were killed, and about 900 have been evacuated by the Government to the Yemenite migration camp at Hashed [i.e. Hashid]. In Maalla, a port, there are no Jewish residents, but premises stored with Jewish goods were looted.

It would be useful to know where the millions of *lakhs* of loot are at present, or whether the Government is taking drastic action to find the looters. But we hear that Arabs are selling their loot at a fifth to a tenth of its value, and that much of it has already removed from the Colony to the interior, despite the police "barriers".

Aden's stricken Jewry expects more than a mere condolence from world Jewry. They require funds to reconstruct their livelihood, and legal aid for a full inquiry and defence of their rights under International Law. They also require the particular attention of the Jewish Agency for migration certificates to Palestine for the whole community as soon as possible ....

In the immediate aftermath of the pogrom in Aden, Elie Eliachar, president of the 160,000-strong Sephardi Community of Palestine, who was visiting London, reported that the number of Jewish fatalities might in actuality have been as high as 145. He noted that Yemeni refugees in the Shaikh (or Sheikh) Othman camp, awaiting removal to *Eretz Yisrael*, had also suffered greatly from Arab attacks, and many feared that the the British government would repatriate them to Yemen.

Daphne Anson blog, 16 May 2011
http://daphneanson.blogspot.co.uk/2011/05/eyewitness-account-of-aden-pogrom-of.html
(Last accessed 26 April 2017)

From Baghdad to an Israeli tent

Avram Piha tells the story of his Iraq-born landlord Eli, who overcame untold hurdles to rebuild his life in Israel.

Eli was born in Baghdad a few months after the *Farhud*. Eli remembers the city well as he spent much time with his father, who was a taxi driver. The *shukim* (open-air markets) are what sticks out most for him, 'They were phenomenal.' His schooling from the age of six through nine was at the local synagogue. He always walked to the synagogue in a group, as the Jewish children suffered daily abuse from Arab children and young adults, everything from verbal to physical. 'It was very tough,' Eli sighed, but he did note that his Arab neighbors always looked out for his family, and, understanding the rules of Shabbat, prepared them tea every Shabbat!

In March 1951, Eli and his family left all their possessions behind and made their way to Israel. All they had with them was their clothing, and Eli described the shock of seeing Iraqi soldiers demand his parents hand over the blanket they were using to keep his baby brother wrapped up and warm.

Though leaving Iraq was traumatic, the new reality of Israel was harsh as well. Along with two other families, Eli's family shared one tent in the Sha'ar Yerushalayim (near Atlit). 'It was an unbelievable shock to us,' Eli explained. 'We went from having a two-bedroom apartment to living in a tent with no running water, electricity or other essentials – with two other families!' I just looked at him, almost in awe, and continued to listen as he continued, 'We weren't angry, we were just happy to be out of Iraq, but this was extremely difficult.' With regards to food, Eli smiled, 'It was terrible, but when you're hungry, you'll eat even *that.*'

After a few months, Eli's family 'upgraded' to a *ma'abara* near Megiddo, where they had a tent to themselves. They soon moved to the Kastal *ma'abara* (near Meva'seret Zion), where Eli's family lived in a *pachon* (tin shack). Though it was better than a tent, life in the *pachon* was also challenging: 'We froze in the winter, faced leaks every time it rained, and burned ourselves on the metal every summer as the weather got hotter.' Despite all these difficulties, Eli stressed that his family remained upbeat and positive and only really worried about their continuing financial struggles. With his father unable to hold a steady job in Jerusalem, the family moved to Beit Yosef in the Beit She'an Valley. Here is where the family would hit rock bottom.

Eli's father tried his hand at agriculture, which was only possible during the autumn and winter months. Unfortunately, he had little success. After seven years of helping out, Eli was drafted to the Armored Corps and rarely had time to help his father. Two years later, Eli's father passed away. Eli was released from his military obligations and became the 'father' to a family of nine (his mother, five brothers and three sisters). After nine unsuccessful agricultural seasons, the family's luck changed and under Eli's handling, they hit the jackpot and earned 10,000 lira for their produce. With this money, Eli bought the family an apartment in Jerusalem and began working many jobs to sustain his family. Sibling after sibling eventually 'made it,' as did Eli, who eventually owned his own building company. Eli smiled, 'I'm so proud of my family, every single grandchild – all children of immigrants – has a university education. That's how I know we really made it.'

'One last question,' I said, 'Would you like to go back to Baghdad one day?' Without hesitation he answered, 'I'd love to go see the city – I was born there and lived there till I was nine, but it's not going to happen due to my health.'

It was time to say goodbye, and I smiled, "'A refugee ... and you made it.'" He returned the smile, and made his way to his car.

'From Baghdad with Love', *Times of Israel* blog by Avram Piha, 13 July 2013
http://blogs.timesofisrael.com/from-baghdad-with-love/(Last accessed 26 April 2017)

Of Etrogim and goats in Yemen

Meet Etrog Man - the 72-year old Yemenite Jew who has made a speciality out of marketing the magical properties of this lemon-like 'vegetable', in great demand for the Jewish festival of Succoth. Uzi-Eli was suckled by a she-goat in Yemen. When the goat was killed to provide meat for his family, then fleeing for Aden and Israel in 1949, Uzi-Eli never got over his loss. Story by Judy Maltz.

They call him the Etrog Man – and for good reason.   Uzi-Eli, as he is otherwise known, is the founder and owner of a one-of-a-kind shop in Jerusalem's Mahane Yehuda market that sells all things etrog, the citron fruit used in religious rituals during the Jewish festival of Sukkot.

The etrog is not eaten during Sukkot, but rather, it serves as one of the four plant species shaken to fulfill the mitzvah associated with this holiday. According to Jewish legend, it's meant to symbolize the heart, and in its bumpy-skinned, lemon-like raw form, it makes an appearance once a year, just before the start of this holiday. But in the bottles, canisters and jars that line the shelves of Uzi-Eli's tiny shop, it's a star all year around.

Among the assortment of derivative products here, there's a spray made from etrog peel that's meant to cure acne, age spots, mouth sores, baldness and even stuttering in young children. There's a cream made from crushed etrog seeds and coconut oil that supposedly smooths out wrinkles. There's a soap made from etrog essence that Uzi-Eli claims is effective in combating dandruff and general itchiness. There's an ointment made from etrog extract, mint, ginger and cayenne pepper he vows will cure sinus problems, hemorrhoids and chronic pain. There's an etrog drink sold in frozen packages that supposedly works wonders on morning sickness in pregnant woman ('If a woman drinks this during her pregnancy, the baby will also come out smelling as fragrant as the fruit,' he assures a prospective buyer.)

There's a special version of the popular Yemenite spice hilbe with a bit of etrog extract mixed in that prevents the body, as Uzi-Eli explains, from giving off the strong odor usually associated with this condiment. And finally, there are the shop's specialty smoothies made from etrog and khat – a plant

Yemenites traditionally chew that is known for its stimulating effect – as well as a delicious etrog liqueur.

In the days leading up to Sukkot, Uzi-Eli's shop is packed. Not only with the usual curiosity seekers interested in sampling his natural remedies, but also, shoppers in the market for an etrog to go with their three-branch lulav (palm frond,) so that they can fulfill the special mitzvah of Sukkot. In order to be considered kosher for the purpose of performing this mitzvah, the etrog must in most cases have an intact pitam, a small extension at the top of the fruit. But those with a damaged pitams are also in demand, says Uzi-Eli, for use as decorations in the hut-like sukkahs where many Jews traditionally eat their meals during the seven-day holiday that starts at sundown on Wednesday.

A robust and jovial 72-year-old with a mop of white curls under his yarmulke, Uzi-Eli and his potions are an unmistakable attraction in the market. Barely has one group of young sight-seers exited the premises when another enters (he gets anywhere from five to 20 groups a day, most of them on organized tours of Jerusalem's storied marketplace.) In broken English, he regales them with tales of his childhood in Yemen. He tells them about his two grandfathers, who happened to be brothers and were both natural healers. He tells them about how one of them concocted a potion to dry up Uzi-Eli's mother's milk when, as a toddler, he refused to wean himself from her breast. He tells them about the goat who replaced his mother as his main provider of food, showing how he would get it to push its leg up in air so that he could crawl under its body. He tells them about how that goat was killed so that the family would have dried meat to eat on their long journey to the port city of Aden, where they eventually boarded a plane to Israel in 1949, and how he never overcame that loss. Then he proceeds to squirt the anti-acne etrog spray on the face of one of his visitors who's agreed to serve as a guinea pig. Another gets a squirt of it in the mouth, and yet another gets Uzi-Eli's finger, with a dab of the special sinus ointment on it, inserted straight up his nose.

'From Sukkot to morning sickness: the magic of the Etrog' by Judy Maltz, *Haaretz*, 5 October 2014

http://www.haaretz.com/jewish/high-holy-days-2014/.premium-1.619254 (Last accessed 26 April 2017)

The Iraqi Jews had the best of everything

This extract by Ameen Al-Mumaiiz from his book, *Baghdad as I know it* (1930), gives a fascinating insight, through the eyes of a Muslim, into how Iraqi Jews were at the forefront of modernising the country. It must be

emphasised, however, that the Jewish upper classes were a small percentage of the community as a whole, most of whom, as per the autobiographies of Nissim Rejwan and Salim Fattal, were poor.

The Iraqi Jews ate the most expensive and rare of fruits and vegetables. As soon as the fruit is available in the market, the Iraqi Jew would buy it no matter how expensive.

He eats a healthy (kosher) meat and chicken diet checked by the Rabbi -- this in obedience to religious edicts which orders them to thank God for the first season fruits, as well as to check the slain animal that no bones are broken and that it is free from any infectious diseases.

The majority of the Jews wear the best quality clothes sewn by the superior Baghdadi tailors (Armenians, Muslims, Jewish or Farma the Indian) to celebrate their festivals as per the Torah edicts. Most of them celebrate in their houses with the best foods, like the fatty chicken breasts and sweets (*Haiwwa*).

The Jewish man will frequent the best snack bars and cafes in Baghdad with names like the River Cafe, al Basha, Shabandar, Moshe, and Mummaiiz Cafe, where he can relax and be entertained, as well as make business deals. He does not care how much he pays to the owner of the snack bar.

They own the best clubs in Baghdad, as well as the high class ones *ie* Al Rashid, Laura Kaddouri. These are exclusively Jewish and no-one else is allowed to join.

They also have the schools with the highest standards, both primary and secondary: The Alliance, Shamash and Frank Iny schools, so that sending their kids to finish their higher education in the American or European universities can be achieved easily with no problem, conditions or limitations.

If, for example, an Iraqi Jew needs to defend himself in court, he can bring in the best lawyers from abroad (as seen in the case of the extremely well off Mr Shemmail Jemaila) when he brought in Mr Parkiton-Ward, the famous English lawyer to do so.

The Jews use the most luxurious and pedigree milking cows, handle the rarest of domestic birds, the parrots, canaries and love birds. They were the first to import American cars into Iraq – for example the Ford agents were Ibrahim and Shafiq Ades.

The agents for General Motors were the Lawee brothers. They appreciate the nutritional value of the *Nabeq* (tiny soft fruit from trees), the *manna, Jammar* (from wood in the trees), roasted beetroots, and they will pay whatever price to get them. The Jews will only buy live fish and buy it directly from the (supplier or fisherman?).

They will put up their summer tents on the riverside only in the best locations like the A'Athamiyyah beach and Al Kahouriya. They only left when threatened by Nu'man al A'thami, as he was afraid they were plotting to make the area all Jewish.

The Jewish Rabbi was the most skilled in circumcision and many Muslim families resorted to using his skills to circumcise their boys.

For foreign languages, the best teachers were Jewish, for example Shummail for French and Heskel Effendi for the English language. The best swimming instructors were Jewish at Said Sultan's Organization and the teacher Saffani was the most able.

The majority of the merchants who imported the hygienic artefacts and instruments from abroad were Jewish ... Salem Shamoun introduced the bathtub and the boiler to bathrooms. The Shasha family imported the variety of cloths in the Saffaffir warehouse. The Hakkak family imported the 'Singer' sewing machines, the gramaphones 'Lady's voice', and 'Pythaphone' records.'

From *Point of No Return*, 29 April 2015
(Last accessed 26 April 2017) Translated by Ivy Vernon
https://jewishrefugees.blogspot.co.il/2015/04/1930s-iraq-jews-have-best-of-everything.html?m=1

Escape from Iran

Eti Sionit Goshen was a 35-year-old mother of two under the regime of the Ayatollahs in Iran. As an employee in a government office she was well-placed to embark on a new career - forging documents for young Jews desperate to escape. (To be drafted into the Iranian army, then at war with Iraq, was a death sentence). Eti was denounced, jailed and tortured and it was ten years before she herself was able to escape to Israel. She tells her hair-raising tale of horror to Yariv Peleg of *Israel Hayom*.

One day, by chance, I saw a top secret document with an order barring Jewish emigration from Iran. I was mortified. I told my husband, and we started thinking about what could be done. Tehran has a rabbi named Baruch Hacham, who would help the young people escape somehow. The smugglers would charge a lot of money and it was a very dangerous road. Many were caught and thrown in jail.

My father-in-law had just died, and they [Houshang's family] decided to try and get two older brothers out [of Iran] through Hacham, but they were caught near the border and thrown in jail. My husband went to get them and was beaten up. But he paid a bribe and got them back. They then decided to try and smuggle the two younger brothers out. They were only 15 and 16, and so many soldiers had died in the war the army was starting to recruit really young boys. "Iranians lend great importance to identity. They would always ask, "'Are you Iranian or Jewish?" Jews were sent to the front line immediately. Going into the army as a Jew –— that was a death sentence.

Q: Were your husband's younger brothers able to escape?
He sent them through Hacham, but they were also caught near the border. Their mother was left alone, she was elderly and lived in another city. They [the authorities] wouldn't issue her a passport because she was Jewish. We were also waiting for passports, but they gave us the runaround. We didn't know what to do.

At that time, in addition to passports and identity cards, there was also a third registry, a notebook that listed the details of the family. To leave Iran, you had to have all three documents. The solution we came up with was to pay Muslims for the documents. I stole stamps from the office where I worked and forged passports. Jews' passports were red and Muslim passports were blue. That's how we started helping Jews leave Iran.

(Placing themselves at considerable risk, the couple launched a forged passport "'industry,'" mostly for young men who were slated to be enlisted.) We never thought of ourselves. We were focused on helping the young people. I would forge passports, replace photos, stamp. I spent hours on end on it. We would buy Muslim passports. They could travel far more easily. But these were delicate transactions. We only got them from people we knew, in my workplace, my husband's or friends we knew before the revolutions. We would spend a long time convincing them. After all, it placed them in danger as well.

(The illegal industry was exposed after a woman they forged a passport for apparently told a government official she had befriended about them.)

One night, we were at home with the kids, and all of a sudden regime officials came into the house. They're not like the police here in Israel – they were like God. They could do whatever the wanted. They could kill with impunity. It's like having Islamic State operatives show up on your doorstep.

Q: Did they find anything illegal?
'They tore the house apart, pulled up tiles, and we weren't allowed to say a word. They blindfolded us, and threw the children to the side [of the room]. We had materials in the house that we used to forge passports. At the time my husband was unemployed and he was involved in illegal money-changing, and there were papers saying he transferred dollars out of Iran, which was illegal. There was also a photo of my cousin, who immigrated to Israel and was in the Paratroopers Brigade, in uniform. God help me, I'm still terrified just talking about it.'

That night ushered in a chapter of horrors for the family. Fortunately, while forging passports, the couple had the sense to pose as Muslims. "'We had documents saying we had converted to Islam. We also had Muslim marriage documents that we had poured tea over, to age them. We also had

Khomeini's book and a Koran, so the police were confused. They didn't really understand who we were or what we did. The police said they were taking us in for interrogation. The landlord heard the ruckus and came over and I asked her to take the children to my sister. I wasn't supposed to speak, so they [the police] hit me and threw me down the stairs. They beat the hell out of us during the interrogation. They used electric shocks ... the torture was unimaginable. Then they showed us the picture the woman who informed on us, and I thought – that's it. This is our death sentence. Then they threw me in a room that was pitch black, without food or water. The next day they took me and my husband to a prison that is known as one of the world's most infamous jails. They say even birds don't fly there. If you go – you never come back. It's a miracle we got out alive. It's a miracle I'm sitting here.

Q: Did your family know how you were doing?
No. We didn't get a phone call, or a lawyer. I had no idea what was going on with the kids. In Israel, an Arab terrorist gets a lawyer and he can go to school while in jail. We got nothing. We were nowhere.

Q: What was prison like?
They separated us immediately. They tied me to the bed and stretched me until I was sure my back had broken. I was beaten with a leather whip until I passed out. The men would beat me, even though they were prohibited to do so by their religion. Because they suspected I was Jewish they enjoyed it. They dragged me across the floor by the chador [full-body-length garment worn by women in Iran when in public]. I didn't eat or drink for three days, I was half dead.

I was interrogated every day. The interrogator would hit me repeatedly. Tell me, you little stinking Jew, how did you fool the Islamic Republic? he would ask. How dare you? Who did you work for? They thought we were a network. But I never broke. I never told them about anyone. I prayed that my husband wouldn't talk. I didn't want to place the families of the young people we helped in danger.

(Between interrogations, Goshen was thrown into a cell with Baha'i women, whose religion was also targeted in post-revolution Iran.) One of the women there taught me the Quran, and I also knew a little from my daughter, who went to kindergarten with Muslim children after the revolution, she recalls.

One day they took me in for questioning by an Imam. He told me to recite something out of a prayer, but Muslims have a purification ritual before [prayers] so I said, I have no water for purification. He told me to go ahead anyway. So I sang what I knew. I did it wholeheartedly, I hoped it would save my life. Then he told me to recite another line that I happened to know from my daughter, then another line, which that woman taught me the night before. By some stroke of luck, he stopped me after the last line I knew. I don't know what I would have done had he asked for even two more words. My mouth was dry and my heart was pounding. It's an indescribable feeling. Every day might be your last. The moment he told me to stop I said Shema Yisrael in my heart.

From *Israel Hayom*, **23 October 2016**

http://www.israelhayom.com/site/newsletter_article.php?id=37329 (Last accessed 26 April 2017)

Bsisa in Libya

On the first day of the month of Nisan Raphael Luzon's would make *Bsisa*, a traditional dish made by Libyan Jews to commemorate the day the *Mishkan* (tabernacle) was erected.

Her swollen fingers kneaded the flower vigorously. Her body was bent over the bowl, her sleeves rolled up, her eyes fixated on the pastry, as she worked her arms tirelessly until it started to take shape. The ingredients are flour, coriander, cumin, almonds, dried fruits, dates and sugar. Once everything was mixed, she would insert small trinkets, including at least one key.

Before tasting this traditional dish we'd pray to God, saying, *Yafetchah, Bla Neftchah, Yaatai, Blamenai, Arzikna warzikmana!* (God, you are the one who can open without keys, always giving a generous hand, giving without compensation. Giving us your goodness so that we can do good to others!)

There is no rejuvenation without *Bsisa*. The sacrament is incomplete without this delicious *bsisa*, as old as the dawn of time. I used to watch my busy mother preparing the meal. She would turn and smile at me and offer her finger to taste the sweet paste. She would laugh as I licked it and continue kneading, going into her own little world.

From *Libyan Twilight* by Raphael Luzon (London: Darf, 2016)

How a Young Woman kept her Promise to Ezra

By the 1990s, there were only a few dozen Jews left in Iraq. O. was one of them. Here is her story.

A young woman – call her O. – attended a Sephardi synagogue in the US some years ago. She struck up a conversation in Arabic with some of the congregants, who came from Iraq. 'What's a Muslim doing in our synagogue?' the congregants muttered to each other -- for the young woman did not speak Judeo-Arabic, with its distinctive accent and pronunciation.

It turned out the young woman was a Jew who had recently arrived from Basra. There had been so few Jews in the city that O. had never learned to speak Judeo-Arabic. As one of the few dozen Jews still living in Iraq under Saddam's rule in the late 1990s, her dearest wish was to leave. But the government were holding the tiny Jewish community as virtual hostages.

It was customary for Jews in Iraq to go on pilgrimage to the tombs of Jewish prophets in order to seek divine intervention to help fulfil their deepest desires. O. decided to go to the shrine of Ezra the Scribe at Uzair, near Basra. She prayed for Ezra to help her to leave Basra. If her wish came about, she promised that she would donate a new *parokhet* (hand-embroidered cover) for the tomb.

Time passed and the young woman fulfilled her wish to leave Basra for the US. But it rankled with her that she was not able to keep her promise to Ezra -- and deliver a new *parokhet* to his tomb.

With the US invasion of Iraq in 2003, the young woman was suddenly presented with the opportunity to go back to Iraq as an interpreter for the Coalition Provisional Administration. The decision was not easy -- after all, for so many years she had wanted nothing more than to leave Iraq.

But she had a promise to keep. She returned to Iraq, bringing with her a rich, velvet, elaborately embroidered *parokhet* for Ezra.

But the Jewish prophet had another reward in store for O. While in Iraq she met her future husband, an American-Jewish diplomat.

She accompanied her husband on his next posting -- to Algeria.

The posting after that was back to Iraq. But at that point, after everything she had done to leave Iraq, O. decided that she had had enough of living in Arab countries.

O. moved to Israel. Her husband is believed to travel back from Iraq to see her at regular intervals.

From *Point of No Return*, 28 June 2010

http://jewishrefugees.blogspot.co.uk/2010/06/how-one-young-woman-kept-her-promise-to.html

(Last accessed 26 April 2017)

My Longest Ten Minutes

After Israel's victory in 1967, Rami Mangoubi's brother Sami was taken away by the Egyptian police and sent to the Abu Zaabal camp as a PoW. His family went through agonies waiting for his return, but they were lucky to have the support of sympathetic neighbours.

During the first three days of the Six Day War, the Egyptian media claimed victory, and Egyptians did not know their army was crushed. Everyone was certain troops were at the doors of Tel Aviv. Rumors spread that thousands of Israeli prisoners were being shipped to Cairo by train to be paraded for all to see in Ramses Square, where the train station is located. The authorities had trouble satisfying this demand, as Egypt had caught no more than a handful of Israeli POWs. But a solution was found. On the first day of the war, at a quarter to five sharp, we heard a knock at the door. We opened. Two policemen in civilian clothes wanted my brother Sami for 10 minutes at the station. He followed them. Two minutes later, Zeinab, the custodian's wife, knocked at the door. Shaken and with tears in her eyes she asked: 'Why did they take him?' Still in shock, we just repeated what we heard: 'He will be back in ten minutes'.

A minute later, our neighbor Set Olfat, who saw from her window my brother taken away in a police truck, arrived. As my mother welcomed her, the slightly obese woman headed quickly toward my father and asked: 'Why did they take him, Mr. Sabet?' The custodian, Am Taher, also came, and told my parents that they should not leave the house; he would run all errands for us. Set Olfat confirmed the warning, assuring us her maid would get us what we needed.

All evening my mother would look at the clock. 'It will not be 10 minutes', my father said. My brother did not come the next day, nor the day after, nor by the end of the week on Friday, June 9, when a cease-fire was declared. That Friday, we asked the custodian to accompany us to Abla Fawzeya's house. She had been the Muslim Arabic language teacher at the Oeuvre de la Goutte de Lait, one of two Jewish schools where my mother was principal. The schools shut their doors a few years back, but Abla Fawzeya remained close to my mother. Since I was a third grader, every two or three Fridays, she would send her daughter, six years older than me, to take me, and I would spend the whole day with the family. My parents and I were welcomed to the guest room, and as Abla Fawziya was wondering why my brother was not with us, my mother cried.

Abla Fawziya stared with her mouth open, speechless. I could see the pain on her husband's face. One of the daughters, Lolla, and the maid, Taheya, heard my mother cry and called on me to join them. When I did, they asked: 'What's going on, Rami?' I told them: 'They came on Monday and took him.' I started crying as Lolla gently put her arms around me, and told Taheya: 'Get him a Coke.'

Two days later, we were sitting in our living room, when we suddenly heard Am Taher's angry voice yell: 'Go away, sons of a dog! Whoever was here you took!' We understood: the authorities had come again. We were certain they were here to take the rest of us away. Thirty seconds later, there was a knock at the door. My father indicated with his hands to my mother that only he would open it, and with a stern look, pointing at me with his finger, he said in French: 'You! Don't move!' As I tried to stretch my neck toward my left shoulder and look through the door to see who was knocking, my mother slapped my wrist. My father walked deliberately to the door and opened it. I heard from the living room Zeinab's reassuring voice: '"They went away."' Am Taher told us three men from the police inquired about my father, but he pretended they were asking for my brother and told them he had already been taken away. Thanks to Am Taher, my father was spared arrest.

It took a month until we learned of my brother's whereabouts. The authorities arrested nearly all Jewish males between the ages of 17 and 60. Those who held foreign citizenship were taken to Alexandria and thrown on a boat, to be disgorged somewhere in southern Europe. They were the fortunate ones. The others, Egyptians and stateless (Jews as a rule were denied citizenship), were taken to the notorious detention camps of Abu Zabaal, near Cairo. On the third day of the war, as a substitute for Israeli PoWs, the authorities decided to parade instead the Jews from Alexandria, who were taken by train to Abu Zabaal by way of Cairo.

The spectacle took place in Ramses Square in front of local mobs, who abused the Jews as they were thrown into open trucks. A Christian friend of my mother, Angèle, lived near the station, and saw the spectacle. She only told me a year later how young and old were throwing stones at the men in the trucks, while shouting '*Yahud*.' The community was almost entirely without young men. The burden fell on women. Women protected their children. They ran from one government office to the next. Women managed family businesses. They watched helplessly as their husband's partners cheated on them, and they sold to customers who bought without paying. They had to keep their mouths shut, as customers and partners routinely threatened to report about relatives in Israel. Many lost their livelihood and, pauperized, relied on the Jewish community for help.

One afternoon, two months later, there was again a knock on the door. It was my aunt and four cousins. Seeing their luggage, I understood immediately how fortunate we were. Their neighbors were not nice like ours. Far from protecting them, they harassed them and forced them to leave. We were so fortunate. Abla Fawziya's family literally adopted us, and visited ever more frequently. She was also worried about her former pupils who left Egypt before the war to live in Israel. Am Taher, Zeinab, and Set Olfat, also protected us like we were their children.

In Abu Zabaal, many detainees were tortured and some, the younger and fair-skinned ones, were sexually molested. Young and old were forced to run daily round and round a small yard, like dogs, and behind them, soldiers beat them with belts. They were screaming. 'Down with Israel. Down with the Jews and with the Zionists.' My uncle was beaten very badly, and had permanent damage to a nerve in his arms. For the rest of his life, he would constantly tick with his left arm.

Six months later, the Jewish men were transferred from Abu Zabaal to another camp, Tourah. Those who were stateless were released after two years and deported. Those with Egyptian citizenship had to endure another year of incarceration before being released and deported. Freedom was made possible thanks to the intervention of Jewish organizations. Several of those incarcerated cannot to this day cope with their experience. Two who were sexually molested committed suicide.

On June 15, 1970, my brother was taken from Tourah prison to the airport at Helipolis. Am Taher was sure what his final destination would be. On the eve of the departure, I heard him say: 'He will go live with the Jews in their country, in Israel'; he was right. Zeinab wanted so badly to come for a last look at my brother, but my father feared she would get in trouble if she was seen with us at the airport. He explained to her: 'He is thrown out, Zeinab.' She cried once more. It was my first visit to an airport. As I watched the Air France Boeing 727 take off, I looked at the black quadrant of my new watch. My mother bought it a week before for the occasion and let me wear it for the first time on that day. It was 10:43 a.m. The 10 minutes were over: They had lasted three years, nine days, 17 hours and 58 minutes.

'My longest ten minutes' by Rami Mangoubi, *Jerusalem Post*, 31 May 2007
http://www.jpost.com/Magazine/Features/My-longest-10-minutes (Last accessed 26 April 2017). http://www.jpost.com/Magazine/Features/My-longest-10-minutes

Bibliography

Abitbol M., *Le Passé d'une Discorde: Juifs et Arabes depuis le VIIe siècle* (Paris: Perrin, 2003).

Achcar G., *The Arabs and the Holocaust: The Arab-Israeli War of Narratives* (New York: Metropolitan, 2009).

Aciman A., *Out of Egypt, A Memoir* (New York: Farrar Strauss Giroux, 1994).

Aharoni A., Israel-Pelletier A., Zamir L. (eds) *History and Culture of Jews of Egypt in Modern Times* (Tel Aviv: Keness Hafakot, 2008).

Aharoni R., *The Jews of Aden: A Community that Was* (Israel: Afikim, 1991).

Allali J-P., *Les réfugiés échangés: Sépharades – Palestiniens* (France: JIPÉA, 2007).

Amir E., *The Dove Flyer* (London: Halban, 2010).

Amir E., *Scapegoat* (London: Weidenfeld & Nicolson, 1987).

Assaraf R., *Une Certaine Histoire des Juifs au Maroc* (Paris: Gawsewitch, 2005).

Bashkin O., *New Babylonians: A History of Jews in Modern Iraq* (Stanford, CA: Stanford University Press, 2012).

Basri C., *The Jews of Iraq: A Forgotten Case of Ethnic Cleansing* (Jerusalem: Institute of the World Jewish Congress, 2003).

Benjamin M., *Last Days in Babylon* (London: Bloomsbury, 2006).

Bat Ye'or, *The Dhimmi: Jews and Christians under Islam* (London: Associated University Press, 1985).

Bat Ye'or, *Understanding Dhimmitude* (New York: RVP, 2013).

Bekhor G.C., *Fascinating Life and Sensational Death* (Israel: Peli, 1990).

Beinin J., *The Dispersion of Egyptian Jewry: Culture, Politics, and the Formation of a Modern Diaspora* (Berkeley, CA: University of California Press, 1998).

Ben-Porat M., *To Baghdad and Back* (Jerusalem: Gefen, 1998).

Bensoussan G., *Juifs en pays arabes: Le grand déracinement 1850–1975* (Paris: Tallandier, 2012).

Bensoussan G., *Les Juifs du monde arabe: La question interdite* (Paris: Odile Jacob, 2017).

Berman P., *The Flight of the Intellectuals* (Melville House, 2011).

Black E., *The Farhud. Roots of the Arab-Nazi Alliance in the Holocaust* (Washington, DC: Dialog Press, 2010).

Bostom A., *The Legacy of Islamic Antisemitism: From Sacred Texts to Solemn History* (Amherst, NY: Prometheus Books, 2008).

Boum A., *Memories of Absence* (Stanford, CA: Stanford University Press, 2013).

Cohen H., *An Army of Shadows: Palestinian Collaborators in the Service of Zion* (Jerusalem: Ivrit - Hebrew Publishing House, 2004) (Hebrew).

Cohen M., *Under Crescent and Cross* (Princeton, NJ: Princeton University Press, 1994).

Cohen M. and Udovitch A. (eds), *Jews Among Arabs: Contacts and Boundaries.* (Princeton, NJ: Darwin Press, 1989).

Douek E., *A Middle Eastern Affair* (London: Halban, 2004).

Durrell L., *The Alexandria Quartet* (London: Faber & Faber, 1962).

Eban S., *A Sense of Purpose* (London: Halban, 2008).

Ellis S., *How to Be a Heroine: Or What I've Learned from Reading Too Much* (London: Chatto & Windus, 2014).

Fattal S., *In the Alleys of Baghdad* (Tel Aviv: Shlomo Levy, 2012).

Fellous C., *Pièces détachées* (Paris: NRF Gallimard, 2017).

Fenton P. and Littman D., *L'Exil Au Maghreb. La Condition Juive Sous L'Islam 1148–1912* (Paris: Université Paris-Sorbonne, 2010).

Fernández-Morera D., *The Myth of the Andalusian Paradise* (Wilmington, DE: ISI, 2016).

Fischbach M., *Jewish Property Claims against Arab Countries* (New York: Columbia University Press, 2008).

Gat M., *The Jewish Exodus from Iraq 1948–1951* (London: Frank Cass, 1997).

Gilbert M., *In Ishmael's House* (New Haven, CT: Yale University Press, 2010).

Goiten S.D., *Jews and Arabs: Their Contacts Through the Ages* (New York: Schocken, 1974).

Haddad H., *Flight from Babylon: Iraq, Iran, Israel, America* (New York: McGraw-Hill, 1986).

Haim S. (ed.), *Arab Nationalism* (London: University of California Press, 1976).

Herf J., *Nazi Propaganda for the Arab World* (New Haven, CT: Yale University Press, 2009).

Hillel S., *Operation Babylon* (UK: Collins, 1988).

Institute of the World Jewish Congress, *Jewish Communities of the World* (Israel: WJC, 1996).

Karsh E., *Islamic Imperialism* (New Haven, CT: Yale University Press, 2006).

Kattan N., *Adieu Babylone* (Montreal: La Presse, 1975).

Kedourie E., *The Chatham House Version, and other Middle Eastern Studies* (New York: Praeger, 1970).

Küntzel M., *Jihad and Jew-Hatred: Islamism, Nazism and the Roots of 9/11* (New York: Telos, 2007).

Lagnado L., *The Man in the White Sharkskin Suit: My Family's Exodus from Old Cairo to the New World* (New York: Harper Collins, 2007).

Langer J. (ed.), *If Salt has Memory: Jewish exiled writers from Africa, Latin America, Europe and the Middle East* (Nottingham: Five Leaves, 2008).

Laskier M., *North African Jewry in the Twentieth Century: The Jews of Morocco, Tunisia and Algeria* (New York: New York University Press, 1994).

Laskier M., *The Jews of Egypt, 1920–1970* (New York: New York University Press, 1992).

Levin I., *Confiscated wealth: the fate of Jewish property in Arab lands*, Policy Forum 22, Institute of the World Jewish Congress, 2000.

Levin I., *Locked Doors: The Seizure of Jewish Property in Arab Countries* (Westport, CT: Praeger, 2001).

Lewis B., *Semites and Anti-Semites: An Inquiry into Conflict and Prejudice* (New York: Norton, 1986).

Lewis B., *The Jews of Islam* (Princeton, NJ: Princeton University Press, 2014).

Ludovitch A. and Valensi L., *The last Arab Jews: The Communities of Jerba, Tunisia* (London: Harwood, 1984).

Luzon R., *Libyan Twilight* (London: Darf, 2016).

Meddeb A. and Stora B., *Encyclopaedia of Jewish-Muslim Relations from their Origins to the Present Day* (Princeton, NJ: Princeton University Press, 2013).

Memmi A., *Portrait d'un Juif* (Paris: Gallimard, 1962).

Memmi A., *La Statue de Sel* (Paris: Gallimard, 1966).

Memmi A., *Portrait du décolonisé* (Paris: Gallimard, 2004).

Meir-Glitzenstein E., *Zionism in an Arab Country: Jews in Iraq in the 1940s* (London: Routledge, 2004).

Morad T., Shasha D. and Shasha R., *Iraq's Last Jews* (New York: Palgrave Macmillan, 2008).

Moreh S. and Yehuda Z., *Al-Farhud: The 1941 Pogrom in Iraq* (Jerusalem: Hebrew University Magnes Press, 2010).

Musée d'Art et d'Histoire du Judaïsme, *Juifs d'Algérie* (Paris: Flammarion, 2012).

Nisan M., *Minorities in the Middle East: A History of Struggle and Self-Expression.* (London: McFarland & Company, 1991).

Patai R., *The Arab Mind* (New York: Hatherleigh, 2002).

Rahmani M., *L' éxode oublié: Juifs des Pays Arabes* (Paris: Raphaël, 2003).

Rejwan N., *The Jews of Iraq* (London: Weidenfeld & Nicolson, 1985).

Roumani M., *The Jews of Libya: Coexistence, Persecution, Resettlement* (Portland, OR: Sussex Academic Press, 2008).

Roumani M., *The Jews from Arab Countries: A Neglected Issue* (Tel Aviv: World Organisation of Jews from Arab Countries (WOJAC,1983).

Rubin B. and Schwanitz W., *Nazis, Islamists and the Making of the Modern Middle East* (New Haven, CT: Yale University Press, 2014).

Russell G., *Heirs to the Forgotten Kingdoms* (London: Simon & Schuster UK, 2014).

Said E., *Orientalism* (New York: Pantheon Books, 1978).

Sansal B., *An Unfinished Business* (London: Bloomsbury, 2008).

Sabar A., *My Father's Paradise* (Chapel Hill, US: Algonquin, 2009).

Satloff R., *Among the Righteous* (New York: Public Affairs, 2006).

Sebbar L. (ed.), *Une enfance juive en Méditerranée musulmane* (Auvergne: Bleu autour, 2012).

Shabi R., *Not the Enemy: Israel's Jews from Arab Lands* (New Haven, CT: Yale, 2009).

Shamash V., *Memories of Eden* (UK: Forum, 2008).

Shiblak A., *Iraqi Jews, A History of the Mass Exodus* (London: Saqi, 2005).

Schulze K.E., *The Jews of Lebanon: between coexistence and conflict* (Brighton: Sussex Academic Press, 2001).

Shulewitz M. (ed.), *The Forgotten Millions* (London: Continuum, 2000).

Sitton D., *Sephardic Communities Today* (Jerusalem: Council of Sephardi and Oriental Communities, 1985).

Sofer D., *The Septembers of Shiraz* (London: Picador, 2007).

Stillman N., *The Jews of Arab Lands: A History and Source Book*, Vols I & II (Philadelphia, PA: Jewish Publication Society of America, 1979).

Stora B., *Les Trois Exils des Juifs d'Algérie* (Paris: Stock, 2006).

Trigano S., *La Fin du Judaïsme en Terres d'Islam* (Paris: Denoël, 2009).

Weinstock N., *Histoire de Chiens: La Dhimmitude dans le Conflit Israélo-Palestinien* (Paris: Mille et Une Nuits, 2004).

Weinstock N., *Une Si Longue Présence: Comment le Monde Arabe a perdu ses Juifs 1947–1967* (Paris: Plon, 2008).

Yehuda Z. (ed.), *Tombs of Saints and Synagogues in Babylonia* (Or Yehuda: The Babylonian Jewry Heritage Center, 2006).

Index

(Bold page numbers denote photographs)

1948 War xix, 104, 244

Abbas, Mahmoud 164
Abda, Lilian 108–9
Abdullah, King of Jordan 8
Abitbol, Michel 55
Abu Rudeis oil fields 155, 177, 178
Achcar, Gilbert 72, 236
Aciman, André 27, 108, 205
Acre, Steve 289–91
Aden 60, 87, 126, 128, 129, **130**, 272, 308–
    10
Ades, Shafiq 107, 136
Aflaq, Michel 12
airlifts xxi, 142, **148**, 152, **170**, 173, 181,
    196
Aix Group 172
Al-Qaeda 95
Aladdin Project 236, 237
Albanians, code of honour and 237
Alexandria 16, 21, 25, 86, **100**, 110
    Jewish property and 176–7, 179, 181,
        185
Algeria xxi, 24, 31, 48, 70–2, 279
    anti-Semitism and 68, 69, 72
    FLN and 69, 72
    France and 54, 55, 71
    French citizenship and 58–9
    independence and 69, 71
    Jews and 69, 71, 173
    music and 65
    nationality code and 107
    pro-Nazi propaganda 104
Allam, Magdi Cristiano xi, 18
Alliance Israélite Universelle (AIU) 11, 53–
    4, 56, **57**, **64**, **68**, 112, 172, 211, **235**
Almohads 35, 37, 38, 139
Amazighen 11, 144, 254
American Jewish Committee 107–8
American Joint Distribution Committee
    xx–xxi, 149
Amir, Eli xxiii, 199, 206

Anglo-American Committee of Enquiry
    232
Anglo-Egyptian financial agreement 176
Anglo-Jewish Association 53–4
anti-Jewish hostility x, 55, 57, 68, 87, 103,
    112, 138
anti-Jewish incidents 59, 87–8, 93, 103, 126
    see also pogroms; riots
anti-Semitism xv, xxv, 53, 74, 96, 107, 121,
    125
    Arab nationalism and 100
    Arab-Israeli conflict and 246–7, 249
    Arabs and 230, 231, 232, 235
    Christians and 81
    colonial 67–70
    ex-Nazi war criminals and 107
    Islam and 38
    Morocco and 33, 140
    Muslims and 80–1, 86–7, 94, 229
    Palestinian nationalism and 104
    perception of 232, 255
    poor Jews and 33–4
    propaganda 55, **56**
    Zionism as solution to 125, 235
anti-Zionism 11, 110, 204, 229, 256
apartheid 163, 230
Arab conquest 7–8, 10, 247
Arab countries
    anti-Jewish measures and 133
    collaboration and 131
    ethnic cleansing and xxi, 73
    Jewish history in 227
    Jewish property losses and 171–2
    Jews and 27, 164, 229, 231, 236, 252
    Jews, mass displacement of 226, 234,
        243
    Nazi war criminals and 95, 107, 237
    pro-Nazi sentiment and 86
    Right of Return and 157
    UN and 133
    see also Jewish refugees, Arab countries
        and

'Arab Jews' 25, 122, 206, 211, 230, 235, 238
Arab League xix, 104, 128, 129, 141, 244
    Draft Law (1947) 265–6
    Plan, Jewish citizens and 131, 132–3
    Political Committee of 129, 131–2, 169
    property claims, refugees and 159
    Zionists and 129, 131
Arab nationalism 12, 71, 94, 100, 102, 103,
    207, 236, 251
Arab Peace Initiative 151
Arab Revolt 83, 87, 115, 134
Arab Spring xiv, 18, 74, 174, 229, 254, 256
Arab-Israeli conflict xvii, xviii, xxi, 104,
    123, 137
    anti-Semitism as root cause 246–7
    Arab narrative of 238
    coexistence projects and 42
    first war 128, 131, 151
    perception of 230
    refugees and 149, 155, 160
    see also Six Day War
'Arab-Jewish' identity 200, 205, 211
Arab-Nazi wartime alliance 230, 246
Arabic 11, 12, 35, 36, 57, 228
    Jews and 42, 199, 200, 206, 215, 216,
    232
Arabism 100
Arabs 256
    dispossession 188
    Holocaust and 84
    identity 12, 248
    of the Jewish faith 204–6, 234
    literacy and 55
    refugees, Palestine and xiv, xviii
    shame/honour code 43, 249
    see also Palestinian Arabs
Arafat, Yasser 154, 238
Aramaic 11, 203, 206
Armenians xvii 21, 59, 89, 110, 127, 255
Ashkenazi Jews xvii, 10, 43, 153, 203, 216,
    236
    dominance of 213, 227
    'false Messiah' and 50, 80
    intermarriage in Israel 157
    Jerusalem site purchased by 186
    Mizrahi and 200, 208, 211
    perception of 200, 205, 254
Ashrawi, Hanan 119, 120
Assyrian Christians xxv, 127, 207, 252, 254
Assyrians xvii, 250, 251, 276
Ataturk 248, 251

Ayalon, Danny 119, 121, 162
Azoulay, André 143

Babylon 6, 8, 9, 206
Babylonian Jews 59
Baghdad ix 7, 16, 18, **19**
    Jews and xiii, xxiv, 6, 27, 29, 31, 137,
    174
    see also Farhud
al-Baghdadi, Abu Bakr 53, 95
Baha'is 252, 259
Bahrain xix, 5, 61, 128, 129
Balfour Declaration 83, 87, 101, 110, 123,
    128
    Egypt and 112, 114
al-Banna, Hassan 82, **82**, 86–7, 94
Bashkin, Orit 235–6
Bechor, Guy 133
Bedouin 11, 34, 61, 206, 292
Begin, Menahem 177, 207, 208
Beinin, Joel 107–8
Beirut xi, 131, 172, 180, 234, **235**
Ben Ali, Zine el-Abidine 225–6
Ben Zvi, Yitzhak 199, 216
Ben-Gurion, David 197, 202, 211, 212, 216
Ben-Porat, Mordechai xxiii, 123, 171
Benjamin, J.J. 49
Bensoussan, Georges 26, 50, 56, 125
Benvenisti, Meron 216
Berber Jews **142**, 206
Berbers 6, 11, 35, 37, 51, 251, 254
    Jews, rainmaking and 52
    Judaism and 71
Berman, Paul 37
Bibas, Yehuda 10, 203
Bigio family 180–1, **180**
bigotry 94, 95, 230
Bismuth, Roger 225–6
Biton Report 162, 214, 227
Black Lives Matter 208
Black Panther movement 207
blood libels xi, 58, 80, 124, 126, 203
'blowback' 123
bombings 108, 122–3, 126
Bostom, Andrew 79, 80
Boukhobsa, Chochana 199
Boum, Aomar 53, 141, 253
boycotts, Jews and 83, 88, 105, 142
British army 86, 89, 126, 223
British government 54, 110, 123
Brooks, J.W., Revd 139, 280–1

Bukharan Jews 203, 206, 217
al-Bukhari, Sahih 80, 81
Burkhardt, J.L. 50
Busnach affair 54, **54**
Byzantine Orthodox 6, 7

Cairo 12, 58, 62, 83, 86, 110, 114
    Groppi Café **29**, 31
    Jewish property **109**, 171, 174, **175**,
        176, 180, 181, 234
    Jews and ix, x, xi, 12, 16, **26**, 62, 72–3,
        86
Calamaro, Lucy 170–1
Camp David II 178, 185, 267
Camp David peace talks 154, 172
Camp David Treaty 177
Canada 122, 151, 160–1, 180, 212
Casablanca xi, **17**, 87, 124, 140, 141, 143,
    144, **257**
Castro family 114, 169, 174, 176
Cattaoui family 62, 174
Chaldean Christians xvii, 207, 252
Chemla, Jean-Pierre 298–301
Chemla, Véronique 236–7
Christian Palestinians 163
Christians/Christianity 8, 12, 13, 38, 139,
    247–8, 252
    anti-Semitism and 81
    Arab Christians 207, 256
    dhimma system and 7, 48
    evil and 53
    exodus from Middle East xiv, xxv, 18
    Islam/Muslims and 41, 50, 80, 248
    Jews and 37, 80
    massacres and 127
    persecution and 248, 259
    as proxies for the West 125
    Reconquista 37
    Saladin and 39
chtaka 61
Cicurel family **109**, 176, 306
Circassians 8, 61, 127
citizenship x, 107
    Jews and xxii, xxiii, xxv, 59, 101, 104,
        105, 109, 120, 132
    Palestinian refugees and 149, 163–4, 246
    see also French citizenship
Clinton, Bill 154, 178, 185, 246, 267
clothing
    dhimmis and 202–3
    Jews and 7, 49, 61

Coca-Cola 180, 181
coexistence 25, 34, 37, 41, 61–2, 104, 107,
    123, 143, 233, 242
    Golden Age of 237
    Mediterranean model of 205
    projects/initiatives 42–4, 208, 209, 232,
        234, 236
Cohen, Edy 182
Cohen, Hillel 112
Cohen, Mark 37–8, 43
Cohen, Ran 121–2, 155
Cole, Peter 36
collective punishment 108, 123–4, 125
colonial rule 61–2, 126, 250, 254
    Jews and 55, 56–7, 59–60, 67–70
colonialism 231, 237
colonisation 53, 244, 247–50
    Arab conquest 7–8, 10, 247
    European 49, 55, 60, 67–70, 71,
        231, 247
    Middle East, Islam and 19
'colonisation of the facts' 228, 229, 231,
    238, 247
Copts xvii, 6, 94, 207, 251, 252, 255
Cotler, Irwin 133, 149, 159, 242
Cox, Sir Percy 59
Crusades/Crusaders 10, 38, 39
Cumming, Major-General Duncan 94
Curiel, Henri 121, 174, **175**

Da'esh xxv, 14, 53, 95, 190, 248, 253 (see
    also Islamic State)
Daghestan, Jews of 8
Dahan, Momi 213
Damascus 14–15, **15**, 103, 127, 171, 172,
    179
Damascus Blood libel xi, 124, 126
Dangoor, Naim 153, 179
Day of Remembrance xiv
decolonisation 57, 69, 70, 109, 228
Décret Crémieux 58, 59, 68, 69, 71
Deek, George 256, 259
denial xiv, xxv, 190, 247, 300
    dhimmi denial 229
    Holocaust denial 26, 95, 96, 236, 243,
        250
    Jewish denial 26–7, 225, 232
    of national minorities 250–2
'desert generation' xxiii
dhimma system 7, 8–9, 11, 48–9, 61, 72, 80
dhimmi denial 229

dhimmi syndrome 27, 38, 44, 224, 225
dhimmis 7, 26, 35, 50–1, 202–3, 281–2
dhimmitude 4, 8, 79, 101, 248
    Jews and 8, 58–9, 79
    liberation from 53–8
Dhu al-Kifl (prophet) 4, 5, 13
diaspora xx, 6, 9, 136, 157, 202, 206, 211, 237
    Ashkenazi-dominated xvii, 159–60, 226
discrimination xxv 72, 128, 211–13
    Christians and 48, 50
    Israel and 211, 254
    Jews and 50, 58, 61, 132
Djerba 10, 40, 202, 277
Doomsday Hadith 80–1
Douek, Ellis 58, 119, 205–6
Dror, Duki (film-maker) 227
Drumont, Edouard 55, **56**

Eastern European Jews 199, 211
education
    Arab nationalism and 102
    arabisation of 105, 107
    Israel and 200, 227–8
    Jews and 55, 56, 57, 67, 136, 137, 202
    see also Alliance Israélite Universelle
Egypt xix, 6, 270–1
    anti-Semitic measures and 107
    Balfour Declaration and 112, 114
    banks and 182
    citizenship 59, 101, 109
    dhimmitude, abolition of 101
    Israel and 110, 155, 177
    Israel, peace agreement and 243, 250
    Jewish heritage and 16, 184–5
    Jewish immigrants and 114
    Nasser's policy and 109–10
    nationality laws and 105, 109
    non-Muslims and 101
    pogroms 83, 94
    property confiscations 174–82
    Suez crisis and 70, 108
    Zionists and 112, 114, 115
Egyptian Jews **xxii**, 25–6, 27, 28–9, 62, 72–3
    arrest as 'Israeli POWs' 72, 125
    bombings and 126
    businesses and 62, 108, 109
    citizenship and 59, 101
    dispossession and 174–82, 243
    Eretz Yisrael and 121

    expulsion of xxii–xxiii, xxiv, xxv, 108–9, 123
    injustice and 156
    multilingualism and 205
    nationality laws and 105
    Operation Susannah and 108, 123
    passports and xxiii, 73, 101
    refugee status and 120
    transit camps and 199
    travel bans 107
    Zionism and 114, 121
Eichmann, Adolph 90, 95
Elbaz, Penina xxi, 33, 103, 125, 282–4
Ellis, Samantha 25, 27
emigration
    Jews and 58, 139–40
    see also immigrants
Encyclopaedia of Jewish-Muslim Relations 238
Enlightenment, the 53, 81, 202, 214
Eretz Yisrael 9, 10, 40, 121, 202, 204
Esses, Joseph Avraham 304–5
ethnic cleansing xviii, 14, 104, 251, 252, 277
    Jews and x, xiv, xxi, xxv, 35, 73, 133, 244
European Jews ix, xi, 36, 85, 93, 138–9, 200, 209, 218, 230, 254
European Union, immigrants and 196
European Union Commission 172
evil
    Christians and 41, 53
    Jews and 41, 53, 83, 96, 249
executions
    Jews and xiii, xxiv, 27, 133, 134, 135–6, 137, 227
    see also massacres
exilarchs 7
extermination plans 84, 89–93
    see also concentration camps
Ezekiel (Yehézqʾel) 3–4
Ezekiel's shrine **1–3**, **5**, 13, **20**, 190, **256**
    Jews and 4, 13–14
    Muslims and 4, 5, 13

Facebook 25, 214
Faisal, Emir 102, **102**, 112
Faisal-Weizmann Agreement 112
Fanon, Frantz 51
Fanonism 255
Farhi, Hayim 50

Farhud 34, 41, 60, 89, **90**, 102, 103, 104, 124, 128, 134
  awareness of 227
  memories of 289–91
  Muslims and 223–4
  survivors of 223–4
Fascists 59, 88, 103, 225, 278
Fattal, Salim 33–4, 223–4, 314
Feast of the Sacrifice (Eid al-Adha) 1
Fellous, Colette 28, 157–8
Fenton, Paul 38, 140
Fernández-Morera, Darío 7
Fez
  Jews of 8, 40
  pogrom 51, 124, **124**, 140, 238
films/film-making 62, **63–4**, 65, 67, 227
Fischbach, Michael 127, 178–9
Fox, Camille xxiii, **69**
France 54, 57, 94, 205, 238
  protectorates 59, 68, 140
French citizenship, Jews and 58–9, 68, 69, 71, 84, 140
Friedman, Matti 218, 253
Front de Libération Nationale (FLN) 69, 72
Futuwwa (youth brigade) 89, 103, 104

Gabay, Dina 141
Gabès pogrom 33, 60, 124
Gaddafi, Muammar 173, 181, 276
Gal, Meir **214**, 227
Gamliel, Gila 162–3
Gaza 95, 164, 186, 188
Geniza records 12, 48, **184**
genocide 127, 243, 255
  Jews and 43, 84, 89, 96
German Jews 55, 236
Germany xx, 5, 86, 89, 101, 129, 133
  Holocaust victims, claims and 178
  Iraqis and 102–3, 223
Ghardaïa 51, 58, 59
Gibraltar 58, 140
Gilbert, Sir Martin 229, **263**, **264**
Goiten, S.D. 87
Golan Heights 188, 273
Goldberg, Arthur 149, 156
Goshen, Eti Sionit 315–18
Gourgey, Percy xiii
Graetz, Heinrich 37
Greece xviii, 54, 110, 203
Greek Orthodox Christians 80, 94, 207

Habbani tribe **xix**, 8
Hachuel, Solika 232, **233**
Haddad, Heskel 51, 171, 174
Hague Convention 184
Hakkakian, Roya 210–11
Hamagen (The Shield) 42
Hamas xxiv, 81, 94, 95, 162, 252
Hanin, Roger 24, 25
Harif xv, 160, **160**
Haroun, Magda 72, 73
Haroun, Shehata 72–3
Harris, Maurice 141
Hassan II, King of Morocco 143, 144
Hayoun, Victor 33
Hebrew 11, 35, 36, 57, 112, 199, 203
  restrictions and 102, 105
Hebron 9, 13, 50, 188, 285
  massacre 41, 60
Herf, Jeffrey 82–3, 84, 229
Heskel, Sir Sasson 18, **19**, 62
Hezbollah 248
Hillah 1, 4, 14
Hillel, Shlomo 122, 127
Himmler, Heinrich 90, 104
Hindus 6, 13, 126
Hirst, David 122
Hitler, Adolf 90, **91**, 103
  Mein Kampf 53, 87, 134
Holocaust Memorial Day 96
Holocaust xiv, 120, 201, 202
  Arabs and 84, 143, 249
  denial of 95, 96, 236, 249–50
  European guilt and 255
  museums 230
  Palestinian *Nakba*, comparison and 228, 229, 237, 249
  schools and 227
  survivors xxiii, 157, 291–3
human rights 159–61, 164, 242–3, 252–3, 255
al-Husri, Sati 12, 102
Hussein, Saddam 27, 181, 182, 190, 209
al-Husseini, Haj Amin (Grand Mufti) 87, 88, **90**, **91**, 102, 230, 238
  anti-Semitism and 246
  extermination plans 89–93

immigrants 11, 114, 201, 212–13
  EU and 196
  Israel and xxiv, 119, 121, 152, 157, 159, 196, 203–4

India xviii, 3, 6, 55, 58, 94, 126, 243, 272
indigenous peoples xvii, 6, 7, 10, 48, 70, 71,
    208, 216, 231
    rights and 252–3, 254, 255
International League Against Racism and
    Antisemitism 60
intersectionality 208
intra-Arab conflicts 243, 259
Iran xiv, xv, 38, 95, 96, 251
    Jews and xv, 210–11, 233, 252, 315–18
    Muslim Brotherhood and 95
Iraq xix, xxi, 49, 133–7, 276–7
    anti-Jewish sentiment 103, 112
    anti-Semitism and 102
    Ba'ath regime xiii, 181
    bombings and 122
    communal property rights, Jews and
        182
    Communist Party 205
    emigrés and 102
    Futuwwa (youth brigade) 89, 103, 104
    Israel and 152
    Jewish history of 13–14
    Jews and xiii, xxii, xxiii, xxiv, 5, 6, 59,
        112
    Kurds and 18
    Mashhad al-Shams shrine 1
    massacre of Assyrian Christians 127
    Muslim graduates and 57
    nationalism 101
    Nazi influence 134
    Palestinian Arabs and 152
    Palestinian refugees, rehousing and
        172
    pro-Nazi government 88–9, 104, 237
    Property Claims Commission 181
    refugee exchange proposal 151–2
    religious persecution and 58
    school curriculum, Nazification of 102
    UN Partition Plan for Palestine and
        129
    US invasion of 153
    Yazidis, treatment of 253
    see also Farhud
Iraqi Jews 18, 25, 33–4, 49, 101–2, 256,
    313–15
    denationalisation of 152
    Denaturalisation Bill and 136
    dispossession/compensation and 179,
        182, 243
    Eretz Yisrael and 121

executions 27, 133, 134, 135–6, 137,
    227
exodus of 27, 119–20, 122, 173, 197,
    223, 310–12
identity and 206
Israel and 199, 230, 255
laissez-passers and **106**
memorial to **228**
nationality and 105
property confiscations and 172–3, 174
restrictions and 136–7
trauma and 209
Zionism and 134, 135
Iraqi Muslims 40, 101
Iraqi-Jewish archive 182–4, 190, 243
Islam 6, 12, 13, 50–1, 81–2, 251
    anti-Semitism and 38
    apostasy and 8
    Arab identity and 12, 248
    Arab states and 248
    Christian conversions to 80
    Christianity and 12, 38
    fundamentalism 10, 81, 82, 247
    Jews, first massacre of 79
    Judaism and 12, 80
    mass apostasy of Jews 38
    religious restrictions and 132
    religious tolerance and 35, 36–7
    sectarian conflicts and 18
Islamic State xxv, 14, 95, 190, 228, 248, 253
    (see also Da'esh)
Islamism 247, 248
Islamophobia 226, 229
Israel Defense Forces (IDF) 44
Israel Democracy Institute 211
Israel xiv, 6, 43, 44, 58, 217, 259
    aliyah (immigration) 120, 121, 203
    ancestral homeland 9, 121, 157, 202,
        247, 253, 254
    Arab dispossession and 188–9
    Arab population 164
    Arts Commission 227
    bombing project and 108
    Central Bureau of Statistics 231
    compensation costs and 172
    creation of State of Israel 123, 129
    cultural wars 214–15
    Declaration of Independence 44
    discrimination and 211, 254
    education and **214**, 227–8
    Egypt and 110, 155

Egypt, peace agreement and 243, 250
Egyptian-Jewish refugees and 178–9
elitists 214, 215
Farhud survivors' stipend 89
immigrants and 119, 121, 157, 196,
    211–13
integration/intermarriage 157, 213
Iran and 95, 96
Iraq and 152
Jewish refugees and 154–5
kibbutzim xxiii, 199
kizzuz policy 153, 154, 170
Knesset xiv, 161, 162, 178, 196, 244,
    270
Labour party 208, 214, 216, 236
land ownership and 188–9
military intelligence 123
Ministry of Justice 169, 170, 177, 226
minorities and 255
national ethos 155
'one-state solution', Muslims and 252
Oslo accords and 154
Palestinian Arabs and xviii
Palestinian compensation demands
    154
Palestinian refugees, resettlement and
    152
perception of 70, 230, 231, 242, 255
racism and 200, 230
refugee claims and 169–71, 244
'refugee-washing' accusation 119
refugees and xxiii, xxiv, 119, 120–1,
    153, 154–6, 157, 169–70, 178–9
Shas party 161, 162, 213
Sinai, invasion of 108
two-state solution/model 161, 245
WOJAC and 159
Zionist immigrants and 121–2
Israel-Egypt Friendship Association 178
Israel-Palestine conflict 228, 229, 246
Israeli Custodian of Absentee Property 188
Italian colonials 59, 94, 275, 291
Italians 110
Italy 84, 88, 93, 171, 275, 278

Jamali, Fadel 102–3, 129
Jerusalem xviii, 10, 50
    East Jerusalem 185, 186, 187, 189, 204
    Jews expelled from 6, 128, 185, 186, 188
    JNF land purchases and 188
    Jordanian occupation of 185, 186, 188

land ownership and 186, 187, 188
    Shimon Hatzaddik's tomb 186, **187**
    West Jerusalem 185
Jewish Agency 196, 201
Jewish heritage 189–91
    Egypt and 184–5
    erasure of 14–18, 190–1
    Iraq and 182–4, 189, 190
    Morocco and 17, 143, 234
    restoration and 17, 143, 189–90, 225,
        234
    Syria and 14–15, 189
Jewish history, Arab countries and 13–14,
    227
Jewish National Fund (JNF) 188
Jewish refugees
    Arab countries and xiii–xiv, xv, 119–20,
        121–2, 157–9, 231
    assets/property losses 171
    claims and 154, 158–9
    compensation and 154, 161, 162, 169,
        244, 246
    as core issue in peace talks 161–3
    cultural differences and 199
    French culture and 205
    human rights and 159–61, 164, 165,
        242–3
    Israel and 153, 154–6, 157
    nation-building and 199
    number of 229
    policy of *kizzuz* and 153
    recognition of 151, 156
    rights and 155, 158–9
    UN and 148, 149, 153, 162
    UNHCR and 120, 149
    Western coverage and 229
    WOJAC and 159
Jewish women, Muslim men and 52
Jews
    animalisation of 51
    Arab League Plan and 131, 132–3
    characteristics 43
    mass apostasy to Islam 38
    Muslim perception of 40–1, 51–2
    Muslim women and 52
    perception of 6, 52, 126
    scapegoating and 128–32
    Shi'a perception of 4
    status 8–9
    violation of rights 131, 132, 142
jihad 7, 38, 80, 81, 95, 247

jihadists 14, 73, 83, 249
JIMENA 160
jizya 8, 48, 55, 61, 139, 248
Johnson, Paul 43–4, 215, 216
Jordan xviii, xix, 128, 129, 163, 172, 250
Jordanian Custodian of Enemy Property
    188
Judaism 9–11, 71, 202–4
    Islam and 12, 50, 80
Judeo-Arabic dialect 11, 217, 227, 228
Judeo-Islamic tradition 10
Justice for Jewish Refugees from Arab
    Countries Conference 162
Justice for Jews from Arab Countries
    (JJAC) 119, 121, 154, 155, 159, 164,
    169, 178, 209, 242

Kadoorie, Sir Elly **57**
Kadoorie, Laura **57**, **64**, 172
Kahina, Queen 71
Kahn, Michelle Devorah 304–5
Kattan, Naim 29, 31, 101–2, 216
Kerry, John 185
Khaybar 79, 80
Khazzoom, Loolwa 210
Khomeini, Ayatollah 94, 95
Kisch, Frederick H. 114
Klarsfeld, Serge 237
Kosansky, Oren 40
Küntzel, Matthias 80–1, 83, 84, 94, 96, 250
Kurdish Jews 51, 206, 211, 212
Kurdistan 9, 254
Kurds 9, 11, 18, 127, 250, 251, 254, 255

labour camps 84, 85, 92, 138, 278
    see also Nazi concentration camps
Lagnado, Lucette **26**
laissez-passer documents xxiii, **106**, 109
land ownership
    compensation, Arabs and 188–9
    Israel and 188
    in Jerusalem 186, 187, 188–9
    Jordanian occupation and 188
Landes, Richard 43
languages 11, 57
    see also Arabic; Aramaic; Hebrew;
        Judeo-Arabic dialect
Lavon Affair 123, 173 (see Operation
    Susannah)
Lazarus, Clemy 212, 301–3
Lebanon xxi, 94, 129, 247, 248, 273–4

Arab League and 128, 133
citizenship and 105
Jewish organisations and 105
Lewis, Bernard 36–7, 53, 79, 80, 251
Libya xix, 275–6
    anti-Jewish incidents and 59, 103
    boycotts, Jews and 105
    deportation of Jews 84
    Giado camp 84
    Italian colonials and 59
    Jewish heritage and 16
    Jewish property sequestered 173
    Jews and xxii, xxiii, **30**, 74, **92**, 93, 105,
        120, 152, 181, 198
    pogrom 41, 60, 93
    riots xxii, 93–4
    Sabbath crisis 59
    travel bans, Jews and 107
Likud 207, 208
Lindt, August 120, 149
Livornese Jews 58
Luzon, Raphael xxiii, 74, 198, 318–19

Macias, Enrico 24, 69, 212–13
Madrid Peace Conference 156
Maghreb xix, 38, 40, 49, 54, 71
Maghrebi Jews 202, 205
Maimonides, Moses 10, 11, 35, 37, 39–40,
    139, 234, 238
Malik, Charles H. 133
Mandaeans xvii, 7, 252
Mangoubi, Rami 319–22
Maronite Christians xvii, 207, 247–8
Martin, Paul 151, 160
Marx, Karl 50
Mashhad al-Shams shrine 1, 2
massacres xi 11, 38, 39, 79, 124, 127, 140
    see also executions
Mecca 4, 41, 53, 290
Medina 79
Meir, Khatoun **30**
Meknes 87–8
Melkite Greek Catholics 207
Memmi, Albert 31–3, 34, 38–9, 61, 86, 235,
    248
Menocal, María Rosa 35
Menuhin, Linda 227
Mesopotamia 6, 13
Messiah, the xxi, 4, 125, 202
Metzger family 180
Michael, Sami 25, 200, 208

Middle East
  academic studies and 229–30
  Christian exodus xiv, xxv, 18
  Christians, treatment of 255
  coexistence projects 42–3
  displacement of Jews xiv, xvii, 231
  exodus of Jews post-1948 104
  Islam's colonisation of 19
  Jewish history and 227
  Jewish population 5, 6, 55
  Jewish schools, arabisation of 105, 107
  Jews and 10, 18
  non-Muslim communities and 8
  peace process 243
  political rights and 250
  Radio Berlin and 88
  travel bans 107
  university expulsions, Jews and 105
  Western views of 230
minorities 250–2, 255
  persecution of 127–8, 255, 259
Mizrahi Democratic Rainbow Coalition
  200
Mizrahi Jews xvii, xxv, 43, 153, 162–3, 196–
  9, 207–8, 210
  Arabs and 236
  Ashkenazi and 200, 208, 211, 214
  culture 211–12, 214, 217–18, 226
  culture, suppression of 200–2
  forgotten exodus and 236
  history textbooks and **214**, 227
  intermarriage in Israel 157, 213
  Israel and 216
  peace initiatives, absence from 209
  perception of 199, 205, 217, 226, 234
  poverty and 226
  transit camps and 196
  Zionism and 200, 201, 202, 205
Mohammed V, Sultan 85, **138**, 141
Mongols 11
Montefiore, Sir Moses 53
Moreh, Shmuel 27, 51, 101, 199, 203, 245
Moroccan Jews 26, 28–9, **32**, 33, 40, 49–50,
  137–44
  compensation and 185
  conversions and 139
  discrimination and 225
  emigration and 139–40, 173–4, 224–5
  French citizenship and 140
  Israel and 197–8
  Jerusalem and 58

  Muslim views on 40, 139, 141
  passports and 142, 143
  Petit-Jean massacre and 140
  ransom, Operation Yakhin and 142
  rights and 253
  slavery and 51
  travel restrictions 107, 142
  violation of civil rights 142
Morocco World News 232
Morocco xix, xxi, xxiv, 59, 61, 137–44,
  274–5
  airlifts and xxi, 142
  anti-Jewish hostility 103, 140
  anti-Jewish violence 87–8
  anti-Semitism and 33, 140
  Arab League and 141
  Arab-Jewish coexistence 234
  boycott of Jewish merchants 105
  confiscation of Jewish wealth 125–6
  dhimmi rules and 61, 139
  French protectorate 140
  independence and 107
  Jewish heritage and 17–18, 143, 234
  Jewish population 5, 18, 137, 232
  Jewish tourists and 143
  Jewish-Arab heritage 232
  Muslim Brotherhood and 142
  nationalism 103
  pogroms 60, 138, 140
  school curriculum, arabisation of 142
  Vichy rule and 84, 138
  wartime labour camps 85, 138–9
  World War II and 85, 86
  Zionism and 140, 141
Morris, Benny 77n77, 122
Mossad xxi, 72, 103, 122, 123, 171, 215
Muallem, Samir 170–1
Muhammad (Prophet) 19, 49, 79, 81, 91
music/musicians 62, 65, **66**, 217–18, **217**
Muslim Brotherhood 82–4, 86–7, 94–5,
  104
  bombing of Baghdad synagogue 122
  Egypt and 115, 126
  Morocco and 142
  Nazism and 86–7
  Palestinian branch 104
Muslim SS divisions 93
Muslims
  anti-*dhimmi* prejudice 249
  anti-Semitism and 80–1
  British army and 86

'Doomsday Hadith' and 80–1
Ezekiel's shrine and 4
Free French army and 86
Jewish women and 52
killings of 127
minorities and 248–9, 250–2
non-Muslim wives and 8
non-Muslims, attitude towards 79, 251
perception of Jews 40–1, 51–3, 249
tolerance and 35, 36–7, 248, 251

Nahmias, Teddy 287–9
Nahmias, Victor 132, 244
najas (unclean) 4, 49
Nakache, Alfred ix, **67**
Nakbas (catastrophes) 244
Jewish, suppression of 231–2
Jewish xiv, 149, 226, 230
Palestinian 149, 155, 161, 209, 227, 228, 229–30, 249
Naldrett-Jays, George 70, 110
Nasser, Gamal Abdel 12, 94, 108, 109–10, 123, 141, 169, 180
Nawi, David 153, 179
Nazi concentration camps
Auschwitz ix, **67**, 291
Bergen-Belsen ix, 84, **92**, 93
see also labour camps
Nazi Germany xx, 107, 133
Arab alliance with 86, 89, 230, 246
Nazis xx, 7, 26, 41, 43, 70, 92–3, 107–8
extermination plans and 84
Iraq and 88–9, 103
'Jewish denial' and 225
Jews, French citizenship and 84
Mufti's collaboration with 89–93
Nuremberg party congress 103
Palestine, collaboration and 112, 244
Palestinian Arabs and 86
war criminals 95, 107, 237
Nazism 81, 82, 83, 84, 236
legacy of 93–4, 95, 236
pan-Arab racism and 104
Nehmad, Aharon 284–6
Netanyahu, Benjamin 161, 209, 214
New York Times 129, **130**, 232
Niddam, Jean-Claude 226
Nobel prize-winners 213
non-Muslims 251
Arab conquest and 7–8

Egypt and 101
emancipation of 55
persecution and 38
Tanzimat reforms and 55
North Africa 10
Christianity and 8, 38
collaboration with Axis powers 104
exodus of Jews post-1948 104
Islam's colonisation of 19
Jews and 5, 6, 10, 11, 55, 58, 71
Radio Berlin and 88
nostalgia 25–6, 28, 34, 230, 256

Obama, Barack 161
Operation Susannah (see Lavon Affair)
Oriental Jews 43
Orphans' Decree 87
Orsher, Gidi 214–15
Oslo Accords 154, 161
Other
ethnic cleansing of 252
intolerance of 249, 251, 252
Otherisation 83, 102
Ottoman Empire 11, 54, 55, 127, 203
collapse of 11, 81, 100, 128, 248, 250, 251
Jews and 11, 35, 40, 54, 58, 232
Oz, Amos 254

Pact of Omar 7, 48
Pakistan xv, xviii, 94, 126, 243, 252
Palestine
anti-Jewish riots 60
Arab refugees and xiv, xviii
Arab Revolt 83, 87, 134
Balfour Declaration and 110, 128
British authorities and 60
collaboration and 112, 244
Jewish property claims and 185–9
Jews and 6, 112
Jews, mass expulsion of 89
Muslim Brotherhood and 104
nationalism 104
Sephardi Jews, treatment of 50
UN Partition Plan xiv, xviii–xiv, 128–9, 135, 149, 244
Western perception of 255
Zionists and 112
Palestine Liberation Organization (PLO) 119, 156, 157, 238
'Palestine Papers' 188

Palestinian Arabs 131, 210, 244
  expulsion of 127
  Israel and 152–3
  Jewish migration to Israel and 244–5
  Jewish refugees and 119
  Nazis and 86, 87
  Zionists and 112, 128
Palestinian emigrés 102, 104
Palestinian refugees xiv, xviii, xxv, 43, 148,
    155, 228
  Arab states and 163
  citizenship and 149, 163–4, 246
  international aid and 149
  Iraq, rehousing and 172
  Palestinian leadership and 164
  property losses, value of 171–2
  refugee status in perpetuity 163, 246
  resettlement and 242, 246
  return and 243
  Right of Return and 156, 157, 163, 165,
    172, 245, 246
  UN and 148–9
Palestinian struggle 70, 71
pan-Arab nationalism 102, 248, 249, 250
pan-Arab racism 104
pan-Arabism 12, 112, 248
paramilitary youth movements 103–4
  see also Futuwwa
passports xxiii
  Israeli **150**
  Jews and 58, 59–60, 73, 101, 107, 140
  travel bans and 107
  Western 212
  see also laissez-passer documents
peace 250
  Egypt/Israel agreement 243, 250
  refugees and 243–6
  treaties 250
Perez, Victor (Young) 67, **67**
Perrault, Gilles 121, 143
persecution 37, 120, 128, 244
  Arab League plan and 132–3
  Christians and 248, 255
  Jews and xviii, 27, 33, 35, 37, 38, 48
  minorities and 127–8, 255, 259
  non-Muslims and 38
  see also executions; massacres;
    pogroms
Persia 3, 6, 11, 49
Persian Jews 49, 52, 61, 121, 203
Pharaonism 207

philo-Semitism 82, 85, 102, 115, 138
Phoenicianism 207
pieds noirs 55, 69, 70, 71
Piha, Avram 310–12
pilgrims/pilgrimages 15, 41, 53, 143, 186,
    319
  Ezekiel's shrine and 1, 2, 4
  Hajj 4, 290
pogroms xix 9, 32–3, 37, 38, 39, 41, 107
  Algeria and 60
  Egypt and 83, 94
  Libya and 93
  Morocco and 60, 138, 140
  post-WWII 93–4
  Tunisia and 60
  Turkey and 251
  see also Farhud; Fez, pogrom; Gabès
    pogrom
Point of No Return (blog) xv, 72, 284, 305
Polish Jews 254
post-colonialism 204–5, 209, 231, 234, 255
post-modern academics 235–6
post-modern trends 237–8
prejudice 128
  anti-*dhimmi* 61, 249
  Israel and xxv, 43, 200
  Jews and 51, 61, 70, 140, 226
  see also discrimination
propaganda 94, 104, 115, 157, 237
  Nazi **88**, 89, 91, 95, 124, 273
property
  dispossession of Jews 174–81
  losses, Palestinians and 171–2
  partial exchange of 172
property confiscations 132, 133, 141, 152,
    153, 169
  Arab criticism of 156
  Arab dispossession in Israel 188–9
  claims and 158–9, 169–71, 176–8,
    181–2
  class action and 153, 179
  compensation and 176, 180, 185, 243
  estimated value of 171
  international fund and 185, 246
  Iraqi government and 172–3, 181
  Jerusalem and 186, 187
  restitution and 179

Qur'an 4, 13, 79, 80, 81
Qutb, Sayyid 83, 94, 95

Rabat x, 87, 124, 283
racial laws, Italy and 84, 275, 278
racism 104, 114, 232, 254
    Israel and 200, 230
Rauff, Walter 84, 86
refugee camps 188
    see also transit camps
'refugee-washing' 119
refugees xviii, **111**
    compensation and 154, 156, 246
    families, dispersal of xxiii
    Iraqi exchange proposal 151–2
    Madrid Peace Conference and 156
    peace and 243–6
    Road Map to Middle East Peace and 156
    UN and 148
    UNHCR definition of 120, 244
Regev, Miri 214, 215
'replacement theology' 254
revisionist academics 223–4
Rhode, Harold 8–9
Rida, Rashid 82
Righteous Gentiles 41, 238
riots xix, xxii, xxiv, 15, 41, 54, 60, 124, 125
    Aden and 126, 128, 129, **130**, 308–10
    Bahrain and 129
    Europeans and 71
    Libya and 93–4, 128
    Morocco and 128
    Palestine and 60, 87
    Syria and 129
Romans xvii, 6, 14, 79
Rosen, Emanuel 170, 171
Rouleau, Eric 114–15, 121
Russian Jews 203, 217

Sabbath crisis 59
Sadat, Jehan 169, 174
Safed 9, 10, 40, 285
Said, Edward 50, 205, 230, 236, 255
Salafism 81, 82
Samama, Albert (Chikly) 65, **66**, 67
Sasson, Amou xiii
Sassoon, David 4, 5, 58
Sassoon, David Solomon 4
Satloff, Robert 26, 34, 144, 225
Saudi Arabia xix 81–2, 129
School of Oriental and African Studies
    (SOAS) 234, 235
Segev, Tom 122
segregation 31, 49

Sephardi Jews xvii, xxv, 6, 10, 11, 40, 43–4,
    153, 213–14
    diaspora and 226
    discrimination and 211
    forgotten exodus and 236
    Holyland and 203
    intermarriage and 213
    Israel and 216
    Jerusalem and 58
    Muslim rule in Palestine and 50, 80
    purchase of Jerusalem site 186
    traditions 212
    Zionist thought and 10
Sfez, Batto xi, 48, 54
Shabi, Rachel 200, 205
Shadow in Baghdad (documentary) 162,
    227
'shared culture' delusion 235–7
sharia law 48, 49, 87, 206, 246, 251, 252
Shavu'oth 4, 12, 223
Shi'a Islam 251, 252, 259
Shi'a *Wakf* 1, 4, 14
Shi'ites 1, 13–14, 49, 61, 94
Shohat, Ella Habiba 204, 205, 211, 236
shrines 12–13, **20**, 190
    destruction of 14
    Islamic State and 14
    Shimon Hatzaddik's tomb 186, **187**
    see also Ezekiel's shrine
Simon Wiesenthal Center 231, 232
Six Day War 72, 110, 125, 142, 149, 185, 188
slavery, Jews and 50, 51, 79
Smouha family 174, 176–7
Solomon, King 8, 73, 277
Somekh, Emil 293–8
Somekh, Sasson 25, 223, 224
Spain 10–11, **39**, 139
    Andalusia 35–6, 37, 238
    Christian *Reconquista* 37
    expulsion of Jews 6
    expulsion of Muslims 6
    Golden Age 10, 35–6, 37, 238
    Granada pogrom 37
    massacre of Jews 38
    tolerance and 35, 36–7
Spain/Granada 37, 38, 41
Spanish Inquisition 6, 35, 40, 71, 203
sports 67
Stewart, Jenny 305–7
Stiebel, Joan xiii
Stillman, Norman A. 235–6

Stora, Benjamin 31, 71–2
Suez crisis 70, 108, 110, 212
Sunni Islam xviii, 38, 81, 115, 251, 259
Sykes-Picot agreement 254
synagogues 14, **15**, 16, **184**, 185, **257–8**
    attacks on xi, 10, 83, 122
    Nebi Daniel **16**, **69**, **100**
    restoration of 17, 225, 234, 290
Syria xix, 86, 103, 128, 273–4
    Ba'ath Party 12, 103, 179
    Golan Heights and 188
    independence and 103, 105
    Jewish heritage and 14–15, 189
    Jews and xxiv, **30**, 50, 57, 105, 114, 120
    riots xxii, 129
    travel bans, Jews and 107
Syrian Jews 203, 304–5
Syrian refugees 164, 228

Tager, Yehuda 122
Talmud 9, 10, 38
Teshuva, Shimon 291–3
Tisha B'Ab 202, 203, 307–8
Torah 69, 182, 184, **190**, **191**, 202
totalitarianism xxv
trade, Jews and 7–8, 40, 55, 62, 107, 109
Trans-Saharan railway 85, 139
transit camps **xx**, xxiii, xxiv, **150**, **151**, 196–
    7, 212
travel restrictions 107, 142
Tritl xix, 124
Tsimhoni, Daphne 27
Tunisia xxi, 10, 59, 225–6, 277–8
    Allied recapture of 86
    anti-Jewish pogroms 60
    colonial rule and 60, 61
    decolonisation and 57
    discrimination, Jews and 61
    entente, Palestinian Arabs and 88
    films and 65
    France and 57, 61
    Jewish heritage and 14
    Jews and 5, 26, 31–2, 57, 58, 105, 157–
    8, 173
    Jews, labour camps and 92–3, **92**
    Nazis and 84, 86
    Vichy rule and 84
Turkey xv, xviii, 11, 61, 127, 248, 251, 252
Turkish Capitulations 55
Turkish language 11, 57

UNESCO 13, 189, 190, 231–2
United Nations (UN)
    Arab states and 133
    Charter, Article 18 252
    Conciliation Commission for Palestine
        171–2
    Declaration on the Rights of
        Indigenous peoples 254
    Economic and Social Council 133
    General Assembly xviii–xiv, 156
    High Commission for Refugees
        (UNHCR) 120, 149, 244, 246
    Human Rights Council 163
    Jewish refugees and 148, 149, 153, 162
    Kalandia refugee camp and 188
    Palestinian refugees and 148–9
    Partition Plan for Palestine xiv, xviii–
        xiv, 128–9, 135, 149, 244
    Reconciliation Commission 152
    Security Council 149, 151, 156
    Universal Declaration of Human
        Rights 164
    Works and Relief Agency (UNWRA)
        149, 244, 245, 246
United States (US)
    census 226–7
    Iraqi-Jewish archive and 182–4
US Congress, Resolution 185 (2008) 160,
    164, 267–9
Uzi-Eli (Etrog Man) 312–13

Vichy regime 84, 85, 138–9, 225
    anti-Jewish laws 61, 68, 71, 85, 140

Wahabism 81, 142
weddings **30**, **31**, **69**, **135**, **142**, **198**
Weinstock, Nathan 5
Weizmann, Chaim 112, 232
West Bank of Jordan xviii, 164, 172, 185,
    186, 188, 204
Wistrich, Robert 100, 232
World Islamic Congress 87
World Jewish Congress xxi, 133, 159–60
World Jewish Relief xiii
World Organisation of Jews from Arab
    Countries (WOJAC) 159, 169, 171, 174
World Organisation of Jews from Iraq 182
World War I 89
World War II 59, 61, 71, 84, 92–3, 103
World Zionist Organization 112

Wurmser, Meyrav 213

xenophobia 110, 121, 124

Yazidis xvii, xxv, 252, 253, 259
Yediot Ahronot 174, **175**
Yehuda, Zvi 172–3
Yemen xix, 6, 49, 88, 129, 272
    Jews and **xx**, xxi, 9, 37, 38, 73, 88, 107
    Orphans' Decree, Jews and 87
Yemenite Children Affair xxvii n28
Yemenite Jews **73–4**, **148**, 187, 196, **197**,
    202–3, 204, 217, 272
Yemini, Ben-Dror 128, 229
Ye'or, Bat 27, 38, 79, 80
Yiddish xxiv 211, 213
Youth Guard 114–15
Yugoslavia 93

Zaslany, R. 112
Zionism 10, 11, 60, 70, 94, 112, 200–2

Algeria and 72
Arab reaction to 125
as cause of exodus 122–3
'collective punishment' for 123–4, 125
criminalisation of 132
Egypt and 114
Egyptian Jews and 114, 121
Mizrahim and 200, 201, 202
Morocco and 141, 142
perception of 70, 125
precursors of 203, 204
as solution to anti-Semitism 125, 235
Zionist Underground xx, 152
Zionists xvii, xxi, 108, 114–15, 121–2, 123,
    224
Arab League and 129, 131
Egypt and 114
Iraq and 134, 135
Palestinian Arabs and 112, 128
Zoroastrians 6, 13, 49, 252